Peace, Culture, and Violence

Value Inquiry Book Series

VOLUME 316

Philosophy of Peace

Edited by

Danielle Poe (*University of Dayton*)

The titles published in this series are listed at *brill.com/vibs* and *brill.com/pop*

Peace, Culture, and Violence

Edited by

Fuat Gursozlu

BRILL
RODOPI

LEIDEN | BOSTON

Cover illustration: "Forest Tree" by LittleCuckoo (Shutterstock).

Library of Congress Cataloging-in-Publication Data

Names: Gursozlu, Fuat, editor.
Title: Peace, culture, and violence / edited by Fuat Gursozlu.
Description: Leiden : Boston : Brill-Rodopi, 2018. | Series: Value inquiry book series, ISSN 0929-8436 ; volume 316. Philosophy of peace | Includes bibliographical references and index.
Identifiers: LCCN 2018001099 (print) | LCCN 2018007799 (ebook) | ISBN 9789004361911 (E-book) | ISBN 9789004361904 (pbk. : alk. paper)
Subjects: LCSH: Violence. | Peace. | Culture.
Classification: LCC HM886 (ebook) | LCC HM886 .P427 2018 (print) | DDC 306--dc23
LC record available at https://lccn.loc.gov/2018001099

Typeface for the Latin, Greek, and Cyrillic scripts: "Brill". See and download: brill.com/brill-typeface.

ISSN 0929-8436
ISBN 978-90-04-36190-4 (paperback)
ISBN 978-90-04-36191-1 (e-book)

This book is printed on acid-free paper and produced in a sustainable manner.

Contents

Editorial Foreword

Since 1981, the organization Concerned Philosophers for Peace (CPP) has been meeting and publishing with the express purpose of critiquing violence, outlining visions of peaceful societies, and explicating the steps necessary to create these societies. In 2015, CPP held its annual meeting at Loyola University Maryland, and presenters from that conference along with other CPP members were invited by this volume's editor, Fuat Gursozlu, to submit papers for possible inclusion. Since violence seems to pervade everyday life in so many ways, it came as no surprise that the call for submissions to both the conference and the book was answered by far more philosophers than could be included.

Gursozlu has focused this volume on the forms of violence that permeate everyday life and how that violence can be changed to create a more peaceful culture. Some of the chapters focus on elements of violence that are readily visible, but their high-visibility also makes them an almost unassailable part of culture. These chapters include those by Andrew Fiala and his inquiry into thug culture, Lloyd Steffen and his exposition of the war on drugs, Sanjay Lal and his analysis of the war against terrorism, David Speetzen and his critique of just war perspectives and police violence, and Alessandro Rovati and his examination of the U.S. culture of war. Other chapters look at the personal toll that violence takes on individuals who are discriminated against because of their religion (Amin Asfari and Ron Hirschbein) or gender (Laleye Solomon Akinyemi). Still other chapters focus on the organizing structures of violence; these include William Gay's chapter on language and violence, Todd Jones's chapter on causes of and conditions for violence. And, no volume in the Philosophy of Peace series would be complete without the chapters that explicate what can be done to create a peaceful society. The conditions for peace are explicated by Gursozlu, Demenchenok, and Hall.

This volume makes an important contribution to the series, as the contributors explore the ways in which violence and militarism are ever-present culture and suggest ways to ameliorate that violence. Further, Gursozlu invites his readers to use this volume to develop their own critical awareness of violence and to cultivate their ability to imagine and create a peaceful society.

Danielle Poe, Professor of Philosophy
University of Dayton
Philosophy of Peace Special Series Editor

Notes on Contributors

Amin Asfari
is an Assistant Professor in the Department of Criminal Justice at Wake Tech College. His research interests broadly include social justice and, intergroup relations, as well as the causes and effects of Islamophobia. His forthcoming book—co-authored with Ron Hirschbein—seeks to expand on the current chapter.

Edward Demenchonok
has worked as a Senior Researcher at the Institute of Philosophy of the Russian Academy of Sciences, Moscow, and is currently a Professor of Foreign Languages and Philosophy at Fort Valley State University, USA. He is listed in *2000 Outstanding Scholars of the 21st Century*. His numerous books and articles are in the fields of the philosophy of culture, social philosophy, and ethics. Recently he edited and contributed to *Between Global Violence and Ethics of Peace: Philosophical Perspectives* (2009); *Philosophy after Hiroshima* (2010); *Intercultural Dialogue: In Search of Harmony in Diversity* (2016); and *The Courage to Hope: World beyond Global Disorder* (with Fred Dallmayr, as co-editor, 2016).

Andrew Fiala
is Professor of Philosophy, Chair of the Department of Philosophy Department, and Director of the Ethics Center at California State University, Fresno. A former President of Concerned Philosophers for Peace, he is the author or editor of more than a dozen books and author of more than fifty scholarly articles and book chapters. Recent titles include *The Peace of Nature and the Nature of Peace* (Brill 2015), *The Bloomsbury Companion to Political Philosophy* (Bloomsbury 2015), and the 9th edition of *Ethics: Theory and Contemporary Issues* with coauthor Barbara MacKinnon (Cengage Publishing, 2017). More information: www.andrewfiala.com.

William Gay
is Professor Emeritus of Philosophy at the University of North Carolina at Charlotte. Within Concerned Philosophers for Peace, he has served as President (1993), Executive Director (1997–1999), Newsletter Editor (1987–2002), and Special Book Series Editor (2002–2012). He has over one hundred journal articles and book chapters on issues of war, peace, and justice and has published *The Nuclear Arms Race* (1987), *On the Eve of the 21st Century* (1994), *Capitalism*

with a Human Face (1996), *Global Studies Encyclopedia* (2003), *Democracy and the Quest for Justice* (2004), *Global Studies Encyclopedic Dictionary* (2014), and *Between Past Orthodoxies and the Future of Globalization* (2016).

Fuat Gursozlu
is Assistant Professor of Philosophy at Loyola University Maryland, where he teaches social and political philosophy and ethics. He is the author of several articles on pluralism and violence, nonviolent political protest, and radical democracy. His recent research focuses on the nature of peace and nonviolent protest from an agonistic perspective. He is beginning a book manuscript, tentatively entitled "Agonistic Peace and Democracy."

Joshua M. Hall
is Assistant Professor of Philosophy at CUNY Queensborough. His current research focuses various historical and geographical lenses on philosophy's boundaries, particularly the intersection of aesthetics, psychology, and social justice. Recent examples include a critically acclaimed coedited anthology on philosophical practices in prisons (entitled *Philosophy Imprisoned*) over two dozen peer-reviewed journal articles (including in *Philosophy and Literature* and *Research in Phenomenology*), and eight anthology chapters (including in *Philosophical Perspectives on the Devil*). His related work in the arts includes one chapbook collection and sixty-five individual poems in literary journals internationally, including multiple Pushcart Prize–winners *Ibbetson St. Magazine, Main Street Rag,* and *Shampoo,* along with twenty years' experience as a dancer and choreographer.

Ron Hirschbein
is a Syracuse Ph.D. He initiated a program in war and peace studies at California State University, Chico. He has also held visiting professorships at University of California campuses in Berkeley and San Diego, and at the United Nations University in Austria. He has authored five books relating to issues of war and peace, and writes for *Tikkun*: a national, Jewish magazine (imprint of Duke University Press).

Todd Jones
is a Professor of Philosophy at the University of Nevada, Las Vegas. He holds degrees in anthropology and cognitive science, as well as philosophy. He is the author of the book, *What People Believe When They Say That People Believe: Folk Sociology and the Nature of Group Intention,* and over forty-five scholarly articles.

Sanjay Lal
is full-time Lecturer of Philosophy at Clayton State University. He has published many articles on the philosophy of Mahatma Gandhi and currently serves as a board member of Concerned Philosophers for Peace.

Alessandro Rovati
earned his PhD in Philosophy at the Università Cattolica del Sacro Cuore di Milano, Italy, in 2015. After his formation in classics and extensive studies in the History of Philosophy, he has specialized in Moral and Political Philosophy, thanks to his graduate research on the thought and legacy of Alasdair MacIntyre. During his graduate work, he studied under the guidance of theologian Stanley Hauerwas at Duke Divinity School to expand his expertise into the fields of Christian Ethics and Political Theology, thus combining his philosophical explorations with reflections on the current life of the church amid contemporary society. He is currently working as an Adjunct Faculty member in the Departments of Theology and Political Philosophy at Belmont Abbey College in North Carolina.

Laleye Solomon Akinyemi
is a Senior Lecturer in the Department of Philosophy at Adekunle Ajasin University, Nigeria. He holds a bachelor of arts degree in Philosophy from Ondo State University, Ado-Ekiti, Nigeria, and a master of arts and doctorate degree in Philosophy from the prestigious University of Ibadan (UI), Nigeria. Laleye has published several papers in reputable journals and books nationally and internationally. He has also attended and participated actively in numerous international conferences, including the Concerned Philosophers for Peace Conference. His research areas are in African Oral and Political Philosophy and Philosophy of Peace. He is married with four children.

David Speetzen
is Assistant Professor of Philosophy and the Director of the War, Peace & Terrorism program at Winona State University in Winona, Minnesota. He writes and teaches about ethics, the philosophy of law, and the morality of war. Recently, his research has focused on extending traditional Just War analyses of the ethics of the use of force to smaller scales of conflict—including the violence inherent to criminal justice and punishment writ large, but especially interpersonal violence, both between private citizens, and between private citizens and law enforcement officers.

Lloyd Steffen
is Professor of Religion Studies at Lehigh University in Bethlehem, PA, where he directs the Lehigh Prison Project. He is the author or editor of eleven books, including *The Ethics of Death: Religious and Philosophical Perspectives in Dialogue,* coauthored by Dennis Cooley; *Ethics and Experience: Ethical Theory from Just War to Abortion*; *Holy War, Just War: Exploring the Moral Meaning of Religious Violence*; and *Executing Justice: The Moral Meaning of the Death Penalty.* An NGO representative to the United Nations for seven years, he currently serves on the National Leadership Council of Americans United for Separation of Church and State.

Introduction

Fuat Gursozlu

Given the pervasiveness of violence and our inability to recognize its different forms, is it possible to remain optimistic about mitigating violence and building cultures of peace? Given the everyday normalization of violence in many different aspects of human affairs such as gender, race, ethnicity, class, religion, nationality, and so on, how do those who aspire for a more peaceful and just society find hope? Johan Galtung's account of cultural violence offers those who are committed to making the world a less violent place grounds for optimism and hope. Galtung has argued that our understanding of violence should extend beyond direct and structural violence. He maintains that some aspects of a culture legitimize and normalize direct and structural violence.[1] Thus, we need to turn our attention not just to direct and structural violence, but also to the aspects of culture that "make direct and structural violence look, even feel, right—or at least not wrong."[2] What needs to be done is to "identify the cultural element and show how it can, empirically or potentially, be used to legitimize direct or structural violence."[3]

Turning our attention to elements in culture in order to understand the sources of violence may render this task more difficult as culture itself is complex and elusive. However, if violence, as Galtung's account suggests, operates in a multiplicity of ways than we have hitherto imagined, we cannot come to grips with its pervasiveness and offer ways to challenge it by simply avoiding "cultural violence." The important point is that if some elements of culture legitimize and normalize violence—and in a way create or mystify reality[4]—, then it should be possible to challenge these elements and replace them with elements that delegitimize violence and normalize peace. If cultural violence creates an account of violent reality within which violence is not recognized or

1 Johan Galtung, "Cultural Violence," *Journal of Peace Research* 27:3 (1990): 291.

2 Galtung, "Cultural Violence," 292 and 296.

3 Galtung, "Cultural Violence," 292 and 296.

4 I briefly discuss this point in my contribution to this volume. The idea here is that if such cultural elements construct reality, it is possible to deconstruct it and offer an account of reality that normalizes nonviolence and marginalizes violence; if they mystify reality and, in doing so, do not allow us to see the true nature of things, then it is possible to demystify and reveal the true nature of reality. Either way the hegemonic account of reality could be contested and replaced with another.

 | DOI 10.1163/9789004361911_002

too easily accepted, what needs to be done is to reveal the violent nature of this reality while, at the same time, offering a nonviolent alternative.

Taking seriously Galtung's theory of cultural violence, the chapters under the title of *Peace, Culture, and Violence* examine the various ways violence functions in different social domains, problematize the discourses operating in the background culture that normalize violence, and explore peaceful alternatives and possible routes to peace. Understanding the deeper sources of violence and how violence operates in different domains allows us not only to challenge violence but also to envision peaceful alternatives. The essays in this volume are unique because they reveal how violence operates and envision ways of achieving a nonviolent world. In that sense, the volume represents an endeavor to seek peace and challenge violence in a world deeply marred by violence and injustice.

In the first chapter, Andrew Fiala discusses the problem of thug culture. Fiala argues that thug culture "makes violence appear to be normal and even heroic." The connection is not a causal one—culture causes violence—rather it is a process of normalization that also makes it "easier for us to express our basic thuggishness and more difficult to see what is wrong with this." A thug culture, Fiala notes, valorizes thuggishness and turns thugs into heroes whose thuggish violence has then been emulated. Fiala also reminds us that thuggishness is learned, but it is contiguous and can be understood as a virus. Fiala suggests that what needs to be done is to challenge these cultural scripts and memes that celebrate thug violence and "continually remind ourselves that thugs are cruel brutes who represent the worst of humanity." To build a culture of peace, Fiala concludes, we should produce and disseminate counter-scripts that valorize peacebuilding and positive peace as heroic activities.

In his contribution to this volume, William C. Gay takes up the relation of language to cultural violence. As Gay rightly notes, language is one of the six domains of cultural violence according to Galtung, but one that remains underdeveloped. Gay argues that understanding the dynamics of cultural violence requires recognizing the central role of language in justifying cultural violence. Gay suggests that it is possible to overcome linguistic violence. To develop his claim that language can eliminate cultural violence, Gay turns to peace linguistics and nonkilling philosophy. He concludes by suggesting that "efforts to eliminate linguistic violence and to advance the practice of linguistic nonviolence" are essential to reducing cultural violence and to advancing social justice.

Todd Jones, in Chapter 3, offers a criticism of the idea of cultural violence. Jones argues that not only is culture an extraordinarily vague and complex term, but "even when we try to work with a relatively clear and concise idea of culture, it isn't a very helpful notion for understanding the causes and solutions to the problem of violence." Most find it attractive to appeal to culture to explain violent behavior, but we should resist this temptation and "try to explain violence in terms of *a much wider* range of disjuncts." This does not mean that cultural factors do not play a big role in producing violence. Rather, Jones argues, "why look at only these, when changing other factors would also make a difference, given the same background conditions?" To reduce violence, we should think about what causes of violence we are able to manipulate and focus most attention on the causes "that are most easily altered and whose alteration would have the strongest effects."

In my contribution, I examine Galtung's theory of cultural violence from the perspective of Laclau and Mouffe's theory of hegemony. Once we take hegemony as a central organizing idea of the social, we recognize that cultural violence is more complex than Galtung takes it to be. Understanding the complexity of cultural violence brings to the fore the insufficiency of Galtung's response to it. For Galtung, what needs to be done to respond to cultural violence is to reveal the way violence is legitimized and normalized. I argue that given the way various discourses of cultural violence shape social reality and the common sense, challenging cultural violence calls for revealing how violent discourses operate as well as disrupting everyday processes. These are the two main approaches the reader will notice in the papers collected in this volume: confront cultural violence by exposing the way it operates and disrupt the existing relations of power by offering an alternative. I suggest that countering the risks of cultural violence and hegemony, agonistic interventions are called for.

In "Two Semites Confront Anti-Semitism: On the Varieties of Anti-Semitic Experience," Amin Asfari and Ron Hirschbein examine the varieties of new and old anti-Semitism and the social and historical forces that derive from them. The authors describe their personal confrontations with old and new anti-Semitism. In sharing their stories of victimization as Semites, they reveal how identity can be a domain of cultural violence. Asfari experienced the old anti-Semitism (hating Jews) when growing up in Kuwait and the new anti-Semitism (Islamophobia) as a Muslim living in New York in the post-9/11 era. Hirschbein experienced the old anti-Semitism as a Jew who has been "taunted by ethnic slurs and bullying" and the new anti-Semitism when, in the 1972 Olympics, Palestinians murdered Israeli athletes. The authors remind us that their experiences may be unique, but the anecdotal experience they offer is not: "The varieties of anti-Semitism we experience reflect ongoing and recent global developments." Asfari and Hirschbein's response to increasing anti-Semitism is personal contact. They were able to overcome their anti-Semitism and being trapped in hatred when they had had experiences with the dreaded "other." At the risk of seeming Pollyannaish, they write, "we believe the enmity turns to amity through personal contact."

Lloyd Steffen's essay examines the problems of mass incarceration and the War on Drugs as a manifestation of cultural violence. Steffen argues that cultural violence "has provided justification for the structural violence to be found in the criminal justice system that has been the instrument for enacting drug war policies." Mass incarceration, which is a consequence of the War on Drugs, has led to the disproportionate incarceration of blacks and devastated the urban African American community. The policy makers' failure to produce and enact just punishment, together with the discriminatory impact of the War on Drugs, has only inflicted harm on the individuals and communities in the name of justice. According to Steffen, what support and sustain a criminal justice system that sanctions harms against persons are the symbols of justice. This is a site where cultural violence operates. Steffen argues that the symbols of justice—jails, prisons, the execution gurney—"can be shown to be symbols of violence rather than justice, yet cultural violence obscures how these symbols function to promote practices that inflict harms on individuals and communities in the name of justice." Steffen notes that given the way culturally accepted symbols function and sanction violence, it will not be easy to dismantle a criminal justice system that perpetuates violence, but it may be possible to challenge the harms against persons in the name of justice by turning to equality of opportunity and equality before the law.

In "Terrorism and the Necessity of Oppositional Clarification in the 'War' against It," Sanjay Lal argues that the West's failure to clarify "what, exactly, is being fought against" in the war against terrorism perpetuates cultural violence. Lal's point is that the ambiguity in defining why we fight the enemy too easily warrants the kind of violence inflicted on "them" on behalf of citizens in the West. Clarifying "what our issue really is with those we believe we should be fighting" would allow us to notice how cultural violence functions in the war against radicals. Lal argues that by uncritically accepting this violence, we inevitably sacrifice our moral standing and thus undermine "the prospect of having a legitimate basis for engaging in such conflicts in the first place." To achieve a more peaceful world and deal with the "radicals," Lal concludes, social institutions in Western societies should "play a more proactive role in developing, among citizens, stronger fealty to liberal values."

In Chapter 8, David Speetzen addresses the ethics of police. Speetzen's aim is to explain what morally permitted use of force by police officers is. He advances a normative account of police force generated from the just war criteria of just cause, necessity, and proportionality. The core idea of Speetzen's ethics of police force is that the use of force by police officers is justified if, and only if, the level of force used is necessary to secure compliance with a legal command, and will not result in more harm than good. Once we adopt Speetzen's normative account, we recognize that "many common beliefs and attitudes about police force are mistaken." Given that such widely shared misconceptions inform public discourse, which in turn supports and sustains police violence, it is crucial to expose them. Speetzen concludes by suggesting that "relative to the appropriate ethical standards, much if not most police force used at present is unjustified." And the prevalence of misconceptions about the use of police together with structural issues warrants taking a "very skeptical stance toward instances of police force."

In "Cultural Violence and Gender Injustice in Africa: The Necessity for Enlightened Self-Interest," Laleye Solomon Akinyemi takes up gender inequality in Africa. Solomon states that "gender inequality and the quest to narrow its gap is one of the challenges confronting twenty-first-century Africa society." However, he argues, both the indigenous cultural practices and the practices imposed by alien cultures perpetuate patriarchy and violence against women in Africa. Due to the prevalence of these cultural practices and belief systems, the institutional efforts to empower African women have had marginal benefits. To reduce or eliminate discrimination and violence against women, Solomon defends gender egalitarianism based on "the ethical principle of enlightened self-interest." Peaceful coexistence in Africa calls for the recognition of equal rights and the understanding that "what is done to enhance the quality of life of another person or group also enhances one's quality of life."

Alessandro Rovati, in "War Is America's Altar: Violence in the American Imagination," is critical of the constitutive role war plays in the contemporary American imaginary. Drawing on Alasdair MacIntyre and Stanley Hauerwas, Rovati argues that "political liberalism has made us blind to the power that war has over our imaginations, thus making us incapable of questioning some of our society's deeply held commitments and blind to the structure of violence that they legitimize." Rovati examines the consequences of the constitutive role of war and argues that confronting this reality is one of the most important tasks for peace theorists and Christian theologians. If war is a constitutive element of our social arrangement, simply exposing the way it exercises power over our imagination may not lead to its transformation. In the absence of an example of peacemaking, community violence would still seem inevitable. At this point, Rovati turns to Hauerwas's pacifism as an alternative model of community. Christian nonviolence, Rovati concludes, offers an alternative model of peaceful community by encouraging mutual forgiveness, reconciliation, and the habits of peace.

Edward Demenchenok, in his contribution to this volume, “Foucault’s Theory of Practices of the Self and a New Anthropology,” examines the promises of Foucault’s theory from the perspective of peace by focusing on the emergence of new philosophical anthropology. The further development of Foucault’s philosophical anthropology is traced in “synergic anthropology,” based on the spiritual tradition and practices of Eastern Orthodox Christian hesychasm. Demenchenok suggests that the newly emerging synergic anthropology could help us respond to the “growing tendency of man toward extreme experiences” such as unprecedented violence, shootings in schools, and suicidal terrorism. It is essential to create “different anthropological possibilities and strategies, capable of satisfying the individual’s needs for full self-realization in a non-destructive, positive way.” The new philosophical anthropology based on the practices of the self and spiritual practices represents an alternative to the ideologies of domination and “culture wars” by promoting “the ideas of human freedom, justice, and peace.” Demenchenok concludes by pointing out the possibility for dialogue and cooperation between different traditions given that, despite their differences, many spiritual traditions share similar spiritual practices.

In the final chapter of the volume, “Toward a New Conception of Socially-Just Peace,” Joshua Hall proposes a new conception of socially just-peace that draws on biology and ecology. According to this account, peace is understood as “sustainable tranquility,” and social justice is understood as “sustainable tranquility through organismic empowerment.” The implication is that peace is unnatural and the result of artful construction, which requires polemical love, generosity, and reimagining, while social justice is natural and requires “the self-disciplined restraint of those armed for force.” Hall’s account of socially just peace resolves a seemingly irresolvable tension between peace and social justice and answers the question of how we can “imaginatively compose peace (as sustainable tranquility) among the just (as empowered organisms) who necessarily have the capacity for divisive harm.” To clarify his conception of peace, Hall turns to King, Aurelius, Arendt, Spinoza, Nietzsche, and Fanon. Finally, he applies his conception of peace to the controversial public debate on gendered justice to illustrate how by “lovingly generous reimagining of the battlefield over gendered justice” it is possible to tip “the scales of justice further to the good.”

CHAPTER 1

A Critique of Thug Culture

Andrew Fiala

> America's first gangsta thugs were Billy the Kid and Jesse James. In the youth thug cultures of both the Wild West and the inner cities, America sees inverted images of its own most iconic values, one through rose-tinted glass, the other through a glass, darkly.
>
> ORLANDO PATERSON[1]

Thugs enjoy violence and celebrate it. No one is born a thug. Thugs are bred by thug cultures. Thug cultures celebrate strong men who employ fists and guns. Thuggishness is gendered. While most men are not thugs, most thugs are men. Mass shootings, terrorism, and war are perpetrated primarily by men. A biological explanation might consider the violence of men as an evolutionary product.[2] But maleness and masculinity are cultural phenomena: cultural meaning gives form to biological antecedents. Thug cultures are masculinist. They exhibit what might be called "toxic masculinity."[3] Thug cultures valorize power and domination. They include misogynist and homophobic elements. They view struggle and the camaraderie of battle as heroic, regardless of the moral content of that struggle. And they celebrate the poetry or aesthetics of violence.

Thug cultures are created through the dialectical processes that create all cultures. Cultures develop by negotiation, reflection, appropriation, rejection, and transformation of ideas and values. The totality of culture includes psychological, social, historical, economic, moral, religious, and philosophical

1 Orlando Patterson, "The Real Problem with America's Inner Cities" *New York Times Sunday Review*, May 9, 2015.

2 See Richard Wrangham and Dale Peterson, *Demonic Males: Apes and Origins of Human Violence* (New York: Houghton Mifflin, 1996).

3 Stephen Asma, "The Weaponised Loser" *Aeon* (June 27, 2016), accessed September 26, 2016. https://aeon.co/essays/humiliation-and-rage-how-toxic-masculinity-fuels-mass-shootings.

 | DOI 10.1163/9789004361911_003

theories, values, and forces. Thug cultures reflect religious, moral, and political images of hierarchy, domination, and hegemonic power. Thug cultures also sell products, provide entertainment, and stimulate wonder and joy. And thug cultures offer an ideal of masculinity that gives form to the male ego, structures gender relations, and impinges upon our most intimate relations.

This paper examines the structure of cultural violence. It provides an overview of thuggishness in contemporary culture. And it delves into the vexing question of causality. My thesis is that thug cultures normalize violence—but do not directly cause it. The causes of violence are many. But thug cultures make violence appear to be normal and even heroic.

Cultural Violence

Johan Galtung, one of the leading theorists of violence, explains that cultural violence is woven into the symbolic realm, where violence is justified and legitimated.[4] He admits it would be very difficult to show that an entire culture is violent. But he also suggests that some cultures are more prone to violence. And he worries that some cultures make violence (whether direct violence or structural violence) "look, even feel, right—or at least—not wrong."[5] The basic idea here is that violent cultures normalize violence.

Human behavior is a product of various forces—psychological, social, biological, and even geographic. It is nearly impossible to trace out all the causal forces contributing to any specific action. So discussions of cultural violence cannot be overly reductionistic. Cultural forces do not directly cause violence. Rather, violent culture normalizes violence, reinforcing certain norms of behavior. The word "norm" means both that which is normally thought to occur (as opposed to what is abnormal or anomalous) and that which ought to occur as a standard of appropriate behavior. To say that violent cultures normalize violence is to say that violent cultures make violence appear to be a regular, typical, morally appropriate, and even heroic feature of our lives.

Cultural images of violence provide models and scripts, which violent perpetrators can follow and emulate. No one is born desiring to shoot innocent people or wanting to torture someone. The desire for mass murder and mayhem is a cultural product. Now it may be the case that violence occurs within intimate relations and on a small scale as a "natural" product of social relations. Dogs growl and fight. Birds chase each other through the

4 Johan Galtung, "Cultural Violence," *Journal of Peace Research* 27: 3 (Aug. 1990): 291–305.

5 Galtung, "Cultural Violence," 291.

air. Predators hunt. Children push and slap one another. And friendship can devolve into fisticuffs. But human behavior is mediated through ideational structures, representations, images, concepts, and—in a word—culture. Premeditated violence—violence that is more than a reactive shout, slap, or punch—is mediated by the cultural imagination.

Human behavior develops out of primary relations between body, perception, and the world. This also includes mediation through the "second nature" of cultural constructs. We mimic, imitate, emulate, learn, evaluate, aspire, and dream. This process occurs through the mediation of language, image, and representation. "Human nature" and individual identity are dialectical products. Human beings and behaviors are the result of interactions that depend upon history, biology, geography, and culture. The human body-mind finds itself situated in an environment that includes other human beings, other species, and the ubiquitous frameworks of various cultural matrices. The individual develops in relation to the culture he or she is born into.

Of course, culture is not monolithic. Individual cultures develop in relation to other cultures. And within a given culture, subcultures develop dialectically in response to the dominant culture. There is much that could be said here about the general question of the philosophy of culture. My focus is not, however, the philosophy of culture. Rather, the object of my focus is violent thuggishness—especially the thuggish culture and ideology that apparently gives rise to violence in the contemporary world: in school shootings, workplace violence, gang violence, terroristic violence—and in backlash against this in police brutality, in the use of torture by military forces, and in reactive war. Other forms of violence are a substantial concern: domestic violence, rape, child abuse, etc. Thug culture is connected to these forms of violence. Perpetrators of mass violence often develop their thuggishness in the home. The *New York Times* reports that in mass shootings, "57 percent of the cases included a spouse, former spouse or other family member among the victims—and that 16 percent of the attackers had previously been charged with domestic violence."[6]

Setting aside this important issue, my focus here is primarily the cultural imaginary that inspires and seemingly fuels the violence that erupts from time to time in random shootings, massacres, and terrorism. A related concern is the calls for thuggishness by political powers and the turn to thuggishness by

6 Amanda Taub, "Control and Fear: What Mass Killings and Domestic Violence Have in Common," *New York Times*, June 15, 2016, http://www.nytimes.com/2016/06/16/world/americas/control-and-fear-what-mass-killings-and-domestic-violence-have-in-common.html?_r=0.

police and military forces. Thug violence is violence that occurs in emulation of the thugs who haunt our cultural imaginary.

Thug violence is, I argue, a cultural artifact—a product of a culture that includes ubiquitous imagery and iconography of the heroic thug. These cultural images do not literally cause violence. But there is a process of normalization that occurs in thug culture. Part of the solution for violence is a critique of thug culture.

The heroes of dominant culture are often cops, soldiers, and warriors—those who use violence in defense of supposedly justified causes. But mainstream culture also celebrates subcultural thugs—individuals who use violence in opposition to the dominant status quo. Cultural images, songs, and films celebrate revolutionaries such as Che Guevara, outlaws like Jesse James, gangsters such as Al Capone, school shooters such as Dylan Kliebold and Eric Harris, and gangster rappers such as Tupac Shakur. It is no wonder that the masculine cultural imagination is full of violence. The cultural imagination reflects the violent heroism of the dominant culture and the memes and myths of subcultural thugs. All of this is quite mainstream. In Chicago, you can buy T-shirts at stores on the Miracle Mile with pictures of Al Capone. College students on campuses across the country wear T-shirts with pictures of Che Guevara or Tupac. Middle class people wave the Confederate battle flag, sport gang tattoos, or bang their heads to heavy-metal or gangsta rap. In the background is the dominant American narrative—the narrative of what Cady calls "warism."[7] This narrative tells of heroic sacrifice and noble violence at Bunker Hill, Gettsyburg, Normandy, and Baghdad. This narrative also appeals to a mythic justification of war that holds that the wars "we" fight must be good wars.[8]

But moral evaluation is really beside the point here. Beneath moral evaluation is a basic love of tough guys. Violent cultures praise avatars of violence; and young men emulate them. It is not surprising then that, on occasion, some man takes up arms and lives out the fantasy of heroic violence or that some politician calls for brutality and violence.

Hegel and Nietzsche pointed us toward the master-slave dialectic, where the struggle for power and recognition is the primary force in social and political evolution. The philosophy of culture that develops after Hegel and Nietzsche recognizes that violence is tightly woven around psychological, social, and cultural processes. We might also cite Freud's discussion of aggression or Marcuse's account of the dialectical struggle between institutionalized

7 Duane Cady, *From Warism to Pacifism* (Philadelphia: Temple University Press, 2010).

8 See Andrew Fiala, *The Just War Myth: The Moral Illusions of War* (Lanham, MD: Rowman and Littlefield, 2008).

violence and the violence of repression.[9] Related ideas are further developed in Girard's notion of mimetic violence. To say that violence is mimetic implies that violence inspires violence—including violence that is ironically used in opposition to violence. According to Girard:

> The more men strive to curb their violent impulses, the more these impulses seem to prosper. The very weapons used to combat violence are turned against their users. Violence is like a raging fire that feeds on the very objects intended to smother its flames.[10]

We see something similar in Foucault's discussions of power. Foucault argued, for example, that history is "Jupiterian." He explained that "history is the discourse of power, the discourse of the obligations power uses to subjugate; it is also the dazzling discourse that power uses to fascinate, terrorize, and immobilize."[11] The history lessons we teach young men celebrate the violence and power of the state, including the violent triumphs of our founding heroes. It is not surprising that some young men develop this lesson in an antiestablishment direction. The forces at play—violence, power, and domination—remain the same, while there are social differences in the way these forces are directed.

The Hegelian and Nietzschean struggle for power and recognition is a central concern for thugs—both dominant and subdominant thugs. What our culture teaches us is that the struggle for recognition can culminate in heroic outbursts of violence. These spectacular violent ejaculations can be seen as sacred, patriotic, aesthetic, and psychological highpoints. Some learn that mastery, dominance, power, and respect are obtained through the barrel of a gun. Struggle and battle explain much of our social psychology—even when most of us sublimate aggression and competition without actually killing anyone. An alternative—a culture of peace—would break free of the dialectical struggle, transforming thugs into brothers or lovers, replacing violent consummations with the joys of friendship, solidarity, compassion, and peace.

More needs to be said in defense of a culture of peace. The goal here is to understand why we need to de-normalize thuggishness in our cultural

9 Sigmund Freud, *Civilization and its Discontents* (New York: Norton, 1961); Herbert Marcuse, "The Problem of Violence and the Radical Opposition" (1967) accessed September 26, 2016, https://www.marxists.org/reference/archive/marcuse/works/1967/violence.htm.

10 René Girard, *Violence and the Sacred,* (London: Continuum 2005), 32.

11 Michel Foucault, *Society Must Be Defended: Lectures at the Collège de France, 1975–76* (New York: Picador, 2003), 68.

imaginary. At present, thug culture has too much power and value. Instead of valorizing thuggishness and transforming thugs into heroes, we need to continually remind ourselves that thugs are cruel brutes who represent the worst of humanity, and that society need not be primarily understood as a field of battle.

From Tupac to Trump

Thug cultures have existed throughout history and across the globe. Wherever men—and I mean "men" in the old-fashioned gendered sense of the term—celebrate swords, fists, and guns, there you will find thug culture. In this section, I focus on some famous contemporary examples, including Tupac Shakur, a rapper who self-consciously appropriated the idea of being a thug. Tupac's thug life has a variety of influences. He influenced a variety of others in the United States and abroad.

Thug culture makes it appear that violence is easy, obvious, heroic, exciting, and manly. While moralists quibble and worry about the justification of war and the excesses of violence, mainstream culture remains brutal and thuggish. Tupac is thus not the only thug. Consider Donald Trump, whose brash braggadocio is typically thuggish. At a rally in Las Vegas in 2016, during his campaign for president, Trump said he would like to punch a protester in the face; Trump said he longed for the old days when security guards would have roughed up the protester who then would have been carried out on a stretcher.[12] The crowd roared in approval. At a debate in Detroit, on March 3, 2016, Trump said that if elected he would command the American military to use torture and brutality against ISIS.

> You look at the Middle East, they're chopping off heads, they're chopping off the heads of Christians and anybody else that happens to be in the way, they're drowning people in steel cages, and now we're talking about waterboarding.... It's fine, and if we want to go stronger, I'd go stronger too. Because frankly, that's the way I feel. Can you imagine these people, these animals, over in the Middle East that chop off heads, sitting around talking and seeing that we're having a hard problem with

12 Jeremy Diamond, CNN, February 23, 2016, accessed September 26, 2016, http://edition.cnn.com/2016/02/23/politics/donald-trump-nevada-rally-punch/index.html.

> waterboarding? We should go for waterboarding and we should go tougher than waterboarding.[13]

More recently, President Trump has made remarks that appear to condone police brutality. At a speech to law enforcement personnel in Long Island in late July of 2017, he encouraged police to be rough, saying:

> Please don't be too nice ... Like when you guys put somebody in the car and you're protecting their head, you know, the way you put their hand over? Like, don't hit their head and they've just killed somebody—don't hit their head. I said, you can take the hand away, O.K.?[14]

Trump celebrates macho toughness, strength, and power—without moral restraint. Trump is a thug. He encourages thuggishness. He also praises thugs, such as the Philippine President Rodrigo Duterte, whom Trump praised and invited to the White House despite the fact that Duterte has bragged about personally shooting criminals. So Trump is not alone. Strongman leaders are a political commonplace—from Pericles to Putin.

People also often cheer on the strongman. According to Philippine folklore, Rodrigo Duterte—before he was President of the Philippines—supposedly pulled a gun on a smoker and threatened to shoot the smoker in the scrotum, unless he swallowed his cigarette. The smoker ate his cigarette. This story may or may not be true. But as a recent report explained, "Duterte's fans love him because he is a thug."[15] Trump is similarly popular among his followers. A number of people cheer on his thuggishness (including both men and women, by the way, which is an indication that masculine thuggishness is not an essential feature of gender and sexuality). Thuggishness is both mainstream and countercultural. It is pervasive—and a fundamental problem for those of us who desire a world beyond violence.

13 Tessa Berenson, "Donald Trump Defends Torture at Republican Debate," *Time*, March 3, 2016, accessed September 26, 2016, http://time.com/4247397/donald-trump-waterboarding-torture/.

14 The White House Office of the Press Secretary, "Transcript: Remarks by President Trump to law enforcement officials on MS-13," *Newsday*, July 28, 2017, accessed August 4, 2017, http://www.newsday.com/news/nation/transcript-remarks-by-president-trump-to-law-enforcement-officials-on-ms-13-1.13863979.

15 Graeme Wood, "The Thug Appeal of Rodrigo Duterte: Making sense of Trump's White House invitation to the Philippine president," *The Atlantic*, May 2, 2017, accessed August 4, 2017, https://www.theatlantic.com/international/archive/2017/05/rodrigo-duterte-donald-trump/525072/.

Some have deliberately adopted thug identities and have embraced the term. Tupac Shakur, for example, had the phrase "THUG LIFE" tattooed across his belly. Thugs often brag about their thuggishness. But this is not new with Tupac. Outlaw bikers, gangsters, pirates, and terrorists celebrate their outsider status, transforming violence into a fashionable mystique. But as we've seen, thuggishness is not merely an outsider phenomenon: outsiders declare themselves to be thugs; but insiders behave thuggishly while condemning the thuggishness of the outsiders they oppose. And so the vicious cycle of thug culture revolves and repeats.

Thug culture has a long lineage and multiple iterations—and thugs from around the world learn from and celebrate one another, borrowing symbols, deeds, and culture from one another. Consider this remarkable story woven around Tupac, who was murdered in 1996. European jihadis have learned from hip-hop and rap artists. European Muslims who turn to jihad sometimes begin as drug dealers, pimps, and rappers—starting out with petty crime and discovering radical Islam in prison. While interviewing some of these young men in Paris in 2015, the journalist George Packer was asked by one of them, "Is it true that Tupac is dead?"[16] One mysterious tale surrounding Tupac holds that his murder was staged so that he could flee to Cuba and somehow escape the thug life. At any rate, it is interesting to note that some of the European youth who drift toward jihad are inspired by Tupac's own thug life—and the violent antiestablishment culture of rap and hip hop. Another example comes from Charles Kurzman, who recounts Tupac's influence on Arab and Palestinian rappers—who are also fascinated with the imagery and ideas associated with Che Guevara and other revolutionaries.[17] Yet another example of the rap-jihad connection is Abdel Bary, who rapped in London under the name L. Jinny, until he went off to join ISIS—where he was suspected of being "Jihadi John," the man who posted Internet videos of himself beheading victims.

Tupac Shakur's parents were Black Panthers—he was named after Tupac Amaru II, a revolutionary fighter of the nineteenth century in Peru—whose name was also used by a Peruvian revolutionary group in the 1980s and 1990s. Tupac's godmother/aunt is Assata Shakur, a terrorist on the FBI's most wanted list, who fled to Cuba after murdering a cop in New Jersey in the 1970s and escaping from prison. Tupac studied theater at the Baltimore School of Performing Arts before becoming a key player in the West Coast rap scene.[18] Tupac's music

16 George Packer, "The Other France," *New Yorker*, August 31, 2015.

17 Charles Kurzman, *The Missing Martyrs: Why There Are So Few Muslim Terrorist* (Oxford University Press, 2011).

18 Chuck Phillips, "Tupac Shakur: 'I Am Not a Gangster,'" *Los Angeles Times*, accessed September 27, 2016, http://www.latimes.com/local/la-me-tupac-qa-story.html#axzz2j2YDkEWE.

supposedly influenced violent acts against the police. Ronald Ray Howard shot a cop in Texas in 1993. He claimed that Tupac's music inspired him, especially Tupac's album *2Pacalypse Now.*[19] This prompted Vice-President Dan Quayle to speak out against hip hop and against Tupac. The album featured classics such as "I Don't give a fuck," which included the lyric

> Better bring the gun, pal
> Cause this is the day we make 'em pay
> Fuck bailing hay, I better spray with an AK

The song concludes with a long list of "fuck you's" to the San Francisco police, Marin County Sheriff, FBI, CIA, etc. For all of his violent bravado, Tupac was also politically aware. Tupac explained that his THUG LIFE tattoo was an acronym for "The Hate You Gave Little Infants Fucks Everyone."[20] He meant this as an indictment of American culture. He claimed that Thug Life was the violent consequence of a culture of violence. He claimed that American culture creates the thug underculture as a logical result of oppression and violence. In an interview from prison, he said the United States was a violent gang: "America is the biggest gang in the world."[21]

Of course, all of that is anecdotal evidence. There is no direct causal relationship between Tupac Shakur, political revolution, and Islamic Jihad. And yet there is a common thread of thug culture that celebrates violence by displaying guns, tattoos, and severed heads. Thugs, gangsters, rebels, and terrorists are politically aware and juiced by violence. They are motivated by revolutionary outrage and the thrill of combat. There is a mix of psychological, social, political, religious, aesthetic, and even sexual motifs in the life and culture of the thug. Sometimes we miss the political message that is easily lost in the macho bravado, violent imagery, excessive brutality, and senseless cruelty. Other times—as in patriotic thuggishness—the political message overshadows the psychosexual dynamic. But this mixed motivation is typical of cultures of violence: multifarious forces give rise to, justify, and valorize violence.

While the example of Tupac and his epigones focuses on countercultural and revolutionary thugs, thuggish violence prompts violent backlash from military and police forces. What a strange story: from Tupac's response to the police to the appropriation of American thug style by jihadis, to

19 Chuck Phillips, "Testing the Limits," *Los Angeles Times,* accessed September 27, 2016, http://articles.latimes.com/1992-10-13/entertainment/ca-225_1_routine-traffic-stop.

20 Michael Eric Dyson, *Holler if You Hear Me: Searching for Tupac Shakur* (New York: Basic Books, 2001), 115.

21 Dyson, *Holler if You Hear Me,* 125.

Donald Trump's thuggish response to the tactics of those jihadis. Rebels can be thuggish. Military and police forces can also turn thuggish. Indeed, in the hands of political leaders like Trump, thuggishness takes on a patina of respectability.

It is possible that some violence can be justified. But in those rare cases, violence is a regrettable last resort and not something to be celebrated, glorified, and bragged about. So let's admit that thugs can have a rationale for violence. Rebellious thugs, violent outlaws, and jihadis are reacting against dysfunction in our society, including structural racism, the lasting impact of prior oppression and imperial power, inequality, lack of opportunity, etc. The Trump response can also be rationalized: bad guys need to be taught a lesson—and brutality is supposed to be the only language the bad guys understand. The problems experienced by the outsiders are real—exclusion and disempowerment are felt directly by immigrants and racial and religious minorities. This does not justify violence. But it helps explain why thug culture is appealing to disaffected young people. At the same time, the problems experienced by dominant groups and the law and order contingent are also real. Terrorism, gang violence, and random school shootings prompt outrage. Dominant forces want to fight back and keep a lid on violence by way of thuggishness of police brutality, military intervention, and tough political talk, including the macho bravado of politicians on the campaign trail.

The phrase "macho bravado" may sound like a cliché. But we see the chest-thumping thuggishness in a variety of places: on the athletic field, in music videos, and at political debates. The thug's braggadocio is part of our image of masculinity. There is a continuum from the shouts and insults of a sporting event or political campaign to the outright violence of war, terrorism, and random violence. A common thread among perpetrators of violence—including gangbangers, jihadis, school shooters, and racist extremists—is that they tend to be young males, who operate in a context in which violence has been normalized, in which power is seen as the primary source of recognition, and in which conflicts are openly resolved through brutality and violence. (Here Trump and the thugs of the political hierarchy may be an exception—in terms of the age dynamic: perhaps older males do retain thuggishness; or perhaps they hope to burnish their masculine mystique by advocating thug violence). Sprinkle in a fascination with weapons and a dose of hypersexualized misogyny, and you have the recipe for thug culture. In addition to political motivation, the thug is turned on by violence, amped up by danger, and stimulated by a desire to fight, cause pain, see blood, and risk everything in battle.

The story of Tupac and his influence on European jihadis may make it seem that thuggishness is confined to the rap and hip-hop thug underground. But consider this as well: American soldiers in Iraq listened to rap and metal to psych up for battle. The military also used rap and metal to recruit young men into the military. As one soldier put it (quoted in Jonathan Pieslak's book *Sound Targets*), "war itself is heavy metal."[22] Pieslak names bands like Slayer, Metallica, and Megadeth. He cites a Slayer video for "Bloodline," and a Drowning Pool song, "Bodies," which has a chorus that consists of a chant of the line, "Let the bodies hit the floor." Megadeth makes the connection with war explicit in its video for "Holy War," which flashes images of Middle East wars—specifically the first Gulf War (since Megadeth's song was from 1990). According to Pieslak, soldiers got "crunked"—amped up for battle—by listening to Metallica, Slayer, and Megadeth (although "crunk" is a term that refers to another form of hip hop that, as far as I can tell, consists of rhythmic swearing—as in "songs" by Lil Jon—crunk also refers to a combination of crazy and drunk).

If war is heavy metal, war is also like a video game and a movie. It is not surprising that our warriors—who are asked to fight in supposedly just wars—are immersed in violent popular culture. Nor is it surprising to find out that military recruiters use rap, metal, and video games to recruit young people.[23] The military apparently also uses video gaming in training. And there is a significant connection between military power and the genre of the war film.[24] Given the cultural impact of rap, metal, and video gaming, it is no wonder that the military is interested in finding young thugs and transforming them into patriotic warriors.

American culture today remains thuggish. Mainstream American culture celebrates violence, enjoys power, and tends to demonize and vilify the other. Trump provides a typical example. Americans deny our own thuggishness, dressing it up in patriotic colors and moralistic language. But we parade our weapons and eulogize military prowess. The sinister obverse of triumphant violence occurs when young men shoot up schools, plant bombs, or take up gangster personae in overt acts of thuggishness. These outbursts reflect the ideas and values of our culture. Violent subcultural aftereffects are a reflection of the ubiquitous imagery of power and violence. The path from Tupac to Trump is not hard to trace.

---

22 Jonathan R. Pieslak, *Sound Targets: American Soldiers and Music in the Iraq War* (Indiana University Press, 2009), 52.

23 See Nick Turse, *The Complex: How the Military Invades Our Everyday Lives* (New York: Metropolitan Books, 2008); and Hamza Shaban, "Playing War: How the Military Uses Video Games," *The Atlantic*, October 2013, accessed September 27, 2016, http://www.theatlantic.com/technology/archive/2013/10/playing-war-how-the-military-uses-video-games/280486/.

24 See Andrew Fiala, "General Patton and Private Ryan" in *Philosophy of War Films*, ed. David LaRocca, (University of Kentucky Press, 2015).

A Word about Words

The word "thug" is a contentious word. I chose to use "thug" in this essay because it is both a word that is used to condemn the violence perpetrated by others and a word that has been embraced by those who affirm violence. The word "bully" or "tyrant" could also be employed. We condemn bullies and tyrants. But it is rare for someone to affirm that they are a bully or a tyrant. It is interesting then that some have embraced the term "thug," declaring themselves to be thugs. That is interesting and troubling. Indeed, across the globe thugs and thuggishness have been celebrated and imitated: thug cultures view violence as a virtue and the thug as a symbol of power and masculinity. It is no wonder that the American empire breeds thuggish subcultures. The deliberate adoption of the thug persona may be a reactionary strategy on the part of those who are already outlawed and classified as thugs. The "outlaw other" simply embraces and celebrates his outlaw status. But I think there is something more sinister and less reactive at work here. Some men enjoy violence and embrace it. And they find scripts and models that give shape to violence readily available in the world.

Some have worried that the word "thug" is a racial epithet. This accusation arose in the aftermath of racialized police and anti-police violence of recent years. Some cops accused blacks of behaving like thugs. John McWhorter claimed in an NPR interview in 2015 that "thug" was a racist word.

> Thug today is a nominally polite way of using the N-word. Many people suspect it, and they are correct. When somebody talks about thugs ruining a place, it is almost impossible today that they are referring to somebody with blond hair. It is a sly way of saying there go those black people ruining things again.[25]

We should be careful to avoid such racist connotations. So please note that there are blond-haired thugs (e.g., Donald Trump). Cops can be thugs. White supremacists are thugs—as are Islamist terrorists and Mexican druglords. Police and military power can become thuggish. The phrase "jack-booted thugs" has long been used to evoke neo-Nazis and authoritarians who threaten

25 John McWhorter, interview by Melissa Block, "The Racially Charged Meaning Behind the Word 'Thug,'" *All Things Considered*, aired April 30, 2015, on NPR, accessed September 27, 2016, http://www.npr.org/2015/04/30/403362626/the-racially-charged-meaning-behind-the-word-thug.

violence. The *Atlantic Monthly*, in a 2015 article about mass violence and attacks on black churches used the word "thug" to condemn white supremacists: "Black churches suffered at the hands of thugs and terrorists throughout the Civil Rights era ... but such attacks are not a matter of remote history."[26] President Obama claimed that Russia's president, Vladimir Putin, was a "thug."[27] Marco Rubio claimed Putin was both a "gangster and a thug."[28] Mike Huckabee has claimed, "the IRS is a rogue, thug agency."[29]

So, the term "thug" is not simply a racial epithet. It is an equal opportunity term, flung in all directions. Mainstream commentators use it as a term of opprobrium, as an insult that aims to condemn brutishness, violence, and cruelty. But as we have seen, the term is used in ideological fashion. A thug is usually someone whose violence we do not respect. In most usages, the term "thug" is directed at excluded others. We condemn them, while ignoring our own thuggishness and the violence of our culture. But, as we have also seen, those excluded others can appropriate the term and embrace the imagery and ideals of thug culture.

A critique of thug culture rejects brutishness, violence, and cruelty in all of its interconnected forms—including the tendencies of thugs to vilify one another and the strange thuggishness of the powerful who use the word "thug" to condemn those they oppress. The complexity of thug culture includes the fact that those who are classified as thugs often accept and adopt this epithet as a badge of honor, as Tupac Shakur did. Here is the problem of the master-slave dialectic. An insulting term used by one party in the struggle can be worn as a badge of honor by the other party in the struggle.

The term "thug" does have racist roots. It can be traced to a group of murderers from India, who supposedly strangled their victims and worshipped Kali as part of a murderous way of life. Some dispute the gruesome details as a

---

26 Conor Friedersdorf, "Thugs and Terrorists Have Attacked Black Churches for Generations," *Atlantic Monthly*, June 18, 2015, accessed September 27, 2016, http://www.theatlantic.com/politics/archive/2015/06/thugs-and-terrorists-have-plagued-black-churches-for-generations/396212/.

27 See *New York Times* editorial September 21, 2015, accessed September 27, 2016, http://www.nytimes.com/2015/09/21/opinion/mr-putins-mixed-messages-on-syria.html.

28 *The Guardian*, October 3, 2015, accessed September 27, 2016, http://www.theguardian.com/us-news/2015/oct/03/vladimir-putin-is-a-gangster-and-thug-says-us-presidential-candidate-marco-rubio.

29 Breitbart News, September 18, 2015, accessed September 27, 2016, http://www.breitbart.com/california/2015/09/18/populist-chief-mike-huckabee-says-humble-roots-connect-americas-working-class/.

colonial and anti-Hindu imposition. But the idea of the Thugs of India caught on, and the term was imported into European contexts.[30]

Mark Twain explores thug culture in India in his account of his travels to India, *Following the Equator: A Journey Around the World*. Twain writes that the secret of thug culture (what he calls *Thuggee* culture) is the "joy of killing." Twain acknowledges some racial issues with the term—since the white colonialists are quick to condemn thuggish behavior in the brown-skinned others, while ignoring their own thuggishness. Twain implies that there have always been thugs who enjoy violence and that there have long been cultures that celebrate thuggishness, including white culture:

> The joy of killing! The joy of seeing killing done—these are the traits of the human race at large. We white people are merely modified Thugs; Thugs fretting under the restraints of a not very thick skin of civilization; Thugs who long ago enjoyed the slaughter of the Roman arena, and later the burning of doubtful Christians by authentic Christians in the public squares....[31]

While I think it is difficult to maintain that the word "thug," is simply a racist code word, I think it is easier to argue that the word is gendered. Thugs are usually men—and thuggishness is a problem associated with male dominance. Of course there are exceptions. But the typical thug is a male—and the typical images of thug culture include substantial amounts of male dominance. Thuggish males have been idolized in various forms throughout history. Achilles and the Greek heroes were thugs. The Roman centurions and gladiators were thugs; as were the medieval knights and Vikings. Wherever men and arms are found, there you will find thugs. Along with the thug you will find thug culture—a cultural matrix that valorizes violence in a way that is often connected with male dominance and images of masculinity.

Cultural Dialectics and Contagious Thuggishness

Thuggishness is contagious. Thuggishness is learned behavior disseminated by thug cultures. Thugs learn from one another. They learn their thuggishness

30 Edward Thornton. *Illustrations of the History and Practices of the Thugs* (London: Nattali and Bond, 1851).

31 Mark Twain, *Following the Equator: A Journey Around the World* (Hartford, CT: American Publishing, 1898), 437.

these days through video games, films, music, and television. They model thuggishness on scripts and memes that celebrate previous thugs and their thuggish misdeeds. Thugs respond to one another with the push and pull of violence and images of violence.

Culture is a dialectical process in which ideas and values arise and are propagated through forces that push and pull in various ways. Attractive and repulsive forces combine and intermingle. And there is no single interpretation or evaluation that guides the whole. A single image—say, Tupac's tattoo—can be interpreted, imitated, and reappropriated in various ways. One person may see Tupac's life and death as a heroic model. Others may see it is as a warning sign. And there is a good chance that these rival interpretations will mix and mingle.

Despite the acknowledgment of the complexity of cultural processes, it seems that thug culture is on the rise. This may be a bit hyperbolic, but I fear we are training our children to be thugs. We celebrate war, power, guns, and brutality. Those on the top of the social hierarchy admire and recommend war and the warrior virtues, while those on the bottom celebrate an inverted version of the same thing. This comes together in the pervasive thuggishness of pop culture—and the impact this has on children (especially boys).

The American Academy of Child and Adolescent Psychiatry explains, "The typical American child will view more than 200,000 acts of violence, including more than 16,000 murders before age 18."[32] A policy statement issued by the American Academy of Pediatrics concludes, "The strength of the association between media violence and aggressive behavior found in meta-analyses is greater than the association between calcium intake and bone mass, lead ingestion and lower IQ, and condom nonuse and sexually acquired HIV infection, and is nearly as strong as the association between cigarette smoking and lung cancer—associations that clinicians accept and on which preventive medicine is based without question."[33]

In a recent article in *The New Yorker*, Malcolm Gladwell explains how school shooters have learned from and imitated the horrors committed by the

32 American Academy of Child and Adolescent Psychiatry, Statement by Eugene Beresin, "The Impact of Media Violence on Children and Adolescents: Opportunities for Clinical Interventions" (2015), accessed September 27, 2016, https://www.aacap.org/aacap/Medical_Students_and_Residents/Mentorship_Matters/DevelopMentor/The_Impact_of_Media_Violence_on_Children_and_Adolescents_Opportunities_for_Clinical_Interventions.aspx.

33 American Academy of Pediatrics, Statement on Media Violence (2009), accessed September 27, 2016, http://pediatrics.aappublications.org/content/124/5/1495.full.

Columbine killers.[34] His explanation draws on the work of Mark Granovetter, who explained how social processes spread by a kind of contagion. Such an account requires a lot of explanation and analysis. But one point seems clear: shooters do have models for their behavior—in the thugs they view as heroes. The difficult problem is this: the fact that someone is a fan of the Columbine killers (or Hitler or Abraham Lincoln, for that matter), provides little in the way of a causal account. Being a fan of thugs does not necessarily lead one to become a thug. Listening to rap or heavy metal does not mean that one will become violent. Many people watch violent movies, play violent video games, and listen to rap music or violent heavy metal without ever killing anyone. Nonetheless, the fact remains that most violent thugs are acting out in emulation of cultural imagery—and violent music and games accompany thuggish outbursts.[35]

Some parts of thug cultural literally give a green light to violence—and should be condemned for this. Certainly it is wrong for a film, text, or game to explicitly call for rape, murder, or genocide. There is thus something quite dangerous about the spread of online videos and manifestos, through which murderers deliberately seek to incite further mayhem.

A more subtle problem occurs when cultural forces serve to obscure violence and inure us to it. We see so much violence that violence is no longer surprising—and that is a very dangerous and disturbing problem.

I suspect there is a connection between thug culture—including the myths and memes that celebrate and justify violence—and the actual occurrence of violence. I've outlined some of this in my account of "the just war myth": the myth that holds that just wars are easily fought (and often fought and won by us) tends to make it more likely that we will go to war. Again, there is no strict or obvious causal story here. Rather, the issue is one of normalizing behavior, valorizing it, and making it seem heroic and even fun.

The American Academy of Pediatrics and the American Academy of Child and Adolescent Psychiatry seem to go a bit further. They appear to affirm a close correlation, which leads them to hint about a causal connection, between thug culture and thuggish behavior. Of course, these are empirical generalizations, which require a lot more evidence and which do not hold absolutely. But I think we cannot deny that thug culture represents violence in a way that

34 Malcolm Gladwell, "Thresholds of Violence: How School Shootings Catch On," *New Yorker*, October 19, 2015. Also see: Elizabeth Winkler, "Malcolm Gladwell Is Wrong about School Shootings," *New Republic*, October 2015, accessed September 27, 2016, https://newrepublic.com/article/123139/malcolm-gladwell-wrong-about-school-shooters.

35 See Jonathan Pieslak, *Sound Targets*.

makes violence seem normal and unproblematic. In this atmosphere, violence is simply taken for granted.

Thug cultures promulgate and propagate violence by normalizing and valorizing it. *Proactive or aggressive thug culture* makes it appear that violence is easy, obvious, heroic, exciting, and manly. Proactive thug culture views violence as a consummation to be celebrated an enjoyed. Related to this is *reactive or defensive thug culture*, which accepts thuggishness as normal, unavoidable, or expected. The reactive thug may not enjoy violence, but he accepts it with a shrug, as an unremarkable and necessary fact of life.

Thuggishness can be understood as a virus, as David Grossman has explained.[36] Grossman argues that popular culture has decreased our natural immunity to violence. As a result, mass killings have increased along with other forms of violence. Indeed, Grossman explains that we do not notice the increase of violence since advances in medical technology have helped increase survival rates. Confirming Grossman's hypothesis about the role of medical advances in decreasing the appearance of violence is a study in the *British Medical Journal* that concludes that murder rates would be five times higher if not for medical advances developed during the past four decades.[37]

Grossman explains that popular culture is engaged in a "systematic process of defeating the normal individual's age-old, psychological inhibition against violent, harmful activity toward one's own species."[38] And, "We are reaching that stage of desensitization at which the inflicting of pain and suffering has become a source of entertainment: vicarious pleasure rather than revulsion. We are learning to kill, and we are learning to like it."[39] One bit of evidence here is that the military uses video games in its own training[40]

Grossman speaks of an indirect way that thug culture propagates itself by lowering our resistance to violence. There are other more direct ways that thuggishness is disseminated, which is related to the reactive/defensive form of thuggishness. The point here is that victims of violence tend to become perpetrators. Just as victims of bullying themselves become bullies (many bullies have themselves been bullied), there is a vicious circle of thuggishness, which is connected to the role of copycat behavior, imitation, contagion, and

36 David Grossman, *On Killing: The Psychological Cost of Learning to Kill in War and Society* (New York: Little Brown, 2009).

37 Roger Dobson, "Medical Advances Mask Epidemic of Violence by Cutting Murder Rate," *BMJ*, 3257365 (September 21, 2002): 615.

38 Grossman, *On Killing*, 304.

39 Grossman, *On Killing*, 311.

40 See Hamza Shaban, "Playing War."

mimesis. More troubling is the fact that some thugs were not bullied—a point that Gladwell emphasizes.

Gladwell's account begs for a cultural explanation. Here's the point: human beings respond to the world with tools and techniques provided by culture. If violence occurs as a normal and natural part of the social world—and if violence is imposed upon us, or images of violence are celebrated and disseminated—then violence will be a first resort instead of a last one. Bullying and thuggishness impose violence on others, which makes violence appear to be normal. This vicious circle is made more vicious by pervasive media, which publicizes violence and thug cultures.[41]

While I believe it is difficult to blame thug culture for directly causing violence, thug culture does make it easier for some people to express thuggishness, while also making it more difficult to see what is wrong with this. Thuggishness is not an essential feature of human nature. Human beings are complex: we love, we hate, we lash out, and we negotiate. But thuggishness develops when violence is normalized and valorized. Thuggish music, film, and video games normalize violence, making it seem that violence is normal, acceptable, and heroic. Some thuggishness is accompanied by myths and ideas that justify violence, which creates an especially volatile mix of cultural images, moral justification, and testosterone. Thugs are not merely dumb brutes. A thuggish culture is not didactic: it does not say "become a thug." Rather, a thug culture turns thugs into heroes, instead of pointing out that the true heroes are those who resist violence. My claim that thug culture normalizes violence stops short of ascribing singular causal efficacy to culture. Films, music, and video games cannot be directly or solely blamed for violence. Consider war films and other violent films, for example.[42] It is unlikely that an individual would watch a thuggish film and suddenly run off on a violent rampage. A film about gangsters, such as the *Godfather*, does not, by itself, cause people to join the Mafia. Nor can a war film by itself cause a person to enlist in the military. Nor can a violent torture film cause someone to engage in torturous violence. But such films form part of a culture of violence that makes violence appear normal, manly, fun, and even valorous.

Or consider video gaming. For some unhinged individuals, there is a blurry line between real life and video gaming. Phil Chalmers recounts stories of murderers who got their ideas from video games such as *Grand Theft Auto*,

41 See Loren Coleman, *The Copy Cat Effect: How the Media and Popular Culture Trigger the Mayhem in Tomorrow's Headlines* (New York: Simon and Schuster, 2004).

42 See Andrew Fiala, "General Patton and Private Ryan."

Manhunt, *Doom*, and *Halo*.[43] Violent video games may have more impact on the psyche than films do: they make it possible for players to be actively involved in causing death and destruction. They normalize violence—even if it is difficult to conclude that they actually cause violence. This is the conclusion that has been drawn recently by an extensive study of psychological research on the power of violent video games conducted by the American Psychological Association. The draft report concludes, "The research demonstrates a consistent relation between violent video game use and increases in aggressive behavior, aggressive cognitions and aggressive affect, and decreases in prosocial behavior, empathy and sensitivity to aggression."[44]

But songs, films, or video games do not directly cause violence. Indeed, there are too many counterexamples for a simple causal story to be told. Many young men listen to violent music, play violent video games, and enjoy violent films—but they do not engage in overt acts of violence. However, cultural violence inures us to violence, normalizing it, and thus preventing us from seeing it and criticizing it; more importantly, thug cultures undermine efforts to promote cultures of peace.

Justifying Violence?

A superstructure may grow upon basic thuggishness that rationalizes, justifies, moralizes, and explains away violence. We often celebrate and enjoy our own thuggishness. We call it justice or entertainment, while condemning the violence perpetrated by others.

Thugs can be politically aware. Trump appears to use his calls for thuggishness as political rhetoric, designed to inspire his followers. But thugs need not be political: some school shooters appear to simply be nihilists obsessed with guns. Others are motivated by revolutionary outrage. White supremacist thugs, black nationalists, and Islamic jihadis are politically motivated, even though the political message is easily lost in macho bravado, violent imagery, excessive brutality, and senseless cruelty. Thuggish violence prompts violent backlash from military and police forces. It is possible that some violence can be

43 Phil Chalmers, *Inside the Mind of a Teen Killer* (Nashville: Thomas Nelson, 2009).

44 American Psychological Association, Draft Report on violent video games (2015), accessed September 27, 2016, https://www.apa.org/news/press/releases/2015/08/technical-violent-games.pdf and American Psychological Association, Press Release on violent video games (2015), accessed September 27, 2016, http://www.apa.org/news/press/releases/2015/08/violent-video-games.aspx.

justified. But in those rare cases, violence is a regrettable last resort and not something to be celebrated, glorified, and bragged about.

So let's admit that thugs can have a rationale for violence. Rebellious thugs, violent outlaws, and jihadis are reacting against dysfunction in our society, including structural racism, the lasting impact of prior oppression and imperial power, inequality, lack of opportunity, etc. And dominant thugs call for torture and brutality as a response to terrorism and random violence. These problems are real—and are felt directly by immigrants and racial and religious minorities. This does not justify violence. But it helps explain why thug culture is appealing to disaffected young people.

A moral claim may be layered on top of this basic violence. But it seems that the moral veneer is often an afterthought. The philosophical and moral discourse of justification is a superstructure built upon the basic psychosexual dynamic of thuggishness. Foucault suggests that this may be the primary explanation of philosophical discourses of justification. I believe this reductive interpretation goes too far, although this is not the place to argue about grounding morality. At any rate, we must admit that men (and here I intend this in the masculine/gendered sense) can be ferocious animals who enjoy killing and dominating other men. I do not think this is innate. Ferocity is one possibility for human beings. But men in the thug cultures of the world are taught to celebrate thuggishness and to find their own masculine identity in ferocity. Indeed, thuggishness is in many cases literally beaten into them, as in the case of those bullies who were themselves bullied. This psychosexual dynamic often comes first. Justifications and rationalizations come after the fact. This is not always true, of course. Some violence can probably be justified as a regrettable last resort (as described in the just war theory). But thug culture makes it difficult to work out the moral calculus of justification. Indeed, the problem of reactive or defensive thuggishness is that when aggressive thuggishness occurs, we can be deluded into thinking the whole world is crazed with violence. It is, therefore, easier to fall back on thuggishness as a response—and the moral discourse of justification and the burden of proof is thus skewed by the background assumptions we bring with us. The peacemaker looks naive in a culture that takes thuggishness for granted and in which the pervasiveness of thugishness appears to call out for violence.

Conclusion

I suspect that thug culture is worse today than it once was—more ubiquitous and more graphically violent. We seem to have moved in the wrong direction since the days of Billy the Kid. Today there are music videos and streaming tunes available on ubiquitous screens and through headphones. There are free rape-porn videos, online beheadings, streaming snuff films, and first-person shooter video games. The lyrics in rap and heavy metal are raunchier and rawer. The imagery is coarse. And graphic cultural scripts for violence can be freely found online. There is a qualitative difference here that is created by new media and by newly evolving standards of acceptable speech and behavior. And I fear things will get worse.

So is there any room for hope? Mark Twain held out hope that we were making progress beyond the thuggishness woven into our culture. "Still we have made some progress: we no longer take pleasure in slaughtering or burning helpless men. We have reached a little altitude where we may look down upon the Indian Thugs with a complacent shudder; and we may even hope for a day, many centuries hence, when our posterity will look down upon us in the same way."[45] A hopeful alternative to thug culture was imagined by Twain's contemporaries, Jane Addams and William James, who articulated the outline of the idea for a moral equivalent or substitute of war.[46] James and Addams recognized that some people—usually young men—enjoyed being thugs. And they imagined that the cure for violence and war was finding a way to channel thuggishness into productive outlets.

If there is to be a solution to the problem of thug culture, it should be imagined from this direction: to build a culture of peace that teaches men how to channel their testosterone through productive scripts and peaceful means. The difficulty, of course, is that in our thug culture, we are awash in destructive scripts. Building a culture of peace requires cultural work: a deliberate attempt to disseminate peacebuilding and positive peace as heroic outlets for the human spirit. Philosophers who are concerned with peace should be concerned with this project.

I have acknowledged that it is difficult to establish a causal relationship between culture and action. Cultural forces are more complicated than any single, reductive causal story admits. Specific acts of violence have complex biological, psychological, social, economic, and geographic roots. Nonetheless, cultures normalize and celebrate certain ideas, actions, and personality types. Thug culture normalizes and celebrates violence. Thug culture is a lubricant that facilitates violence and a virus that spreads it. Violence would continue

45 Twain, *Following the Equator*, 437.

46 Jane Addams, *Newer Ideals of Peace* (New York: McMillan, 1911); William James, "The Moral Equivalent of War" in *Essays in Religion and Morality*, ed. William James, (Cambridge, MA: Harvard University Press, 1982).

to occur without thug culture; but it would not appear so heroic, exciting, and sexy. Thug culture is dangerous—and one should rightfully criticize the ways it normalizes and celebrates violence.

Let me conclude with a bit of hope. The work of theorists such as Galtung, Girard, Foucault, and others—along with the sorts of empirical research discussed above—is opening our eyes to the idea of cultural violence. We are beginning to understand the power of cultural violence. I hope we are also beginning to understand the nihilism of thug culture. Some young men will continue to be turned on by violence. But one hopes that disciples of the thug life can find ways to direct their violence in less destructive ways. When would-be thugs make music videos instead of making mayhem in the streets, we may, in fact, be on our way toward a better world. Ironically, then, the media that permit the spread of thug cultures may also provide a kind of solution. But what's required in order to move forward is an ongoing critique of thug culture.

Bibliography

Addams, Jane. *Newer Ideals of Peace.* New York: McMillan, 1911.

American Academy of Pediatrics. Statement on Media Violence (2009). http://pediatrics.aappublications.org/content/124/5/1495.full.

American Academy of Child and Adolescent Psychiatry. Statement by Eugene Beresin. "The Impact of Media Violence on Children and Adolescents: Opportunities for Clinical Interventions." (2015). https://www.aacap.org/aacap/Medical_Students_and_Residents/Mentorship_Matters/DevelopMentor/The_Impact_of_Media_Violence_on_Children_and_Adolescents_Opportunities_for_Clinical_Interventions.aspx.

American Psychological Association. Draft Report on violent video games (2015a). https://www.apa.org/news/press/releases/2015/08/technical-violent-games.pdf.

American Psychological Association. Press Release on violent video games (2015b). http://www.apa.org/news/press/releases/2015/08/violent-video-games.aspx.

Asma, Stephen. "The Weaponised Loser." *Aeon.* (June 27, 2016). https://aeon.co/essays/humiliation-and-rage-how-toxic-masculinity-fuels-mass-shootings.

Cady, Duane. *From Warism to Pacifism.* Philadelphia: Temple University Press, 2010.

Chalmers, Phil. *Inside the Mind of a Teen Killer.* Nashville: Thomas Nelson, 2009.

Coleman, Loren. *The Copy Cat Effect: How the Media and Popular Culture Trigger the Mayhem in Tomorrow's Headlines.* New York: Simon and Schuster, 2004.

Dobson, Roger. "Medical advances mask epidemic of violence by cutting murder rate." *BMJ* 325(7365): 615 (September 21, 2002).

Dyson, Michael Eric. *Holler if You Hear Me: Searching for Tupac Shakur.* New York: Basic Books, 2001.

Fiala, Andrew. *The Just War Myth: The Moral Illusions of War.* Lanham, MD: Rowman and Littlefield, 2008.

Fiala, Andrew. "General Patton and Private Ryan." In *Philosophy of War Films,* edited by David LaRocca. Lexington: University Press of Kentucky, 2015.

Foucault, Michel. *Society Must Be Defended: Lectures at the Collège de France, 1975–1976.* New York: Picador, 2003.

Freud, Sigmund. *Civilization and Its Discontents.* New York: Norton, 1961.

Friedersdorf, Conor. "Thugs and Terrorists Have Attacked Black Churches for Generations." *Atlantic Monthly,* June 18, 2015. http://www.theatlantic.com/politics/archive/2015/06/thugs-and-terrorists-have-plagued-black-churches-for-generations/396212/.

Galtung, Johan. "Cultural Violence." *Journal of Peace Research* 27: 3. (August 1990): 291–305.

Girard, René. *Violence and the Sacred.* London: Continuum, 2005.

Gladwell, Malcolm. "Thresholds of Violence: How School Shootings Catch On." *New Yorker,* October 19, 2015.

Grossman, David. *On Killing: The Psychological Cost of Learning to Kill in War and Society.* New York: Little Brown, 2009.

James, William. "The moral equivalent of war" in William James, *Essays in Religion and Morality.* Cambridge, MA: Harvard University Press, 1982.

Jeffries, Michael P. *Thug Life: Race, Gender, and the Meaning of Hip-Hop.* Chicago: University of Chicago Press, 2011.

Kurzman, Charles. *The Missing Martyrs: Why There Are So Few Muslim Terrorists.* New York: Oxford University Press, 2011.

Marcuse, Herbert. "The Problem of Violence and the Radical Opposition" (1967). https://www.marxists.org/reference/archive/marcuse/works/1967/violence.htm.

McWhorter, John, interview by Melissa Block, *All Things Considered,* April 20, 2015. http://www.npr.org/2015/04/30/403362626/the-racially-charged-meaning-behind-the-word-thug.

Packer, George. "The Other France." *New Yorker,* August 31, 2015.

Paterson, Orlando. "The Real Problem with America's Inner Cities." *New York Times Sunday Review,* May 9, 2015.

Pieslak, Jonathan R. *Sound Targets: American Soldiers and Music in the Iraq War.* Bloomington: Indiana University Press, 2009.

Shaban, Hamza, "Playing War: How the Military Uses Video Games." *The Atlantic,* October 2013. http://www.theatlantic.com/technology/archive/2013/10/playing-war-how-the-military-uses-video-games/280486/.

Thornton, Edward. *Illustrations of the History and Practices of the Thugs.* London: Nattali and Bond, 1851.

Turse, Nick. *The Complex: How the Military Invades Our Everyday Lives.* New York: Metropolitan Books, 2008.

Twain, Mark. *Following the Equator: A Journey Around the World.* Hartford, CT: American Publishing, 1898.

Winkler, Elizabeth. "Malcolm Gladwell Is Wrong about School Shootings." *New Republic,* October 2015. https://newrepublic.com/article/123139/malcolm-gladwell-wrong-about-school-shooters.

Wrangham, Richard and Dale Peterson. *Demonic Males: Apes and Origins of Human Violence.* New York: Houghton Mifflin, 1996.

CHAPTER 2

The Role of Language in Justifying and Eliminating Cultural Violence

William C. Gay

In this essay, I address the relation of language to cultural violence. More specifically, I present how my treatments of linguistic violence and linguistic nonviolence can occupy a central place within investigations into how cultural violence is justified and how it can be eliminated. To present my position, I begin with some comments on defining violence and a review of Johan Galtung's concepts of direct, structural, and cultural violence and his presentation of language as one type of cultural violence. Next, I address the positions of Slavoj Žižek and Paul Ricoeur on the relation of language to violence and indicate why I do not find their approaches to be satisfactory. Then, after reviewing my own work on linguistic violence and nonviolence, I turn to the work of Patricia Friedrich and others in peace linguistics and nonkilling linguistics in order to develop a more helpful approach and present how in philosophy Irene Comins Mingol and Sonia París Albert apply the related concept of nonkilling philosophy. I end by reviewing how the linguistic positions I have supported contribute to reducing cultural violence and to advancing social justice.

Defining Violence and Cultural Violence

Violence and Human Affairs

Typically, violence involves the use or presence of force. In this essay, when I use the term "violence," I am referring to human affairs. In human affairs, many of the most obvious cases also involve the intention to hurt or harm, although hurt and harm that count as violence can occur without the perpetrator being conscious of or intending such a result, or can even occur with no specific perpetrator being identifiable. While most people also refer to some natural events as violent, this use of the term is distinct from the one I am following. Even in human affairs, while violence involves force, not all force is violence. When someone's tooth is removed, force is used. However, we typically do not use the term "violence" when consent is present. So, in human affairs, a central

 | DOI 10.1163/9789004361911_004

characteristic of the obvious forms of violence concerns whether force or some use of restraint or discrimination occurs without consent. When such consent is absent, violence is present—although in some cases, even when such consent is present, violence is also present.

The preceding remarks show some of the problems in trying to define violence. One way to deal with the confusion would be to turn to the work of the later Wittgenstein. In trying to define violence, we may have a situation like what Wittgenstein described as language games, where no single definition of a term will work.[1] Instead, we initially need to look at how a word is used in various language games. We may be able to group several such language games according to family resemblance, but we are not going to get a clear, definite, universal, essential, and unambiguous definition. We then can show that some ways a word is used are not part of one of the language games we are playing (such as when a forceful storm is called "violent"). From the perspective I have presented, I find misdirected the response of some that we need an objective standard for defining violence if we are to avoid relativism or a use of the term "violence" that merely rationalizes our own desires or feelings. For many terms, legal to scientific, such objective standards are lacking, but the use of the terms can still be meaningful and reasonable and not just a subjective rationalization. Nevertheless, since we can come to see matters differently, the definition of such terms should not be viewed as "chiseled in stone." We change laws, and we change scientific paradigms—from eliminating unjustified racial and gender discrimination to changing scientific paradigms that have too many anomalies to be practical for accurate predication of the course of nature. Of course, changes in legal and scientific definitions often have relied partly or even largely on violence. My preference is for such change to come about, as Socrates would say, as the result of the "force of the better argument"—not because of the force of the "better club" or other instrument of nonrational persuasion.

To present my argument in relation to cultural violence, I need to consider typologies of the violence in human affairs that include moral and ethical considerations. Specifically, I will trace and accept the views of Johan Galtung. Then, I will show why I find less than satisfactory the views of Slavoj Žižek and Paul Ricoeur. Once I have made these clarifications, I will proceed with my discussion of cultural violence and the role of language in relation to it.

1 Ludwig Wittgenstein, *Philosophical Investigations*, trans. G.E.M. Anscombe (New York: Macmillan, 1953); William Gay, "Wittengenstein and Applied Philosophy," *The International Journal of Applied Philosophy* 9, n1 (Summer/Fall 1994a): 15–20.

Galtung on Language as a Domain of Cultural Violence

In 1969 Johan Galtung introduced his concept of "structural violence" as a complement to "direct violence."[2] Twenty-one years later he added the concept of "cultural violence." He says, "direct violence is an *event*; structural violence is a *process* with ups and downs; cultural violence is an *invariant*, a 'permanence.'"[3] Direct violence is more obvious and is usually visible and done by an individual or a group. Murder is a frequently cited example; it also includes war. Direct violence is usually intentional, although cases such as involuntary manslaughter can be unintentional. Structural violence is less obvious and is often invisible and viewed as "ordinary," "normal," or "natural." Examples include forms of discrimination against specific groups, such as denying women the right to vote or racial segregation of schools. Structural violence is detected more by an examination of consequences rather than intent (or lack thereof). Cultural violence involves meaning, specifically systems that justify or legitimate direct or structural violence. The "superstructures" of a society, exemplified by its ideologies, provide the explanation for direct and structural violence and are needed by them. Cultural violence is frequently very difficult to detect because it is part of the "taken for granted" assumptions perpetuated within a society.

In making cultural violence a "permanence" or constant, Galtung is viewing cultural violence like a normative lens that is a socially constructed and pervasive phenomenon that functions like Duane Cady's "warism."[4] Cultural violence and warism, as normative lenses, constrict our vision and action. We so much take violence for granted that we do not envision the possibility of a society without it. Violence is a means to ends; at most, we judge some occurrences to be excessive, illegal, or unethical. Particular cases are questioned, not the use of violence in general.

By introducing cultural violence, Galtung greatly extends the range and types of phenomena considered as violence, especially in relation to the justification of direct violence and structural violence. He defines cultural violence as "those aspects of culture, the symbolic sphere of our existence … that can be used to justify or legitimize direct or structural violence."[5] In this essay, he

2 Johan Galtung, "Violence, Peace, and Peace Research," *Journal of Peace Research* 6:3 (1969): 167–199, accessed July 25, 2014, http://www.jstor.org/stable/422690.

3 Johan Galtung, "Cultural Violence," *Journal of Peace Research* 27:3 (August 1990): 294, accessed August 31, 2015, http://www.jstor.org/stable/423472.

4 Duane Cady, *From Warism to Pacifism: A Moral Continuum*, 2nd ed. (Philadelphia: Temple University Press, 2010).

5 Galtung, "Cultural Violence," 291.

presents language as one of the six "cultural domains" that he cites, along with religion, ideology, art, empirical science, and formal science. His section on language, however, contains only two relatively brief paragraphs and, in relation to means of reducing cultural violence, focuses on efforts at nonsexist writing. Although he later publishes a little more on language, he attends to it primarily in relation to peace education and language instruction. For this reason, I connect my two decades of research into exposing and overcoming linguistic violence with Galtung's call for broader endeavors within peace education, including ones concerning cultural violence.

Galtung also contrasts direct violence as being personal and structural violence as as involving social injustice.[6] This distinction parallels Newton Garver's concepts of personal and institutional violence.[7] Both direct and structural violence, like Garver's personal and institutional violence, can be physical or psychological. Also, Galtung adds, in parallel forms, intended and unintended direct violence and manifest or latent structural violence. In addition, each of these types of violence can be with objects or without objects.[8] Galtung presents the absence of direct (personal) violence as negative peace and the absence of structural violence (social injustice) as positive peace.[9] He concludes by suggesting that peace research, as he frames it, aims for both the absence of direct (personal) violence and the presence of social justice.[10]

Galtung makes various additional distinctions regarding violence. At times some of his distinctions become a bit fuzzy. This point can be illustrated with a further consideration of Garver's distinctions. Garver has overt personal, covert personal, overt institutional, and covert institutional, and, correspondingly, Galtung has physical personal and psychological personal, and physical structural and psychological structural. Then later, when Galtung adds cultural violence, it seems to be covert institutional in Garver's terms or, in Galtung's own earlier terms, psychological structural violence. Nevertheless, any points of omission or even confusion in the details of Galtung's view, expressed over three decades, are minor. The thrust of his work remains central to the field. He has the most extensive set of terms that are very widely used and well constructed. Rather than carp further about Galtung's terminology and treatment of violence, I wish to contrast the value of his contribution with the more

6 Galtung, "Violence, Peace, and Peace Research," 173.

7 Newton Garver, "What Violence Is," *The Nation* 209 (24 June 1968): 817–822.

8 Galtung, "Violence, Peace, and Peace Research," 173.

9 Galtung, "Violence, Peace, and Peace Research" 183.

10 Galtung, "Violence, Peace, and Peace Research," 186.

problematic position of Slavoj Žižek and the more limited contribution of Paul Ricoeur.

Žižek and Ricoeur on Violence and Language

Žižek and the Problem of Whether Violence is Justified

I give more detailed attention to Slavoj Žižek not only because his work is less well known but also because it undercuts efforts to highlight the problem of cultural violence and to advance a philosophy of nonviolence. Žižek's most often cited work in this area is his book *Violence: Six Sideways Reflections.*[11] In relation to this book, Harry van der Linden provides a thorough analysis and critique of how Žižek's view can too easily justify revolutionary violence "as counter-violence to systemic violence," as well as a variety of confusions and suspect assertions in Žižek's reflections.[12]

At first glance, Žižek's distinctions on violence have parallels to ones in Galtung. Žižek has three forms of violence: subjective and objective, with objective being divided into symbolic and systemic. Respectively, these three forms roughly correspond to direct, cultural, and structural in Galtung. Žižek sometimes refers to subjective violence as direct or physical and to objective violence as ideological.

Concerning objective violence, Žižek says that the first form (symbolic) is "embodied in language and its forms, what Heidegger would call 'our house of being'" and continues "there is a more fundamental form of violence still that pertains to language as such, to its imposition of a certain universal meaning."[13] So, examples of both the "obvious" and "more fundamental" are ones of symbolic violence. Continuing with objective violence, Žižek says, "Second, there is what I call 'systemic' violence, or the often catastrophic consequences of the smooth functioning of our economic and political systems."[14] Hence, objective violence can be symbolic or systemic and pertain to language or economic and political systems.

Regarding the relation of subjective and objective violence, he makes an important point regarding subjective violence as visible and as seen against a

11 Slavoj Žižek, *Violence: Six Sideways Reflections* (New York: Picador, 2008).

12 Harry van der Linden, "On the Violence of Systemic Violence: A Critique of Slavoj ŽiŽek," *Radical Philosophy Review* 15:1 (2012): 2, accessed August 19, 2015, http://digitalcommons.butler.edu/cgi/viewcontent.cgi?article=1249&context=facsch_papers.

13 Žižek, *Violence,* 2.

14 Žižek, *Violence,* 2.

nonviolent zero level, and objective violence as invisible and as the violence that is inherent in what we take to be normal: "The catch is that subjective and objective violence cannot be perceived from the same standpoint: subjective violence … is seen as a perturbation of the 'normal,' peaceful state of things. However, objective violence is precisely the violence inherent to this 'normal' state of things. Objective violence is invisible since it sustains the very zero-level standard against which we perceive something as subjectively violent."[15] These points are quite similar to ones made by Galtung. His objective violence is like Galtung's cultural violence, except that Žižek does not present how it is a social construct that justifies or legitimates violence.

In the section on "The Violence of Language" in his chapter on "Fear Thy Neighbor As Thyself!" he says: "As Hegel was already well aware, there is something violent in the very symbolization of a thing.… Language simplifies the designated thing, reducing it to a single feature. It dismembers the thing, destroying its organic unity, treating its parts and properties as autonomous."[16] Later, using Hegelian concepts, he says, "when we perceive something as an act of violence, we measure it by a presupposed standard of what the 'normal' non-violent situation is—and the highest form of violence is the imposition of this standard with reference to which some events appear as 'violent.' This is why language itself, the very medium of non-violence, of mutual recognition, involves unconditional violence. In other words, it is language itself which pushes our desire beyond proper limits, transforming it into a 'desire that contains the infinite,' elevating it into an absolute striving that cannot ever be satisfied."[17] So, he does say that language "involves unconditional violence." Somehow this unconditional violence is connected with the insatiability of human desire. While I concede to Hegel that desire brings negation into the world, I do not concede to Žižek that all desire and all language involve violence—even though I admit both too often lead to a great deal of unjustified violence.

In his final chapter, he says, "Better to do nothing than to engage in localized acts the ultimate function of which is to make the system run more smoothly."[18] He continues, "The threat today is not passivity, but pseudo-activity, the urge to 'be active'.… People intervene all the time … academics participate in meaningless debates, and so on. The truly difficult thing is to step back, to withdraw. Those in power often prefer even a 'critical' participation, a dialogue,

15 Žižek, *Violence,* 2.
16 Žižek, *Violence,* 61.
17 Žižek, *Violence,* 64–65.
18 Žižek, *Violence,* 216.

to silence—just to engage us in 'dialogue,' to make sure our ominous passivity is broken."[19] He ends, "If one means by violence a radical upheaval of the basic social relations, then, crazy and tasteless as it may sound, the problem with historical monsters who slaughtered millions was that they were not violent enough. Sometimes doing nothing is the most violent thing to do."[20] Given such claims, Žižek can leave the individual confused, if not paralyzed or even inappropriately violent, in relation to responding to the multifarious forms of violence.

Ricoeur and the Problem of Whether Speech is Violent

Several phenomenologists have described effectively the subjective experience and meaning of violence, particularly on the basis of the work of Maurice Merleau-Ponty and Alfred Schutz.[21] However, I discuss here only the work of Paul Ricoeur, since he explicitly treats violence in relation to language in his essay "Violence and Language."[22] Here he presents violence and language as standing in "formal opposition."[23] He views language itself as "innocent" or neutral, saying, "Language as speech ... is the place where violence reaches expression."[24] He contrasts the way in which "violence speaks" in a tyranny with the way in which philosophy aims at "judicious discourse" and denounces tyranny because it invades language. Ricoeur is also aware of how language can be usurped by persons in power: "Tyranny makes its way by seduction, persuasion, and flattery; the tyrant prefers the services of the sophist to those of the executioner."[25] Beyond Ricoeur, I need to add that this problem is not just one for oppressors; it is a danger as well for delegates for the oppressed, as Pierre Bourdieu makes clear.[26]

19 Žižek, *Violence*, 217.

20 Žižek, *Violence*, 217.

21 William C. Gay, "Probability in the Social Sciences: A Critique of Weber and Schutz," *Human Studies* 1:1 (January 1978): 16–37; William C. Gay, "Merleau-Ponty on Language and Social Science: The Dialectic of Phenomenology and Structuralism," *Man and World* 12:3 (1979): 322–338; Michael Staudigl, "Towards a Phenomenological Theory of Violence: Reflections Following Merleau-Ponty and Schutz," *Human Studies* 30 (2007): 233–253.

22 Paul Ricoeur, "Violence and Language," in *Political and Social Essays* [of Paul Ricoeur], eds. David Stewart and Joseph Bien, trans. Joseph Bien (Athens: Ohio University Press, 1975), 88–101, accessed April 13, 2015, jffp.org/ojs/index.php/jffp/article/download/410/404.

23 Ricoeur, "Violence and Language," [from web source], 33.

24 Ricoeur, "Violence and Language," [from web source], 34.

25 Ricoeur, "Violence and Language," [from web source], 34.

26 Pierre Bourdieu, *Language and Symbolic Power*, ed. John B. Thompson and trans. Gino Raymond and Matthew Adamson (Cambridge: Harvard University Press, 1991), 209–214;

Ricoeur goes in a different direction that is more like Martin Heidegger when he suggests that the poet, in surrendering to Being, "forces things to speak."[27] Žižek, too, makes this connection, saying that Heidegger associates ontological violence with "language itself" and presents this "essential violence" as grounding or opening up "explosions of ontic or physical violence."[28] Still, Ricoeur retains the hope that language can move us toward "rational meaning" if we respect that "the multiplicity, diversity, and hierarchy of languages is the only way ... to work towards rational meaning."[29] My criticism here is like one I made of Žižek. What Ricoeur says of poets may be true of many of them, but I am not prepared to make a blanket statement, as I suspect from much of his other work, Ricoeur also would not want to do.[30] Moreover, despite Ricoeur's effort to orient language to expressing the truth, his efforts, like those of other phenomenologists, retain the focus on subjectivity and generally stop short of dealing with the more objective features of cultural violence.

Given my initial comments on defining violence, I obviously am not including within my discussion of violence in general and cultural violence in particular phenomena such as cosmic explosions or the view of nature as "red in tooth and claw." Cosmic violence and even ontological violence, if one wishes to use these terms, are not what I am discussing. Likewise, I am not discussing violence among nonhuman animals. Use of these terms confuses our understanding of those forms of violence about which we should be concerned, about which we should hold some people responsible, and about which we can do something to reduce or eliminate their occurrence.

The notion of "fighting fire with fire" is also of limited value in discussion of violence in human affairs. Of course, quite literally, sometimes to effectively fight fire one needs to use fire. One clear example is the burning of fire lanes to reduce the risk of the spread of wildfires. In the case of human affairs, however, such an analogy begs the question of whether violence needs to be countered with violence. Even if cases exist where violence is needed to reduce or stop violence, other methods are generally available and, normatively, may be preferable. Just as you should not throw water on a grease fire, I contend you

---

William C. Gay, "Bourdieu and the Social Conditions of Wittgensteinian Language Games," *The International Journal of Applied Philosophy* 11:1 (1996): 15–21.

27 Ricoeur, "Violence and Language," [from web source], 37.

28 Žižek, *Violence*, 70.

29 Ricoeur, "Violence and Language," [from web source], 41.

30 William C. Gay, "Ricoeur on Metaphor and Ideology," *Darshana International* 32:1 (January 1992): 59–70.

should not use violence that fans violence in an effort to stop its spread—since other effective nonviolent means are available.

Regarding Žižek and Ricoeur, I thus ask the following question: Is the locus of violence in human affairs as general as the cosmos or as specific as language? In reading Žižek you can wonder if violence is a characteristic of the universe quite apart from human beings, and in reading Ricoeur you can wonder if the culprit is speech itself. To refer to the cosmos as violent characterizes its physical forces like some that are distinctive to creatures with volition and choice. The physical forces of the cosmos or nature are better characterized as indifferent, neutral or, more accurately and to avoid anthropomorphism, as consequences of physically determined causal chains. Properly, as I am using the term, violence pertains to creatures with volition and choice—although, as I have noted previously, persons can commit or experience violence in ways where consent is unrecognized or even absent. In relation to human beings, violence likely precedes or is pretty much coeval with human speech, but this violence was and is done by creatures with volition and choice. Speech may well often, if not initially, express the occurrence of the violence that precedes it and even occurs through it. However, while much speech may be violent, speech itself is not violent. The violence of speech, linguistic violence, arises from language and how it is used.[31]

In summary, by questioning the utility of Žižek and Ricoeur for my project, I am advocating a middle ground that is narrower on the scope of violence in the sense that I am not considering it apart from human affairs or as a function of language per se. Moreover, since alternatives to the ways language is used are possible, these choices can reduce or avoid violence. So, where are we left in reflecting on language and violence, specifically on the relation of language to cultural violence?

Linguistic Violence and Linguistic Nonviolence

In answering my question on the relation of language to cultural violence, I will review the position on linguistic violence and linguistic nonviolence that I have been developing since the 1990s. Then I will present some of the work of Patricia Friedrich, a linguist at Arizona State University who is originally from Brazil.

31 Gay, "Bourdieu and Social Conditions"; William C. Gay, "Nonsexist Public Discourse and Negative Peace: The Injustice of Merely Formal Transformation," *The Acorn: Journal of the Gandhi-King Society* 9:1 (Spring 1997): 45–53.

Language and Violence

How can language do violence? For Stephanie Ross, a U.S. feminist, offensive language hurts us, while language that harms us is oppressive.[32] Some words that are directed at us can hurt us psychologically, and language in general can perpetuate the harm of a system of oppression, regardless of whether individuals consciously experience the hurt of its transgressions against them. Since the claim that language can do violence we are unaware of is more difficult to support, Ross restricts her analysis to the efforts at exposing and eliminating offensive forms of language. While I agree language that hurts does what I term linguistic violence, I go beyond what Ross argues by contending that language that harms us also does linguistic violence and also should be eliminated.[33] Likewise, I maintain that linguistic nonviolence can occur, and we may or may not be aware of it.[34] We can be aware of how the use of some terms uplifts us, although we may not be aware of how other aspects of a language system can provide recognition and affirmation of us. Since language is part of our culture, use of the concepts of linguistic violence and linguistic nonviolence allows me to expose aspects that contribute to cultural violence and injustice and to advance aspects that contribute to cultural nonviolence and justice.

With my concepts of linguistic violence and linguistic nonviolence, I try to do several things. First, I show how the concept of violence is applicable to language. Second, I suggest that the forms of linguistic violence can be conceived along a continuum that ranges from very subtle to very grievous forms. Third, I contend that a practice of linguistic nonviolence is possible. To support my position, I defend the following five theses on language.[35]

1. Language is a social institution, and one of the most conservative ones in any society.
2. Language is inseparable from the distribution of power in society, and these relations are unequal in every society.
3. Language is frequently an instrument of covert institutional violence.

---

32 Stephanie Ross, "How Words Hurt: Attitude, Metaphor, and Oppression," in *Sexist Language: A Modern Philosophical Analysis*, ed. Mary Vetterling-Braggin (Huber Heights, Ohio: Littlefield, Adams, 1981), 197.

33 William C. Gay, "Linguistic Violence," in *Institutional Violence*, eds. Deane Curtin and Robert Litke (Amsterdam: Rodopi, 1999), 13–34.

34 William C. Gay, "The Practice of Linguistic Nonviolence," *Peace Review* 10, n4 (1998b): 545–547.

35 William C. Gay, "Exposing and Overcoming Linguistic Alienation and Linguistic Violence," *Philosophy and Social Criticism* 24, n2/3 (1998a): 138.

4. Language shapes, but does not determine, human consciousness and behavior.
5. Language that appears to ameliorate conditions of social violence can actually represent a merely formally sanctioned sphere of less violent discourse that leaves unchanged the cultural base that spawns and sustains various forms of social violence.

To convey the range of linguistic violence, I employ a continuum that progresses from subtle, through abusive, to grievous forms. I also give a few examples of each. (See Table 2.1)

Unfortunately, the lack of linguistic determinism does not imply that, once recognized, linguistic violence will be overcome. On the contrary, linguistic freedom and linguistic creativity can be used to impose additional restrictions on social groups and further distort perceptions of them, just as much as they can be used to empower social groups and enrich our understanding and appreciation of human diversity. Nevertheless, one can reduce linguistic violence by simply refraining from using offensive and oppressive terms, since alternative more neutral or positive terms are almost always available or can be coined. However, just because linguistic violence is not being used, a genuinely peaceful discourse is not necessarily present. Nonviolent discourse, like the condition of peace, can be negative or positive.[36] The peaceful discourse that is analogous to negative peace can actually perpetuate injustice.

I have done much more work on linguistic violence than I have on linguistic nonviolence. For this reason, since I ultimately want to advance nonviolence and social justice, I have searched for works that address advancing the practice of linguistic nonviolence. In the remainder of this essay, I will summarize the most important of these investigations that I have found.

TABLE 2.1 *Forms of linguistic violence* (GAY, "EXPOSING AND OVERCOMING LINGUISTIC ALIENATION," 146 (MODIFIED)).

Subtle forms	**Abusive forms**	**Grievous forms**
Children's mean jokes	Heterosexist language	Warist language
Literacy restrictions	Racist language	Nuclear discourse
Official languages	Sexist language	Genocidal language

36 Gay, "Nonsexist Public Discourse," 45–53.

Friedrich and the Use of English to Advance Peace

As a linguist, Friedrich describes empirically how language can foster violence and nonviolence, and she argues normatively that we should use nonviolent language to foster nonviolent society. So, just as language can function as an instrument of cultural violence that justifies or legitimates direct and structural violence, language can also function as a means to reduce and avoid linguistic violence. In this regard, through tracing how she connects my work on linguistic violence with treatments of cultural violence, I have been introduced to the very promising fields of peace linguistics and nonkilling linguistics.

Friedrich's book *Language, Negotiation and Peace*, published in 2007, is very useful for reflecting on language and the quest for peace.[37] She begins her first chapter by addressing "Theories of peace and conflict and their relationship to language." While philosophers are familiar with the challenges of formulating a precise definition, Friedrich notes the additional problem of the word "peace" as it is associated with different terms in different languages. She is making the point that the word "peace" stands in opposition to different words in different languages such that the scope of the term varies by language. For example, German uses *Frieden* for external peace and *Ruhe* for inner peace. Nevertheless, in trying to amalgamate various definitions of peace from a variety of languages, she focuses on the term being the opposite of "war" but in ways that can be negative or positive.[38] Hence, from an academic perspective, she connects her use of the term with Galtung's account that also stresses the distinction between negative and positive peace.

Friedrich begins with how languages, particularly ones imposed by hegemony, can function linguistically in a manner parallel to negative peace. In the 1990s some linguists introduced the term "linguistic imperialism" to refer to "the spread of English as a new form of imperialism, one imposed by the English speaking 'centre' and absorbed by the so-called 'periphery.'"[39] Nevertheless, she rejects the view that this status of English necessarily thwarts the pursuit of linguistic peace. First, imperialism itself is more of "a political, military, and economic mechanism of dominance which employs language simply (but effectively) as a tool," and, second, she points to the vast number of researchers and educators (and I would add social activists) who are

37 Patricia Friedrich, *Language, Negotiation and Peace: The Use of English in Conflict Resolution* (London: Continuum, 2007).

38 Friedrich, *Language, Negotiation and Peace*, 4.

39 Friedrich, *Language Negotiation and Peace*, 8.

"mobilized to present alternatives to counteract the possible ill effects of the widespread use of English."[40]

Since Friedrich cites in particular Robert Phillipson's 1992 book *Linguistic Imperialism*, I will make a few comments on his position. His concept of linguistic imperialism could be viewed as a pervasive and key component in cultural violence, which gets manifested internationally in cultural imperialism. Phillipson says, "Galtung's theory does not refer to linguistic imperialism, but this can be seen as a sub-type of what he refers to as cultural imperialism."[41] In addition, Phillipson coins the term "linguicism," which he says "is distinct from other '-isms,' such as sexism and racism, in so far as it is language rather than gender or race which is the crucial criterion in the beliefs and structure which result in unequal power and resource allocation."[42] He continues, "*Linguicism* involves representation of the dominant language, to which desirable characteristics are attributed, for purposes of inclusion, and the opposite for dominated languages, for purposes of exclusion," and English linguistic imperialism is one of its subtypes.[43]

In his treatment of linguistic imperialism and linguicism, Phillipson also connects what he terms "anglocentricity" with professionalism.[44] Just as ethnocentricity gives primacy to one group of people, anglocentricity gives primacy to the English language, particularly the version supported by a central political authority and professionals in academia and elsewhere. However, he does not say much about what is to be done, although he does advocate linguistic rights. Nevertheless, he was writing before the UNESCO "Universal Declaration of Linguistic Rights" (UNESCO 1996).[45] Moreover, since the 1990s numerous responses have been made that, while affirming the reality of linguistic imperialism, do not advocate ending the globally dominant status of English. Athelstan Suresh Canagarajah, for example, cites recent orientations to language that at least partly free "subjects to reclaim their agency, negotiate the different subjectivities and ideologies offered by completing discourses, and adopt a subject position favorable to their empowerment."[46] Beyond the

40 Friedrich, *Language Negotiation and Peace*, 8–9.

41 Robert Phillipson, *Linguistic Imperialism* (Oxford: Oxford University Press, 1992), 51.

42 Phillipson, *Linguistic Imperialism*, 54.

43 Phillipson, *Linguistic Imperialism*, 55.

44 Phillipson, *Linguistic Imperialism*, 47.

45 UNESCO, "Universal Declaration on Linguistic Rights," World Conference on Linguistic Rights. Barcelona, Spain, 9 June 1996, accessed July 24, 2015. http://www.unesco.org/cpp/uk/declarations/linguistic.pdf.

46 Athelstan Suresh Canagarajah, *Resisting Linguistic Imperialism in English Teaching* (Oxford: Oxford University Press, 1999), 30.

efforts of Paulo Freire, he mentions in particular the work of bell hooks.[47] Of course, efforts to establish English as the official language, at least of the United States if not the world, persist.[48]

Like Phillipson, Friedrich appeals to linguistic human rights. However, she is writing after the adoption of the "Universal Declaration of Human Rights." She says, "Upholding human rights is one of the primary tasks in building positive peace. If individuals have their basic needs respected and catered for, they will theoretically be less likely to try and pursue justice by means of violence."[49] Among treatments of human rights, a few philosophers have given some attention to language. For example, David Boersema has addressed free expression, and Will Kymlicka and Alan Patten have addressed language rights, but they do not explicitly make ties with the UNESCO declaration or with efforts to achieve peace.[50]

Within linguistics, Friedrich is the one who directly connects pursuit of linguistic rights and human rights, sometimes simply called "linguistic human rights," with efforts to attain peace. In fact, in her book *Language, Negotiation and Peace*, she appends the UNESCO Declaration of Linguistic Rights. Despite the difficulties and challenges, Friedrich concludes, even before her work with nonkilling linguists, "at present no other language is in a better position to seek and mediate peace than English."[51] For this reason, she adds we can and should "seek positive peace through English."[52]

In relation to this debate, my position is the following. If the thesis of linguistic determinism is correct, conscious efforts to change language cannot succeed.[53] If the thesis of linguistic imperialism is correct, conscious efforts to change language may be incapable of overcoming the hegemonic power of the official language. Nevertheless, if linguistic volunteerism is possible,

47 Canagarajah, *Resisting*, 35.

48 Eduardo Hernández-Chávez, "Language Policy in the United Sates: A History of Cultural Genocide," in *Human Rights: Overcoming Linguistic Discrimination*, eds., Tove Skutnabb-Kangas and Robert Phillipson in collaboration with Mart Rannut (Berlin: Mouton de Gruyter, 1994), 141–158.

49 Friedrich, *Language, Negotiation and Peace*, 66.

50 David Boersema, *Philosophy of Human Rights: Theory and Practice* (Boulder, CO: Westview Press, 2011); Will Kymlicka and Alan Patten, eds., *Language Rights and Political Theory* (Oxford: Oxford University Press, 2003).

51 Frederich, *Language, Negotiation and Peace*, 5.

52 Frederich, *Language, Negotiation and Peace*, 6.

53 William C. Gay, "Nuclear Discourse and Linguistic Alienation," *Journal of Social Philosophy* 18:2 (Summer 1987): 42–49; Gay, "Exposing and Overcoming Linguistic Alienation," 137–156; William C. Gay, "Linguistic Violence," 13–34.

linguistic resistance is possible. Since conscious efforts to change language sometimes succeed, the thesis of linguistic determinism is not correct. Moreover, since efforts to practice linguistic resistance sometimes succeed, the thesis of linguistic imperialism needs to be qualified to admit that within an official language, individuals can speak and write in ways that can challenge and transform not only these linguistic structures but also the social structures that it legitimates and supports.[54]

Advancing Linguistic Peace and Linguistic Justice

Returning to Friedrich's main argument, in her section on "Offsetting violence," she discusses both Galtung's notion of cultural violence and my concept of linguistic violence. Noting how I contend that the issue is whether linguistic violence can be eliminated, she concludes, "The mere fact that I wrote this book should be enough to determine that I believe in the possibility of change and the power of conscious effort."[55] Noting the inability of artificial languages, such as Esperanto and Volapük, to function as a global language and how instead English currently fulfills such a need, Friedrich, while admitting the problems of linguistic violence and hegemony in English, aims for more equality and for linguistic peace. She states, "This search has given rise to peace linguistics, an interdisciplinary branch of linguistics and peace studies which concerns itself with relationships between language, communication, education and peace. As a branch of linguistics, it is situated alongside sociolinguistics and pragmatics in so far as all three consider issues of language in use, its effects and implications."[56]

For moving toward her version of a practice of linguistic nonviolence, she provides a useful chart. She commends:

> Instead of reinforcing the negative, we can reinforce the positive by adding to our vocabulary the terms in the right-hand column below, and adjusting our reasoning accordingly.... The greatest threat lies in the misuse of language as instruments of oppression rather than understanding. (See Table 2.2)

54 Gay, "Nonsexist Public Discourse"; Gay, "Exposing and Overcoming Linguistic Alienation"; Gay, "Practice of Linguistic Nonviolence," 545–547; William C. Gay, "Supplanting Linguistic Violence," in *Gender Violence*, eds. Laura L. O'Toole, Jessica R. Schiffman, and Margie L. Kiter Edwards, 2nd ed. (New York: New York University Press, 2007b), 435–442.

55 Friedrich, *Language, Negotiation and Peace*, 10.

56 Friedrich, *Language, Negotiation and Peace*, 12.

TABLE 2.2 *Terms of disagreement and agreement* (FRIEDRICH, *LANGUAGE, NEGOTIATION AND PEACE*, 70 (QUOTE AND TABLE)).

Disagreement-fostering terms	Cooperation-fostering terms
Linguistic violence	Linguistic peace
Linguicism	Communicative peace
Linguistic separatism	Linguistic rights
Killer languages	Linguistic justice
Linguistic genocide	Linguistic diversity
Linguistic imperialism	Linguistic choice
Linguistic hegemony	Languages of wider communication

In this regard, she cites my work in making her further point that changing terms that have negative meanings is insufficient if the underlying social structures that perpetuate inequality are not transformed as part of the effort to achieve positive peace. She is correct in characterizing my argument as meaning that "the unequal distribution of power that exists in every society and extends itself to linguistic power needs to be reshaped if we are to achieve linguistic justice."[57]

Interestingly, Friedrich's chart points toward the alternatives that need to be developed and are being developed in peace linguistics and elsewhere. These alternatives can also be seen as a response to Žižek. Of particular importance are the aims to move from linguicism to communicative peace, from linguistic imperialism to linguistic choice, and from linguistic hegemony to languages of wider communication. Communicative peace would be part of the practice of linguistic nonviolence. Linguistic choice is part of what I discuss below in addressing how bell hooks regards alternative cultural production and alternative epistemologies. Languages of wider communication include the aim within linguistics to document and advocate what are termed "World Englishes."[58]

As already noted, bell hooks is recognized as someone who has made significant contributions to reclaiming English for the oppressed. In *Teaching to Transgress*, bell hooks cites Adrienne Rich's poem, "The Burning of Paper Instead of Children" and quotes her line "This is the oppressor's language yet

57 Friedrich, *Language, Negotiation and Peace*, 7.

58 Andy Kirkpatrick, *World Englishes: Implications for International Communication and English Language Teaching* (Cambridge: Cambridge University Press, 2007).

I need it to talk to you."[59] bell hooks continues, "Standard English is not the speech of exile. It is the language of conquest and domination; in the United States, it is the mask which hides the loss of so many tongues, all those sounds of diverse, native communities we will never hear, the speech of the Gullah, Yiddish, and so many other unremembered tongues."[60] She adds, "It is difficult not to hear in standard English always the sound of slaughter and conquest."[61]

What does Rich mean by saying of the oppressor's language that "I need it to talk to you"? The oppressed need to use the oppressor's language (to speak what I term "the linguistic coin of the realm") in order to achieve personal power and to forge the space for and practice of alternative cultural production. Standard English, which globally is increasingly the linguistic coin of the realm, is "not the speech of exile," but this "language of conquest and domination" can be put to a different use; it can function in a different language game with emancipatory intent that can be understood by speakers of Standard English and potentially can even persuade enough of them to bring about social change that nonviolently advances social justice. In this way, Standard English, despite its echoes of "slaughter and conquest" can be reclaimed, contrary to the view of linguistic absolutists, who claim that the etymology and history of use of terms cannot be transcended.[62]

Why is English needed for resistance? Two questions first need to be asked. First, why use language to resist? Second, if language is used to resist, what type of language should be employed? In relation to the first question, while language is not the only form of resistance, it can be very effective. In relation to the second question, just because a method can be effective is not a sufficient justification. The language used needs to be understood and, I contend, needs to be as linguistically nonviolent as possible. In many cases, oppressors do not know the language of the oppressed or have very limited skills in or sympathy for it. In order to respond to oppression without turning to the violent means of the oppressor, the oppressed need do communicate with the oppressors in a language that the oppressors understand. On a global scale, English has held hegemonic sway for a long time and likely will continue to do so for quite a long time. So, from resistance by persons forcefully (violently) brought to the

59 bell hooks, *Teaching to Transgress: Education as the Practice of Freedom* (New York: Routledge, 1994), 167.

60 bell hooks, *Teaching to Transgress*, 168.

61 bell hooks, *Teaching to Transgress*, 169.

62 Lynne Tirrell, "Derogatory Terms: Racism, Sexism, and the Inferential Role Theory of Meaning," in *Language and Liberation: Feminism, Philosophy, and Language*, eds. Christina Hendricks and Kelly Oliver (Albany: State University of New York Press, 1999), 41–79.

United States from Africa as slaves to many other forms of resistance to U.S. global hegemony, the oppressed, in order to be heard, need to use English. Fortunately, the oppressed can use English that is both effective and nonviolent.

For resistance, we need the oppressor's language—we need English. As bell hooks says, "Learning English, learning to speak the alien tongue, was one way enslaved Africans began to reclaim their personal power within a context of domination."[63] bell hooks makes a point here that continues to be relevant under contemporary circumstances of linguistics imperialism and English linguicism. For bell hooks, we need to resist more than white supremacy; we also need to create spaces for "alternative cultural production and alternative epistemologies—different ways of thinking and knowing" in order to create "a counter-hegemonic worldview."[64] A language of linguistic nonviolence, of linguistic peace and linguistic justice, can reduce the manifestations of cultural violence found in linguistic violence, in linguistic imperialism, and hegemony. Just as language has been used to justify cultural violence, language can be used to reduce, even if it cannot ever fully eliminate, cultural violence. The fault is not with language, but the responsibility is with us in how we speak and act.

Moving beyond Cultural Violence

In efforts to move beyond cultural violence, I expand on my work on linguistic nonviolence by drawing from Patricia Friedrich's edited book *Nonkilling Linguistics*, published in 2012, in which she introduces this new field.[65] I also draw from the work of Irene Comins Mingol and Sonia París Albert to introduce nonkilling philosophy. Their works are among a small group that both challenge cultural violence and seek to develop alternatives to it.

Friedrich and Nonkilling Linguistics

In his book *Nonkilling Global Political Science* and through his Center for Global Nonkilling, located in Honolulu, Glen Paige introduced the nonkilling perspective.[66] His Center for Global Nonviolence began in 1994 and in 2008 developed into the Center for Global Nonkilling. Its mission is "to promote

63 bell hooks, *Teaching to Transgress*, 170.

64 bell hooks, *Teaching to Transgress*, 171.

65 Patricia Friedrich, "Introduction," in *Nonkilling Linguistics: Practical Applications*, ed. Patricia Friedrich (Honolulu: Center for Global Nonkilling, 2012a), 11–13.

66 Glen Paige, *Nonkilling Global Political Science* (Honolulu: Center for Global Nonkilling, 2002 and 2009).

change toward the measurable goal of a killing-free world" and now involves over six hundred scholars from three hundred academic institutions in seventy-three countries from twenty disciplinary fields.[67] Paige says his book is the first to have "nonkilling" in its title and notes that the book has now been translated into forty languages. He begins with the fact that "despite their lethal capability most humans are not and have not been killers."[68] He then contends that "nonkilling capabilities already have been demonstrated in a wide range of social institutions that, if creatively combined and adapted, can serve as component contributions to realize nonkilling societies."[69]

Linguistics and philosophy are among the more recent disciplines to become involved in the nonkilling project, and their focus on language connects with exposing cultural violence and forging alternatives to it. Patricia Friedrich, expanding on her work in peace linguistics, led this effort. In her Introduction to *Nonkilling Linguistics*, Friedrich says:

> It is true that we have the concepts of peace and nonviolence to lead us in a quest for a fairer and more just world and a meaningful social experience for all individuals. Indeed, these concepts are great light posts to guide us along the way. Their existence, however, does not obviate the kind of concrete goal that nonkilling can provide. Here we are talking about an absolutely measurable objective, one that can manifest itself both literally and figuratively. That is, nonkilling speaks both to the goal of preserving the physical lives of individuals, communities, other species, the environment as well as the more metaphorical but also extremely important survival of languages, cultures, histories (oral and written), literary manifestations, etc. The list is vast and varied, and the good news is that a nonkilling mentality can be applied to all these realms and lives.[70]

In the first chapter Friedrich and Francisco Gomes de Matos address the central role of language in establishing a nonkilling society. Their treatment of language is guided by two fundamental principles and pleas:

> *First fundamental principle*: "Language is a system for communicating in nonkilling ways."

67 Center for Global Nonkilling, accessed July 28, 2016, www.nonkilling.org.
68 Paige, *Nonkilling*, 9.
69 Paige, *Nonkilling*, 9.
70 Friedrich, *Nonkilling Linguistics*, 11.

> *Second fundamental principle*: "Language users should have the right to learn to communicate nonkillingly for the good of humankind."
>
> *First plea*: "Let us be communicative Humanizers, treating all language users with compassion and dignity."
>
> *Second plea*: "Let us opt for communicatively nonkilling uses of language."[71]

From this perspective how we regard and employ language can contribute significantly toward advancing positive peace.[72]

They go on to argue that peace linguistics and other academic subfields that focus on peace can contribute to "the building of a nonkilling society."[73] The application of this perspective to philosophy, however, had already begun with the 2009 essay "Nonkilling Philosophy" by Irene Comins Mingol and Sonia París Albert.[74] I turn to this essay to sketch the contribution that philosophy can make to the application of the nonkilling perspective not only to exposing cultural violence but also and more importantly to forging alternatives to cultural violence.

Comins Mingol and París Albert on Nonkilling Philosophy

Comins Mingol and París Albert, two philosophers from University Jaume in Spain, base their position on works in discourse ethics and care ethics. Regarding discourse ethics, they rely primarily on Jürgen Habermas, particularly his notions that discourse presupposes truth as an ideal and that truth should be operative at the level of the statements of speakers, the intentions that lie behind their words, and the actions that flow from them. In relation to care ethics, they rely primarily on Carol Gilligan, Betty Reardon, and Sara Ruddick, particularly the way in which their ethics of care facilitates an orientation toward nonviolence and peace. Both of these perspectives are part of an "epistemological turn" in philosophy, initiated by Vicent Martínez Guzmán, that rejects the orientation toward the "objectivity" and "neutrality" associated with logical positivism and supports the positions I cited earlier that reject

71 Patricia Friedrich and Francisco Gomes de Matos, "Toward a Nonkilling Linguistics," in *Nonkilling Linguistics: Practical Applications*, ed. Patricia Friedrich, (Honolulu: Center for Global Nonkilling, 2012b), 20–21.

72 Friedrich and Gomes de Matos, "Toward a Nonkilling Linguistics," 25.

73 Friedrich and Gomes de Matos, "Toward a Nonkilling Linguistics," 20.

74 Irene Comins Mingol and Sonia París Albert, "Nonkilling Philosophy," in *Toward a Nonkilling Paradigm*, ed. Joám Evans Pim (Honolulu: Center for Global Nonkilling, 2009), 271–286.

the supposed availability of objective standards and that affirm the need for language games that are explicitly normative.

Making use of these perspectives, Comins Mingol and París Albert stress the relational and intersubjective character of science and other human enterprises. They regard such activities as value laden in ways that are more realistic than ones found in supposedly object- and value-neutral approaches. Moreover, they contend that these activities involve an orientation toward care and the affirmation of diversity. The result for Comins Mingol and París Albert is a view that philosophy should be oriented to sustaining life by advancing nonviolence and peace. Before giving some key details in their other philosophical contributions, I want to say a little more about discourse ethics and care ethics.

Discourse ethics "presupposes the liberty and equality of all speakers" and has "truth in what is being said" as central to the validity claims of speech.[75] In the early 1970s, Habermas initiated his argument that the formal properties of practical discourse provide the objective grounds for assessing normative validity claims.[76] Then he elaborated on this argument during the 1980s and 1990s.[77] Comins Mingol and París Albert regard "peaceful communication" as a method based on the principles of discourse ethics.[78] In the effort to try to implement this version of discourse ethics, Comins Mingol and París Albert also use John Austin's speech act theory.[79] They contend that when this theory is applied properly, "what is said ends up being what is done."[80] However, even if the norms of rational discourse entail a universal morality that is related to truth, the problem remains that social actors may not follow such norms.[81] Nevertheless, if what *is* said in rational discourse is what rational actors *should* do, a basis is provided for a grounded social criticism—insofar as actions are rational. Habermas holds on to the prospect of rationality and contends that even in relation to a fascist regime it "will not be able to guarantee recognition in the long run."[82] I remain cautious about such optimism, noting the

75 Comins Mingol and París Albert, "Nonkilling Philosophy," 278.

76 Jürgen Habermas, *Legitimation Crisis*, trans. Thomas McCarthy (Boston: Beacon Press, 1975), 99.

77 Jürgen Habermas, *The Theory of Communicative Action* (Cambridge: Polity, 1989); Jürgen Habermas, *Moral Consciousness and Communicative Action* (Cambridge: MIT Press, 1993).

78 Comins Mingol and París Albert, "Nonkilling Philosophy," 278.

79 John Langshaw Austin, *How to Do Things with Words* (Oxford: Oxford University Press, 1976).

80 Comins Mingol and París Albert, "Nonkilling Philosophy," 278.

81 William Gay, "Justification of Legal Authority: Phenomenology vs Critical Theory," *Journal of Social Philosophy* 11:2 (May 1980): 3.

82 Habermas, *Theory*, 100.

observation of John Stuart Mill that "It is a piece of idle sentimentality that truth, merely as truth, has any inherent power denied to error of prevailing against the dungeon and the stake."[83] However, regimes and languages do change, and critical discourse analysis and practice can contribute to such a change.[84]

Fortunately, Comins Mingol and París Albert also rely on care ethics that shows a different way forward. They begin by noting, "Women and the non-western countries have had their voices excluded from epistemological paradigms."[85] Basically care ethics provides an alternative to a deontological ethics and strengthens efforts to use a pragmatic or consequentialist ethics.[86] Through its stress on particularity and connection, care ethic avoids the problems that arise from seeking a universalized or generalized foundation. Using Gilligan and Ruddick, Comins Mingol and París Albert present the nonkilling paradigm as leading to the cultivation of characteristics such as empathy, responsibility, and patience.[87] For them, as for Betty Reardon, "above all a culture of peace would be a culture of caring."[88] In the final analysis, care ethics rejects the punitive orientations found in corporal punishment, capital punishment, and international war and replaces them with an orientation that complements strategies of nonviolence during conflict and after conflict. Still, care ethics can lapse into gender essentialism (a dichotomy in which men pursue justice and women pursue care). Nevertheless, care ethics can be formulated in ways that go beyond such a reductive view. For example, Maurice Hamington seeks to erase the gap between the genders and argues for an ethics of care that applies to all human beings.[89]

I think Comins Mingol and París Albert have articulated a plausible entry point to the nonkilling perspective for philosophers in both the deontological

83 John Stuart Mill, *On Liberty* (London: J.W. Parker, 1859), 17.

84 William C. Gay, "Language, War, and Peace," in *Handbook of Language and Communication: Diversity and Change*, eds. Marlis Hellinger and Anne Pauwels (Berlin: Bouton de Gruyter, 2007a), 493–521; Gay, "Bourdieu and Social Conditions."

85 Comins Mingol and París Albert, "Nonkilling Philosophy," 279.

86 Andrew Fiala, "Forgiveness, Justice, and Care: A Pragmatic Balance," *Ethical Perspectives* 17:4 (2010): 580–602.

87 Carol Gilligan, *In a Different Voice: Psychological Theory and Women's Development* (Cambridge: Harvard University Press, 1996); Sara Ruddick, *Maternal Thinking: Toward a Politics of Peace* (New York: Women's Press, 1989).

88 Betty Reardon, *Education for a Culture of Peace in Gender Perspective* (Paris: UNESCO, 2001), 85.

89 Michael Hamington, *Embodied Ethics: Jane Addams, Maurice Merleau-Ponty, and Feminist Ethics* (Chicago: University of Illinois Press, 2004).

and consequentialist ethical traditions. Also, discourse ethics provides the needed focus on language, and care ethics provides the needed attention to human relations. At the least, Comins Mingol and París Albert recognize the nonkilling perspective needs philosophical foundations and provide a good initial articulation of these foundations from within two widely employed ethical approaches. While further problems may need to be addressed, I will forego in this essay a more critical treatment of discourse ethics and care ethics.

Of equal importance to the efforts by Comins Mingol and París Albert to lay the philosophical foundations for the nonkilling perspective is how they proceed to show how philosophy can assist with applying the nonkilling perspective by (1) noting further concrete steps that can and should be taken and (2) providing philosophical support for alternatives to our inclination toward cultural violence. In particular, Comins Mingol and París Albert highlight a distinctive view of how to respond to conflict. They characterize the traditional academic approaches of conflict resolution and conflict management as negative in that they try to either eliminate or administer conflict. Instead, they recommend that we "*disaccustom* ourselves to violence" and replace this inclination by cultivating the practice and then the habit of conflict transformation.[90] Instead of seeking to eliminate or administer conflict, conflict transformation seeks "peaceful alternatives that avoid the use of violence."[91] "*Peace as a habit*" becomes possible when we "*disaccustom* ourselves to violence."[92] In this regard they support philosophical methods for the peaceful, nonviolent transformation of conflict. However, they do not turn to works in psychology, such as ones by Marshall Rosenburg, or works in political science, such as ones by Ellen Gorsevsk—both approaches that I have treated elsewhere.[93] Instead, as I have already noted, they employ discourse ethics and care ethics to guide our language and our behavior to foster their goal of connecting a "culture of peace" with a "culture of caring."[94]

In their conclusion, Comins Mingol and París Albert assert "a nonkilling philosophy is necessarily a philosophy committed to the recuperation of and the recognition of human potential for peace."[95] They reject the view that

90 Comins Mingol and París Albert, "Nonkilling Philosophy," 275.

91 Comins Mingol and París Albert, "Nonkilling Philosophy," 276.

92 Comins Mingol and París Albert, "Nonkilling Philosophy," 276.

93 William C. Gay, "Nonviolent Rhetoric in Geopolitics," in *Positive Peace: Reflections on Peace Education, Nonviolence, and Social Change*, ed. Andrew Fitz-Gibbon (Amsterdam: Rodopi, 2010), 31–37 and 152–153.

94 Comins Mingol and París Albert, "Nonkilling Philosophy," 278 and 281.

95 Comins Mingol and París Albert, "Nonkilling Philosophy," 283.

human beings are naturally violent. On the contrary, they assert that human beings have capacities for "harmonious coexistence, for reciprocal care and the peaceful transformation of conflicts."[96] Linguistically, this effort involves moving from what I term and analyze as a language of war and linguistic violence to a language of peace and linguistic nonviolence.[97]

Like Friedrich, Comins Mingol and París Albert emphasize the positive. They cite peace researcher Francisco Muñoz, who notes the cognitive dissonance of strongly desiring peace but primarily thinking about and publishing on violence, which he terms the "*violentology perspective*"—an orientation that Comins Mingol and París Albert say has the "perverse effect of … making it seem as though violence is more present."[98] They also use studies in anthropology to support Paige's position that human beings can avoid war. In particular, they rely on David Fry's *The Human Potential for Peace*, in which he contends that an emphasis on the supposed inevitability of war and violence is not supported by the empirical evidence.[99] These cultural beliefs are often taken for granted, respectively, by those persons who see the world through the normative lens of what Cady terms "warism" and what Robert Holmes terms "violentism."[100]

Comins Mingol and París Albert summarize their position with two premises. First, they reiterate the thesis that "violence, killing and war are not inevitable" and that "human beings have a great capacity for peaceful coexistence and for dealing with conflict nonviolently." Second, they stress that cultural beliefs in what Cady and Holmes term warism and violentism "skew our interpretations and affect our vision of human nature, to such an extent that they blind us to the possibilities of developing alternatives to killing, war and violence."[101] At the close of their article, they note how cultural violence "dulls our moral responsibility," while a nonkilling philosophy, first, should make visible and remove "the veil of cultural killing, with its discourses that marginalize, exclude and ultimately serve to legitimize structural and cultural killing,"

96 Comins Mingol and París Albert, "Nonkilling Philosophy," 283.

97 William C. Gay, "The Language of War and Peace," in *Encyclopedia of Violence, Peace, and Conflict*, vol. 2, ed. Lester Kurtz, 2nd ed. (Oxford: Elsevier, 2008), 1115–1127.

98 Comins Mingol and París Albert, "Nonkilling Philosophy," 283.

99 Douglas Fry, *The Human Potential for Peace: Peace and Conflict, Development and Civilization*. (London: Sage, 2006).

100 Robert L. Holmes, "Violence and Nonviolence," in *The Ethics of Nonviolence: Essays by Robert L. Holmes*, ed. Predrag Cicovacki (New York: Bloomsbury, 2013), 149–167. [Essay originally published in *Violence*, Jerome A. Schaffer, ed. David McKay Co., 1971: 103–135.]

101 Comins Mingol and París Albert, "Nonkilling Philosophy," 283–284.

and, second, should "construct and reconstruct discourses that legitimize and promote nonkilling."[102]

At this point, I want to add a further point on the perspective of Comins Mingol and París Albert. My point concerns two different ways in which their goals in communication can be achieved. Correlative to the distinction between negative and positive peace is the distinction between coercive and nonviolent methods of advancing peaceful discourse. Just as I advocate pacifism as the proper response to the physical violence of war, even so I advocate peaceful discourse as the proper response to linguistic violence. Some think that insofar as the violence of language is to be countered, force will have to be exercised. I am also among those who maintain that holding fast to linguistic nonviolence as a means is as important as aiming for linguistic nonviolence as a goal. Politically correct discourse can be achieved through legal or even physical coercion. Even if needed and successful, the use of legal or physical coercion to end hate speech or establish politically correct discourse entails the abandonment of nonviolence. When people are silenced by the threat posed in the words of law or by the constraint imposed through the deeds of authorities, verbally or physically violent means have been employed. By contrast, individuals can intentionally choose to eschew hate speech and to use politically correct discourse. They also can use linguistically nonviolent tactics to persuade others to do so as well. By recognizing and addressing these two different ways of moving toward the goals of communication, we can better facilitate the pursuit of nonkilling discourse that will remain true to its nonviolent intentions.

Final Reflections on Language and Violence

I conclude with a brief summary of the topics I have addressed and then give a few final reflections.

I began by noting problems in defining violence. To move beyond the absence of any objective and universal standards for defining violence, I used the later Wittgenstein to highlight how meaningful discourse on the wrongness of violence in human affairs can be found in various language games that have normative components. I then considered a typology of violence in human affairs that includes cultural violence. I noted that cultural violence, as discussed by Galtung, depends on linguistic justifications and, often, employs linguistic violence. I suggested that while "linguistic violence" is narrower

102 Comins Mingol and París Albert, "Nonkilling Philosophy," 285.

than "cultural violence," it permeates cultural violence and provides its central justifications.

I turned next to some perspectives that I cautioned pose obstacles for efforts to eliminate cultural violence, particularly in the position of Žižek. In his assertions, Žižek is not so much giving an argument as he is giving a definition of violence. Moreover, I noted that Žižek's analysis too often lacks sufficient conceptual clarity and specific concrete suggestions on how to advance peace and justice. Sometimes, to paraphrase Albert Camus, we simply need to side with the victims and do what we can to heal, knowing more forms of disease continue to plague humanity and better treatments might even be possible. Sometimes we simply need to do what we can in the here and now for the particular victim or the particular violence that we encounter.

Next, I reviewed my work on linguistic violence and linguistic nonviolence. Then, I turned to Friedrich who situates much of her work within peace linguistics (by analogy to peace psychology) and, more recently, within nonkilling linguistics. Friedrich and bell hooks recognize how English oppresses, but they also affirm that English can be used by the oppressed to speak and to transform, to resist oppression and to advance peace and justice. I then addressed how Comins Mingol and París Albert extend this nonkilling perspective into philosophy.

For Comins Mingol and París Albert, nonkilling philosophy is inseparable from the human potential for peace. They note that Francisco Muñóz, however, refers to the cognitive dissonance experienced by people who, although they search for and value peace, continue to think in terms of violence and to focus on its occurrences. He coined the term "violentology perspective" to characterize this disconnect, and the nonkilling perspective helps us move forward with a focus on ways that so much in the lives of individuals and societies takes place apart from violence. Comins Mingol and París Albert build on this fact. They assert two premises that I noted earlier, but, by way of summary, I quote them in full:

> There are two premises that justify and award working toward a nonkilling paradigm: violence, killing and war are not inevitable; on the contrary, human beings have a great capacity for peaceful coexistence and for dealing with conflicts nonviolently. Secondly, cultural beliefs regarding the inevitability of violence, killing and war skew our interpretations and affect our vision of human nature, to such an extent that they blind us to the possibilities of developing alternatives to killing, war and violence.[103]

103 Comins Mingol and París Albert, "Nonkilling Philosophy," 283–284.

They continue, "Our work as philosophers publicly commits us to transform the suffering of both humans and nature by peaceful means."[104] Their nonkilling philosophy is inclusive and is "committed to the recognition of human diversity, intercultural solidarity and peace."[105]

How far can this perspective be taken? Nonkilling societies are possible, but their achievement and security require more work than I have sketched so far. Other nonviolent approaches could easily complement the nonkilling perspective. I will note briefly two of these approaches, namely, restorative justice and civilian defense.

Restorative justice is a relatively new alternative to retributive practices of justice. Restorative justice began with efforts to repair the harm of criminal behavior and seek cooperative resolutions that include victims, offenders, and the community. Even at the level of an alternative to punishment, particularly incarceration, restorative justice has clear advantages for advocates of nonviolence and nonkilling. Philosophically, restorative justice also has a lot in common with care ethics.[106] Moreover, part of the appeal of restorative justice for the nonkilling perspective is that its application has been broader than that of care ethics. Internationally, it has been applied across many disciplines on interpersonal to international levels. I will give just a few examples. In primary and secondary education, Dennis Wong employs restorative justice in response to the current verbal and physical abuse of LGBTQ youth, especially in the United States.[107] David Karp and Thom Allena look specifically at the use of restorative justice in college settings as a means to promote student responsibility and campus community.[108] Restorative justice is also used with defendants in courts, with parolees, and even with prison inmates, as Barb Toews and M. Kay Harris have noted.[109] At the furthest frontiers, restorative justice also fits with efforts at responding to the atrocities of war and genocide.

---

104 Comins Mingol and París Albert, "Nonkilling Philosophy," 28–285.

105 Comins Mingol and París Albert, "Nonkilling Philosophy," 285.

106 William C. Gay, "Restorative Justice and Care Ethics: An Integrated Approach to Forgiveness and Reconciliation," in *Explorations of Forgiveness: Personal, Relational, and Religious*, ed. Court Lewis (Wilmington, DE: Vernon Press, 2016), 31–58.

107 Dennis Wong, "Adolescent Bullying: The Whole-School Approach," in *The Promise of Restorative Justice: New Approaches for Criminal Justice and Beyond*, eds. John P.J. Dussich and Jill Schellenberg (Boulder: Lynne Rienner Publishers, 2010), 181–194.

108 David R. Karp and Thom Allena, eds., *Restorative Justice on the College Campus: Promoting Student Growth and Responsibility, and Reawakening the Spirit of Campus Community* (Springfield, IL: Charles C. Thomas, 2004).

109 Barb Toews and M. Kay Harris, "Restorative Justice in Prisons," in *Social Work and Restorative Justice: Skills for Dialogue, Peacemaking, and Reconciliation*, eds. Elizabeth Beck,

Nancy Amoury Combs, for example, meticulously documents the constructive role that can be played by plea bargaining in response to genocide and crimes against humanity as a means to obtain guilty pleas and to increase the proportion of offenders who can be prosecuted.[110] Peter Reddy even envisions a "peace operatives corps" as an alternative to military peacekeepers or, at least, in some sort of "hybrid" organization that is "equipped with skills that range from protective and security tasks through negotiation, language, mediation and conflict de-escalation skills."[111]

While restorative justice can complement the nonkilling perspective in several beneficial ways, the issue remains of how to move altogether past the very large scale killing involved in war. In this regard, one of the last hurdles will be the development and implementation of nonviolent models of national security. Elsewhere, I have argued we can move from military defense to civilian defense.[112] A transition to nonviolent national security involves (1) moving from the threat posed by a standing military organization to the pledge of massive noncooperation by civilian defenders, (2) moving from use of military strikes to nonviolent civilian resistance, and (3) moving from a theory of victory to a practice of non-defeat. While war is the continuation of politics by different and violent means, civilian defense is politics by the same means. Of course, the levels of nonviolence can take on more intense dimensions. As Gene Sharpe has shown, we can move from discussion, through negotiation, to arbitration and from protest through noncooperation to intervention.[113] However, each of these intensifications can remain nonviolent and can foster the nonviolent transformation of conflict in the pursuit of social justice. Moreover, as several researchers have shown, empirical evidence increasingly shows the greater effectiveness of civilian defense.[114]

Nancy P. Kropf, and Pamela Blume Leonard (Oxford: Oxford University Press, 2011), 118–148.

110 Nancy Amoury Combs, *Guilty Pleas in International Criminal Law: Constructing a Restorative Approach* (Sanford, CA: Sanford University Press, 2007).

111 Peter Reddy, *Peace Operations and Restorative Justice: Groundwork for Post-conflict Regeneration* (Farnham, Surrey, England: Ashgate Publishing, 2012), 222.

112 William C. Gay, "The Prospect for a Nonviolent Model of National Security," in *On the Eve of the 21st Century: Perspectives of Russian and American Philosophers*, eds. William C. Gay and Tatiana A. Alekseeva (Lanham, MD: Rowman and Littlefield, 1994b), 119–134.

113 Gene Sharp, *The Politics of Nonviolent Action* (Boston: Sargent, 1973).

114 Erica Chenoweth and Maria J. Stephan, *Why Civil Resistance Works: The Strategic Logic of Nonviolent Conflict* (New York: Columbia University Press, 2011); Peter Ackerman and Jack Duvall, *A Force More Powerful: A Century of Nonviolent Conflict* (New York: St. Martin's Press, 2000).

I wish to end with a few final thoughts on the theme of this essay—the role of language in justifying and eliminating cultural violence. Peaceful discourse that is analogous to positive peace facilitates and reflects the move from a lull in the occurrence of violence to its negation. Efforts to establish a practice of linguistic nonviolence are part of a larger struggle to reduce cultural violence.

Breaking our silence concerning the many forms of violence is an important first step in reducing cultural violence. We need to recognize that often silence is violence. Frequently, unless we break the silence, we may be guilty of complicity or duplicity in relation to the violence of a situation. However, in breaking the silence, our aim should be to avoid counter-violence, in its physical forms and in its verbal forms. Efforts to advance peace and justice should occupy the space between silence and violence. A positively nonviolent discourse can provide a communicative means to overcome linguistic violence that does not contradict or compromise its goal at any point during its pursuit.

We can speak and act nonviolently. We can take on the cause to stop the killing—not just at the local level but globally as well. A nonkilling philosophy when focused on efforts to eliminate linguistic violence and to advance the practice of linguistic nonviolence could play a central role in efforts at reducing cultural violence and expanding social justice.

Bibliography

Ackerman, Peter and Jack Duvall. *A Force More Powerful: A Century of Nonviolent Conflict*. New York: St. Martin's Press, 2000.

Austin, John Langshaw. *How to Do Things with Words*. Oxford: Oxford University Press, 1976.

Beck, Elizabeth, Nancy P. Kropf, and Pamela Blume Leonard, eds. *Social Work and Restorative Justice: Skills for Dialogue, Peacemaking, and Reconciliation*. Oxford: Oxford University Press, 2011.

bell hooks. *Teaching to Transgress: Education as the Practice of Freedom*. New York: Routledge, 1994.

Boersema, David. *Philosophy of Human Rights: Theory and Practice*. Boulder, CO: Westview Press, 2011.

Bourdieu, Pierre. *Language and Symbolic Power*. Edited by John B. Thompson. Translated by Gino Raymond and Matthew Adamson. Cambridge: Harvard University Press, 1991.

Cady, Duane L. *From Warism to Pacifism: A Moral Continuum*. 2nd ed. Philadelphia: Temple University Press, 2010.

Canagarajah, Athelstan Suresh. *Resisting Linguistic Imperialism in English Teaching*. Oxford: Oxford University Press, 1999.

Chenoweth, Erica and Maria J. Stephan. *Why Civil Resistance Works: The Strategic Logic of Nonviolent Conflict*. New York: Columbia University Press, 2011.

Cicovacki, Predrag, ed. *The Ethics of Nonviolence: Essays by Robert L. Holmes*. New York: Bloomsbury, 2013.

Combs, Nancy Amoury. *Guilty Pleas in International Criminal Law: Constructing a Restorative Approach*. Sanford, CA: Sanford University Press. 2007.

Comins Mingol, Irene, and Sonia París Albert. "Nonkilling Philosophy." In *Toward a Nonkilling Paradigm,* edited by Joám Evans Pim. 271–286. Honolulu: Center for Global Nonkilling, 2009.

Curtin, Deane, and Robert Litke, eds. *Institutional Violence*. Amsterdam: Rodopi, 1999.

Dussich, John P.J. and Jill Schellenberg, eds. *The Promise of Restorative Justice: New Approaches for Criminal Justice and Beyond*. Boulder and London: Lynne Rienner Publishers, 2010.

Fiala, Andrew. "Forgiveness, Justice, and Care: A Pragmatic Balance." *Ethical Perspectives*. 17:4 (2010): 580–602.

Fitz-Gibbon, Andrew, ed. *Positive Peace: Reflections on Peace Education, Nonviolence, and Social Change*. Amsterdam: Rodopi, 2010.

Friedrich, Patricia. *Language, Negotiation and Peace: The Use of English in Conflict Resolution*. London: Continuum, 2007.

Friedrich, Patricia. "Introduction." In *Nonkilling Linguistics*, edited by Patricia Friedrich, 11–13. Honolulu: Center for Global Nonkilling, 2012a.

Friedrich, Patricia, ed. *Nonkilling Linguistics: Practical Applications*. Honolulu: Center for Global Nonkilling, 2012b.

Friedrich, Patricia, and Francisco Gomes de Matos. "Toward a Nonkilling Linguistics." In *Nonkilling Linguistics*, edited by Patricia Friedrich. 17–36. Honolulu: Center for Global Nonkilling, 2012.

Fry, Douglas. *The Human Potential for Peace: Peace and Conflict, Development and Civilization*. London: Sage, 2006.

Galtung Johan. "Violence, Peace, and Peace Research." *Journal of Peace Research* 6:3 (1969): 167–199. Accessed July 25, 2014. http://www.jstor.org/stable/422690.

Galtung, Johan. "Cultural Violence," *Journal of Peace Research* 27:3 (August 1990): 291–305. Accessed August 31, 2015. http://www.jstor.org/stable/423472.

Garver, Newton. "What Violence Is." *The Nation* 209 (24 June 1968): 817–822.

Gay, William C. "Probability in the Social Sciences: A Critique of Weber and Schutz." *Human Studies* 1:1 (January 1978): 16–37.

Gay, William C. "Merleau-Ponty on Language and Social Science: The Dialectic of Phenomenology and Structuralism." *Man and World* 12:3 (1979): 322–338.

Gay, William C. "Justification of Legal Authority: Phenomenology vs Critical Theory." *Journal of Social Philosophy* 11:2 (May 1980): 1–10.

Gay, William C. "Nuclear Discourse and Linguistic Alienation." *Journal of Social Philosophy* 18:2 (Summer 1987): 42–49.

Gay, William C. "Ricoeur on Metaphor and Ideology." *Darshana International* 32:1 (January 1992): 59–70.

Gay, William C. "From Wittgenstein to Applied Philosophy." *The International Journal of Applied Philosophy* 9, n1 (Summer/Fall 1994a): 15–20.

Gay, William C. "The Prospect for a Nonviolent Model of National Security." In *On the Eve of the 21st Century: Perspectives of Russian and American Philosophers*, edited by William Gay and Tatiana A. Alekseeva. 119–134. Lanham, MD: Rowman and Littlefield, 1994b.

Gay, William C. "Bourdieu and the Social Conditions of Wittgensteinian Language Games." *The International Journal of Applied Philosophy* 11:1 (1996): 15–21.

Gay, William C. "Nonsexist Public Discourse and Negative Peace: The Injustice of Merely Formal Transformation." *The Acorn: Journal of the Gandhi-King Society* 9:1 (Spring 1997): 45–53.

Gay, William C. "Exposing and Overcoming Linguistic Alienation and Linguistic Violence." *Philosophy and Social Criticism* 24:2/3 (1998a): 137–156.

Gay, William C. "The Practice of Linguistic Nonviolence." *Peace Review* 10:4 (1998b): 545–547.

Gay, William C. "Linguistic Violence." In *Institutional Violence,* edited by Deane Curtin and Robert Litke. 13–34. Amsterdam: Rodopi, 1999.

Gay, William C. "Language, War, and Peace." In *Handbook of Language and Communication: Diversity and Change*, edited by Marlis Hellinger and Anne Pauwels. 493–521. Berlin: Bouton de Gruyter, 2007a.

Gay, William C. "Supplanting Linguistic Violence." In *Gender Violence: Interdisciplinary Perspectives*. 2nd ed., edited by Laura L. O'Toole, Jessica R. Schiffman, and Margie L. Kiter Edwards. 435–442. New York: New York University Press, 2007b.

Gay, William C. "The Language of War and Peace." In *Encyclopedia of Violence, Peace, and Conflict*. 2nd ed., Vol. 2, edited by Lester Kurtz. 1115–1127. Oxford: Elsevier, 2008.

Gay, William C. "Nonviolent Rhetoric in Geopolitics." In *Positive Peace: Reflections on Peace Education, Nonviolence, and Social Change*, edited by Andrew Fitz-Gibbon. 31–37 and 152–153. Amsterdam: Rodopi, 2010.

Gay, William C. "Restorative Justice and Care Ethics: An Integrated Approach to Forgiveness and Reconciliation." In *Explorations of Forgiveness: Personal, Relational, and Religious*, edited by Court Lewis. 31–58. Wilmington, DE: Vernon Press, 2016.

Gay, William C. and Tatiana A. Alekseeva, eds. *On the Eve of the 21st Century: Perspectives of Russian and American Philosophers*. Lanham, MD: Rowman and Littlefield, 1994.

Gilligan, Carol. *In a Different Voice: Psychological Theory and Women's Development.* Cambridge: Harvard University Press, 1996.

Habermas, Jürgen. *Legitimation Crisis.* Translated byThomas McCarthy, Boston: Beacon Press, 1975.

Habermas, Jürgen. *The Theory of Communicative Action.* Cambridge: Polity, 1989.

Habermas, Jürgen. *Moral Consciousness and Communicative Action.* Cambridge: MIT Press, 1993.

Hamington, Michael. *Embodied Ethics: Jane Addams, Maurice Merleau-Ponty, and Feminist Ethics.* Chicago: University of Illinois Press, 2004.

Hendricks, Christina, and Kelly Oliver, eds. *Language and Liberation: Feminism, Philosophy, and Language.* Albany: State University of New York Press, 1999.

Hernández-Chávez, Eduardo. "Language Policy in the United States: A History of Cultural Genocide." In *Human Rights: Overcoming Linguistic Discrimination,* edited by Tove Skutnabb-Kangas and Robert Phillipson in collaboration with Mart Rannut. 148–158. Berlin: Mouton de Gruyter, 1994.

Holmes, Robert L. "Violence and Nonviolence." In *The Ethics of Nonviolence,* edited by Predrag Cicovacki. 149–167. New York: Bloomsbury, 2013. [Essay originally published in *Violence,* Jerome A. Schaffer, ed. (David McKay Co., 1971): 103–135.]

Karp, David R. and Allena Thom, eds. *Restorative Justice on the College Campus: Promoting Student Growth and Responsibility, and Reawakening the Spirit of Campus Community.* Springfield, IL: Charles C. Thomas, 2004.

Kirkpatrick, Andy. *World Englishes: Implications for International Communication and English Language Teaching.* Cambridge: Cambridge University Press, 2007.

Kurtz, Lester, ed. *Encyclopedia of Violence, Peace, and Conflict.* 2nd ed. Oxford: Elsevier 2008.

Kymlicka, Will, and Alan Patten, eds. *Language Rights and Political Theory.* Oxford: Oxford University Press. 2003.

Lewis, Court, ed. *Explorations of Forgiveness: Personal, Relational, and Religious.* Wilmington, DE: Vernon Press, 2016.

van der Linden, Harry. "On the Violence of Systemic Violence: A Critique of Slavoj Žižek." *Radical Philosophy Review* 15:1 (2012): 33–51. Accessed August 10, 2015. http://digitalcommons.butler.edu/cgi/viewcontent.cgi?article=1249&context=facsch_papers.

Mill, John Stuart. *On Liberty.* London: J.W. Parker, 1859.

O'Toole, Laura L., Jessica R. Schiffman, and Margie L. Kiter Edwards, eds. *Gender Violence: Interdisciplinary Perspectives.* 2nd ed. New York: New York University Press, 2007.

Paige, Glen. *Nonkilling Global Political Science.* Honolulu: Center for Global Nonkilling, 2009.

Phillipson, Robert. *Linguistic Imperialism.* Oxford: Oxford University Press, 1992.

Pim, Joám Evans, ed. *Toward a Nonkilling Paradigm*. Honolulu: Center for Global Nonkilling, 2009.

Reardon, Betty. *Education for a Culture of Peace in Gender Perspective*. Paris: UNESCO, 2001.

Reddy, Peter. *Peace Operations and Restorative Justice: Groundwork for Post-conflict Regeneration*. Farnham, Surrey, England: Ashgate Publishing, 2012.

Ricoeur, Paul. "Violence and Language." Translated by Joseph Bien. In *Political and Social Essays* [of Paul Ricoeur], edited by David Stewart and Joseph Bien. 88–101. Athens: Ohio University Press, 1975. Accessed April 13, 2015. jffp.org/ojs/index.php/jffp/article/download/410/404.

Ross, Stephanie. "How Words Hurt: Attitude, Metaphor, and Oppression." In *Sexist Language: A Modern Philosophical Analysis*, edited by Mary Vetterling-Braggin. 194–213. Huber Heights, Ohio: Littlefield, Adams, 1981.

Ruddick, Sara. *Maternal Thinking: Toward a Politics of* Peace. New York: Women's Press, 1989.

Sharp, Gene. *The Politics of Nonviolent Action*. Boston: Sargent, 1973.

Skutnabb-Kangas, Tove, and Robert Phillipson, eds., in collaboration with Mart Rannut. *Linguistic Human Rights: Overcoming Linguistic Discrimination*. Berlin: Mouton de Gruyter, 1994.

Staudigl, Michael. "Towards a Phenomenological Theory of Violence: Reflections Following Merleau-Ponty and Schutz." *Human Studies* 30 (2007): 233–253.

Tirrell, Lynne. "Derogatory Terms: Racism, Sexism, and the Inferential Role Theory of Meaning." In *Language and Liberation: Feminism, Philosophy, and Language*, edited by Christina Hendricks and Kelly Oliver. 41–79. Albany: State University of New York Press, 1999.

Toews, Barb, and M. Kay Harris, "Restorative Justice in Prisons." In *Social Work and Restorative Justice: Skills for Dialogue, Peacemaking, and Reconciliation*, edited by Elizabeth Beck, Nancy P. Kropf, and Pamela Blume Leonard. 119–148. Oxford: Oxford University Press, 2011.

UNESCO. "Universal Declaration on Linguistic Rights." World Conference on Linguistic Rights. Barcelona, Spain, 9 June 1996. Accessed July 24, 2015. http://www.unesco.org/cpp/uk/declarations/linguistic.pdf.

Vetterling-Braggin, Mary. *Sexist Language: A Modern Philosophical Analysis*. Huber Heights, Ohio: Littlefield, Adams, 1981.

Wittgenstein, Ludwig. *Philosophical Investigations*. Translated by G.E.M. Anscombe. New York: Macmillan, 1953.

Wong, Dennis. "Adolescent Bullying: The Whole-School Approach." In *The Promise of Restorative Justice: New Approaches for Criminal Justice and Beyond*, edited by John P.J. Dussich and Jill Schellenberg. 181–194. Boulder: Lynne Rienner Publishers, 2010.

Žižek, Slavoj. *Violence: Six Sideways Reflections*. New York: Picador, 2008.

CHAPTER 3

Getting at the "Root Cause": Why a "Culture of Violence" is the Wrong Place to Focus

Todd Jones

Introduction

In academic literature, there are numerous important discussions of cultural violence, a term first introduced by Johan Galtung. Galtung's notion of cultural violence centers on harms that are done to people (or legitimized) by sets of ideas that a society holds. When people are interested in cultural violence, they are likely interested in how violence is caused and may be prevented in general and in culture's role in causing and preventing violence. Because of this, it's likely that those interested in cultural violence would also be interested in the related notion of a "culture of violence." The idea of a "culture of violence" is widespread in both academic and popular literature. (See, for example, John Devine's monograph *Maximum Security: The Culture of Violence in Inner City Schools* or James's Bennett's recent *Atlantic Monthly* article, "A Culture of Violence: Revisiting the Legacy of Martin Luther King Jr. in a Time of Police Shootings and Church Murders.")[1] "Culture of violence" seems to refer to circumstances in which a group has social processes that dispose many of its members to violent behaviors. People seem most apt to talk about violence in terms of culture when they want to stress the idea that, if you want to help stop violence, you have to get at the deep root causes that have to do with these long-standing social pressures. Galtung himself likened physical violence to an earthquake and culture as the deep longstanding fault lines.[2]

In this chapter, I will be focusing on the notion of a culture *of* violence, the more common way of talking about violence and culture in popular and academic literature.

1 John Devine, *Maximum Security: The Culture of Violence in Inner-City Schools* (Chicago: University of Chicago Press, 1996); James Bennett, "A Culture of Violence: Revisiting the Legacy of Martin Luther King Jr. in a Time of Police Shootings and Church Murders," *Atlantic,* September, 2015.

2 Johan Galtung, "Cultural Violence," *Journal of Peace Research* 27, 3 (1990): 294.

 | DOI 10.1163/9789004361911_005

I'll talk about a set of problems for thinking about violence and its causes and cures in terms of culture. The problems begin with the fact that "culture" is an extraordinarily vague and complex term. Raymond Williams, one of the founders of cultural studies, called it "one of the two or three most complicated words in the English language."[3] Edward Tylor, one of the founders of anthropology, wrote that culture was "the complex whole which includes knowledge, belief, art, morals, law, custom, and any other capabilities and habits acquired by man as a member of society."[4] Quite a lot folded into one concept! "Culture" also seems to refer both to what is *produced by* certain social processes (e.g., "French culture is full of femme fatale figures.") and to the very processes producing the result (e.g., "Only French culture could have produced the femme fatale figure."). The vagueness and complexity of "culture" can cause a lot of confusion about what people mean when they talk about culture causing violence. But I want to argue here that even when we try to work with a relatively clear and concise idea of culture, it isn't a very helpful notion for understanding the causes and solutions to the problem of violence.[5]

Why Explain with Culture?

Why are we tempted to explain violent behavior using a notion as complex as culture? Let's look at a (fictionalized) example of the kind of violent behavior people feel most comfortable discussing in terms of culture—one I've discussed in other works. People certainly use these terms to discuss American mass shootings or inner city gang activity. But the "culture of violence" seems even more apt for discussing certain attitudes and practices that are often prevalent in preliterate societies. Suppose an anthropologist were to explain that Wally, a member of the Wahiri tribe, killed Cato, a member of the rival

3 Raymond Williams, *Keywords: A Vocabulary of Culture and Society*, rev. ed. (Oxford: Oxford University Press, 1983), 87.

4 Edward Bennett Tylor, *Primitive Culture: Researches into the Development of Mythology, Philosophy, Religion, Art, and Custom*, Vol. 1. (London: John Murray, 1871), 1.

5 The notions of *cultural* violence and *culture of* violence differ from each other in several ways. When people speak of a culture of violence, they tend to be talking about a group where physical violence, caused by culture, is widespread. Galtung's *cultural violence* is a set of harm-causing ideas that are likely present to some degree in all societies, whatever physical violence is or isn't present. A society with many violent physical *acts* could have a low degree of cultural violence, and a society with a lot of violence-supporting cultural ideology need not have lots of physical violence. In this essay I am focusing on the notion of culture *of* violence.

Calami headhunting tribe, by saying that it is part of Wahiri culture to kill Calamis. Clearly, in cases like this, something about Wally's *psychological* state and his circumstances inclined him to try to kill Cato. So why would such behavior be explained in terms of *culture?*

In several works (2010,[6] 2012[7]), I've argued that there are good reasons why people are often inclined *not* to explain actions like this in terms of things like Wally's particular psychological state. When social scientists and others say that a killing or other act was done because of culture, they usually mean there is a *disjunctive set* of social factors present, any one of which would have caused that result in the right circumstances. Many of the features of the actual causal chain involved in producing this event were not strictly necessary, for if this set of circumstances had not produced this result, a related set would or could have. We talk about "culture" (and cognate terms like "norm" and "custom") producing certain results, when we think that various different related social and psychological processes all could have produced that result.[8]

Suppose what had happened in the case at hand was that Wally saw Cato bathing in a river and thought about how his fellow tribesmen would make fun of him if they heard that he'd come upon a Calami and made no attempt to kill him. Thinking about this led Wally to attack and drown Cato. This is an example of a type of social pressure leading Wally to do what he did. But there are other sorts of social pressure. Wally likely also would have killed Cato if, instead of thinking about being made fun of (or other sorts of gestures of disapproval), he had thought about how his fellow tribesmen would sing songs of praise about him for taking a Calami life. "Fear of disparagement" would seem to be something of an inappropriate explanation, as its presence was unnecessary for the result, since "desire for praise" also would have led to the same result. We tend to talk about "cultural" forces being at work when there is a disjunction of different types (and subtypes) of social forces involved in

6 Todd Jones, *What People Believe When They Say That People Believe* (Latham, MD: Rowan and Littlefield, 2010).

7 Todd Jones, "Do Customs Compete with Conditioning? Turf Battles and Division of Labor in Social Explanation" *Synthese* 184: 3 (2012): 407–430.

8 We are especially inclined to say that a disjunction of factors is responsible when we are talking about a world where the result is over-determined (or pre-empted) by each of the various disjuncts—a world where, when the A-cause is removed, the B-cause is already present. But we are also inclined to credit a disjunction when, were A to be removed, there is a decent likelihood that B would be present. The less likely it is that a B that *could* produce that result in these circumstances (or ones like them) would *actually be* present were the A-cause to be removed, the less likely we are to say that result is caused by A *or* B.

causing a result. Social pressure—worrying about others' approval and disapproval (which can take various forms)—is a kind of cultural force.

But we tend to think that social pressure doesn't fully explain things if other sorts of cultural forces are present. Social conditioning is another such force. Suppose that, over time, Wally and his compatriots were rewarded for trying to kill Calamis and punished for not trying to kill them. Because of this history of social conditioning, Wally would likely have been automatically inclined to try to kill Cato, without stopping to think about it—whether any fears of ridicule or hope of praise had been present or not. Suppose, also, that one of the forces present here was Wally's inclination to *imitate* others he had seen trying to kill Calamis. All of these forces are considered part of Wahiri culture, which causes Wahiris to kill Calamis whenever they are seen. Typically we use culture to explain an action done either because of social pressure, social conditioning, or social imitation. We should consider culture to be the cause because none of the more particular causes is counterfactually necessary.[9] Consider an analogous case: If a bull were to charge when a red flag was waved, but it would also have charged had the flag been green, it seems inappropriate to say that the redness of the flag caused the bull to charge. It's really seeing an instance of redness or greenness that caused the bull to charge. Similarly, it wasn't fear of ridicule that caused Wally to kill Cato. It was ridicule, or conditioning, or the tendency to imitate that did it. We feel the presence of a certain set of similar social factors, all capable of producing X in similar circumstances, is so common that we have a particular name for it—that name is "culture." Thus, we are inclined to say that Cato was killed because of the Wahiri culture of violence.

Problems with Explanations Based on Culture

Undermining from Below

We can see how appealing to "culture" provides an attractive explanation. It doesn't focus on overly specific factors that are unnecessary. There's a feeling

9 Various social scientists (e.g., Max Weber) have stressed the importance of giving explanation in terms of finding the factors that were counterfactually necessary for a results happening (see H.L.A. Hart and Tony Honore, *Causation in the Law* Oxford: Clarendon, 1959). Counterfactual analysis is at the center of David Lewis's celebrated theory of causation (David Lewis, *Philosophical Papers,* Vol. 2. Oxford: Oxford University Press, 1986). When we do a counterfactual analysis of whether X causes Y, we ask: Was X really necessary for Y? In a world where X was removed, would Y not be the case? While there are many different ways of understanding causation, I will assume, in this chapter, that this is the right way to think of causal explanation.

that we are getting at the broad disjunctive set of factors that actually ensures this result. But there are numerous problems with talking about culture as the cause of anything. Elsewhere, I've labeled one family of problems the "undermining from below" worries.[10]

Undermining from below happens when there is good reason to think that what's frequently called a "lower level" account is a better explanation of X than a "higher level" account. We get one version of the problem if it turns out there *can't really be* disjunctive causal explanations (which explanations involving "culture" seem to be). The philosophical literature is full of arguments and examples aiming to show that there really are no disjunctive causes. (See, for example, works by Armstrong; Lewis; Kim; and Audi.[11]) Jaegwon Kim discusses that a woman's painful joints may be caused by arthritis or may be caused by lupus, but they are unable to be caused by the disjunctive property of [arthritis or lupus]; there are no such disjunctive properties, he argues.[12] If the arguments against the possibility of disjunctive causes and explanations are correct, and if explanations using culture (like norm or custom explanations) really are attempts to give disjunctive explanations, then a large class of attempted social scientific explanations is in deep trouble. If there are no disjunctive explanations, it simply can't be the case that the correct explanation of Cato Calumi's death is that Wally, as a Wahiri, was being conditioned by his peers to do Y or feared his peers would punish him for not doing Y or believed his peers thought he should do Y or imitated the behavior of his peers, etc.[13]

Another "undermining from below" problem is that, even if disjunctive properties *could be* legitimate explainers, many of the various disjuncts (e.g., social pressure, imitation) are *insufficient* explainers of the result, making the explanation inadequate. The disjunctive cultural explanation says that any

10 Jones, "Do Customs Compete?".

11 David Armstrong, *A Theory of Universals* (Cambridge: Cambridge University Press, 1980); David Lewis, *Philosophical Papers*, Vol. 2. (Oxford: Oxford University Press, 1986); Jaegwon Kim, *Mind in a Physical World* (Cambridge, MA: MIT Press, 2000); Paul Audi, "How to Rule Out Disjunctive Properties" [Issue online], *Noûs*, 47, 4 (2013): 748–766. DOI: 10.1111/nous.12016.

12 Jaegwon Kim, *Mind in a Physical World* (Cambridge, MA: MIT Press, 2000).

13 One might reply to the criticism that there are no disjunctive properties by saying that when someone says that culture caused X, meaning that [social pressure or conditioning or imitation] caused X, this disjunction is not meant to be a property. One is simply claiming that the cause of X is one of these disjuncts, but we know not which. If this is what is meant, then saying that culture causes something is just saying that we don't know which of a bunch of possible things caused something. Hopefully, people who want to *explain* things in terms of culture are trying to claim more than this.

one of either imitation or conditioning or social pressure could cause the killing. (Each one is unnecessary, but having one or another of the three disjuncts is necessary for the effect to happen, given other background conditions.) But it's unlikely that each of the disjuncts making up the unit of Wahiri culture we are discussing really is *sufficient* for explaining the precise event of Cato's actual death. If Wally kills Cato because he is imitating other Wahiris, he would likely do so in a different manner than if he does so because of social pressure. Indeed, a tendency to imitate might not be enough to make Wally kill at all if he has never heard of a case of killing a Calami by drowning him in a river. If we are explaining things like Cato's actual death, and not various possible ones, then the only things that can do so are the actual state of Wally's mind and surrounding circumstances, not various disjunctive states that make up a "cultural" inclination.

Perhaps we can avoid this problem if we say that what we want to explain is why Wally killed Cato *that morning*, rather than why Cato had the precise death event he had. I think the problem of the likely insufficiency of a disjunctive account still looms. In the circumstances where we are most likely to give a cultural explanation of an event, there are often numerous social factors that all help make the even happen. Pressure, imitation, and conditioning likely all play a role in encouraging a Wahiri like Wally to kill a Calami. But if it's really the case that *all* the disjuncts were involved in that killing or ones like it, then it isn't really the case that *any one* of the disjuncts will produce the result (as the cultural explanation allows). A disjunctive (rather than a conjunctive) cultural explanation will be inadequate.

But couldn't we say that all of these social factors are important parts of Wahiri culture, in that, when they don't *all* contribute to a given Calami death, *one or another* of them is bound to be present and will likely produce the result in question? For example, if Wally hadn't been feeling the social pressure, his conditioning would likely have kicked in and he still would have killed Cato. It's not clear that we can say this. If we are talking about circumstances (i.e., a possible world) in which people like Wally *don't* feel social pressure to kill Calamis, it's not clear that this is a world where people have come to be conditioned to kill Calamis. A world where Wahiris have been conditioned to automatically try to kill Calamis is usually a world where there have been lots of social rewards for doing so and social punishments for not doing so, resulting in feelings of social pressure. A world with no feelings of social pressure is also probably a world that doesn't have conditioning. So we can't say that if one isn't present, we can assume that the other is likely available.

Now in the technical philosophy literature on possible worlds, this problem is usually avoided by forbidding possible worlds with "backtracking" counterfactuals. What can and can't happen in a non-backtracking counterfactual world is something philosophers debate. But it is assumed that, if we are assessing what would happen in a world that has conditioning but no social pressure, we should not consider a world where the past is so altered that the removal of social pressure must also change the presence of social conditioning. Note, though, that this possible world, with non-backtracking counterfactuals, is going to be a strange one. This is a world where people are conditioned but they don't have the other effects of the social pressure forces that usually create that conditioning. This is a world where there are features that ensure feelings of compulsion to do and avoid certain things, but also features that keep away worries about what other people will think. I think it is hard to tell what will go on in such a strange world. (David Lewis, the leading theorist of counterfactual analysis, admits that "miraculous" events must occur.) But it is especially hard to give relatively *specific* diagnostics of what will go on, along the lines of "Wally would kill Cato that morning." We can't say this is what would happen in a world where we have only one or another of these disjuncts. So, even if we are trying to explain a somewhat wider target than that exact death event at the hands of Wally, I think that saying a culture of violence produced it is insufficient. One or another of a disjunctive set of things that incline group members to violent behavior (along with other background conditions) may not be enough to produce that sort of killing, so the disjuncts comprising culture can't explain the killing.

Another related "undermining from below" problem stems from what Jaegwon Kim and others call the "causal exclusion principle." One of the simplest versions of the principle is described by Kim this way: "If an event e has a sufficient cause c at t, no event at t distinct from c can be a cause of e (unless this is a genuine case of causal overdetermination)."[14] The causal exclusion principle can be used to undermine a cultural explanation "from below" if it's shown that we can give a completely sufficient explanation, say, of Cato's death in terms of Wally's psychology. If we can, then the explanation in terms of a culture of violence is superfluous—the event has already been explained. Now we should certainly be able to give an account of many of the details of Wally's actions on the basis of the circumstances and Wally's psychology (something a cultural explanation can't do). This gives us a reason to try to explain the event in terms of Wally's psychology. The higher level account is thus "screened off" by the preferred lower level one. Indeed, some argue that if the mind is just the brain, then a detailed explanation of *the physics of the brain* and surrounding

14 Jaegwon Kim, *Physicalism, or Something Near Enough* (Princeton: Princeton University Press, 2005), 17.

events should also screen off a psychological explanation. (See, for example, Kim's *Mind in a Physical World.*)

Note that the causal exclusion principle could screen off a *disjunctive explanation* by holding that, if we can explain A in terms of B, this screens off an explanation of A in terms of [B or C or D]. But causal exclusion can also rule out high-level accounts that are not disjunctive at all. This means that cultural explanations could be "undermined from below" even if they turn out not to be disjunctive explanations. Suppose that my analysis of culture is mistaken, and that there is a shared *general* property that various instances of cultural shaping have. An explanation in terms of this shared high-level general property is still going to be screened off by a lower level account of the killing given in terms of the more particular psychological realizer of that general cultural property. Causal exclusion again renders a high-level cultural explanation superfluous.

Overcoming "Undermining from Below" Problems

"Undermining from below" problems pose important challenges to explanations in terms of something like a culture of violence. There are, however, some ways these challenges might be met. To begin with, one can argue that disjunctive properties can perfectly well be causal, after all. A number of philosophers have held that in certain cases, disjunctions really can be causes. (See, for example, Bennett; Mackie; Mellor; and Sartorio.[15]) A broad defense of disjunctive explanations would be to argue that if, in specific conditions C, the addition of any one of a number of different factors F could have caused Y, then we should say the true cause of Y is the appearance of some or other member of F. Anything else is overkill. In his classic anti-reductionist article, "1953 and All That: A Tale of Two Sciences," Philip Kitcher argues against giving various particular low-level accounts of cellular meiosis.[16] He writes:

> Yet simply plugging a molecular account into the [high-level] narratives offered at previous stages would *decrease* the explanatory power of those narratives. What is relevant to answering our original question is the fact that nonhomologous chromosomes assort independently. What is

15 Jonathan F. Bennett, *Events and Their Names* (Indianapolis: Hackett, 1988); J.L. Mackie, "Causes and Conditions," in *Causation and Conditionals,* ed. Ernest Sosa (Oxford: Oxford University Press, 1993); D.H. Mellor, *The Facts of Causation* (London: Routledge, 1995); Carolina Sartorio, "Disjunctive Causes," *Journal of Philosophy* 103, 10 (2006): 521–538.

16 Kitcher, Philip. "1953 and All That. A Tale of Two Sciences." *The Philosophical Review* 93, No. 3 (1984): 335–373.

> relevant to the issue of why nonhomologous chromosomes assort independently is the fact that the chromosomes are not selectively oriented toward the poles of the spindle.... In neither case are the molecular details relevant. Indeed, adding those details would only disguise the relevant factor.

One can imagine using Kitcher's injunctions against irrelevant detail as part of the defense of a disjunctive causation. Naming a particular disjunct as the cause is to be guilty of giving irrelevant detail since just being *any one of* the members of the disjunctive class would cause the result. Using a general term (like culture), on the other hand, that covers a range of disjuncts can correctly specify the set of factors necessary for making that effect happen in those conditions. Naming the disjunction, on this view, gives us a better explanation than providing particular antecedent conditions. Moreover, I don't think we have a good way of demarcating when we have a disjunction of two properties and when we have two subtypes of the same property. Many perfectly respectable explanations can be construed as disjunctive property causation.

One could also argue that, even if disjunctions cannot cause single events, they are the best explanation for a *general* result. *Whenever* a Wahiri spots a Calami, you always have an attempted Calami killing. Why? The norm of Calami-killing in the culture ensures this. Any time a Wahiri sees a Calami, the Wahiri either wants to imitate his Calami-killing uncles, or worries about how his friends will treat him if he doesn't kill, or has a reflex brought on by a lifetime of Calami-killing conditioning. Even if you don't need a disjunction to explain a particular case, you need the disjunction to explain why there is a high frequency of Calami-killing in this region.

If we are explaining a *general* disposition toward Calami-killing among Wahiris, we also no longer have worries about sufficiency. Each of the disjuncts in the set comprising culture, even if they can't explain a particular Calami killing, is capable of explaining a high rate of Calami killing. Culture—social pressure, or conditioning, or imitation—is sufficient to explain a high rate of Calami-killing. A non-disjunctive shared cultural feature (if it exists) would also be sufficient. Meanwhile, if we are explaining the general rate of killing, citing a particular kind of low-level psychological state as a cause is inappropriate, because it is especially unnecessary for that result. That means that low-level accounts will not be able to screen off disjunctive or other high-level accounts as superfluous. The higher level will *not be excluded* by more specific lower level properties. These more detailed lower level sorts of properties are not in the explanation since they are unnecessary to the result. If causal exclusion is to play a role at all, the argument goes, it's to exclude the *lower* level account.

Undermining from Above

But these same considerations that suggest a higher level account is more appropriate than a lower level account also suggest that even a *cultural* explanation for violence may be overly specific. If disjunctions can be causal, there is nothing wrong with an explanation that cites the presence of a cultural norm in Wahiri society as the cause of a high rate of violent Calami deaths. The problem is that the same considerations that suggest we should attribute cause to a larger disjunctive *set* (like culture), rather than to one of the disjuncts (like imitation), would also suggest that we should attribute the cause to an *even larger* set of disjuncts—a set like [culture *or fear*]. Imagine, as is likely, that in addition to conditioning and/or imitation, *fear* of Calamis makes Wahiris try to kill their rivals. A counterfactual-oriented notion of causation, along with the requirement not to give more specificity than is required for the effect, mandates that culture ([imitation or conditioning or pressure]) provides a better explanation for Calami-killing than imitation. Even for an individual killing, it didn't need to be Wally's imitation of other Wahiris that caused him to kill Cato, since *any* way the custom of Calami-killing was implemented would do it. But this also mandates that [culture or fear] (call this the "kill-on-sight disposition") is a better causal explanation than the cultural one. Opponents of disjunction often hold that disjunctive explanations are undermined "from below," with lower level accounts being the real explanations for various results. But if disjunctive explanation advocates are correct and disjunctive accounts are legitimate, then cultural accounts themselves can also easily be undermined *from above* by still larger disjunctive sets that include more potential causers.

Note that this is *not* merely the logical worry that if A or B causes X, then A or B or C must as well. The only disjunctions we should consider as being good candidates for disjunctive *causes* should be disjunctions that are counterfactual supporting. Conditioning or imitation (or any other form of culture) would also have produced a certain result in these circumstances, so we name the general property (culture), rather than something unnecessarily specific. Thus, we are not saying that if we are able to say "A or B [imitation or conditioning] caused Wally to kill Cato Calami," then we are just as able to say "A or B or C [imitation or conditioning or praying to a monkey-god] caused Wally to kill Cato Calami." We are saying merely that in the case of the culture, here, if C or D [imitating killers or being-conditioned-to-kill] is a more accurate description of the cause of Cato's death than C [imitating killers] alone, then E or F [killing out of custom or killing out of fear] is a more accurate description of the cause of Cato's death than E [killing out of custom] alone. The disjunction can only grow larger while still being a true cause, so long as each disjunct would have the same effect in those circumstances. I am not claiming, then, that any large disjunct will "undermine from above" all subvening subset disjuncts. But it is plausible that, for most cases where what could cause an effect are the disjuncts making up a *culture*, other variables could cause the same effect as well. This makes the *larger* disjunct consisting of the cultural factors *along with these other factors* a better cause; thus "undermining from above" the narrower cultural cause. The idea that disjunctive causes can be "undermined from above" in this manner has been little noticed (Franklin-Hall's "High-Level Explanation and the Interventionist's 'Variables Problem'" is an important exception[17]). But it is a problem that advocates for an explanation using culture would do well to be aware of.

There are similar worries about undermining from above if it turns out that culture is a high-level non-disjunctive property. The causal power of culture could easily often be "undermined from above" by the presence of *even higher* level properties in the same way that causal disjunctions could be undermined from above by wider disjunctions. Suppose someone could demonstrate that, in cases like the Calami killing, it's really the presence of the high-level property of having this social custom, and not the low-level psychological mechanism "realizing" the social custom (e.g., fear of ridicule), that explains Wally's ensuing behavior. The problem is that in the majority of circumstances where one can give this kind of cultural explanation, one can also give an even higher level *rationality* or *optimality* explanation that should "screen off" the lower level culture account.

Since Ancient Greek times, numerous scholars have sought to explain things with variants of rationality or optimality accounts: Organisms do Y because Y is a very good way of conferring important benefits on the organism. (See Bueno de Mesquita for good examples of this style of explanation.[18]) It's easy to envision someone arguing that the Calami-killing cases that others explain with a culture-based account should really be explained this way: In the forests where the Wahiri and the Calami live, there are not enough resources to support both tribes. There are even fewer resources in nearby regions. Tribes that have survived in this region are ones that have been able systematically to eliminate their rivals. Developing a strategy of killing all Calamis is, thus, a rational strategy for Wahiri survival. For this reason, Calami-killing has been socially selected. Sometimes Wahiris kill Calamis after thinking about what

17 L.R. Franklin-Hall, "High-Level Explanation and the Interventionist's 'Variables Problem.'" *British Journal for the Philosophy of Science* (2014) axu040v.

18 Bruce Bueno de Mesquita, *The Predictioneer's Game: Using the Logic of Brazen Self-Interest to See and Shape the Future* (New York: Random House, 2009).

can be done about resource scarcity. Other times they act because of the social pressure that has developed.

As in most rationality or optimality explanations, the exact low-level mechanism leading to the action is held to be irrelevant. Biological adaptationist versions of optimality generally pay little attention to questions of how mutations arise and create the mechanism for doing some task. In the case of "social adaptationism" (or what used to be called "functionalism"), it is similarly taken for granted that useful structures will arise over time by some means or other, and then be selected for their usefulness. Whatever lower level psychological mechanisms lead any individual Wahiri to kill a Calami, the right explanation for the killing, this argument goes, is that it is highly rational for a Wahiri to do so.[19] Advocates for higher level explanations might be right that we have good reasons for thinking that cultural explanations actually "screen off" and exclude lower level accounts like those in terms of imitation. But it looks like those same considerations should suggest that cultural accounts are themselves often screened off by accounts at an even higher level. Arguments advocating the more general account as being the truly causal one end up undermining cultural accounts "from above" with regards to both higher level and disjunctive accounts.

Our situation then seems to be this: Cultural explanations of violent behavior like Calami-killing among Wahiris are inadequate. They are undermined from both above and below. If we are trying to explain a particular historical event like Wally's killing Cato, then that very event can be explained only by a very *particular* causal chain. Cultural explanations for such things tend to be *insufficient*. Various "undermining from below" criticisms of higher level explanations for such events are correct. At the same time, if we are trying to explain the occurrence of a more *general* kind of event, like the frequency of Calami-killings, the factors comprising cultural explanations are *unnecessary*. The main reason for preferring a high-level disjunctive cultural explanation is the idea that each of the particular psychological processes involved in things like a Calami killing are unnecessary for explaining the frequency. If any of

19 To see an example of an actual social scientist making an argument like this, consider this one, written by a popular economist and columnist. (Tim Hartford, "The Logic of Life: The Economics of Marriage," *Slate* January 2008): 'But "black culture" doesn't explain why the single moms are disproportionately in the states where lots of young black men are in prison. Economics does: women's bargaining power is badly dented by the imprisonment of potential husbands. The better-educated guys stay out of jail, and they are smart enough to realize that with the competition locked up, they don't have to get married to enjoy themselves. "Culture" is no explanation; that women respond rationally to a tough situation is a much better one'.

these processes were not present, we would still have a frequency of killings from the other processes. The counterfactual view of causation suggests that none of these particular processes should be thought of as causing that result. Lower level accounts do not tell you what is counterfactually necessary for the kind of violence being explained to occur. But these same "undermining from above" criticisms can also be directed at the set of disjunctive factors that make up cultural explanation. The initial advantages of the cultural account disappear in favor of the superiority of an *even higher level* account. The reasons why people in groups like the Wahiri commit many violent acts are probably not limited to the disjunctive factors comprising culture: imitation, conditioning, and social pressure. That particular disjunction of factors is not necessary for violence toward Calamis to occur. We've seen that, if they were absent, the violence may well still occur.

What this means is that it's not correct to say that the root cause of violence is a *culture of violence*. The undermining from above critique suggests we should try to explain frequent violence in terms of *a much wider* range of disjuncts. Note this is not just the worry that culture is one of many different things that can cause violence. (Nor is it the worry that there are always additional auxiliary factors that must be there in addition to the "main" causes.) The worry is that the three or four disjuncts comprising "culture" creates an arbitrary concoction that doesn't really give us the necessary or sufficient conditions for causation (even assuming other stable background conditions). There's no special reason to focus on three disjuncts instead of seven. And if it's three, there's no special reason to focus on *these* three. There's certainly no reason to focus on *culture* as a privileged "root cause," as it's often treated. Looking at a "culture of violence" is too limited. It directs us to look at a set of features involved in producing violence that are somewhat similar, and for which we happen to have a common term—"culture." But we don't have very good reasons to focus merely on *similar* factors involved in violence (if, indeed, they are that similar).

Better Explanations of Violence than Culture

When we try to figure out what causes something, what contributes *to making a difference* to a result, we need to think about what would have to be added to a world *that didn't have* this result, to make sure that it did. We are trying to figure out what is necessary by figuring out what would and wouldn't have produced this result in what many philosophers talk about as "close possible worlds." We can think about close possible worlds in terms of similarities and differences regarding what we consider the *main* causal variables. Figuring out what caused the bull to charge, in the case we mentioned earlier, we ask: What would the bull have done in a world where the waved flag was green? What if it had been blue? But we can also think of differences in *other* conditions that *might have been* present. What if there had been a loud noise? Meanwhile, there is no special reason we need to assume *the same background* conditions must be on hand in other possible worlds, when we think about what might have caused the result. Their potential changeability makes these additional "background" conditions always a part of the counterfactually necessary ones for a cause, such that if they were changed, the effect wouldn't take place in the same way. (See Lewis 1986 for an argument that "background" conditions do not differ from "main" ones.[20]) When we think about what causes what, we should generally be thinking about differences in combinations of "background" conditions that make a difference to something's happening. A red *or green* flag would have caused the bull to charge—*but not if* the bull were wearing blinders. A loud noise would also have caused the bull to charge—*unless* the wind were blowing strongly in the opposite direction.

Ultimately, the number of various combinations of conditions that could lead to a large set of violent behaviors *still* being produced in possible worlds like ours, even if some of the main causers were removed, might still be very large—especially when the "background conditions" are allowed to vary. So what are the different possible worlds with different "main variables" and different "background conditions" that we should actually be looking at when we are contemplating counterfactual worlds? What set of possibilities should we be contemplating as possible?[21]

I suggest we let pragmatic considerations be our guide. When we are thinking about the causes of violence, we should be thinking in terms of what we are able to do about manipulating violence. Manipulationist theories of causation (e.g., von Wright; Menzies and Price; Woodward[22]) hold that this is how we

20 David Lewis, *Philosophical Papers*, vol. 2 (Oxford: Oxford University Press, 1986).

21 Theorists of causation like David Lewis's (see note above) and others tend to put firm restrictions on which possible worlds we should be looking at when trying to assess cause. But this is because such theorists are interested in using counterfactuals to assess what caused what in the *existing* world. If we are interested in *altering* the world (as we should be when we are thinking about how to decrease violence), it is important to think about *all kinds* of circumstances that could possibly be. We should look at what enables or prevents what in this wider set of possible worlds.

22 George Henrik von Wright, *Explanation and Understanding* (Ithaca, New York: Cornell University Press, 1971); Peter Menzies Peter and Huw Price, "Causation as a Secondary Quality," *British Journal for the Philosophy of Science* 44 No. 2 (1993): 187–203; James Woodward,

should understand the *basic metaphysics of causation* itself. Whether or not this is the case, I think that how we can intervene in the world is usually the main thing we want to *know about* when we want to know about causation. When we are asking about what causes violence, we usually want to know about the kinds of things that would have to be added to an area of a world *without* high rates of violence to turn it into an area *with* high violence. We want to know what variables we could subtract to make this area less violent. So we should be thinking about possible worlds that are like ours with *all sorts of combinations* of added or subtracted conditions that could increase or decrease the rate of violence.[23]

Among the conditions we should be most interested in are those in possible worlds that are the most easy to create: the ones in worlds that are (a) most like ours and/or (b) require the fewest resources to get to. Also, we should be especially interested in the causal conditions that have the most *powerful and robust* effect on the results we are studying. These include conditions that require the fewest types of *additional* necessary conditions to reach the result. Other robust powerful conditions are ones that still will tend to produce the same result, even if we add lots of different types of additional conditions.

So what are things that tend to produce increasing or decreasing rates of violence that we should be focusing on when we think about the causes of violence? What are the things we can most easily affect, and have the most robust results? Certainly a set of various social mechanisms producing a disposition for violent behaviors (a culture of violence) could be part of the focus. But that might turn out to be one of the most well entrenched features of a society, and one of the hardest to change. But there are many other things that we might focus on. We could look at what might change other sorts of beliefs that make individuals think violence is a good course of action. Perhaps many people are inclined, in the right circumstances, to commit violent acts against members of certain groups because they think members of these groups are bad people. This might have little to do with peer pressure, but instead be due to how members of these groups are depicted in popular media, or how they are

Making Things Happen: A Theory of Causal Explanation (Oxford: Oxford University Press, 2003).

23 I believe that the main reason we want to understand the causes of violence is to reduce it. But whatever states we ultimately want to bring about, we can talk only about what is possible, given certain assumptions about what *other* factors we will assume stay the same in the world and what factors are allowed to change in this or that way. In theory, we can make any nomologically possible assumptions about what does and doesn't change. In practice we should focus on what it is about the world we most and least *want* to change, and on what is most and least changeable in the world.

talked about by national leaders. Rates of violence could plausibly be brought down by changes in how mistreated groups are depicted. Sometimes high rates of violence are due partly to individuals' beliefs that violent action (e.g., armed robbery) is the only or the easiest way to get resources. If so, then setting up ways of making resources available to community members through a variety of other means could potentially reduce violence. Another way to help might be to make people more aware of existing resources available to them. Violence might also be prevalent because people in a community do not think they have the ability to redress grievances in court. They consequently take matters into their own hands, dispensing "vigilante justice." But if they come to feel that more legal resources are available to them, rates of violence should go down. (See Pinker's *The Better Angels of Our Nature* for an account of how this indeed has frequently happened.[24])

Even if individuals feel social pressure to be violent or have strong individual motivations to be violent, rates of violent behavior could still be reduced if people came to have different beliefs about the likelihood of punishment. Some studies have shown that the costs of punishment don't have that much effect on crime or violence, but that the likelihood of punishment does. (See Wright 2010.[25]) One of the chief causal factors in determining whether people commit violent acts can be the presence or absence of their belief that they would likely be caught and serve a prison sentence. There is no reason, then, that such beliefs shouldn't be thought of as among the "root causes" of violence.

Other things that could likely have a strong effect on rates of violence are people's *opportunities and abilities* to inflict violence on others. Certain types of violent acts are reduced when it's clear that others can see what's happening. Simple improvements in street lighting, then, could be a cause of lower rates of violence, and so could the presence of more patrol cars, community policing, playground monitors, and more "eyes on the street" of various sorts. Violence could also be reduced simply because people are spending that time engaged in other activities. This is why activities like church group meetings, midnight basketball leagues, or *the lack thereof*, can be seriously considered as a cause of increased or decreased violence.

---

24 Steven Pinker, *The Better Angels of Our Nature: Why Violence Has Declined* (New York: Viking, 2011).

25 Valerie Wright, "Deterrence in Criminal Justice. Evaluating Certainty vs. Severity of Punishment," The Sentencing Project (November 2010), accessed September 19, 2016, http://www.sentencingproject.org/publications/deterrence-in-criminal-justice-evaluating-certainty-vs-severity-of-punishment/.

Of course, among the main factors leading to an increase or decrease of serious violent activities is the availability of deadly weapons. Various studies indicate that by simply reducing the number of weapons available to people, we can decrease the number of violent deaths (e.g., Hepburn and Hemenway 2004[26]). Even where there is no reason to suspect any changes at all in cultural or individual proclivities toward violence, differences in the availability of weaponry makes big differences in what happens. Less access to handguns or assault weapons simply means fewer violent deaths in a society. Common sense indicates that something similar is likely true of international warfare. If various classes of weapons aren't available because of treaty restrictions, financial restrictions, or what have you, potential combatants have an incentive to negotiate, rather than fight. This means that the availability of weaponry is part of the set of conditions counterfactually necessary for certain rates of violence to occur. Reduce this availability, and you will reduce the violence. I suspect that national legislation making gun availability more difficult is easier to achieve than changing engrained habits and networks of pressures in a community. But whether or not it is, gun restrictions, if achieved, would likely have a strong effect, no matter what other changes in conditions are or aren't added to the mix.

It is important to see that I am not merely noting that there can be lots of different causes of violence in different sorts of cases, and that we should look at all of them. I am arguing that even where there seems to be a single predominant cause of violence, there is often a disjunction of potential causers such that even if one were absent, the others would likely still be there. Removing one sort of cause may not be effective if the others are still there, so we should, indeed, be looking at many potential causes. But we should be focusing *most* attention on the causes that we can alter most easily and, in so doing, would create the strongest effects. At the same time, any causal condition's effects rarely happen without a large conjunction of *additional necessary conditions*. If we altered any of these conditions, the effects would be altered. This means that sometimes, even if we could do nothing at all to effect some of the main causes of violence (e.g., peer approval), violence could still be dramatically curtailed if the *other conditions necessary* for violence (e.g., the availability of weapons) were curtailed. These are the sorts of conditions we should be focusing on most.

An in-depth discussion of the various factors that contribute to violence and the most promising ways to reduce violence is obviously beyond the scope

26 Lisa Hepburn and David Hemenway, "Firearm Availability and Homicide: A Review of the Literature" *Aggression and Violent Behavior: A Review Journal* 9 (2004): 417–440.

of this paper. But it should be clear that, given all of these factors that can play a role in increasing or decreasing violent behaviors, there's no reason that a "culture of violence" should be the dominant focus of the discussion of the "root causes" of violence, despite many people's inclination to focus there.

Concluding Remarks

Many thinkers, when discussing violent behavior, believe it's important to get at the "root causes" of the violence. Among the root causes, a "culture of violence" is often discussed as a primary culprit. In this chapter, I have discussed reasons why this focus is problematic. We talk about violence being caused by culture when we think that if one set of social factors would not have caused an act or rate of violence, then another set of social factors would have. We give this somewhat diverse set of disjunctive causes the unifying label "culture." But the diversity of these different causes presents one family of problems: each of these different sorts of causes likely creates different sets of effects. Each is not sufficient for explaining the particular event that happened. Someone who is inclined to imitate the violent behavior of people around him or her is likely to perform somewhat different sorts of actions than someone who has been repeatedly punished for not performing violent actions. Although we call both sorts of social influences "culture," the particular results are likely to be different. The diverse forms that "cultural" influences can take tend to produce difference effects.

But the different sorts of social forces labeled "culture" also have a certain similarity about them, and that similarity is a source of problems of its own. Thinking of a culture of violence leads us to concentrate on a small set of similar-seeming social forces involved in violence, all of which could lead to a certain sort of effect, given a set of background conditions. But if what we want to do is to somehow intervene in the world to change a resulting state of affairs, there is no reason to have such a narrow focus. Indeed, if we merely want to say what can make a difference as to whether an effect is there, we should be considering a much bigger range of potential "main causes" and "auxiliary" background enablers.

There tend to be numerous disjunctive sets of conditions that can cause an effect, even within a set of background conditions. We need not be focused on the same sorts of producers (e.g., the "cultural" ones) if we want to change that effect. Neither do we want to assume that certain sorts of background conditions must necessarily be there (readily available guns), when these can change too. I think we will give better accounts of violence if we are *more restrictive* regarding explaining particular results and *more open* regarding explaining general sorts of results, than when we explain them in terms of factors like "culture." If we want to do something to reduce the amount of violence in the world we live in, we should understand that violence is the result of a vast number of different *disjunctions* of *conjunctions* of various conditions. We need to think outside the box, and one of those limiting boxes is the notion of a "culture of violence."

Bibliography

Armstrong, David. *A Theory of Universals*. Cambridge: Cambridge University Press, 1980.

Audi, Paul. "How to Rule Out Disjunctive Properties." *Noûs* 47, 4 (2013): 748–766. doi: 10.1111/nous.12016.

Bennett, James. "A Culture of Violence: Revisiting the Legacy of Martin Luther King Jr. in a Time of Police Shootings and Church Murders." *Atlantic*, September 2015.

Bennett, Jonathan F. *Events and Their Names*. Indianapolis: Hackett, 1988.

Bueno de Mesquita, Bruce. *The Predictioneer's Game: Using the Logic of Brazen Self-Interest to See and Shape the Future*. New York: Random House, 2009.

Devine, John. *Maximum Security: The Culture of Violence in Inner-City Schools*. Chicago: University of Chicago Press, 1996.

Franklin-Hall, L.R. "High-Level Explanation and the Interventionist's 'Variables Problem.'" *British Journal for the Philosophy of Science*. (2014). doi: axu040v1.

Galtung, Johan. "Cultural Violence." *Journal of Peace Research* 27, 3 (1990): 291–305.

Harford, Tim. "The Logic of Life: The Economics of Marriage." *Slate* (January 2008). Accessed September 19, 2016. http://www.slate.com/articles/arts/the_undercover_economist/features/2008/the_logic_of_life/the_economics_of_marriage.html.

Hart, H.L.A., and Tony Honore. *Causation in the Law*. Oxford: Clarendon, 1959. Hepburn, Lisa, and David Hemenway. "Firearm Availability and Homicide: A Review of the Literature." *Aggression and Violent Behavior: A Review Journal* 9 (2004): 417–440.

Jones, Todd. *What People Believe When They Say That People Believe*. Latham, MD: Rowan and Littlefield, 2010.

Jones, Todd. "Do Customs Compete with Conditioning? Turf Battles and Division of Labor in Social Explanation." *Synthese* 184: 3 (2012): 407–430.

Kim, Jaegwon. *Mind in a Physical World*. Cambridge, MA: MIT Press, 2000.

Kim, Jaegwon. *Physicalism, or Something Near Enough*. Princeton: Princeton University Press, 2005.

Kitcher, Philip. "1953 and All That. A Tale of Two Sciences." *The Philosophical Review* 93, no. 3 (1984): 335–373.

Lewis, David. *Philosophical Papers.* Vol. 2. Oxford: Oxford University Press, 1986.

Mackie, J.L. "Causes and Conditions." In *Causation and Conditionals,* edited by Ernest Sosa. Oxford: Oxford University Press, 1993.

Mellor, D.H. *The Facts of Causation.* London: Routledge, 1995.

Menzies, Peter and Huw Price. "Causation as a Secondary Quality." *British Journal for the Philosophy of Science* 44 no. 2 (1993): 187–203.

Pinker, Steven. *The Better Angels of Our Nature: Why Violence Has Declined.* New York: Viking, 2011.

Sartorio, Carolina. "Disjunctive Causes." *Journal of Philosophy* 103, 10 (2006): 521–538.

Tylor, Edward Bennett. *Primitive Culture: Researches into the Development of Mythology, Philosophy, Religion, Art, and Custom.* Vol. 1. London: John Murray, 1871.

von Wright, George Henrik. *Explanation and Understanding.* Ithaca, NY: Cornell University Press, 1971.

Williams, Raymond. *Keywords: A Vocabulary of Culture and Society.* Rev. ed. Oxford: Oxford University Press, 1983.

Wright, Valerie. "Deterrence in Criminal Justice. Evaluating Certainty vs. Severity of Punishment." The Sentencing Project, 2010. Accessed September 19, 2016. http://www.sentencingproject.org/publications/deterrence-in-criminal-justice-evaluating-certainty-vs-severity-of-punishment/.

Woodward, James. *Making Things Happen: A Theory of Causal Explanation.* Oxford: Oxford University Press, 2003.

CHAPTER 4

Cultural Violence, Hegemony, and Agonistic Interventions

Fuat Gursozlu

Introduction

In everyday usage "violence" refers to the visible actions of an agent who uses physical force against oneself or another person with the intention to cause harm or injury. This common understanding of the term presupposes a visible action that causes the harm and an agent who intends to bring about this consequence. Johan Galtung offers an alternative to the commonly accepted account of violence that associates violence with "direct violence" by first introducing the concept of "structural violence" and then the concept of "cultural violence." Galtung's aim is to challenge the "common sense" and the "settled" understanding of violence so as to make the recognition of deeper and more pervasive forms of violence possible.

The concept of structural violence aims to address the insufficiency of the concept of direct violence in identifying forms of violence that are not committed by intentional agents.[1] If by violence we mean only direct violence, Galtung argues, we have to admit that "highly unacceptable social orders would still be compatible with peace."[2] An extended concept of violence is needed for the theorization of certain forms of harm and injury that are invisible to society and that are not caused by the actions of an intentional subject. The concept of structural violence addresses this problem by extending the types of injuries and harms considered as violence. Galtung defines structural violence as the type of violence where the harm and injury cannot be attributed to an intentional subject, but is built into the structure and shows up as unequal power, uneven distribution of resources, and consequently as unequal life chances.

Galtung's philosophical strategy is to challenge the discursive limits of intelligibility through an intervention on the discourse of violence. Thus, his account of structural violence broadens the dominant understanding of

1 Johan Galtung, "Violence, Peace, and Peace Research," *Journal of Peace Research* 6:3 (1969): 167–199.

2 Galtung, "Peace Research," 168.

 | DOI 10.1163/9789004361911_006

violence while allowing for the theorization of a host of social relations such as exploitation, domination, poverty, and social exclusion as forms of violence. Galtung pursues a similar strategy in his later work when he introduces his account of "cultural violence," which extends violence even beyond direct and structural violence.[3] Galtung's account of "cultural violence" consists of three significant parts. The first part provides the definition of the concept of cultural violence and presents it as a normative problem. According to Galtung's definition, cultural violence refers to "those aspects of culture, the symbolic sphere of our existence that can be used to justify or legitimize direct or structural violence."[4] The concept of cultural violence radically deepens the dominant understanding of violence by defining certain discursive elements in a culture as violent. Violence does not refer only to direct intentional harm perpetrated by an actor, but it includes symbolic and discursive aspects of cultures. The concept of cultural violence makes it possible to theorize discourses that make violence acceptable. Galtung suggests that violence operates in a multiplicity of ways and is more pervasive and insidious than we imagine.

The second part of Galtung's theory of cultural violence explains how cultural violence operates. Galtung points out that "one way cultural violence works is by changing the moral color of an act from red/wrong to green/right or at least to yellow/acceptable; an example being 'murder on behalf of the country as right, on behalf of oneself wrong.' Another way is by making reality opaque, so that we do not see the violent act or fact, or at least not as violent."[5] Here Galtung describes the two moments of cultural violence. The first is the moment of revaluation of an action, which changes its moral color and thus makes it morally acceptable. The second moment is one of mystification. Cultural violence operates by obscuring reality. In doing so, it makes invisible what would otherwise be visible.[6] In both moments, cultural violence functions by transforming the discursive conditions that determine the limits of intelligibility and thus whether we recognize a certain act as violent or not.

In the first two parts of this paper, I will discuss the complexity of Galtung's account of cultural violence. I argue that to understand the complexity of cultural violence, it is necessary to approach it from a perspective that takes the concept of hegemony seriously. Once we take hegemony as a central organizing idea of the social, it becomes possible to recognize that cultural violence operates by constituting reality. My claim is that approaching cultural violence

3 Johan Galtung, "Cultural Violence," *Journal of Peace Research* 27:3 (1990): 291–305.
4 Galtung, "Cultural Violence," 291.
5 Galtung, "Cultural Violence," 292.
6 Yves Winter, "Violence and Visibility," *New Political Science* 34(2012): 198.

from a hegemony-based perspective reveals three moments that could lead to violence: the hegemony of a discourse of cultural violence over and within its own domain, a discourse of cultural violence exercising power over several social domains, and the possible violence of a hegemonic discourse.

Approaching cultural violence from the perspective of hegemony also allows us to recognize why Galtung's response to cultural violence remains weak. The third part of Galtung's theory of cultural violence provides an account of what needs to be done to respond to the problem of cultural violence. Galtung maintains that since cultural violence "makes direct and structural violence look, even feel, right—or at least not wrong," we should "identify the cultural element and show how it can, empirically or potentially, be used to legitimize direct or structural violence."[7] This is what Galtung means by getting at the roots of the problem: reveal how cultural violence operates and render what we fail to recognize—violent acts and processes—visible and recognizable. In the last two sections of this paper, I suggest that given the pervasive nature of the discourses of cultural violence and the way they shape social reality and the common sense, it is not sufficient simply to reveal how these discourses operate. I argue that challenging cultural violence calls for agonistic interventions. I defend two strategies of agonism—a politics of contestation and a politics of disruption—as possible ways to counter the three risks introduced by cultural violence and hegemony.

Hegemony and Cultural Violence

The concept of hegemony as used by Antonio Gramsci refers to the ideological dominance of a particular social class over the others.[8] Gramsci's theory of hegemony offers an alternative to the production of relations of domination through coercion. Gramsci uses the term to explain how the bourgeoisie perpetuated its supremacy over the working class by securing their consent. According to Gramsci, hegemony operates by creating and maintaining social reality that expresses the interests of the ruling class. Hegemony as a mechanism of social power produces consent by naturalizing the worldview of the dominant groups and thus constructing an ideological and political consensus. This consensus presents a particular account of social reality while excluding, suppressing, or dominating other possible accounts. Within this hegemony,

7 Galtung, "Cultural Violence," 292 and 296.

8 Antonio Gramsci, *Selections from Prison Notebooks*, ed. and trans. Q. Hoare and G.N. Smith (New York: International Publishers, 1971).

dominated groups experience their domination not as domination, but as the way things "really" are. As such, the dominated class voluntarily accepts their domination and in general supports the social order and follows its institutions of civil society, which reproduce and disseminate hegemonic power.

Ernesto Laclau and Chantal Mouffe's theory of hegemony draws on Gramsci's account of hegemony, but their approach decouples hegemony and class while keeping hegemony as the central explanatory category of the social realm.[9] According to Laclau and Mouffe, Gramsci's theory of hegemony, despite its attempt to break from the economic determinism of Marxist thought and to recognize the relative independence of the superstructure from the base, still keeps the "inner essentialist core" of Marxism by asserting that hegemony must always correspond to a fundamental economic class. For Laclau and Mouffe, this is a regressive move that not only reaffirms "determination in the last instance by the economy" but also limits the logic of hegemony, since it predicates the economy as the fundamental domain that "constitutes an insurmountable limit to society's potential for hegemonic recomposition."[10] Laclau and Mouffe abandon class-essentialism of Marxism and recognize the contingency of the social. In taking hegemony as the central organizing principle of the social, Laclau and Mouffe theorize hegemony as a fluid and dynamic category that denotes identities, interests, and relations of power beyond the confines of economic relations. This understanding of hegemony opens up the category of hegemony so as to include every aspect of the social world—organizations, institutions, social categories, meanings of concepts, identities and social relations, and so on. The central idea, as Mouffe notes, is that "reality is not given to us; meaning is always constructed. There is no meaning that is just essentially given to use; there is no essence to the social, it is always constructed."[11] Social objectivity is constituted through acts of power, and thus every order is the result of hegemony struggle.[12] The social, Mouffe writes, "is the realm of sedimented practices, that is, practices that conceal the originary acts of their contingent political institution and which are taken for granted, as if they were self-grounded."[13] The social is not possible without these sedimented social practices, which are themselves given shape by the power

9 Ernesto Laclau and Chantal Mouffe, *Hegemony and Socialist Strategy* (London: Verso, 1985), 65–71.

10 Laclau and Mouffe, *Hegemony*, 69.

11 Nico Carpentier and Bart Cammaerts, "Hegemony, Democracy, Agonism and Journalism: An Interview with Chantal Mouffe," *Journalism Studies* 7(2006): 967.

12 Chantal Mouffe, *The Democratic Paradox*, (London: Verso, 2000), 99–100, and Chantal Mouffe, *On the Political*, (London: Verso, 2005), 17–18.

13 Mouffe, *On the Political*, 17–18.

relations. Mouffe recognizes that there are different forms of hegemony, some more democratic than others, but any social order is the product of a hegemonic political articulation.[14]

An important characteristic of Laclau and Mouffe's theory of hegemony that help us better grasp the complexity of cultural violence is their rejection of the approach that theorizes society as a unified field of struggle with a center structured by hegemony. When Laclau and Mouffe argue that hegemony constitutes social reality, their point is not that a hegemonic form of power takes over the center of the social. Rather it is that in a given social formation, "there can be a variety of hegemonic nodal points."[15] They argue that no hegemonic logic can account for the totality of the social realm.[16] This account of hegemony allows the theorization of multiple hegemonies. One needs to recognize the ongoing struggle for hegemony within and over multiplicity of domains of social and political life such as race, gender, sexual identity, nationality, religion, morality, and law, as well as the multiplicity of struggles that aim to problematize, contest, and transform relations of power in these domains.

The hegemony-centered account of the social changes the way we theorize the problem of cultural violence. Since the aim is to understand what makes acceptable structural and direct violence, what we need to recognize is that the social domain as a terrain of struggle provides an opportunity for discourses that defend violence to become hegemonic. The destructive potential of cultural violence is unleashed when discourses of violence are the ones that give shape and legitimize the social order. Put differently, what Galtung calls cultural violence occurs when a discourse of cultural violence becomes hegemonic.[17] Galtung's example of national socialism illustrates this violent moment. As Galtung writes, national socialism with its category of the Chosen/Self and the Unchosen/Other exalted the value of the Chosen while debasing the value of the Other. It has successfully defined the Other as the "'dangerous it' the 'vermin,' or 'bacteria' (as Hitler described the Jews)," who is then blamed for all the suffering of the Chosen.[18] By dehumanizing and converting the Other into an "it," this form of nationalism has set the stage for any kind of violence against the Other. Thus, "extermination becomes a psychologically possible duty. The SS guards become heroes to be celebrated for their

---

14 Mouffe, *On the Political*, 17–18.

15 Laclau and Mouffe, *Hegemony*, 139.

16 Laclau and Mouffe, *Hegemony*, 142.

17 I follow Galtung's definition of cultural violence. Any discourse that justifies and legitimizes violence could be defined as a discourse of cultural violence.

18 Galtung, *Cultural Violence*, 298.

devotion to duty."[19] The social order then exists to exalt the Chosen, which requires the elimination of that which threatens it. Institutionalization of the violent structure and the internalization of the violent culture render direct violence "institutionalized, repetitive, ritualistic, like a vendetta."[20] Galtung describes this normalization of violence as an aspect of culture legitimizing violence by revaluing the moral code of an action. However, this is not a simple revaluation of a particular action. Rather it is a discourse of cultural violence, such as national socialism instituting a *social reality* that creates identities, hierarchies, interests, and institutions. When a discourse of cultural violence becomes hegemonic, that is, when a discourse of cultural violence successfully defines social reality, it does more than legitimizing and making direct or structural violence "look right—or at least not wrong," but it naturalizes and normalizes violence by presenting an account of reality that defines violence as reasonable, ordinary, inevitable, and part of everyday life.

The issue is not that there are aspects of culture that legitimize violence. Each culture is complex and has its own share of such violent aspects. The issue is the hegemony of a discourse that defends violence. The true destructive potential of cultural violence appears when a discourse of cultural violence becomes the dominant discourse within its domain of hegemony struggle. Many discourses compete to structure meaning within a particular domain; however, as long as a discourse of cultural violence is not the one that is able to fix meaning and create a hegemonic point, it fails to naturalize violence. When a discourse becomes hegemonic, the definition of social reality constructed by that discourse becomes the only sensible one. And when a discourse of violence dominates its domain, the society—or at least the majority of those living in that society—has no reason to think that this violence is problematic. The interests, identities, social norms, and practices created by this dominant discourse of cultural violence become part of "what we see as the 'natural order' at a given moment which is always accompanied by a 'common sense.' This is what hegemony really entails: the 'mutual collapse' of objectivity and power."[21]

Viewed from the perspective of the hegemony-centered view, Galtung's description of a violent culture, which refers to "a culture in which a set of aspects are so violent, extensive and diverse, spanning all cultural domains," should be reformulated as a social world where many discourses of cultural violence are hegemonic in their particular terrains and deeply structure the common sense

19 Galtung, *Cultural Violence*, 298.

20 Galtung, *Cultural Violence*, 302.

21 Mouffe, *On the Political*, 17–18, and Mouffe, *Democratic Paradox*, 99.

in such a way that the normalization of violence in those domains spills over and influences other social domains. This chain of violence weakens the position of nonviolent discourses struggling for hegemony in other social domains, and thereby making violent discourses look more reasonable and acceptable. This is a society where violence becomes a nodal hegemonic point and "may constitute points of condensation of a number of social relations and, thus, become the focal point of multiplicity of totalizing effects."[22] This is what Laclau and Mouffe call "overdetermination." Consider, for instance, neoliberalism and how it not only fixes the web of meanings in the domain of economy and economic relations, but also operates in many spheres such as environment, politics, education, and so on—fixing meanings, creating subject positions, forms of struggle and points of resistance, and relations of power. Similarly, in a violent culture we see violence as a nodal hegemonic point constituting the central organizing concept in a variety of relatively autonomous spheres. This overdetermination nears a total hegemony of violence as it excludes, marginalizes, and renders invisible the peaceful alternatives to violent discourses. Since the overdetermined hegemonic discourse marginalizes points of resistance to the point of invisibility, there remains no "reasonable" counter-discourse that could challenge the dominant violent discourses. It structures the common sense almost as whole and thereby determines the limits of intelligibility and the limits of our imagination. A violent culture of this sort has tremendous potential for violence. This is the second threat of cultural violence.

The first type of cultural violence refers to the hegemonization of a discourse of cultural violence and thereby structuring the common sense in relation to a particular sphere. The second type refers to the multiplication of the discourses of cultural violence over the discursive field and hegemonization of several discourses of cultural violence over their particular domains and thus constructing violence as a hegemonic nodal point over several domains. The post-structuralist account of hegemony enables us to theorize another form of cultural violence: "hegemonic violence." The point here is not the unavoidable violence of hegemony itself. As Duane Cady states while criticizing the hegemony of the discourse of development, "when we do not see plurality in the very structure of a theory, we see hegemony. This is why hegemony is violent; it violates, distorts, coerces, dismisses, reduces, diminishes, and devalues what it embraces."[23] The violence of hegemony then resides in the fact that it eliminates plurality, reduces complexity of the world, and "forces adaptation

22 Laclau and Mouffe, *Hegemony*, 139.

23 Duane Cady, "Hegemony as Violence," *Acorn* 11(2002): 18.

to the hegemonic uniformity."[24] Hegemony always constrains. However, for Cady, hegemony is always imposed from "the outside." The virtue of Laclau and Mouffe's post-structuralist theory of hegemony is that it theorizes the social as a discursive realm of contest among discourses for fixing meaning. Hegemony is not something necessarily imposed from the outside, but it is already the central organizing principle of any society. Viewed thus, there is no unlimited play of differences left untouched by discursive articulations. Galtung was very well aware of this inevitable violence. He writes, "A major task of peace research, and the peace movement in general,. is that never-ending search for a peace culture—problematic, because of the temptation to institutionalize that culture, making it obligatory with the hope of internalizing it everywhere. And that would already be direct violence, imposing a culture."[25] Thus viewed, even a society where discourses of peace are hegemonic and where peace becomes the hegemonic nodal point would owe its existence to violence, since this particular social regime would be constituted by a version of social reality, albeit a peaceful one, claiming to represent the whole and in its constitution would have favored and normalized certain identities, norms, and institutions while sheltering its own exclusions and marginalizations.

The third type of cultural violence comes about when a discourse that is not violent becomes hegemonic and thus appears natural and deeply structures the common sense. The logic of hegemony, as Laclau and Mouffe point out, necessarily introduces the concept of antagonism. Hegemony is an empty form, a type of relation of power that excludes and marginalizes other discourses vying for hegemony. When a discourse becomes hegemonic, it fixes and stabilizes meaning in a particular domain and exercises hegemonic affects that marginalize the other contestants. Every hegemonic articulation inevitably defines an enemy and draws a line that excludes. Thus, insofar as there is hegemony there is antagonism. As Mouffe states, "every order is based on a particular structure of power relations that exclude other possibilities: to be hegemonic one form of power has to repress the other possibilities that can always be reactivated."[26] However, this also introduces the possibility that every hegemonic order can be challenged by practices that demand new articulations of power and establish a new hegemony. Mouffe argues that when antagonistic principles of legitimacy coexist within the same political association, this introduces a serious threat to the existing hegemonic order. Thus, she

24 Cady, "Hegemony," 16.

25 Galtung, "Cultural Violence," 291.

26 Mouffe, *On the Political*, 18.

concludes, "hegemonic discourses have to discriminate between discourses that would be tolerated and discourses that would be excluded."[27] This is a dynamic and an ongoing process of "sorting out"—the political moment of defining who the enemy is. Once a dominant discourse successfully structures the common sense and the social reality created by it settles down and thus erases its traces of contingency, it may appear natural to use violence to contain that which threatens the "natural" order of things. Hegemonic articulations tend toward closure, stabilize meaning, and naturalize their exclusions since that's how they become hegemonic. They marginalize and reify the Other. And when the Other is perceived as a threat, it can be destroyed. This is different from a discourse of violence becoming hegemonic. A discourse of violence already defends violence, and if it becomes hegemonic, the kind of violence it defends would be perceived as reasonable and acceptable. Hegemonic violence, on the other hand, is the possible consequence of hegemony itself. Any discourse has the potential to accommodate or legitimize violence when it becomes hegemonic. The violence of hegemony does not reside only in its authoritative ordering of the social and homogenization of plurality, but also in its naturalization of violence in the name of securing what is part of the common sense and the normal—nation, religion, ethnicity, gender relations, democracy, development, environment, honor, and even peace.

Struggles against Hegemony

Once we take seriously the idea of hegemony, it becomes possible to recognize that Galtung's theory of cultural violence fails to grasp the complexity of the problem of cultural violence. Seen from the perspective of hegemony, it becomes clear that cultural violence has three different variants: first, naturalization of a discourse of cultural violence by becoming hegemonic over and within a particular social sphere; second, violence constituting a hegemonic nodal point—a chain of violence—and thus impacting several social domains; and third, the potential violence of any hegemonic discourse. These three risks introduce mainly three questions: How is it possible to prevent a discourse of cultural violence from becoming hegemonic? How is it possible to respond to the tendency of commonalities or settlements to sediment and naturalize? How is it possible to weaken hegemony?

The first two questions bring attention to the prevention of hegemonic violence in the latent stages. One might give priority to the third question and

27 Mouffe, *On the Political*, 121.

argue that, given the already existing hegemonies and the commonness of hegemonic violence, it is urgent to focus on theorizing ways to weaken existing hegemonic articulations and to transform relations of power that naturalize violence. However, what is at least as important as undoing existing hegemonies is to find ways to prevent the hegemony of discourses of violence and, more importantly, the hegemony of a discourse within a particular domain.[28] John Paul Lederach observes that once a conflict reaches the proportions of a humanitarian disaster, it draws the attention of the public and creates a crisis mentality. But, he continues, "little preparation is made for sustaining the peace process over the medium and long term."[29] If we consider hegemony as the crisis moment that exercises its inevitable violence without most people perceiving this as violence, what needs to be done, in addition to developing ways to weaken hegemony, is to devise strategies of prevention that would address the problem in its latent stages. Preventing hegemony is a crucial task in minimizing violence because, unlike Lederach's approach, which aims to respond to a commonly recognized conflict, the main problem hegemonic violence introduces is that once hegemony structures the common sense and guides everyday life, not only we do not have any reason to think that hegemonic violence is problematic, but also those who resist would find it very difficult to formulate hegemonic violence as a problem. Since hegemony structures the background of social meaning, which marginalizes points of resistance beyond this discursive horizon, the demands of those who resist would not make sense within that particular social order. They would be heard as "noise," becoming invisible and having no business being heard or seen.[30] As such, it is crucial to explore the possibility of a politics that would prevent the naturalization of commonalities and settlements that constitute the social order.

28 I assume that preventing hegemony as such would also address the problem of hegemony of a discourse of violence. I recognize that the hegemony of a discourse of violence may have more violent consequences than the hegemony of a discourse whose constitutive features do not include defending and promoting violence. For instance, it is reasonable to assume that the hegemony of militarism would have far more violent consequences than the hegemony of human rights although I recognize that when radicalized the discourse of human rights could justify intervention, forced democratization, and regime change. The difference between the two is significant: the former is essentially violent, whereas the latter is not but could lead to the legitimization of violence.

29 John Paul Lederach, *Building Peace: Sustainable Reconciliation in Divided Societies* (Washington, DC: United States Institute of Peace, 1997), 74.

30 Aletta Norval, "Democracy, Pluralization, and Voice," *Ethics and Global Politics* 2(2009): 48.

My suggestion is that struggles against hegemony should be considered an ongoing and unending process, given the tendency of commonalities and settlements toward closure which incur the risk of naturalization of violence. One obvious response to hegemony is to reject all settled commonalities—collective identities, social rules, ethical codes, traditions, social habits, institutions, and so on. In a way, this means embracing the Heraclitian "flux."[31] The logic underlying this response is that if there are no settlements or commonalities, there can be no hegemony. This would be a social world of a series of differences, which are always in the dynamic process of becoming. This response gets to the root of the issue and appears to have eliminated the problem of hegemony once and for all. The approach I'd like to defend here—strategic agonism—as a way of responding to the problem of hegemonic violence rejects the possibility and desirability of this response since it downplays the role and significance of settlements and commonalities in human life. Consider, for instance, identity as a settlement established in relation to a series of differences. As William Connolly writes, identity is an indispensable part of every stable way of life.[32] It is, Connolly suggests, "what makes one what she is and how she appears to others. It is the dense self from which choosing, wanting, and consenting proceed."[33] For Connolly identity is the density without which one "would not be, do, or achieve anything."[34] A life without a particular identity is neither possible nor desirable. However, identity introduces certain risks. Identities secure themselves by congealing into fixed forms. They are "thought and lived as if their structure expressed the true order of things."[35] When experienced this way, identity triggers the drive to marginalize, demonize, and convert some differences into otherness. The dogmatization of identity leads to violence toward differences. The problem then is not identity, which is both inevitable and desirable, but how an identity is constituted and experienced.

31 Fragments such as "Changing it is at rest" and "Upon these who step into the same rivers, different and again different waters flow" express the idea that change is what preserves stability and identity. I follow Richard McKirahan's interpretation here. See Richard D. McKirahan, *Philosophy Before Socrates: An Introduction with Texts and Commentary* (Cambridge: Hackett Publishing, 1994), 122 and 124. The ultimate goal of hegemony is to stabilize meaning and thus to end or manage change.

32 William Connolly, *Identity/Difference: Democratic Negotiations of a Political Paradox* (Minneapolis: University of Minnesota Press, 1991), 158.

33 Connolly, *Identity/Difference*, 64.

34 Connolly, *Identity/Difference*, 158.

35 Connolly, *Identity/Difference*, 158.

Agonism recognizes that "human beings require meaning in order to make sense of the world." Settlements and commonalities serve as the sources of meaning that construct narratives for social life in a given time or culture.[36] These foundational claims are what make social order possible and provide human life with a degree of security, stability, and meaning. In that sense, settlements and commonalities are unavoidable, necessary, and essential to human life.[37] Agonism also recognizes that each settlement contains "subjugations and cruelties within it."[38] When these settlements begin to *sediment,* the cruelties—exclusion, marginalization, oppression, domination, injustice—created by these settlements appear as natural. For agonism the aim is not to eliminate settlements and commonalities, without which stability and social order would not be possible, but it is to find ways to prevent them from appearing inevitable and natural, that is, hegemonic.

The type of agonism I defend here draws a distinction between "hegemony" and "settlement." Hegemony is an expression of sedimented and naturalized forms of settlements. Despite their tendency toward closure, commonalities do not necessarily become hegemonic if countered and disturbed by agonistic strategies. This does not mean a settlement is not an expression of hegemonic power. Rather, it is to say that there is a distinction between the early stages of hegemony—"settlement," which is an expression of weak hegemonic power—and late stages of hegemony—"sedimentation," which is an expression of established hegemonic power. In the early stages, hegemonic articulations are weak, vulnerable, and have not yet successfully structured the common sense. Neither its place in the social nor its exclusions have been naturalized. Weak hegemony embodies a sense of contingency and fallibility, which allows for the critical evaluation of hegemonic power and renders possible the recognition of alternatives as legitimate. The idea of weak hegemony allows us to respond to the paradox of settlement—that we need commonalities, but when commonalities naturalize, they incur the risk of violence—by introducing a third alternative that goes beyond the binary of hegemony and radical contingency.

Strategic agonism I defend here goes beyond the confines of Foucaultian agonism while keeping its spirit of resistance. For Foucault, agonism is a strategy of resistance that opens up a space for the transformation of relations of power that tightly tie the individual to her identity, which is inherent in the process

36 Edward Wingenbach, *Institutionalizing Agonistic Democracy* (Burlington: Ashgate Publishing, 2011), xvi.

37 Wingenbach, *Agonistic Democracy*, 7.

38 Connolly, *Identity/Difference*, 94.

of subject formation.[39] Foucault's main concern here is the emergence of new forms of subjectivity and the relationship between self and other. Strategic agonism has a broader scope and conceives of society as an agon where contestation extends to all elements of the social—deeply ingrained assumptions of society, seemingly apolitical cultural norms and set of traditions, cultural expectations and institutions, reservoir of meanings and accepted meanings of social values, identities, life styles, and practices. The aim is to contest the naturalization of these settlements and thus to prevent the emergence of a hegemonic consensus while exposing and problematizing exclusions and marginalizations that are inherent in and sheltered by every social order. Sedimented forms of settlement are expressions of strong hegemony, but settlements are possible without sedimentation as long as spaces of contestation are open and there are other competitors in the field of political contestation who challenge the dogmatization of settlements.[40] Seen from this perspective, the possibility of weak hegemony defines the task of strategic agonism: to envision contestational political strategies through which hegemonic power can be resisted and weakened and its sedimentation can be prevented.

Agonistic Interventions

Coming to terms with the ever-existing risk of violence introduced by strong hegemony and the tendency of weak hegemony to transform into strong hegemony requires developing political strategies to counter hegemonic power. Agonism proposes mainly two political strategies—contestation and disruption—through which it may be possible to challenge hegemonic power and to prevent sedimentation of social practices.[41]

Politics of Contestation

The aim of politics of contestation is to unmask the true nature of hegemonic power and thus set the stage for the pluralization of discourses competing for hegemony. Galtung neatly sums up how the political strategy of unmasking

39 Michel Foucault, "The Subject and Power," in *Michel Foucault: Power*, ed. James Faubion (NewYork: The New Press, 2000), 330.

40 Connolly, *Identity/Difference*, x.

41 For varieties of agonism see Andrew Schaap, introduction to *Law and Agonistic Politics* (Burlington: Ashgate, 2013), 1; Wingenbach, *Agonistic Democracy*, 43–78. For agonism as a strategic approach see Mark Wenman, *Agonistic Democracy Constituent Power in the Era of Globalisation* (NY: Cambridge University Press, 2013), 39 and 54.

works when he writes, "identify the cultural element and show how it can, empirically or potentially, be used to legitimize direct or structural violence."[42] The strategy of unmasking is an important aspect of politics of contestation, but hegemony critique requires more than exposing how a dominant discourse of cultural violence operates. Weakening hegemonic power also calls for revealing the contingency of hegemony, which is concealed throughout the process of sedimentation. Given the need for meaning and stability in human life and thus the significance of settlements, simply revealing how these dominant narratives operate may not necessarily expose their contingent nature. What needs to be done is to constantly put the self-groundedness of sedimentations and the practices they authorize into question. Put differently, the political institution of hegemony should be revealed and challenged.

An essential requirement for an agonistic politics of contestation is the existence of multiple competitors in the field of hegemonic struggle. Politics of contestation is based on the idea that exposing the historicity of settlements and social practices and contesting the common sense could keep the hegemonic competition alive. The underlying idea is that when spaces of democratic contestation are safe and vibrant, and when there are several contenders vying for hegemony, the dynamics of agonistic exchange would most likely prevent the domination of the social field by any one narrative and assume a hegemonic character. From the perspective of the agonistic approach the inevitable tensions between stability and change, sedimentation and disruption, and closure and fissures are what keep democratic contestation alive.[43] As long as the dynamics of this tension is healthy and not resolved in favor of either side of each binary, the agon as the site for perpetual contest and politics would not be closed and settled, and thus the struggles over the institution of society and meaning could be kept democratic. Agonistic political strategies then aim to provide the means for creating possibilities of resistance to hegemony and keeping spaces for democratic contestation open in order to contain the tendency of settlements to sediment and naturalize.

At this point, it is important to note that the aim is not to relativize everything, as that would mean unsettling all settlements and conventions without which society cannot exist. Rather the aim is to pluralize the social by expanding "the range of possible expressions of meaning within the contingency of social life" while at the same time rendering the social order more attentive

42 Galtung, "Cultural Violence," 296.

43 Bonnie Honig, *Political Theory and the Displacement of Politics* (Ithaca, NY: Cornell University Press, 1993), 200.

to the exercise of power and to its exclusions.[44] The idea of weak hegemony promises a more peaceful society, but the risk of hegemonic violence is inherent to it as it has the potential to naturalize and transform into strong hegemony. Consider, for instance, the hegemony of liberal democracy. From an agonistic perspective, democracy is an achievement that needs to be cherished and cared for. However, democracy in its liberal and representative form is one version of democracy among many other forms of democracy. What is happening today is that the hegemony of one particular version of democracy within the domain of political order leads to the marginalization of other alternatives, and those who defend other alternatives are not taken seriously. The hegemony of liberal representative democracy is so strong that the use of "liberal" and "representative" are almost redundant as "democracy" simply refers to representative democracy in its liberal form. Similarly, democracy as a political regime is one way of organizing society among many others. Not only are the alternatives to democracy rarely voiced in the political public spheres of democratic countries, but they also do not make sense to the public when they are voiced. This is an expression of how deeply discourse of democracy has shaped the common sense in established democracies. The issue is that the hegemony of liberal democracy over and within this domain renders it inevitable and natural, which easily justifies interventions, friend/enemy categorization and ordering of the international arena, and marginalization of those who are against democracy. The aim of politics of contestation here is not to subvert democracy itself, but to weaken its hegemony to loosen its tight grip on our collective consciousness so as to prevent it from being used as a discourse of cultural violence.

Another important example is national identity. Galtung identifies national identity as a possible site of cultural violence and places it in the domain of "ideology," which is one of the six main domains of cultural violence according to him.[45] Galtung observes that the problem with nationalism is that it reduces the identity of the people to one attachment—ethnicity—and naturalizes it, which then could legitimize violence toward nonmembers when the hierarchies implicit in the national identity are radicalized. To be sure, it is possible to decouple nationalism and ethnicity and advance different forms of nationalism that do not take ethnicity as the basis of the nation. However, each form of nationalism would be defined in terms of a commonality—ethnic, religious, historical, linguistic, cultural, civic, and so on—and would inevitably reduce

44 Wingenbach, *Agonistic Democracy*, 52.

45 According to Galtung the six domains of cultural violence are ideology, religion, art, language, empirical science, and formal science.

the identity of the people to one or more of these attachments. The domination of the social by one of these interpretations would introduce the possibility of hegemonic violence. Thus, the aim of the agonistic approach is to open up the concept of national identity to new attachments and multiply possible interpretations. Each attempt to define the identity of the people is a political moment and an expression of a particular normative vision. The identity of the people organizes the social order since it answers the question of who "we" are as a people while drawing a political boundary that decides who should be included and who should be excluded. Agonistic contestation by putting multiple interpretations of the "we" in play aims to prevent the closure of any meaning of the identity of the people. At times a particular understanding of the "we" might gain dominance, thereby attempting to fix the meaning of the "we" once and for all. In this case, the aim is to contest this meaning to prevent its sedimentation.

The pluralization of the "we" not only aims to counter internal violence—marginalization and exclusion of the hegemony of one particular meaning of national identity—but it may also counter xenophobic potential of the "we" by altering the way "we" relate to the foreigners. As Bonnie Honig puts it, pluralizing the national attachments may "interrupt and counter some well-established scripts."[46] The point is not to confront the xenophobic with the xenophilic, which might fuel the xenophobic drives and intensify the us/them distinction, but to offer a new vantage point that allows us to offer different accounts of democratic citizenship, including transnational ones. It is not to get rid of the "nation," which is very important for many people and is still very strong, but to pluralize possible attachments that might help us recognize the validity of other attachments and might loosen our attachment to one particular meaning of national identity. Honig notes that politics of contestation and the pluralization of national attachment that it would bring about could shift the perspective from what should we do about the foreigner to "what problems does foreignness solve for us, as a democracy?"[47] It is important to formulate the question this way, as it may prevent us from comfortably holding the foreign responsible for our problems, which may change the way we perceive the immigrant. This new perception may foster a more positive and welcoming attitude toward "them." Ultimately, the political strategy of contestation "may break, or at least loosen the grip of the xenophobic structure,"[48] thereby

46 Bonnie Honig, "What Is Agonism For? Reply to Woodford, Finlayson, Stears," *Contemporary Political Theory* 13(2014): 209.

47 Honig, "What Is Agonism For?" 209.

48 Honig, "What Is Agonism For?" 209.

responding to possible cultural violence that originates in the domain of national identity.

Politics of Disruption

At first glance a politics of disruption might appear to be redundant, given that a politics of incessant contestation could prevent the naturalization of dominant settlements and conventions. When a politics of contestation functions well, the agonistic competition among the discourses vying for hegemony could preclude the emergence of strong hegemony. The agonistic game would have no ultimate winners that could shut down the agon. Thus, the argument concludes, there is no need for political strategies of disruption that might have polarized the political discourse and encourage further conflict which might lead to violence and undermine the agon itself. This is an important point that cannot be easily dismissed.

One reply to this argument is that when there is a healthy agonistic exchange among the competing parties, and when there is a commonly accepted ethos of contestation, which is subject to contestation itself, as there are many different accounts of an ethos of agonism, a politics of disruption may indeed be redundant. The agonist may concede that in an ideal world there may be no need for a politics of disruption since in the ideal world there would not be strong hegemony to disrupt because of well-functioning dynamics of agonistic contestation. In that ideal world, differences would coexist peacefully and recognize the others striving for victory, not as enemies but as competitors who have a right to attempt to stabilize meaning and to challenge the dominant settlements and conventions. Ideally, differences would extend an understanding and a fair hearing to the others while being attentive to the possible violence of one's own attachments and the contestability of one's own position.[49] However, it is clear that the actual world is radically different from this ideal. And the one we live in calls for politics of disruption as there are many established strong hegemonies in many different spheres.

Another reply to this argument points out the deeply pervasive and constitutive nature of hegemony. Hegemony refers to the naturalization of a particular

---

49 I am proposing an ethos based largely on Mouffe's that takes tolerance as its key value and Connolly's ethos of engagement that defends agonistic respect and critical responsiveness as the two crucial virtues of agonistic democracy. Elsewhere I argued that each has merits as well as problems and an ethos for agonistic politics should bring the valuable elements of the two ethics together. See Fuat Gursozlu, "Pluralism, Identity, and Violence," in *Peace Philosophy and Public Life: Commitments, Crises, and Concepts for Engaged Thinking*, eds. *Greg* Moses and Gail Presby (Amsterdam:Rodopi, 2014), 101–109.

version of social reality, which appears as the only sensible way of seeing the world. Galtung recognizes how hegemony operates when he notes, "when the violent culture is institutionalized and internalized, direct violence becomes repetitive and ritualistic."[50] But, because he fails to recognize the nature of hegemony, he believes that a politics of contestation could successfully respond to cultural violence. For Galtung, what allows the repetition and reproduction of violence is its invisibility. Once we rendered violence visible by lifting the veil that hides it, it would be possible to stop it. However, as Yves Winter rightly argues, it is "not invisibility that allows violence to be repeated and reproduced, but that repetition and reproduction make violence invisible."[51] The normalcy of everyday violence is not hidden behind a veil but is in plain sight, which is sanctioned, practiced, and repeated daily such that violence is part of everyday routines and the common sense. It is not that we do not recognize various manifestations of violence, rather we think that some of these manifestations are inevitable and some are acceptable and reasonable. Thus viewed, a common response to politics of contestation may very well be an even stronger affirmation of the existing hegemonies that authorize and normalize violence. Given how deeply hegemony guides the everyday and conditions identities and social practices, the strategy of unmasking the true nature of sedimented forms of settlements and rendering operations of power visible may be fruitless in weakening existing hegemonies. The constitutive and pervasive nature of hegemony brings to the fore the need for political strategies that would disrupt established settlements. Such disruption may lead to the suspension of extant social conventions. This suspension opens up a space for questioning the violence created and sheltered by the existing social order and for the emergence of viable alternatives. Then the aim is not only to reveal the contingency of hegemony and subvert social fixity, which in part could be achieved by politics of contestation, but it is also to disrupt the routine processes of the everyday and the pressures of hegemonic power in order to open little cracks in the social order and "to get citizens to think seriously about what until then they may have found normal and acceptable."[52]

It is possible to review many other historical examples of politics of disruption undertaken by ordinary people, from the nomination of Victoria Woodhall—the first woman to run for president in the United States—in 1872 to Rosa Parks' refusal to move to the back of the bus and surrender her seat to

50 Galtung, "Cultural Violence," 302.

51 Winter, "Violence and Visibility," 202.

52 Iris M. Young, "Activist Challenges to Deliberative Democracy," *Political Theory* 29(2011): 675.

a white passenger, and from Muhammed Ali's refusal to serve in the army and fight in Vietnam to the recent decisions of public sphere movements to occupy public squares and parks to make the public aware of injustices in economic distribution and the undemocratic nature of existing democracies. Such acts of disruption call attention to violence caused by the existing social order. In doing so they call attention to ignored and suppressed issues and introduce the possibility of a more peaceful social order.

Consider, for instance, the disruptive politics of Martin Luther King Jr.'s Birmingham campaign. As King emphasizes, the problem in Birmingham was not simply one of visibility: that the white majority failed to see how racism operated and justified direct and structural violence.[53] King states that the violence of the system was already well documented. Despite the visibility of such harms, "the political leaders consistently refused to engage in good faith negotiations," and when they negotiated and made some promises, they quickly broke them.[54] It is clear that the issue in Birmingham was not one of unmasking and rendering visible how racism operates and how racist power structures harm African Americans in Birmingham. The problem was the hegemony of racism and the dominant version of social reality it constituted. The racist narrative based on the superiority of the white over the black has deeply shaped the common sense and the dominant social norms, rules, practices, and identities. This is why a politics of unmasking and contestation, both of which had been tried before the Birmingham campaign, failed to weaken the impact of white supremacy in Birmingham. And this is why King turned to disruptive strategies. In his defense of the method of nonviolent direct action, King points out that "non-violent direct action seeks to create such a crisis and foster such a tension that a community which has constantly refused to negotiate is forced to confront the issue. It seeks to dramatize the issue so that it can no longer be ignored."[55] This is not disruption for the sake of disruption, but a constructive disruption, the aim of which is to bring about a creative tension. This is a type of constructive nonviolent tension that "will help men rise from the dark depths of prejudice and racism to the majestic heights of understanding and brotherhood."[56]

53 Martin Luther King, Jr, "Letter from a Birmingham Jail," *The King Center*, April 16, 1963, accessed August 4, 2015, http://www.thekingcenter.org/archive/document/letter-birmingham-city-jail-0.

54 King, "Letter," 4.

55 King, "Letter," 5.

56 King, "Letter," 5.

A more contemporary example of politics of disruption is the political performances of the Serbian student movement Otpor! When resistance to Milosevic's authoritarian power had a high cost in Serbia, the student resistance group Otpor! used street theater and pranks to spread their message. The group's most famous prank involved displaying Milosevic's effigy in public, which passersby could punch for a small fee. In 2000, to celebrate the new year, Otpor! organized a concert in Belgrade. At midnight, they projected the images of war victims on a big screen in the city center followed by an announcer saying, "these are the victims of the regime, the head of which is still in power. How much longer?"[57] The creative political protests of Otpor! have been immensely influential in disrupting the everyday and encouraging the public to resist Milosevic's oppressive government.

In both of these examples the purpose of engaging in a politics of disruption is the creative disruption of sedimented social arrangements. The Birmingham campaign disrupted the routine processes of everyday in an attempt to force those who partake in the perpetuation of violence to negotiate the terms of the social order and to encourage them to rethink the existing relations of power. The purpose of the disruptive political acts of Otpor! was to empower the public and to undermine the hegemonic narrative that presented a particular political regime as inevitable. Both campaigns exemplify the ultimate aim of strategies of disruption: to create the possibility for transforming existing symbolic order by weakening strong hegemony and by introducing a better alternative.

Conclusion

Mouffe argues that political philosophy has an important role to play in the emergence of a new common sense since it shapes the "definition of reality."[58] Galtung's theory of cultural violence should be seen as part of an endeavor to constitute a social reality that would authorize and shelter less violence than the one that is dominant today. The most important contribution of Galtung's theory of cultural violence in challenging violence is its emphasis on the necessity to contest violence on a discursive level. However, I have argued, Galtung's

57 Srdja Popovic, *Blueprint for Revolution* (New York: Spiegel and Grau, 2015), 101. See also Tina Rosenberg, "Revolution U," *Foreign Policy* February 17, 2011, accessed August 23, 2015, http://foreignpolicy.com/2011/02/17/revolution-u-2/.

58 Chantal Mouffe and Paul Holdengräber, "Radical Democracy: Modern or Postmodern?" *Social Text* no. 21 (1989): 42.

theory of cultural violence fails to theorize the real risks of cultural violence and offers a limited response to counter it since it lacks an understanding of hegemony. Ours is an age of strong hegemony. In several domains, there are decisive winners that have successfully defined reality and the social, thereby shaping the common sense. What we should be concerned about is not simply the hegemony of a discourse of cultural violence over and within a particular social sphere. We should also pay attention to the possible violence of any form of hegemony. We care for our favorite values, social norms, identities, and lifestyles and tend to cherish the dominance of narratives that have constructed them. What we need to keep in mind is that even the most peaceful settlement and convention have the potential to legitimize violence when it becomes hegemonic and appears as natural.

The even greater risk to nonviolence today is global hegemony. The shrinking global village has introduced the possibility of global hegemonies. We already speak of the global hegemony of capitalism, first-world development, consumerism, possessive individualism, militarism, militarization of the police, elite model of liberal democracy and a notion of passive citizenship, liberty understood only in negative terms, a Western interpretation of human rights, anthropomorphism, and so on. To counter global hegemony, it is important to resist at a local and national level and try to link together local resistances. Local politics of everyday life is one of the essential sites of resistance. But when hegemony is global, the politics that can counter it should emerge from global solidarities. In addition to linking together local disturbances, it is essential to forge transnational alliances and points of resistance. Despite its pervasiveness, hegemony is never complete and hegemony always creates points of resistance. The question is whether it is possible to transform existing local and global hegemonies toward more peaceful articulations and to construct relations of power in such a way that it is attentive to its own exclusions and possible violence.

Bibliography

Cady, Duane. "Hegemony as Violence." *Acorn* 11 (2002): 13–19.

Carpentier, Nico and Bart Cammaerts. "Hegemony, Democracy, Agonism and Journalism: An Interview with Chantal Mouffe." *Journalism Studies* 7 (2006): 964–975.

Connolly, William. *Identity/Difference: Democratic Negotiations of Political Paradox*. Ithaca, NY: Cornell University Press, 1991.

Foucault, Michel. "The Subject and Power." In *Michel Foucault: Power*, edited by James Faubion, 326–347. New York: New Press, 2000.

Galtung, Johan. "Violence, Peace, and Peace Research." *Journal of Peace Research* 6 (1969): 167–199.

Galtung, Johan. "Cultural Violence." *Journal of Peace Research* 27 (1990): 291–305.

Gramsci, Antonio. *Selections from Prison Notebooks*. Edited and translated by Q. Hoare and G.N. Smith. New York: International Publishers, 1971.

Gursozlu, Fuat. "Pluralism, Identity, and Violence." In *Peace Philosophy and Public Life. Commitments, Crises, and Concepts for Engaged Thinking*, edited by Greg Moses and Gail Presby, 93–109. Amsterdam: Rodopi, 2014.

Honig, Bonnie. *Political Theory and the Displacement of Politics*. Ithaca, NY: Cornell University Press, 1993.

Honig, Bonnie. "What Is Agonism For? Reply to Woodford, Finlayson, Stears." *Contemporary Political Theory* 13(2014): 208–217.

King, Martin Luther Jr. "Letter from a Birmingham Jail." *The King Center*, April 16, 1963. Accessed August 4, 2015. http://www.thekingcenter.org/archive/document/letter-birmingham-city-jail-0.

Laclau, Ernesto, and Chantal Mouffe. *Hegemony and Socialist Strategy*. London: Verso, 1985.

Lederach, John Paul. *Building Peace: Sustainable Reconciliation in Divided Societies*. Washington, DC: United States Institute of Peace, 1997.

McKirahan, Richard D. *Philosophy Before Socrates. An Introduction with Texts and Commentary*. Indianapolis: Hackett Publishing, 1994.

Mouffe, Chantal. *Democratic Paradox*. London: Verso, 2000.

Mouffe, Chantal. *On the Political*. London: Verso, 2005.

Mouffe, Chantal, and Paul Holdengräber. "Radical Democracy: Modern or Postmodern?" *Social Text* 21 (1989): 31–45.

Norval, Aletta. "Democracy, Pluralization, and Voice." *Ethics and Global Politics* 2 (2009): 297–320.

Popovic, Srdja. *Blueprint for Revolution*. New York: Spiegel and Grau, 2015.

Rosenberg, Tina. "Revolution U." *Foreign Policy* (February 17, 2011). Accessed August 23, 2015. http://foreignpolicy.com/2011/02/17/revolution-u-2/.

Schaap, Andrew. *Law and Agonistic Politics*. Burlington, VT: Ashgate Publishing, 2013.

Wenman, Mark. *Agonistic Democracy Constituent Power in the Era of Globalisation*. New York: Cambridge University Press, 2013.

Wingenbach, Edward. *Institutionalizing Agonistic Democracy*. Burlington, VT: Ashgate Publishing, 2011.

Winter, Yves. "Violence and Visibility." *New Political Science* 34 (2012): 195–202.

Young, Iris Marion. "Activist Challenges to Deliberative Democracy." *Political Theory* 29 (2001): 670–690.

CHAPTER 5

Two Semites Confront Anti-Semitism: On the Varities of Anti-Semitic Experience

Amin Asfari and Ron Hirschbein

The authors, an Arab and a Jew, present irony-assisted narratives interpreting their confrontations. These narratives reflect the dialectic interplay between the personal and political. We hasten to add that, contrary to popular views, like Jews, Arabs are Semites. As Hebrew scripture reminds us, Noah's son, Shem, was the progenitor of Arabs; indeed, "Semite" is derived from "Shem." And Freud entertained the possibility that Moses really was an Egyptian prince. There's no need to speculate or stress common linguistic roots. To cite a headline from the Israeli paper *Haaretz*: "Jews and Palestinian Arabs share genetic roots." They are "blood brothers."[1]

Amin experienced both varieties of anti-Semitism, and so did Ron. Growing up in Kuwait, Amin experienced the old variety: hating Jews was as natural as the searing desert sun. Even if he succumbed to such hatred, he couldn't act upon it—there were no Jews. Propagandists promoted Jews as *the* evil abstraction, an "other" responsible for all problems, real and imagined. Migrating to New York changed everything: Jews became real, particular human beings with all the virtues and vices that inform humanity.

Unfortunately, Amin experienced the signature of post-9/11 America, the new anti-Semitism—Islamophobia. He knows more about the new anti-Semitism than he cares to. Of course, none dare call Islamophobia anti-Semitism—consider the implications. Trump dismissed criticizing Islamophobia as political correctness. But anti-Semitism—directed at Jews—remains a grievous offense, a charge even Trump had to deny when one of his ads featured a Star of David, "Crooked Hillary," and piles of cash.

In the aftermath of 9/11, Amin set out to prove to his fellow countrymen that he could be both American *and* Muslim. Little did he know that some people refuse to accept him as either. An antagonistic relationship with his professor as an undergraduate student at an evangelical university proved

1 "Blood Brothers: Palestinians and Jews Share Genetic Roots," Haaretz.com, Last modified October 20, 2015, http://www.haaretz.com/israel-news/science/1.681385.

 | DOI 10.1163/9789004361911_007

to be the first of an unfolding saga of vitriolic attacks and marginalization. Indeed, the daily stares became inconsequential compared to the overt practices of "othering" that Amin—as well as his family and friends—experienced; which suggested in no uncertain terms *"you're not like us, you're not welcome!"* Family and friends—to understate the case—also experienced Islamophobia at an alarming rate. Amin writes of the tragedy that befell family members murdered execution style by a self-declared anti-theist.

The second section narrates Ron's confrontations. Taunted by ethnic slurs and bullying, he experienced the old anti-Semitism. To be sure, it was nothing like the pogroms and Holocaust that tormented and killed his ancestors—it was anti-Semitism-lite. Nevertheless, for a time, it instilled a sense of shame about his ethnicity. However, by the time he reached college, he celebrated his heritage, regaling friends with embellished tales of Hebrew school and climaxing in his shotgun bar mitzvah.

Ron's early attitudes toward fellow Semites—Arabs—reflected the times. During his childhood, Arabs were as unreal as the ancient tribes depicted in Hebrew school lessons: make-believe people from faraway places with strange-sounding names. During those long-ago Saturday matinees, magical Arabs flew magic carpets in Disney cartoons. He had no method of fact-checking what the dominant culture read into the abstract Arab. He had nothing against Hittites *or* Arabs; neither tribe occupied his suburban neighborhood. He never met an actual Arab till he attended college. Befriending Suhail disabused Ron of the abstract Arab and introduced him to individuated particulars; Suhail's influence endures to this day.

Looking back, the Munich massacre changed everything: magical no more, the Arab became monster. In 1972 Palestinians murdered Israeli athletes. He came to fear that Jews throughout the world might well suffer the same fate; would he be next? Like other Americans, he reacted to the 9/11 tragedy with horror and disgust. But unlike his countrymen, by that time, he realized that what they do to us and what we do to them are not unrelated. He was alarmed and disgusted by the prevailing notion of collective guilt. In the eyes of some, speaking out against Islamophobia seals his identity as a self-hating Jew. (Funny thing: A Protestant speaking out against the treatment of Catholics in Northern Ireland isn't called a "self-hating Presbyterian.")

This collaboration between a Jew and an Arab confronts the varieties anti-Semitism. Our paper may be unique but our anecdotal experience is not—we wish it were. The varieties of anti-Semitism we experience reflect ongoing and recent global developments. Accordingly, this paper narrates a dialectic between the personal and the political.

1 Anti-Semitism: A Global Phenomenon

Recent global developments usher in a rise in xenophobia against people of Jewish *and* Arab descent. Consider the popularity of European far-right groups—neo-Nazis and hardline anti-immigration groups such as the National Front in France. Surveys show that 43 percent of the French public believe that Islamic influence is "too large" in France.[2] The recent attacks in Paris have increased anti-Muslim views in France. This sentiment echoes throughout the European continent in Switzerland, France, Sweden, Austria, and elsewhere: France's far-right leader Marine Le Pen was tried but exonerated for inciting racial hatred by comparing Muslim prayers in public to Nazi occupation.[3] Even a cursory look at online sites such as the Southern Poverty Law Center reveals scores of domestic groups promoting traditional hatred of Jews and the newfound anti-Semitism—Islamophobia. Trump has no monopoly on hatred.

Resentment between Semites stands out in stark relief in the Middle East—there's a history. Such animosity can be traced to the warring tribes of Arabia when Jews and Arabs came into conflict, often for geopolitical purposes. (Given British dissembling at the close of World War I, the Holy Land can rightly be called "The Twice Promised Land.") Contemporary forms of anti-Semitism, however, are manifested through political agitation for vested interests—often domestic politics. In the American-led War on Terror, the Arab is demonized and portrayed as the savage from a strange, hostile, and uncivilized land. The late Edward Said referred to this practice of creating the "other" in reference to Arabs as orientalism.[4] By so doing, the American public has no hesitation in supporting aggressive, often inhumane, military and embargo campaigns against Arabs—the idée fixe of the global war on terror.

Jewish history also chronicles the construction of the Jew as alien—an ineffable other. Germans, Russians, and some influential Americans (e.g., Henry Ford) used the czarist-fabricated polemic *The Protocols of the Elders of Zion* to propagate an anti-Jewish message. According to the *Protocols*, Jewish leaders planned to extend their pernicious influence into the global political arena, to rule the world by dominating banking systems, global trade, and

2 "Survey Exposes French Anxieties over Islam," France24.com, last modified January 26, 2012, http://www.france24.com/en/20121025-france-muslim-opinion-poll-survey-exposes-french-anxieties-over-islam-mosque-far-right.

3 "Le Pen to Be Tried over Anti-Muslim Remarks," *America*. aljazeera.com, last modified September 22, 2016, http://america.aljazeera.com/articles/2015/9/22/french-rightist-le-pen-to-be-tried-over-anti-muslim-remarks.html.

4 Edward Said, *Orientalism* (New York: Pantheon Books, 1978).

worldwide political bodies. Ford funded the printing and distribution of nearly 500,000 copies translated into many languages. Today, American and European anti-Semitic groups refer to this conspiracy of Jewish global domination as ZOG (Zionist Occupied Government). Indeed, so prevalent is the anti-Jewish ideology that it has infiltrated the academic world in the form of Holocaust denial, most notably the now debunked Institute for Historical Review, which consisted of pseudo-academics[5]—all of whom adhered to a white supremacist ideology.

What Drives Anti-Semitism?

Given the limitations of this paper, we only suggest possibilities for further inquiry: the cunning of domestic politics and the fatal attraction of tribalism. Freud's rumination regarding group psychology resonates in the abundant psychological literature on intergroup relations, a literature that concludes that humans remain tribal beings. The evolutionary process reinforced group narcissism restricting our concern and affection to those with whom we share cultural, religious, racial, and even economic traits. An affinity to one's own group typically excludes and degrades other groups—a screen for projecting one's undesirable traits and unthinkable thoughts. This process of exclusion is commonly referred to as "othering."

Not surprisingly, theories on the ways in which humans exclude members of the out-group remain indebted to psychoanalysis. Adorno and his colleagues developed an understanding of prejudice and exclusion that rooted in the authoritarian personality—a byproduct of child-rearing practices reinforcing discipline and harshness.[6] Such practices produce children who mature into stern and often intolerant people. Later theoretical approaches focused on socio-political causes of exclusion, accounting for economic, cultural, racial, and religious differences as causal mechanisms of othering and other forms of prejudice—see, for example: *Intergroup Relations* by Messick and Mackie for a partial list of contemporary theories of intergroup relations.[7]

The persistence of tribalism tempers faith in progress. What Freud called; "the narcissism of minor group difference" sparks hostility between Catholics and Protestants in Northern Ireland, Sunni and Shia in Iraq, and Semites in

5 Lynne Snowden and Bradley Whitsel, *Terrorism: Research, Readings, and Realities*, (New York, Pearson, 2004). See David Lobb in references for more on this topic.

6 Theodor Adorno, Else Frenkel-Brunswik, Daniel Levinson, and Nevitt Sanford, *The Authoritarian Personality* (New York: Harper and Brothers, 1950).

7 David M. Messick and Diane M. Mackie, "Intergroup Relations," *Annual Review of Psychology* 40, (1989): 45–81.

the Holy Land. The creation of the "other" springs from a deep-seated desire to identify oneself as part of an elect, social group. To belong, be it a racial group, an ethnic tribe, a socioeconomic caste, or a religious group, is primordial to all societies, spanning time and geography. Freud referred to this trait as the "oldest psychology": a universal, virtually indelible propensity reinforced by the evolutionary process.[8]

However, not until the age of Enlightenment did we conceptually articulate what we call "the newest psychology": understanding of out-groups from a scientific and philosophical perspective—as fellow human beings. Indeed, because of the contributions of Karl Von Linne, Georg Hegel, and Michel Foucault,[9] we now categorize societies and individuals according to socially developed constructs such as "oriental," "insane," "criminal," or "deviant." This fragile, hard-won newest psychology readily vanishes amid trying circumstances as events illustrate in the Middle East, in Europe, and—as we write—in the United States. Tribalism—the Oldest Psychology—exerts its indelible influence: It's as if elites and their subjects cannot live without enemies.

We are not the first to note that political players and other elites exploit anti-Semitism for their advantage. Elites construct the "other" to promote group solidarity, to distract attention from their perfidy, and to justify the mistreatment and misery visited upon their subjects—to say nothing of the despised out-group. Slavery, cultural cleansing, racist policies, and war without mercy illustrate this mistreatment with painful clarity. An analysis of recent policy trends illustrates the interrelationship between increased anti-Semitic violence and victimization, tougher immigration laws, and unprecedented government reach into the private lives of citizens—a pretext for restoring law and order by quelling sectarian violence and distracting attention from elite malfeasance. These are not archaic policies and practices from the days of yore; consider the practice of transporting, caging, and displaying humans from Africa, Asia, and elsewhere as forms of amusement: human zoos remained open until the 2000's.[10] As drones buzz overhead and fanatics kill one another along with the innocent, man's inhumanity to man continues

8 Sigmund Freud, *Group Psychology and the Analysis of the Ego,* trans. James Strachey (New York: Boni and Liveright, 1922). Bartleby.com, 2010. www.bartleby.com/290/.

9 Masoud Kamali, "Conceptualizing the 'Other,': Institutionalized Discrimination, and Cultural Racism," CORDIS, accessed September 17, 2015, ftp://ftp.cordis.europa.eu/pub/improving/docs/ser_racism_kamali_session2.pdf.

10 M.B. David, "Deep Racism: The Forgotten History of Human Zoos," *Popular Resistance,* accessed September 17, 2015, https://www.popularresistance.org/deep-racism-the-forgotten-history-of-human-zoos/.

unabated. Nevertheless, as Freud marveled, we think ourselves refined and beyond reproach.

Theological versus Political Sources of Arab Anti-Semitism toward Jews

Arab anti-Semitism may be explained as a religiously-based phenomenon stemming largely from *interpretations* of Quranic injunctions against the Jews; although injunctions may be episodic rather than systematic and endemic. A subtle exegesis suggests that such injunctions generally address a particular group of Jews at the time of Muhammad, or Israelites prior to Islam's arrival. It calls attention to the fact that Arabs of various religions, including non-theists, account for some of the anti-Jewish sentiment of the Middle East. The rise of Muslim anti-Semitism may be explained, in some measure, by religious reasons. A subtle exegesis must contextualize by stressing the political forces within a historical milieu that drive the interpreters of the text: Theology is not a God-like revelation from the heavens; it is informed by politics and by much else.

During the latter part of the sixth century, the Arabian Peninsula was composed mainly of polytheists, Christians (most of whom were located in the south, near modern-day Yemen), as well as Jews (predominantly residing in Yathrib—today's Medina). In the northern, Christian-controlled portions of the Roman Empire, Jews suffered at the hands of Christians as a result of theologically based anti-Semitism. However, the advent of Islam during the seventh century was accompanied by an exodus of the Prophet Muhammad and his small community out of Mecca and into what he perceived as a welcoming community of Jews; after all, Jews were well known as thinkers, and fellow monotheists. However, with the spread of Islam, resentment would soon form between the two communities: Islam, no longer seen as a docile compatriot, threatened the existence of the Jewish community inhabiting Arabia with a certain degree of amity. Indeed, as a result of the growing enmity between the two groups, some verses of the *Quran* describe the Jewish community in undesirable terms. One of the prominent incidents of souring relations between the two communities took place at *ghazwatul khandaq*, or the battle of the trench. As the polytheists of Mecca advanced to eradicate Islam by targeting the Muslims of Medina, Muhammad and his companions decided to dig a trench to protect themselves from the advancing forces. Given Medina's mountainous topography, the Muslims felt protected from all but two sides: the one where they were digging the trench and the other from their rear, where the large Jewish tribes of *Al-Aws* and *Al-Khazraj* resided. Muhammad would make an agreement with his Jewish neighbors, seeking protection from the rear, an agreement betrayed. As a result of the betrayal, the Muslims experienced casualties but ultimately won the battle. Muhammad would then decree that the treasonous Jews be executed.

> The *Quran* very clearly articulates the shock, disappointment, and anger that Muhammad must have felt at the betrayal of recognized monotheists. Sometimes the anger is directed metaphorically toward the ancient Israelites (Q. 2:40–96, 211, 3:181–188, 4:46–47), sometimes directly to Jews contemporary to Muhammad (2:146, 159, 3:78–79, 5:41–44, 64, 62:6–8), and sometimes the two are conflated (4:153–161, 59:2–4).[11]

We hasten to add that the history of Islam is not a unique chronicle of conquest, betrayal, and atrocity. Even a cursory glance at the *Old Testament* reveals a saga of atrocities ignored if not celebrated by all Abrahamic faiths. Indeed, Islamophobes read the Quran tendentiously, just as critics of Judaism dwell upon atrocities at Jericho and overlook Isiah's concern with peace and justice.

If *Quranic* injunctions are the main cause of anti-Semitism, then one would expect anti-Jewish fervor to remain constant since the founding of Islam. Thus, the preceding explanation fails to explain the erratic flare-ups of Muslim anti-Semitism. Consider the recent attacks against Jews in Europe following Israel's war in Gaza in 2014. In Austria, youths holding up Turkish and Palestinian flags stormed the soccer field where the Israeli team, Maccabi Haifa, played, in an attempt to assault the players.[12] Such hostilities mark the onset of political events, and are rarely based on an exegesis of scripture. Even so, for some, tendentious hermeneutics remains relevant. Firestone asks us to consider the factors that inflame "scriptural anti-Semitism into an operational state." Here, we turn our attention to the political expediency that promotes anti-Jewish fervor.

As we've seen, Muslim scripture criticizes Jewish Arabian tribes and the Ancient Israelites; however, Islam per se is not hostile to the Jewish faith. Nevertheless, it's a commonplace that Muslims (and by proxy, Arabs) hate Jews. Why is this so? To properly ascertain the cause of Arab anti-Semitism, we turn

---

11 See Rueven Firestone, "Contextualizing Anti-Semitism in Islam: Choseness, Choosing, and the Emergence of New Religion," *International Journal of Applied Psychoanalytic Studies* 4 (3) (2007): 235–254, doi: 10.1002/aps.139.

12 Melissa Eddy, "Anti-Semitism Rises in Europe Amid Israel-Gaza Conflict," *New York Times*, accessed July 11, 2016, http://www.nytimes.com/2014/08/02/world/europe/anger-in-europe-over-the-israeli-gaza-conflict-reverberates-as-anti-semitism.html?_r=0.

our attention to the political process that activates Jewish hatred from time-to-time, often for opportunistic political benefit. A brief historical reflection reminds us that anti-Semitism and Anti-Jewishness are two different concepts. Indeed, the early European Christian conception of anti-Semitism was nothing more than a theologically based enmity manifested at "those who killed Jesus, our Lord and Savior."[13] Christian anti-Semitism requires cognitive dissonance—if not cognitive insolence. Never mind that Jesus, Joseph, and Mary were Jews, as were the disciples. Of course, if the old anti-Semitism were impurely theological, one could not direct hatred toward Jews if they accepted "the Truth" and were saved. Jews would become part of Christendom. In order to turn Jews into a despised other, anti-Semites had to reconstruct Jewish identity. To do so, and to create a permanent focus of hatred and hostility, intellectuals of nineteenth century Germany worked to frame Jewishness as a race and not a religion—an immutable variable.[14]

Race-based anti-Semitism (aimed at Jews) is now a crime in Germany and other European regimes. It wasn't always so. Nazis promoted Jew-hatred to account for the folly of World War I and the decline and fall of the Weimar Republic. The Hitler regime knew how to galvanize German solidarity. Race-based hatred of Jews prevails in certain Arab regimes. It wasn't always so. Jews, Christians, and Muslims lived in relative harmony during the Moorish occupation of Spain. The Golden Age vanished when the Catholic monarchs exiled Jews; Ottoman and Arab empires offered refuge. And a semblance of amity existed between Jews and Palestinians prior to the advent of militant Zionism. Unfortunately, numerous current efforts to promote harmony between Jews and Arabs are unworthy of primetime—if it bleeds it leads.

A Personal Revelation

My first real experience with a Jew was with Dr. Rosenthal, an oncologist at Long Island College Hospital who treated my mother as she underwent the pain and anguish of her newly discovered breast cancer. Dr. Rosenthal was a source of solace for me (being only ten years old at the time), comforting me as I travelled to and from the hospital and the house. He consoled me by smiling at me, laughing with me, and sometimes presenting me with valuable

---

13 This is more commonly known as the blood libel.

14 Sindre Bangstad and Matti Bunzl, "'Anthropologists Are Talking' about Islamophobia and Anti-Semitism in the New Europe," *Ethics: Journal of Anthropology* (2010): 217. Bangstad and Bunzl expand this idea by discussing it in anthropological terms, differentiating between the emic and etic. "Emic categories are the categories a population itself uses. Etic categories are categories from the outside that you would impose as an analyst."

treasures in the form of chocolate and assorted candies. It was he who I hugged first after arriving to the hospital that morning at 1 a.m. to view the body of my newly deceased mother.

How could this be? A Jew! A monster! I was fortunate to have a progressive, rational father, who graciously explained to me that Islam is *not* a religion of intolerance. "Remember, son," my father said, "Prophet Muhammad had a Jewish neighbor who used to dump trash on his door out of hatred for him; then one day, when the Messenger was leaving his house, he noticed that no trash was there, so he went next door to inquire about his neighbor, only to find him sick. So he visited with him and asked if he could be of assistance…" This was life changing for me; it led me to the reality that not all Jews are fundamentalist Zionists and not all bad! How could Kuwaiti imams be so wrong?

The New Anti-Semitism

Latter-day anti-Semitism—Islamophobia—traffics in both cultural and biologic anti-Semitism. Indeed, cultural anti-Semitism is more malleable and can manifest itself in different contexts, aimed at different Semitic groups—Islamophobia is one such manifestation. Consider current global events in the "war on terror," where the Semitic Arabs have become the idée fixe of military strategists, media pundits, and hate groups alike. Sartre explained the anti-Semite as one who "localizes all evil of the universe in the Jew. If nations war with each other…it is because the Jew is there behind the governments, breathing discord. If there is class struggle…it is because Jewish demagogues…have seduced the workers."[15] Islamophobia is a variation of this familiar theme: The Muslim (Arab) must be behind all atrocious attacks on civilians around the world.

Jews are well integrated and assimilated in today's America: Bernie Sanders came surprisingly close to capturing the presidential nomination. The idea of a Muslim candidate, let alone president, remains unthinkable, for Muslims lurk in the shadows ready to strike at a moment's notice. Time and again, the Muslim reveals his or her true persona: a blood-thirsty jihadist, willing to execute unspeakable acts in line with religious commandments. (Never mind that these days, most atrocities committed against American civilians are the work of street gangs, racists attacking black churches, and deranged students attacking schools.)

15 Jean-Paul Sartre, *Anti-Semite and Jew* (New York: Schoken Books, 1965) cited in Michael Dobkowski, "Islamophobia and Anti-Semitism: Shared Prejudice or Singular Social Pathologies," *Crosscurrents* 65, no 3 (2016): 328.

Despite evidence to the contrary many presuppose that (1) Islam is inherently a violent religion, and (2) Muslims are a monolithic group whose lives are dictated by their religion, and they will all carry out violence because their religion calls them to do so.

Today, the two terms "anti-Jewish" and "anti-Semitic" are conflated. Thus, if academics—and by extension average people—cannot deconstruct the new anti-Semitism, politicians can opportunistically use the concept to create a perpetual state of hate toward the other. Therefore, semantics are important in understanding the political process.

Turning attention to the current manifestations of othering, we notice the implementation of efforts to place social groups beyond the bounds of American and European identity. With regard to adherents of the Jewish faith, popular culture continues to perpetuate the notion that Jewishness is a racial category, being heedless of the intellectual framework that casts Jewish people of all nationalities beyond a national identity. Likewise, use of the term "Hispanic" oversimplifies the nuanced and diverse cultural heritage of those from Latin America. Lastly, Muslims, while not a monolithic group, endure similar attempts at being framed as a homogenous, undifferentiated entity. One need only to look at an employment application to recognize that the Arab (Muslim or otherwise) is not listed as an independent ethnic category. However, with the increasing Arab American population, attempts are being made to ameliorate this identity problem; specifically, the Census Bureau is now exploring the addition of new categories that would more accurately represent those of Middle Eastern or North African descent as Arabs.

The addition of an ethnic category does not, however, address the larger problem of framing the Arabs or the Jews as other. Indeed, while the intellectuals toil in the universities, think-tanks, and special interest groups to develop a theoretical framework for integrating those who appear different from most, it is the *machinery* of popular culture that perpetuates the negative stereotypes and misperceptions of certain groups; cementing such ideas in the minds of the masses.

Most notable among these machines is Hollywood. In his influential work, Jack Shaheen[16] exposes the historical reality concerning the use of Hollywood as a machine for the propagation of negative stereotypes about Arabs.

> It is acceptable to advance anti-Semitism in film—provided the Semites are Arabs. I call this habit of racial and cultural generalization "The New

16 Jack Shaheen, *Reel Bad Arabs: How Hollywood Vilifies a People* (Northampton: Olive Branch Press: 2009).

> Anti-Semitism." I call it "new" not because stereotypical screen Arabs are new (they aren't) or because anti-Semitism against Jews is dead (it isn't). I use the word "new" because many of the anti-Semitic films directed against Arabs were released … at a time when Hollywood was steadily and increasingly eliminating stereotypical portraits of other groups.[17]

By tracing the evolution of American and British films, Shaheen offers insight into a well-orchestrated effort to cast Arabs throughout the Western world as demonic, vengeful, sex-driven madmen, whose only objective in life is to live lavishly and be over-sexed and determined to destroy all that is good in the world, most notably, Western civilization.

Persona Non-Grata

Turning to personal anecdotes, Amin's outing commences shortly after 9/11 while still a college student. As a new transplant in the South, Amin was questioned by curious peers, who inquired, "since you're Muslim, tell us what you think of 9/11?"—as if I spoke for one and a half billion Muslims! The spotlight shone brightly on me; they demanded answers. Fellow students expected a compelling explanation—surely I had inside information. This line of questioning presupposes a Muslim monolith: sub rosa communication and planning—the envy of an ant colony.

My antagonistic relationship with my professor began when he corrected an inquiry of mine by prefacing his remarks with a pontifical "In this country…" Later as a teacher, I recall a student's inquiry amid the "ground zero mosque" debate. He approached and inquired vociferously so that others might hear, "What do *you* think of a mosque being built near ground zero; isn't *that* disrespectful?" Yet again, the inquisition removed me from the "us category"; I was to answer for "them."

Friends and family report Islamophobia's unnerving ubiquity. In a nearby state, a relative chairs a committee in an Islamic center in need of expansion; the Islamophobes won't have it. After months of national publicity and protests, the Islamic center is open, but the journey was fraught with malevolent acts: The construction company had its machinery burned down. My relative found his personal information plastered online: An encouragement to those would do him harm. The message was unmistakable—watch out! My relative (with a wife and five children) was forced to purchase a gun.

Grownups can handle exclusion better than children; the psychological impact is not nearly as detrimental on the former. My wife's closest friend went

---

17 Jack Shaheen, *Reel Bad Arabs*.

shopping with her five-year-old boy. Because she wears the *hijab* (head scarf), she was noticeable—so was her son. An elderly man approached, looked at the boy and demanded, "What's your name?" The boy replied "Muhammad," prompting a belligerent demand: "Tell your mom that she should take you back home where you come from; you're not an American and y'all need to leave." Unbeknownst to the man, the boy's mother is an American convert, quite possibly tracing her roots to Columbus! Goethe was right: "Nothing worse than ignorance in action."

The finality of this last story is overwhelming—the murder of my cousin, his wife, and her sister. A dental student at a reputable university, my cousin—on his way to a bright future—was recently married and moving his wife's belongings into his apartment. A disgruntled neighbor took note of the new Muslim neighbors when he saw the *hijab*-wearing wife. He approached the woman and her mother as they were moving and scoffed, "I hate that stuff you wear"—his gun visible in the holster by his side. The mother advised her daughter, "let's repel evil with good, maybe if we're nice, he'll come around. It's not his fault. Look at what he's fed by the media." Indeed, the media initially downplayed the incident, towing the official line—it was over a parking spot (little did they know that the woman's cars were found on a public street). In the world according to the media, the murders were just a bit of road rage—certainly not terrorism. (An all-too-resonant commonplace: "Not all Muslims are terrorist, *but* all terrorists are Muslims!")

A few days thereafter, the story of the execution-style murder of three young Muslims made international headlines. Heads of state from Muslim-majority countries called and visited to give the parents condolences on their loss.[18] My cousin wasn't as fortunate as I; he and his bride, along with her sister, were permanently outed.

Somehow, there's a silver lining to these disheartening tales: American Muslims, like their Catholic, Jewish, African American, Hispanic, and Japanese predecessors see the writing on the wall—the time is ripe for civic engagement and social justice initiatives. Indeed, much of the credit for spurring the American Muslim community can be given to the Republican Party, specifically, their presidential candidate, Donald Trump. Statements made by Mr. Trump have invigorated civil libertarians of all nationalities and religious affiliations—as well as non-theists—and moved them to take action. Mr. Trump continues to assert that Islam is the enemy and that Muslims should be specifically

18 Margaret Talbot, "The Story of a Hate Crime: What Led to the Murder of Three Muslim Students in Chapel Hill?" *New Yorker*, June 15, 2015, accessed August 6, 2016, http://www.newyorker.com/magazine/2015/06/22/the-story-of-a-hate-crime.

targeted by policies of overt exclusion solely based on their religious affiliation. To him, all Muslims are personae non gratae! Fortunately, there is opposition. It would be impolite to not give credit where credit is due: a recent publication by the Center for American Progress details the funding of Islamophobia and exposes some of the most fervent Islamophobes and hatemongers. According to the report, “seven charitable foundations spent $42.6 million between 2001 and 2009 to support the spread of anti-Muslim rhetoric.”[19]

It's heartening to discover that a variety of progressive Jewish organizations join their Semitic, Arab brethren in indicting Islamophobia.[20] Of course, as Ron learned, one gets labeled a “self-hating Jew” for fighting Islamophobia and opposing Israeli treatment of Palestinians. Ron's personal confrontation follows.

11 Philosophy as Self-Confession

“Jew” and “Swiss.” “Lutheran or Catholic?” I take a personal—if not painful—approach to these binaries; I offer a first-person account of encounters with the varieties of anti-Semitism. It would be perversely entertaining to dwell upon an Internet encounter with anti-Semitism—a foray into “cognitive insolence”: Salient facts are not merely ignored; they're treated with contempt. There's the ever-popular claim that Jews run the world. That's not all: Flat earth sites indict Jews for promoting the view that the Earth is a globe revolving around the sun: a cosmology obviously devised to degrade our God-given place at the center of the universe. You can also learn that Jews are shape-shifting lizards assuming human form. It's easy to mock these sites. But it's disturbing when progressive friends—I should say former friends—insist that the Israeli Mossad brought down the towers on 9/11.

It would be more academic respectability—never my strong suit— to reiterate what's well known about anti-Semitism:

- The irony: Some professed Christians hate Jews and worship a Jew as God. (Cognitive dissonance or cognitive insolence?)

19 Matthew Duss, Yasmine Taeb, Ken Dude, and Ken Sofer, “Fear, Inc. 2.0: The Islamophobia Network's Efforts to Manufacture Hate in America,” *Center for American Progress*, February 11, 2015, accessed August 6, 2016, https://cdn.americanprogress.org/wp-content/uploads/2015/02/FearInc-report2.11.pdf.

20 See, for example, Rabbi Michael Lerner's *Tikkun* magazine, an imprint of Duke University Press.

- Both Sartre and Freud recognized that Jew-hatred springs from denial and projection: In order to cleanse the personality of unthinkable traits, they're projected upon the "other." (Could this explain those Internet sites?)
- Elites have long promoted such hatred to deflect attention from their failures and perfidy. (Consider massacres and pogroms.)

This essay, however, begins with a gloss on the anti-Semitism I know best: personal experience. As Freud argued, the child is the father of the man. Childhood experiences profoundly color and refract anti-Semitism as a lived experience—how could it be otherwise? I'm the child of good fortune, merely facing first-world problems. The worst anti-Semitism I experienced was within myself. During my early years—no matter how much I detest the term—I was a self-hating Jew. To give the next section more philosophical gravitas, I hazard a phenomenological gloss on self-hatred: a gloss attentive to unthought, unquestioned a priori categories introjected and naturalized at an early age. The a priori stands out in stark relief when we consider the hermeneutics of everyday usage: the nuance and connotations of those binaries just mentioned.

Self-Hatred

Who or what was to blame for self-hatred? There's no metric or proper sense of proportionality. Was it cowardice, an all-American desire to conform or fit in? I'm not sure, but I remember the context of those earliest days.

Consider the nouns "Jew" and "Swiss." Along with learning English as a native language, I learned that "Jew" had derogatory connotations. (Calling a person "Jewish" rather than a "Jew" softens the pejorative connotations.) Consider the difference between declaring: "He's a Jew." versus "He's Swiss." Conceptualized on a sliding scale, the former conjures up defamatory images of an unscrupulous businessman trying to get the best of you. (All-American Yankee traders get better press.) In any case, I suspect I'm not the only one who's heard colleagues boasting of "Jewing him down." Shylock's persona still lives.

It gets worse: Consider Mel Gibson's sacred snuff film, *The Passion of the Christ*—Jews as Christ-killers—an all-too-familiar genre. Even if Jews didn't commit deicide, they nevertheless deserve eternal damnation. Pastor Rick Warren who, prior to presenting the invocation at Obama's 2008 inauguration, avoided personal responsibility for condemning Jews with the following jeremiad. Jews belong in hell—it ain't his fault:

> A woman comes up and she says to me: "I'm Jewish. I'm not going to accept Jesus as my savior. Am I going to hell?" ... Jesus said, "No one comes to the Father but by me. .... I *am* the way." I'm betting my life that He was

> telling the truth. Now see what I did? I took it off of me, and making me the authority.[21]

The Swiss fare better: at least the vast majority who embrace the Christian faith. The Swiss, unlike the Jews, are not an "other," despite the fact that they're famously involved in practices attributed to Jews—finance and banking. As I write, some of these prominent banks are indicted by U.S. authorities for feloniously conspiring to shelter the assets of wealthy Americans from Internal Revenue scrutiny. Nevertheless, you won't hear a Zurich banker derided for "Swissing someone down." Despite their neutrality during World War II and notorious financial practices, the Swiss almost invariably get good press. In addition to milkmaid Heidi, "Swiss" connotes cheese, chocolate, and storybook villages surrounded by luminous peaks. A Swiss may denounce her canton, but she wouldn't be demeaned as a "self-hating Swiss."

I didn't choose Swiss parents. When I was six, kids in the new neighborhood—we were the only Jews—introduced *their* world of intelligibility, a binary world: "Are you Lutheran or Catholic?" I answered "Lutheran." Well into high school I desperately wanted to fit into this all-American, Christian world and pass as a generic gentile. (Portnoy's attempts in Roth's *Portnoy's Complaint* are biographical.) But life changed—for the better—after a painful experience.

A girl I will call Judy Salvatore, invited me on a hayride to celebrate her sixteenth birthday. (Hormone-driven adolescent fantasies neared fulfillment—so I prayed despite my doubts about the God petitioned in synagogue.) Just before the anointed hayride, Judy looked up my number in the phonebook and saw the listing for dad's Independent Kosher Meat Market. I became the "Other"—outed. The ride through the subzero Wisconsin landscape proved frigid indeed! It was little solace to realize that, had Judy invited her Lord and Savior, He too would have met with the same rejection.

Perhaps, because I could pass as a gentile, the Anti-Defamation League recruited me for espionage. My mission: attend right-wing meetings and report anti-Jewish rhetoric—then as now, criticism of Israel was code for anti-Semitism. Maybe I didn't look hard enough. My clearest memories harken back to overheated church basements where kindly, elderly women served cocoa and cookies as I listened to patriotic programs honoring the flag and our boys overseas.

21 See "Rick Warren Is an Insulting Choice," *Los Angeles Times*, December 22, 2008, accessed <November 10, 2016>, http://www.latimes.com/opinion/la-oe-pollitt22-2008dec22-story.html.

No longer a double agent with the Anti-Defamation League—*or within myself*—I abandoned the self-hatred and embraced my ethnic heritage—as distinct from religious Judaism. In a Yiddish accent picked up at dad's butcher shop, I regaled friends with embellished stories from the kosher meat business and its Old World customers. (Don't ask about the rancid chicken fat.) Funny thing: I remain a self-hating Jew in the eyes of fundamentalist Zionists. Two reasons:

1. I take exception to narratives of Israeli exceptionalism.
2. I indict Israeli treatment of Palestinians in the Occupied Territories.

Rejecting Fundamentalist Zionism

Suhail, my first Middle Eastern friend, made me aware of the plight of Palestinians. The injustice visited upon the Palestinian people violated the best of Judaism: the universal moral precepts of the prophets. Palestinians were driven from their ancestral homes to make way for the Zionists. An immigrant from Israel, Suhail, advocated "pan-Semitism": a single state of Jews and Arabs. He knew that enmity could become amity: He had a Jewish mother and Arab father. I asked God whether Suhail's dream would ever come true. God said, "Yes, but *not* in My lifetime." Hope becomes quixotic when fundamentalist Zionists traffic in entitlement and shame.

Entitlement

Reverting to my anecdotage, a childhood example comes to mind. I boarded a bus with my other eight-year-old rowdy friends; we took the best seats. A crippled man boarded after us. We knew—virtually reflexively—we had to move. He was entitled!

Theodore Herzl, the founder of modern Zionism, was painfully aware of the long history of persecution; pogroms were variations on a familiar theme. Given all that Jews endured, surely we were entitled to a safe haven, a land of our own. Subsequent followers would do whatever was necessary to end British rule, and to remove the native inhabitants. Not without reason, the Brits referred to militant Zionists—such as the Irgun and Stern Gang—as terrorists.

The Holocaust made a Jewish homeland an exigent imperative. Surely Jews, crippled in mind and body by the Holocaust, were entitled to a land of their own, a homeland. Too bad for the natives—they had to move! Questioning Zionist entitlement meets with derision. In Herzl's words: Those questioning plans to create a Jewish state in Palestine are "disguised anti-Semites of Jewish origin."

Unlike my ancestors, I didn't endure the Holocaust. With a few exceptions—such as a cold shoulder during the hayride, I haven't suffered from persecution. And yet, due I suppose to some mythic connection with King David, I'm entitled to the Right of Return, and maybe even a nice condo in the Occupied Territories. My Palestinian friends, Ali, Khalid, and Abeer can't return—despite (or because of?) their deeply rooted identity with Palestine. Stressing this injustice didn't win friends and influence among the fundamentalist Zionists.

More than fifty years have passed since Hannah Arendt guaranteed her status as a self-hating Jew. She urged that the horror of the Holocaust no longer justified the rhetoric of entitlement. Zionism, she explained, has outlived the conditions from which it emerged, and it's becoming a "living ghost amid the ruins of our time."

Shame

Indeed, Hannah Arendt became the quintessential self-hating Jew with the publication of *Eichmann in Jerusalem*.[22] She portrayed Eichmann as a vapid bureaucrat rather than *the* personification of evil. Worse yet, she reminded readers that—with notable exceptions—there was little resistance to the "Final Solution." Hundreds of thousands of Jews were rounded-up and passively met their doom. (What could they do surrounded by machine guns and dogs about to tear them apart?) And yes, some Jews, "Kapos," collaborated with the Nazis to save themselves, or, perhaps, they hoped cooperation might save others. Who among us might have done otherwise?

Understandably, Israeli and diaspora Jews vow "Never Again!" Yiddish, the diaspora language of the ghetto, is derided as the feckless cant of the oppressed. A robust, nativist return to Hebrew became the confident lingua franca of the strong, liberated Jew, the Sabra, the native-born Israeli. History won't repeat itself! Enemies of the Jewish people, real and imagined, will be crushed—no questions asked later.

True, in their struggle for a homeland and for revenge, Palestinians commit atrocities. However, as the destruction of Gaza illustrates, the Israeli response is disproportionate, if not draconian. Thousands of Palestinians perish, along with their homes and orchards. Prominent intellectuals such as Noam Chomsky, Michael Lerner, and Tony Judt are derided as self-hating Jews for calling the injustice to the public's attention.

It's gotten worse. Efforts are underway—with some measure of success—to punish critics of Israel. The U.S. State Department suggests that such criticism

22 Hannah Arendt, *Eichmann in Jerusalem* (New York: Penguin, 1965).

is tantamount to anti-Semitic hate speech. (Even if it is hate speech, shouldn't hate speech be protected? Was it Justice Brandeis who insisted that free speech means nothing unless it's afforded to those we find repulsive?)

Pressure is brought to bear at the University of California to punish those hazarding strident criticism of Israeli policy.

One of the Regents most vocally advocating for the most stringent version of the speech code is Richard Blum, the multi-millionaire defense contractor who is married to Sen. Dianne Feinstein of California. At a recent Regents meeting, reported the *Los Angeles Times*, Blum expressly threatened that Feinstein would publicly denounce the university if it failed to adopt far more stringent standards than the ones it appeared to be considering, and specifically demanded they be binding and contain punishments for students found to be in violation.[23]

A coda from playwright Tony Kushner seems appropriate:

> In every religious or ethnic group, one finds irascible people who arrogate unto themselves the job of policing who is and who isn't a good and loyal member of the community. Such people rarely contribute anything to the community other than pain, and always fail to understand that it is the heterogeneity of the community … that gives it life.[24]

Coda

We pray for peace between the Semitic peoples, and, given our common heritage, our prayers bear a family resemblance—*shalom* and *as salaam*. Even so, there is no peace. Semites are hated and too often hate each other with the same passion. What can be one?

We've described personal confrontations with the old and the new anti-Semitism, and we've suggested a path for interpreting this affliction. However, to paraphrase Marx, merely interpreting the world won't do; the point is to change the world. We doubt the power of formalistic "thou shalt not" approaches. Media-based propaganda promoting the Muslim threat trumps those venerable Kantian or religious maxims.

Empirical approaches meet with the same fate. Citing evidence that most domestic mayhem these days is committed by white supremacists, gangs, and deranged fanatics massacring in schools and movie theaters seems rarely

23 "UC Goes Back to the Drawing Board on Controversial Revamp of Free-speech Policy," *Los Angeles Times*, September 17, 2015.

24 See Tony Kushner interview by Juan González, "Playwright Tony Kushner Hails Obama's Support for Same-Sex Marriage: 'I Felt the Earth Move,'" Democracy Now, May 10, 2012, www.democracynow.org/…/exclusive_playwright_ton.

persuasive. This is the post-factual, anti-intellectual world of the political spectacle.

At the risk of seeming Pollyannaish, we believe the enmity will become amity through personal contact. Amin's animosity toward Jews vanished when he migrated to New York and experienced an epiphany with the dreaded "other"—a Jewish doctor. Likewise, Ron's post-Munich hostility toward Arabs dissipated when an Iraqi physician comforted him and his mother during his father's final illness. We pray for a more tolerant society and close with a reminder by Albert Einstein: "'Peace cannot be kept by force; it can only be achieved by understanding'."

Bibliography

Adorno, Theordor, Else Frenkel-Brunswik, Daniel Levinson, and Nevitt Sanford. *The Authoritarian Personality.* New York: Harper and Brothers, 1950.

Arendt, Hannah. *Eichmann in Jerusalem.* New York: Penguin, 1965.

Bangstad, Sindre, and Matti Bunzl. "'Anthropologists are talking' about Islamophobia and Anti-Semitism in the New Europe." *Ethnos: Journal of Anthropology* 2010: 213–228.

"Blood Brothers: Palestinians and Jews Share Genetic Roots." Haaretz.com. October 20, 2015. http://www.haaretz.com/israel-news/science/1.681385.

David, M.B. "Deep Racism: The Forgotten History of Human Zoos." *Popular Resistance.* 2013. Accessed September 17, 2015. https://popularresistance.org/deep-racism-the-forgotten-history-of-human-zoos/.

Dobkowski, Michael. "Islamophobia and Anti-Semitism." *Crosscurrents* 65, no. 3 (2015): 321–333.

Duss, Matthew, Yasmine Taeb, Ken Dude, and Ken Sofer. "Fear, Inc. 2.0: The Islamophobia Network's Efforts to Manufacture Hate in America." *Center for American Progress* (February 2015). Accessed August 6, 2016. https://cdn.americanprogress.org/wp-content/uploads/2015/02/FearInc-report2.11.pdf.

Eddy, Melissa. "Anti-Semitism Rises in Europe Amid Israel-Gaza Conflict." *New York Times*, August 1, 2014. Accessed July 11, 2016. http://www.nytimes.com/2014/08/02/world/europe/anger-in-europe-over-the-israeli-gaza-conflict-reverberates-as-anti-semitism.html?_r=0.

Firestone, Reuven. "Contextualizing Anti-Semitism in Islam: Chosenness, Choosing, and the Emergence of New Religion." *International Journal of Applied Psychoanalytic Studies* 4, no. 3 (2007): 235–254.

Freud, Sigmund. *Group Psychology and the Analysis of the Ego.* Translated by James Strachey. New York: Boni and Liveright, 1922. Bartleby.com, 2010. www.bartleby.com/290/.

Gordon, Larry. "UC Goes Back to the Drawing Board on Controversial Revamp of Free-speech Policy." *Los Angeles Times*. September 15, 2015. Accessed September 13, 2016. http://touch.latimes.com/#section/-1/article/p2p-84448493/.

Kamali, Masoud. "Conceptualizing the 'Other,' Institutionalized Discrimination, and Cultural Racism." n.d. Accessed September 17, 2015. ftp://ftp.cordis.europa.eu/pub/improving/docs/ser_racism_kamali_session2.pdf.

Kushner, Tony. Interview by Juan González. "Playwright Tony Kushner Hails Obama's Support for Same-sex Marriage: 'I felt the Earth Move.'" Democracy Now. May 10, 2012. Accessed September 13, 2016. http://www.democracynow.org/2012/5/10/playwright_tony_kushner_hails_obama_support.

"Le Pen to Be Tried over Anti-Muslim Remarks." *America*. aljazeera.com. Last modified September 22, 2016. http://america.aljazeera.com/articles/2015/9/22/french-rightist-le-pen-to-be-tried-over-anti-muslim-remarks.html.

Lobb, David C. "The IHR and Holocaust Denial." In *Terrorism: Research, Readings, and Realities*. Edited by Lynn Snowden and Bradley Whitsel. 309–339. New York: Pearson, 2004.

Messick, David M, and Diane M Mackie. "Intergroup Relations." *Annual Review of Psychology* 40 (1989): 45–81.

Said, Edward. *Orientalism*. New York: Pantheon Books, 1978.

Sartre, Jean-Paul. *Anti-Semite and Jew*. New York: Schoken Books, 1965.

Shaheen, Jack. *Reel Bad Arabs: How Hollywood Vilifies a People*. Northampton: Olive Branch Press, 2009.

"Survey Exposes French Anxieties over Islam." France24.com. Last modified January 26, 2012. http://www.france24.com/en/20121025-france-muslim-opinion-poll-survey-exposes-french-anxieties-over-islam-mosque-far-right.

Talbot, Margaret. "The Story of a Hate Crime: What Led to the Murder of Three Muslim Students in Chapel Hill?" *New Yorker*, 2015. Accessed August 6, 2016. http://www.newyorker.com/magazine/2015/06/22/the-story-of-a-hate-crime.

"Tikkun: To Heal, Repair, and Transform the World." n.d. Accessed September 13, 2016. http://www.tikkun.org/nextgen/.

CHAPTER 6

The War on Drugs as Harm to Persons: Cultural Violence as Symbol and Justification

Lloyd Steffen

Introduction

"Cultural violence makes direct and structural violence look, even feel, right—or at least not wrong."[1] This statement from Johan Galtung, who introduced the idea of "structural violence" and may have been the first to have used the term "cultural violence," goes a long way in a short space to point out how actual harms to people may be done in the name of justice. By using the term "cultural violence," Galtung is offering the insight that if cultural supports are sufficiently strong and thus widely accepted, then policies and societal attitudes that sanction violence may pass largely unnoticed or may rise to consciousness as actions deemed allowable—not desired but also "not wrong"—within a larger framework of justification.

As a meaningful framework within which violence can be justified, cultural violence is expressed in all manner of cultural practices, beliefs, attitudes, and institutions. My purpose here is to explore the cultural violence that provides justification for the structural violence to be found in the criminal justice system, and I shall address that question by offering a moral analysis of three issues. First is the claim that criminal justice is racially discriminatory and that mass incarceration serves as an instrument of social control. Has the criminal justice system created an underclass sustained by a culture of repression and legitimated violence—a "caste" in Michelle Alexander's words?[2] If so, those caught up in the system are denied opportunity for flourishing, which is then a threat to social well-being for specific communities and ultimately for society at large. If harsh and punitive measures have led to such consequences and are justified as the most appropriate response to crime, then the justification for the harms caused by such social structures will direct attention to the cultural

1 Johan Galtung, "Cultural Violence," *Journal of Peace Research* 27, 3 (August 1990): 291.

2 Michelle Alexander, *The New Jim Crow: Mass Incarceration in the Age of Colorblindness* (New York: The New Press, 2012).

 | DOI 10.1163/9789004361911_008

violence that sustains those structures. The second issue concerns policy decisions that have focused on punishment for nonviolent drug offenses in the so-called "War on Drugs." Although punishment is a central feature of the criminal justice system, the argument can be made that policy makers advanced the War on Drugs in ways that legitimate and sustain a culture of violence in two ways: first, by articulating social policy goals that emphasize retribution and the visiting of harms on nonviolent drug offenders, which prevents restoring such offenders to their families and communities, and, secondly, by failing to articulate and enact a clear notion of just punishment in the context of a reasonable social policy. A third issue concerns the culture of violence in relation to symbols of justice. Jails and prisons—and the execution gurney—can be shown to be symbols of violence rather than justice, yet cultural violence obscures how these symbols function to promote practices that inflict harms on individuals and communities in the name of justice, which is to say that the wider society can sanction such harms as allowable—even desirable—within a larger framework of justification. If evidence can be brought to bear to show that institutions like the jail and prison, or practices like execution, symbolize violence rather than justice, then the case can be made that these culturally accepted symbols actually incite, maintain, and extend violence and subvert the objective of creating social harmony and a culture of peace. All three of these issues point to the role the criminal justice system plays in advancing and perpetuating cultural violence.

Mass Incarceration Policies and the War on Drugs

Research data about the criminal justice system abound. Data always need a context for interpretation, and ethical inquiry provides a context for considering relevant moral issues like fairness in sentencing, just punishment, racial disparities in incarceration policies, and other criminal justice issues involving discrimination. Data relevant to ethical investigation of criminal justice as an evolved system of mass incarceration might well begin by noting the size and reach of criminal justice in the United States. The United States has the highest per capita prison population rate in the world,[3] and over eleven million people "churn" through local jails in the United States each year according to the

3 Roy Walmsley, "World Prison Population List, 10th Edition," *International Center for Prison Studies* (University of Essex), accessed January 5, 2016, http://www.apcca.org/uploads/10th_Edition_2013.pdf.

Prison Policy Initiative.[4] With 5 percent of the world's population, the United States incarcerates 25 percent of the world's prisoner census; and if one takes into account those who are on probation or other supervision, one in thirty-one adults, or over 3 percent of the American population, "is under some form of correctional control."[5]

Race is an incarceration variable that from a statistical point of view is sure to raise eyebrows. One million of the over 2.2 million people incarcerated in the United States are African American; African Americans are incarcerated at six times the rate of whites;[6] and "if current trends continue, one in three black males born today can expect to spend time in prison during his lifetime."[7] Additionally, African Americans make up well over half of those in the states incarcerated for drug offenses,[8] with blacks comprising 80 percent of those sentenced under federal crack cocaine laws, despite the fact that two-thirds of crack cocaine users in the United States are white or Hispanic.[9] Blacks also are sent to prison for drug offenses at ten times the rate of white offenders even

4 "Mass Incarceration: The Whole Pie 2015," Prison Policy Initiative, accessed January 10, 2016, http://www.prisonpolicy.org/reports/pie2015.html.

5 This information is widely available and has been published in various popularly read venues. For example, Michelle Ye Hee Lee, "Does the United States Really Have 5 Per Cent of the World's Population and One Quarter of the World's Prisoners?" *The Washington Post,* April 30, 2015, accessed November 23, 2015, https://www.washington post.com/news/fact-checker/wp/2015/04/30/does-the-united-states-really-have-five-percent-of-worlds-population-and-one-quarter-of-the-worlds-prisoners/. Information in this paragraph is also available from the *NAACP Criminal Justice Fact Sheet,* accessed November 23, 2015, http://www.naacp.org/pages/criminal-justice-fact-sheet and the U.S. Bureau of Justice Statistics, *Correctional Populations in the United States,* 2011, 1, 3 tbl2, November 2012, accessed July 29, 2016, http://sentencingproject.org/wp-content/uploads/2015/12/Race-and-Justice-Shadow-Report-ICCPR.pdf.

6 George Gao, "Chart of the Week: The Black-White Gap in Incarceration Rates," Pew Research Center, July 18, 2014, accessed November 19, 2015, http://www.pewresearch.org/fact-tank/2014/07/18/chart-of-the-week-the-black-white-gap-in-incarceration-rates/.

7 U.S. Bureau of Justice Statistics, "Prisoners in 2011," 8 tbl.8 (Dec. 2012), quoted in U.S. Bureau of Justice Statistics, *Correctional Populations*, 1.

8 U.S. Bureau of Justice Statistics, "Prisoners in 2014," *Bureau of Justice Statistics, Summary/NCJ24 8955*, September 2015, accessed July 30, 2016, http://www.bjs.gov/content/pub/pdf/p14_Summary.pdf.

9 Thomas P. Bonczar, "Prevalence of Imprisonment in the U.S. Population, 1974–2001," Washington, DC: Bureau of Justice Statistics, 2003, accessed July 30, 2016, http://sentencingproject.org/wp-content/uploads/2016/01/Trends-in-US-Corrections.pdf. See also NAACP, *Criminal Justice Fact Sheet.*

though whites use drugs at a rate five times that of African Americans.[10] And racial disparities in the criminal justice system are especially evident when it comes to the death penalty, with the United States Supreme Court having acknowledged the validity of research findings that showed that blacks who killed whites were more likely to receive the death penalty than were whites who killed blacks.[11] In Georgia, a black person convicted of killing a white person was twenty-two times more likely to be sentenced to death than a black person convicted of killing another African American.[12]

These statistics indicate the presence of racial disparities in sentencing for certain kinds of offenses, namely drug offenses and felony murder, for which the death penalty is imposed. Drug offenses are my main object of concern here—I have addressed racial disparities in the death penalty elsewhere[13]—for they are the cornerstone of the mass incarceration phenomena that has emerged from the criminal justice system over the last four decades. Compared with whites, blacks suffer disproportionate hardship in that system. Blacks are sentenced at higher rates than whites for the same crime and serve longer periods of incarceration. For example, in 1991 incarceration rates for blacks were nearly seven times higher than those of whites, and that year 42 percent of young black males in Washington and 56 percent of black males in Baltimore aged eighteen to thirty-five were under control of the criminal justice system.[14] This research begs an interpretive question: Do blacks commit more crimes than whites, or is this skewed result the product of a racist criminal justice system?

---

10 "Written Submission of the American Civil Liberties Union on Racial Disparities in Sentencing: Hearing on Reports of Racism in the Justice System of the United States, Submitted to the Inter-American Commission on Human Rights, 153rd Session," October 27, 2014, 5 and footnote 53, American Civil Liberties Union, accessed January 7, 2016, https://www.aclu.org/sites/default/files/assets/141027_iachr_racial_disparities_aclu_submission_0.pdf. See also U.S. Bureau of Justice Statistics, *Correctional Populations*, 15.

11 *McClesky v. Kemp*, 481 U.S. 279 (1987). The Supreme Court did not dispute the statistical findings but also could not accept such statistics as determinative for judicial action, since it would have had the effect of requiring the dismantling of the criminal justice system, or so I read the decision. The court, rather, imposed the requirement that when charging racial discrimination, a defendant must prove that such discrimination was present in the individual's case, an exceedingly difficult standard to meet.

12 Michael Tonry, *Malign Neglect: Race, Crime, and Punishment in America* (New York: Oxford University Press, 1996), 42.

13 Lloyd Steffen, *Executing Justice: The Moral Meaning of the Death Penalty* (Eugene, OR: Wipf and Stock, 2006), 121–128; and Lloyd Steffen, *Ethics and Experience: Moral Theory from Just War to Abortion* (Lanham: Roman and Littlefield, 2012), 145–172.

14 Tonry, *Malign Neglect*, 4.

The answer to this interrogative is surprising, for neither of those options explains why the incarceration rates for young black males rose so precipitously. The cause cannot simply be laid at the doorstep of local police, prosecutors, and judges who intended to imprison blacks disproportionately compared with whites; neither can these disparities be attributed to an increase in African American crime. The cause can be located in a national policy first pushed in the Nixon Administration and then pursued by the Reagan and first Bush administrations in what has come to be called the "War on Drugs." Here is how Michael Tonry has described the background for what has happened in the criminal justice system:

> [F]irst, the rising levels of black incarceration did not just happen. They were the foreseeable effects of deliberate policies spearheaded by the Reagan and Bush administrations and implemented by many states. Anyone with knowledge of drug-trafficking patterns and of police arrest policies and incentives could have foreseen that the enemy troops in the War on Drugs would consist largely of young, inner-city minority males .... Second, and worse, support for repressive crime control policies, with their foreseeable disproportionate impact on blacks has been national Republican policy at least since the presidential campaigns of Richard Nixon .... Third, and perhaps worst of all, the crime control policies of recent years have undermined achievement of the overriding national goal of full unbiased incorporation of black Americans into the nation's social, political and economic life .... [T]he effects of crime control have been a major contributor to declining levels of lawful employment by young black males.[15]

That whites use drugs at a rate much higher than blacks—yet blacks make up 60 percent of those imprisoned for drug offenses (in 1998)[16]—is an outcome directly tied to crime control policy decisions related to the War on Drugs. Those policies institutionalized structural violence through mandatory sentencing laws that were instituted as part of the drug war. Drug war policies led to dramatic increases in the numbers of young black males arrested and sentenced to prison, an outcome that was sustained by the cultural violence that justified this result while overlooking the damage criminal justice measures were

15 Tonry, *Malign Neglect*, 4–6.

16 Dorothy Roberts, "The Social and Moral Cost of Mass Incarceration in African American Communities," *Stanford Law Review*, 56, 5, *2004 Stanford Law Review Symposium: Punishment and Its Purposes*, (April 2004): 1275.

having on black males, their families, and communities. Mandatory sentencing policies, justified as a harsher yet fairer response to crime, have swollen America's prison population and led to the social phenomenon of mass incarceration, which many American citizens today view as the acceptable consequence of effective law enforcement. Widespread awareness of, and critical engagement with, these policies has not been a part of the public discourse over the past decades, and only recently has mass incarceration become an issue in political campaigns.[17]

The disproportionate increase in black incarceration could not have occurred without public support for harsher retributive sentencing policies. These policies were formally justified by concerns for public safety even as they also expressed a culturally embedded view among many whites that blacks were mainly responsible for crime. "Whites who more strongly associate crime with racial minorities are more supportive of punitive policies," concludes a Sentencing Project Report.[18] Despite the fact that violent crime has declined since the mid-1990s, 68 percent of Americans say there is more crime in America than in the previous year,[19] that drug-related crimes are disproportionately committed by persons of color, and that violent crime, also disproportionately committed by persons of color, is on the increase. Although these beliefs turn out to be unfounded, they persist. Beliefs associating crime with race are embedded in community-reinforced assumptions and sustained by a fear of crime connected to the enduring power of racial stereotyping. This has led to a criminal justice system that has instituted policies that harm offenders, especially members of racial minorities caught in the structures of that system; and because these policies have met with societal approval, they persist and resist legal reform, which then reinforces and even justifies harsh and punitive retribution in the name of public safety. Between the destructiveness of the policies resulting in mass incarceration and the belief that those policies are justified—and fair—is to be found the cultural violence that sustains this system even as it continues to inflict harms on individual offenders and their communities.

---

17 Candidates as far apart politically as Rand Paul and Bernie Sanders addressed mass incarceration in their respective Republican and Democratic 2016 presidential campaigns.

18 Nazgol Ghandnoosh, *Race and Punishment: Racial Perceptions of Crime and Support for Punitive Policies*, The Sentencing Project, 2014, accessed July 31, 2016. http://www.sentencingproject.org/wp-content/uploads/2015/11/Race-and-Punishment.pdf.

19 Lydia Saad, "Most Americans Believe Crime in U.S. Is Worsening," *Gallup*, October 31, 2011, accessed July 30, 2016, http://www.gallup.com/poll/150464/americans-believe-crime-worsening.aspx.

The cultural violence relevant to criminal justice and mass incarceration can be located in the race-based attitudes toward crime embedded deep within American political culture. Taking a historical overview to see trends that then sustain a deeper cultural view of mass incarceration, Michael Tonry has noted that between 1962 and 1980 arrests of blacks for violent crimes did not increase, but the percentage of blacks sent to prison after 1980, when the War on Drugs began in full swing, increased to 54 percent by 1991.[20] The drug war came to embody the cultural violence of a politics that encouraged interpreting crime through the category of race, and evidence that policy makers sought and encouraged wide public support for such an interpretation has recently come to light. Former Nixon aide John Ehrlichman, who helped construct the Nixon War on Drugs effort, was interviewed in the 1990s about the Nixon administration's drug war policies. When sharing insights about the deeper motivations for the president's launch of the drug war, Ehrlichman revealed that the Nixon White House had identified black people as "enemies," going so far as to also say that drug war policies were being devised with the intention of associating race and crime, and specifically, blacks with drugs. In this recently revealed interview, Ehrlichman said that by "criminalizing" black drug use "heavily," "we could disrupt those communities." He added: "Did we know we were lying about the drugs? Of course we did."[21]

The movement toward mass incarceration can be tied directly to the War on Drugs. Drug war policies were borne of associating crime with race and inciting fear of crime by stereotyping blacks—and the black community—as drug-using "enemies." Drawing on racial stereotypes, policies were devised that had the effect of transforming blacks into criminals to be feared, and from that point, blacks became dangerous social threats to safety against whom white Americans needed protection.

The desire to criminalize drug use among blacks "heavily" led to major policy initiatives in the War on Drugs. Of singular importance was the move to impose harsher—and more harmful—mandatory penalties on drug offenders. This led to higher incarceration rates, with no corresponding reduction in crime rates attributable to those harsher sentences. Harsher sentencing has been an ineffective tool in efforts to reduce crime—crime rates fluctuate and are subject to even seasonal effects, and crime rate reduction is usually

20 Michael Tonry, "Racial Politics, Racial Disparities, and the War on Crime," *Crime and Delinquincy* 40, 4 (October 1994): 481.

21 Tom LoBianco, "Report: Aide Says Nixon's War on Drugs Targeted Blacks, Hippies," CNN, March 25, 2016, accessed, July 28, 2016, http://www.cnn.com/2016/03/23/politics/john-ehrlichman-richard-nixon-drug-war-blacks-hippie/.

attributable to employment opportunities and the degree of robustness in the economy.[22] The Reagan and Bush administrations advanced new sentencing initiatives in the drug war, but the impact on crime rates due to sentencing manipulation was, as Tonry noted above, "foreseeable": "In this and in other countries, practitioners and scholars have known that manipulation of penalties has few, if any, effects on crime rates."[23]

Policy makers who foresaw that harsher sentences would lead to increased incarceration rates, especially among urban black males even as the crime rates would not be affected, helped nurture the culture of violence that the War on Drugs brought to the black community. Although I shall say more about this momentarily, the War on Drugs destabilized the African American community, increasing economic hardship as males—fathers and husbands and breadwinners—were removed from families to serve prison sentences, some exceedingly lengthy—first offenders for simple possession can get from two to ten years in prison in Kentucky.[24] And since prison corrections policies themselves were not focused on drug treatment or rehabilitation, incarceration proved to be a learning environment for increased likelihood of a return to prison. For America's drug offenders in federal prison, the high rates of recidivism within three years of a prisoner's release, according to the Bureau of Justice Statistics, hovers around 77 percent.[25]

The policies that led to mass incarceration have visited harms on offenders, a form of legitimated structural violence related to the punishment objectives of retribution. And the harms experienced by inmates, families, and communities have either passed largely unnoticed or have been received as an acceptable consequence that is warranted within a larger framework of justification related to personal security and public safety. Fear of crime still makes a powerful political appeal and provides motivation for continuation of mass incarceration policies, with one candidate in the 2016 presidential contest going so far as to adopt Nixon's fear-of-crime appeal directly and declare himself, as Nixon had almost five decades ago, the "law and order" candidate.[26]

22 Nathan James, "Is Violent Crime in the United States Increasing?" Congressional Research Service, accessed July 28, 2016, https://www.fas.org/sgp/crs/misc/R44259.pdf.

23 James, "Violent Crime," 478.

24 "Drug Possession Penalties and Sentencing," *FindLaw*, accessed July 29, 2016, http://criminal.findlaw.com/criminal-charges/drug-possession-penalties-and-sentencing.html.

25 "Recidivism," National Institute of Justice, June 17, 2014, accessed July 28, 2016, http://www.nij.gov/topics/corrections/recidivism/pages/welcome.aspx.

26 Dan Roberts and Ben Jacobs, "Donald Trump Proclaims Himself 'Law and Order' Candidate at Republican Convention," *The Guardian*, Friday, July 22, 2016, accessed July 31, 2016,

Aside from such political developments, however, several policy initiatives have led to increased rates of arrest and incarceration: harsher federal drug enforcement policies, mandatory sentences, and Byrne Grants that encourage every federal grant participant to help fight the War on Drugs.[27] Byrne Grants funnel federal financial incentives to police departments to stimulate increased drug arrests and reward those able to show "productivity records" in drug convictions.[28] Taken together, these various initiatives have reinforced a culture in which harsh responses that prove to be harmful to individuals, especially black males, and destructive to their communities are deemed acceptable responses to the problem of drug-related crime.

As Michael Tonry has argued, those who engineered the War on Drugs could have reasonably foreseen that people of color and low-income people, African Americans in particular, would become the easiest targets for arrest in the drug war policing policies. Nixon domestic policy adviser, John Ehrlichman, confirmed that this was the case. And the incarceration rates responded to the policy changes, drastically increasing the numbers of those imprisoned and eventually accounting for half of those incarcerated in the federal incarceration system.[29] The War on Drugs has been aptly described as a "prisoner generating machine" that "defied gravity," for it functioned to increase incarceration rates at a time when crimes rates were actually dropping.

The War on Drugs did little to impact the drug trade, but it had a profound effect on the African American community. Drug war policies led to aggressive law enforcement in predominantly black urban neighborhoods and resulted in harsh mandatory sentencing for even minor offences. Today incarceration is an expected and predictable experience for African American males in their twenties, with blacks now eight times more likely than whites to spend time in prison.[30] According to Michelle Alexander, 80 percent of those incarcerated in federal prisons in the 1990s for drug offenses were there for marijuana use, and,

---

https://www.theguardian.com/us-news/2016/jul/21/donald-trump-epublican-national-convention-speech.

27 "Byrne JAG Program," The National Criminal Justice Association Center for Justice Planning, accessed January 24, 2016, http://www.ncjp.org/byrne_jag.

28 Aaron Cantu, "How the Government Bribes Police to Arrest People for Smoking Pot," *Alternet*, June 5, 2014, accessed September 30, 2015, http://www.alternet.org/civil-liberties/how-government-bribes-police-arrest-people-smoking-pot.

29 Roberts, "The Social and Moral Cost of Mass Incarceration," 1275; see also, "Drug Policy," The Sentencing Project, accessed October 3, 2015, http://www.sentencingproject.org/template/page.cfm?id=128.

30 Roberts, "The Social and Moral Cost of Mass Incarceration," 1274.

while this statistic is arguable,[31] the majority of those incarcerated for drug offenses at the state level had no history of violence and no history of serious selling activity.[32] Those who defend the War on Drugs have argued that the purpose of the new policies was to go after violent drug dealers. That was the aim but not the result. Evidence shows that those incarcerated in the War on Drugs have been overwhelmingly low-level nonviolent offenders.[33]

The War on Drugs has destroyed the lives and futures of drug law offenders, but attention has been given recently to the ways mass incarceration has devastated communities. Michelle Alexander's book, *The New Jim Crow: Mass Incarceration in the Age of Colorblindness,* makes a powerful argument that the crime control features of the War on Drugs have decimated the black community. Alexander notes that in Illinois white drug offenders are rarely arrested, and 90 percent of those sentenced for drug offences are African American. "The total population of black males in Chicago with a felony record (including both current and ex-felons)," she writes, "is equivalent to 55 percent of the black adult male population and an astonishing 80 percent of the adult black male workforce in the Chicago area."[34]

The War on Drugs has destroyed economic viability and social networks. With so many males imprisoned, families "lose income, assistance with child care, and bear expenses related to supporting and maintaining contact with incarcerated family members."[35] The stress of family maintenance falls on women caregivers who "are struggling to manage budgets consumed by addiction," as

31 The Bureau of Justice of Justice Statistics in its report, "Prisoners in 2007," puts drug offenders by race at 29% white, 20% Hispanic, and 45% black, which is lower than Alexander presents but still considerably disproportionate according to race. Heather C. West and Sebastian Sabol, "Prisoners in 2007," *Bureau of Justice Statistics Bulletin,* revised February 2, 2009, accessed July 29, 2016, http://www.bjs.gov/content/pub/pdf/p07.pdf.

32 Michelle Alexander, "The New Jim Crow: How Mass Incarceration Turns People of Color into Permanent Second-class Citizens," *The American Prospect* 22, 1 (Jan/Feb, 2011): A21. From 1993 to 2011, there were 30 million arrests for drug crimes, 24 million for possession, and blacks are three to four times more likely to be arrested for drug crimes and nine times more likely to go to a state prison for a drug crime. See Jonathan Rothwell, "Drug Offenders in American Prisons: The Critical Distinction between Stock and Flow," The Brookings Institute, November 25, 2015, accessed July 28, 2016, https://www.brookings.edu/2015/11/25/drug-offenders-in-american-prisons-the-critical-distinction-between-stock-and-flow/.

33 "The Impact of the War on Drugs on U.S. Incarceration," Human Rights Watch, accessed January 18, 2016, https://www.hrw.org/reports/2000/usa/Rcedrg00-03.htm.

34 Alexander, *The New Jim Crow,* 189.

35 Roberts, "The Social and Moral Cost of Mass Incarceration," 1282.

they hold families together, bear the stigma and shame of incarceration, and try "to prevent their children from becoming casualties of the war on drugs."[36]

The claim that cultural violence sustains mass incarceration is perhaps nowhere more powerfully supported than in the fact that the criminal justice system imposes on offenders and communities a life-altering inescapability. Policies that heightened the likelihood of drug offenders entering prison continue to work their effect on inmates after release. Convicted felons lose many citizenship privileges. Some of those privileges are formal—for instance, thirty-two states ban convicted felons from voting. Some are informal, such as ex-convicts not being able to get a job or go back to school because of a criminal record that is often inquired about on application forms. The "Ban the Box" movement is a recent response to this suppression of educational and employment opportunity through its efforts to remove the check boxes on applications that require acknowledgement of any felony convictions.[37]

A suppressed philosophical essentialism underlies this refusal to let a felon escape the "once a felon always a felon" system of social control, and it is cultural violence that extends this control past the designated period of incarceration. This essentialism takes form as a continuing discrimination that limits opportunity and prevents meaningful social and economic reentry into society. The idea of an offender paying a debt to society and then being free to live again outside such control is now akin to the person with a huge credit card debt who can pay on only the minimum balance, who keeps using the card with high interest rates and accumulating more debt, and is thus never debt free. As some credit card users come to realize that living in a culture of indebtedness is hard to escape, mass incarceration has led to a pervasive system—a culture—of limited opportunity, economic debilitation, social dislocation, poverty, and relationship fracturing. These are harms—violence—perpetrated against individuals and their communities, and the high recidivism rates of those released indicates the continuing influence of cultural violence in the post-incarceration experience.

The culture of violence that has so harmed the African American community through policies leading to mass incarceration has led to other unexpectedly harmful consequences as well. For instance, some researchers have noted that mass incarceration has incited distrust of the justice system, so

36 Roberts, "The Social and Moral Cost of Mass Incarceration," 1282.

37 Michelle Natividad Rodriguez and Nayantara Mehta, "Ban the Box: U.S. Cities, Counties, and States Adopt Fair Housing Policies," National Employment Law Project, December 1, 2015, accessed, January 15, 2016, http://www.nelp.org/publication/ban-the-box-fair-chance-hiring-state-and-local-guide.

that abused women are reluctant to rely on that system as a remedy to intervene in other kinds of violence, such as domestic abuse.[38] Mass incarceration incites a spiral of self-defeating and reinforcing poverty and rejection, and this is the foundation for the argument that Alexander advances—that mass incarceration has created a "caste" system. This is not an idle comparison. Mass incarceration has led to social consequences akin to the Indian Varna ("caste") system, at least with respect to the ancient Vedas, which presents caste as simply inescapable—at least in this lifetime. Individuals who enter the criminal justice system as the result of the War on Drugs seem unable to find any way out of it.

The drug war has prevented drug users whose offenses are nonviolent, and most likely the result of self-medication in the face of despair, from reentering society equipped with saleable and socially useful skills. It has excluded persons from a living-wage labor market, created social-civic isolation, and subverted the foundations of equal opportunity that are at the heart of a liberal democracy. Mass incarceration, the main product created by the War on Drugs, is a societal phenomenon that subverts the goods of life, which are necessary for flourishing in the moral life; and it has blunted the possibility of a return to civic life based on human dignity and equality of opportunity. It has created a response to offense against law that amounts in its effects to racial repression. Mass incarceration, as a system, has inflicted the harms of violence on offenders and on the families and the communities of those incarcerated. It has targeted certain groups—especially black males—to suffer an inescapable system of opportunity-limiting destructiveness and social control; and the harms visited on offenders remain in place and resist reform since they are justified by the supports of cultural violence.

This first and most important issue this paper proposed to investigate was whether criminal justice in the United States today is a racially discriminatory instrument of social control. If the criminal justice system impedes the restoration of incarcerated individuals to meaningful citizenship, if it expresses discriminatory policies or sustains racist practices, if it contributes to the impoverishment of families and communities and does not lead to greater social harmony and peace, then this system is infected with structural violence that then persists because of deeper cultural supports. Such supports identify the presence of cultural violence.

Let me summarize my argument thus far. War on Drugs policies were publically defended as an effective means for controlling crime, but this objective morphed into an even more pervasive method of social control by means of

38 Roberts, "The Social and Moral Cost of Mass Incarceration," 1287.

specific War on Drugs policies. The result has been that the American criminal justice system created an inescapable and apparently permanent underclass—thus does Michelle Alexander's analysis rely on the word "caste" to describe it; and those caught up in the system are denied opportunity for flourishing by forced entry into an economically and socially deprived way of life. The suppression of opportunity that is a consequence of mass incarceration poses a threat to social well-being for specific communities and ultimately for society at large. This presents a social justice issue for those committed to equality of persons; for offenders who as citizens have a legal and moral right to expect equal and proportionate treatment in the criminal justice system; and for a society dedicated to promoting opportunity and human flourishing.

Retribution versus Just Punishment

The role of punitive punishment in the War on Drugs is a second issue worthy of attention. Scholars have noted that rehabilitation, the effort to transform law offenders into law abiders, has been thoroughly eclipsed since the War on Drugs began, and rather than moving in the direction of rehabilitation or drug treatment for nonviolent offenders, the criminal justice system has committed to punitive, non-rehabilitative punishment.

> [T]he ideological landscape [in corrections] has been transformed to the point that it is substantially unrecognizable. Today [2000], commentators often assume that punitive responses to offenders—what Todd Clear (1994) calls "penal harm"—have achieved hegemonic status in the United States.[39]

Incarceration constitutes a punishment that does nothing to treat drug offenders, rehabilitate them, or prepare them for return to society and flourishing lives. Involvement in the incarceration system does just the opposite. Incarceration places a stifling burden on offenders—the burden of a felony conviction—that will prove an obstacle to flourishing for the rest of an offender's life.

---

39 Francis T. Cullen and Paul Gendreau, "Assessing Correctional Rehabilitation: Policy, Practice, and Prospects," *Criminal Justice 2000: Policies, Processes, and Decisions of the Criminal Justice System,* Vol. 3 (2000): 111, accessed January 16, 2016, http://www.d.umn.edu/~jmaahs/Correctional%20Assessment/cullen%20and%20gendreau_CJ2000.pdf. Embedded reference is to Todd R. Clear, *Harm in American Penology: Offenders, Victims, and their Communities* (Albany: State University of New York Press, 1994).

The War on Drugs was initiated with commitment to sentencing reform, but the mandatory sentences have tied judges' hands so that, lacking the ability by law to exercise discretion with nonviolent offenders, they are unable to return nonviolent offenders to their homes where they can assume responsibilities as contributors to family incomes and family nurture. The War on Drugs, now understood as a racialized activity and biased social policy with devastating consequences in black communities, positioned retributive punishment as central to the drug war effort. Such retribution was pursued without a clear idea of what would constitute a just punishment, especially in light of the nonviolent nature of most drug offenses. Moreover, the retribution policy canceled other options for addressing illicit drug use, including the possibility of reframing America's drug problem as a public health issue for which medical, psychological, and social support was needed. Policy makers were of course free to go the retribution route, but the question is why has the policy of retribution continued when its consequences have been so dramatically disastrous?

Were the problem of illicit drugs reframed as a public health issue, the massive expenses of incarceration—estimated to be $80 billion in 2010[40]—could be redirected toward treatment, work release, and rehabilitation. This would make it possible for offenders to move toward reintegration into society by means of education and job training, the very things the current social control system of retributive punishment and prison warehousing undermines and actually prevents.

A philosophical contribution to the retributive incarceration preference pursued under War on Drugs policy would be to consider the meaning of "just punishment" in the criminal justice system. Fashioning a response to offenders on a theory of "just punishment" would in all likelihood lead to results akin to those that result from an approach to corrections that endorses work release, job training, treatment, and rehabilitation for nonviolent offenders. An ethics model for just punishment can be found in a natural law–based set of justice-related criteria akin to those that guide deliberation on the use of force in "just war" thinking. With "just war" providing a model, I would offer the following criteria as relevant to determining the conditions that, if satisfied, would allow us to avow a punishment as just:

40 Melissa S. Kearney, Benjamin H. Harris, Elisa Jácome, and Lucie Parker, "Ten Economic Facts about Crime and Incarceration in the United States," The Hamilton Project, The Brookings Institute Policy Memo, (May 2014): 2, accessed December 10, 2015, http://www.hamiltonproject.org/assets/legacy/files/downloads_and_links/v8_THP_10CrimeFacts.pdf.

1. Punishment and sentencing of offenders must be legitimately authorized.
2. There must be just cause for inflicting a punishment, which is to say the offense itself must be sufficiently grave that society itself is aggrieved and the community well-being is adversely affected.
3. The motivation for punishment must be justice, not vengeance.
4. Punishments must be distributed and administered fairly, without accidental features such as race, religion, class, or sex affecting administration of the punishment.
5. Punishment and sentencing must express cherished values and be a part of a sanction that seeks to restore peace and harmony to society and even restitution for aggrieved parties.
6. Punishments ought not to be cruel and dehumanizing but should observe the law of parsimony (i.e., the least harsh sentence) and aim at restoring offenders to their rightful place in the moral community.
7. Punishment ought to be sought as a last resort, with every effort made to restore the relationship of offender and offended by means of restitution for an offended person's pain, loss, and suffering.
8. Punishment ought to restore a value equilibrium distorted and upset by the wrongdoing.
9. Punishment policies must observe a principle of proportionality in a social justice sense, for if not all persons have the same opportunity to participate in society, economic and social disadvantage must be seen as "affect[ing] the benefits of autonomy that produce obligation." The sentencing system should therefore demonstrate willingness to mitigate sentences by taking into account both social injustices and the personal circumstances of individual offenders.[41]

The punishment model upheld and institutionalized in the justice system that has produced mass incarceration violates all but the first of these provisions. Prison sentences following upon drug convictions, especially for nonviolent offenders, have proven cruel and dehumanizing. Little attention has been given to restoring individual offenders to peace and social harmony through rehabilitation, and, as mentioned, imprisonment burdens felon offenders with weights so heavy they cannot be restored to citizenship, return to full civic life, and enjoy the benefits of living in a liberal democracy. This is why Michelle Alexander condemns the current system as a caste system that spreads joyless social fracturing in its wake. The just punishment perspective would seek to restore an individual to society and then take the steps necessary to accomplish

41 Steffen, *Ethics and Experience*, 165–166.

that end. So offenders in need of drug treatment would receive such treatment, and undergoing that discipline would be the corrective pathway to restoration in community. Just punishment, framed in a restorative framework, would intervene in self-harming illicit drug activities and yield a result akin to a public health approach to the American drug problem.

Research evidence shows that drug use is not rampant in disadvantaged neighborhoods compared with those not disadvantaged, although the problems attendant to illicit drug use in disadvantaged neighborhoods are more serious when they do arise. Residents in disadvantaged neighborhoods see dealers rather than users as the central problem; and reports of drug use are higher in disadvantaged neighborhoods because of higher visibility of drug use in such neighborhoods, "so [the view] that poor and minority areas are assumed to be the focus of the problem of drug use, is plainly wrong."[42] In addition, it is often overlooked in the War on Drugs that the *demand* for drugs reflects deeper moral and spiritual dynamics in contemporary society. Illicit drug use is often a self-medication route for those living without hope or engagement in meaningful social structures, or who are living in poverty, or who lack meaningful employment and educational opportunities. The authors of a study of drug use in a public housing community in Canada concluded that "Poverty-induced despair is also a key determinant of illicit drug use and consumption of large quantities of alcohol .... Only policies specifically designed to eliminate poverty and unemployment will enhance the 'severely distressed's' physical and psychological well-being."[43]

The drug war has been a supply-side effort focused on law enforcement and interdiction, but addressing illicit drug use from the demand side emphasizes that drug use is often a means to confront the pain of despair, which, among other causes, may be "poverty induced." Pope Francis, in his 2015 environmental encyclical, *Laudato Si'*, commenting on the current state of human well-being, said that human beings are made for love, yet "people no longer believe in a happy future; they no longer have blind trust in a better tomorrow based

42 Leonard Saxe, Charles Kadushin, Andrew Beveridge, David Livert, Elizabeth Tighe, David Rindskopf, Julie Ford, and Archie Brodsky, "The Visibility of Illicit Drugs: Implications for Community-Based Drug Control Strategies," *American Journal of Public Health* 91, 12 (December 2001): 1988, accessed January 14, 2016, http://www.ncbi.nlm.nih.gov/pmc/articles/PMC1446920/pdf/0911987.pdf (PMCID: PMC1446920).

43 Walter DeKeseredy, Shahid Alvi, Martin D. Schwartz, and Andreas E. Tomaszewski, *Under Siege: Poverty and Crime in a Public Housing Community* (Lanham, MD: Lexington Books, 2003), 119.

on the present state of the world and our technical abilities."[44] If this comment rings true in assessing the state of the world from an ecological point of view, it may also ring true for those caught up in the hopelessness and despair of a drug world and the criminal justice system determined to crush drug offenders by harsh retribution. The spiritual aspect of the "demand for drugs" problem was not addressed adequately by the architects of the War on Drugs. Their reconstruction of law and law enforcement to create what has become the culture of mass incarceration bespeaks a monumental failure of imagination and humanity toward those caught in spiritual despair, including that caused, at least in part, by social and economic disadvantage. Attending to a just punishment model would provide one means of countering the cultural violence of mass incarceration with a culture of peace, where the objective is individual and social harmony.

Cultural Violence and Criminal Justice

I have argued that mass incarceration, the product of the War on Drugs, springs from a justice system that delivers neither justice nor correction but positive harm toward people, not only to convicted felons but also to families and communities and even to society as a whole. Those harms are so repressive, so much an expression of bias and assault on human dignity, and so debilitating in that they reinforce poverty and impede social advancement, that they deserve to be interpreted as expressions of structural violence. That violence is apparent in the harms that criminal justice as a system delivers to persons and social networks. The announced intention of America's drug war policy originally was to get violent offenders and drug kingpins off the streets, but the main effect of drug war policies was to disproportionately incarcerate poor people and racial minorities. The onus of arrest and conviction has fallen mainly on black males, but it has also affected black females, who are today the largest growing population of inmates in prison.[45] Not only does this result expose the failure of the War on Drugs to achieve its publically stated purpose,

44 Pope Francis, *Laudato Si': On Care for Our Common Home,* paragraph 113, 33, accessed December 10, 2015, http://w2.vatican.va/content/francesco/en/encyclicals/documents/papa-rancesco_20150524_enciclica-laudato-si.html.

45 The number of women in prison increased by 646% between 1980 and 2010, rising from 15,118 to 112,797. See "Incarcerated Women," The Sentencing Project, accessed October 2, 2015, http://www.sentencingproject.org/doc/publications/cc_incarcerated_women_factsheet_sep24sp.pdf.

but this result is inconsistent with citizenship based on human dignity, equality before the law, and equal opportunity, which are often touted as core values of liberal democratic societies.

When we ask "How did we get here?" the answer lies in a combination of factors. Michael Tonry's mention of fear of crime playing a part in elections, even presidential elections, is relevant since many Americans experienced an increased fear of crime during the 1970s and 80s, not because of actual increases in crime rates but because of perceptions of greater insecurity and vulnerability to crime fed by the media. The 1991 *Time* magazine article about "Crack Kids," subtitled "*Their mothers used drugs, and now it's the children who suffer,*" may have been the primary media example of heightening public awareness and support for tougher responses to illicit drug use, but other factors played a part. Articles submitted to medical journals dealing with the debilitating effects of prenatal drug exposure "had a significantly higher chance of being published than more careful research finding no adverse effects."[46] Despite the fact that cocaine is not uniquely or even inevitably harmful to the in utero fetus,[47] even less so than alcohol and cigarette smoking, the publicity given in the media to the phenomenon of crack babies, the politics of crime control and the drug war, and even research that seemed skewed to support popular perceptions of increasing harm, all contributed to lulling popular opinion into an uncritical acceptance of the War on Drug as an optimal policy. Attention did not fall on the 70 percent of drug-addicted women who were victims of violent sexual abuse, nor on the fact that the "crack babies" who were the subjects of numerous popular news exposes were coming from impoverished homes and social settings. As Lynn Paltrow has noted, crack kids' symptomology cannot easily be separated from other poverty-related problems for non-flourishing children, including low-birth weight, malnutrition, lead poisoning, and abuse; and the media presentation, which put an urban black face on the problem of illicit drug use, provoked a political response of support for a "crack down" on crack users.[48] All of this occurred at a time when the crime rate was in decline.

So fear of crime and the electoral politics related to such fears, as well as media involvement that perpetuated research inaccuracies and transmitted

46 Gideon Koren, Karen Graham, Heather Shear, and Tom Einarson, "Bias Against the Null Hypothesis: The Reproductive Hazards of Cocaine Use and Pregnancy Outcome: A Meta-Analysis," *Teratiology* 44 (1991): 405–414, cited in Lynn Paltrow, "Punishment and Prejudice: Judging Drug-Using and Pregnant Women," in *Taking Sides: Clashing Views on Bioethical Issues,* ed. Carole Levine (Dubuque, IA: McGraw-Hill, 2008), 152.

47 Paltrow, "Punishment and Prejudice,"153.

48 Paltrow, "Punishment and Prejudice,"153.

stereotyping myths that bracketed social ills consequent to poverty, created a "culture" where more arrests and harsh sentencing were deemed justified, especially when it appeared that children were the ones most adversely affected by illicit drug use. When the need to protect babies and children was added to the justification for the drug war effort, public support for the mass incarceration policies also increased. Policies that visited harms on many drug-using persons were not placed in check because of those harms but were advanced and justified as the acceptable cost of dealing with the drug problem. The harms inflicted by the policies either passed unnoticed or were deemed allowable, perhaps not desired but certainly "not wrong."

Mass incarceration has been a policy response to the War on Drugs, and my argument has been that the War on Drugs, as it came to reality, embodied cultural violence. My view is that the War on Drugs commenced with a low level of informed conversation about those who could reasonably be expected to be disproportionally affected by the drug war policy changes, namely young black males and the urban African American community; and this was accompanied by a lack of attention to research on relevant questions pertaining to the impact of incarceration, mandatory sentencing, and prospects for flourishing by those caught up in nonviolent drug offenses. Political leadership focused attention on criminalization and away from alternatives, such as work release and employment training, housing and childcare assistance, and drug treatment and support for expanded educational opportunity. "Tough on crime" attitudes came to dominate approaches to criminal justice, and widespread public acceptance that such approaches were just and justifiable obscured how the policies were devastating communities of color. Political leadership and media attention did not challenge this story, thus allowing it to persist. The phenomenon of mass incarceration, rather than being seen as a failure to meet the objectives of the drug war, actually came to be interpreted as evidence of the war's successful prosecution.

Only recently have alternative voices, such as those of Michael Tonry and Michelle Alexander, gained sufficient attention that the myths perpetuated by the drug war are undergoing exposure as myths. A counter-story is being allowed to gain traction, which is that the War on Drugs itself became the social instrument that delivered not justice but violence and social oppression to the black community, and it did so by means of mass incarceration. When Michelle Alexander points out that there are more African Americans under control of the criminal justice system today than were enslaved in ante-bellum America, and that a racial caste system has been created, these realities speak to a flawed and biased criminal justice system that has failed the objectives of liberal democracy. Those objectives are inseparably related to equality: equal opportunity and equal protection of the law. While addressing this situation will require commitment to racially blind policies that stress decarceration, one sad but ironic consequence of the War on Drugs is that it has perpetuated the violence of racism by articulating an anti-drug policy that avoids all mention of race. As Alexander notes, "The War on Drugs, cloaked in race-neutral language, offered whites opposed to racial reform a unique opportunity to express their hostility toward blacks and black progress, without being exposed to the charge of racism."[49]

Today, there is evidence of bipartisan support to re-examine the legal supports for mass incarceration, and some actions have been taken, such as President Obama's signature on the *Fair Sentencing Act*, which reduced sentencing based on powder versus crack cocaine. The disparity in sentencing for a difference in drug delivery rather than pharmacological effect was widely criticized for targeting African Americans, who were much more likely to use crack cocaine than whites, whose cocaine of choice was powder.[50] Still the view is widely held that only harsh sentencing and focus on the offender is or should be at issue in addressing America's drug problem, and this attitude, which correlates to racialized perspectives and attitudes, sustains mass incarceration. Policy makers continue to resist changing policies around mandatory sentences and incarceration for drug offenses. Cultural violence persists.

Conclusion: Cultural Violence, Essentialism and Symbols

Certain symbols of justice provide access to the cultural violence of criminal justice and mass incarceration. The prison is still a symbol of justice to many. The execution gurney is still a symbol of just retribution for many despite evidence that the system of capital punishment is infected with racial bias. As symbols, the prison and the gurney uphold a worn-out philosophical essentialism that, as previously mentioned, takes form in the idea of "once a criminal always a criminal." The criminal justice system reinforces this essentialism by providing a felon with no way to escape the press of criminal justice oversight and return to responsible and participatory civic life. That essentialism is powerfully present in the uncritical acceptance of the justifications for the

49 Alexander, *The New Jim Crow*, 54.

50 CNN Wire Staff, "Obama Signs Bill Reducing Cocaine Sentencing Gap," August 3, 2010, accessed January 3, 2016, http://www.cnn.com/2010/POLITICS/08/03/fair.sentencing/.

structural violence of criminal justice system policies. The structural violence of this system is sustained by a deeper cultural violence and suggests the more invidious presence of a *violent culture*. Death sentences are imposed on the assumption that the conditions persons were in when they committed a homicide are irrelevant to the idea of rehabilitation, yet the reality is that for some condemned individuals death row is the most stable environment they have ever known. Criminal justice in the United States does not accept that an offense creates a debt to society, and that once paid, it is paid. The system does not confront the offender with a sentence, see that sentence concluded, and then instruct, "Go and offend no more, we're done with that part of your life—how can we help make the next part better?" Such a response is impossible because of the essentialist constraints imposed on offenders by the criminal justice system itself, and prison leads not to rehabilitation and restoration and peace but, in a majority of cases, to repeat offenses and a high likelihood of recidivism.

The cultural violence revealed by the criminal justice system operates in accord with an essentialist metaphysic that denies the humanity of persons who are "in essence" neither criminals nor drug users—a human life ought not be reduced to such a one-dimensional trope. The willingness of so many to identify a offender with an essential criminality, often because of racial associations, is where cultural violence is most apparent in contemplating how the drug war has played out in the criminal justice system in the United States. The symbols of cultural violence reinforce such a view as they associate prison with offenders whose illegal activity is assumed to be a product of race and whose punishment is a just—harsh and punitive—desert, and from such offenders society needs protection. These views are often held beyond the reach of linguistically explicit awareness and arise in the unexamined justifications for harsh, punitive retribution against offenders even when they are not violent, even when cracks in the justice system appear flawed and the symbols of justice fail to reinforce culturally embedded assumptions. The flaws come to light—to consciousness—when there is public discussion about nonviolent black drug offenders receiving disproportionately harsh sentences compared with whites for the same crime or when offenders sentenced to death are exonerated. There is still support for the repressive measures, however, because structural violence remains in place sustained by the cultural violence that justifies it. Even when the structural violence of criminal justice and mass incarceration is pointed out and reasonable people can admit that it "does not feel right," the culture so directs perceptions and interpretations that the sustaining and perpetuating systems are accepted as—in Galtung's words—"at least not wrong."

The criminal justice system that has produced mass incarceration will be difficult to dismantle. Mass incarceration has spawned a new type of prison system, the private-for-profit prison, and the construction of ever more prisons fits other economic and political goals, such as creating jobs especially for unemployed rural whites. Economic concerns related to corporate profit and employment opportunities continue to govern the system that has evolved to sustain mass incarceration, so the culture of retribution and violence continues. Mass incarceration is a product of social, political, and economic policies that have gained wide acceptance; and so integrated are they into political culture that it is difficult for the critical voices to be heard.

This situation may be changing right now—there are some signs, including wider public and even political conversation about the effects of mass incarceration.[51] Mass incarceration, however, is embedded in widely held perspectives on political questions that involve issues of social unrest and fears about "others," whether they are immigrants or drug users or racial minorities or the poor. From a moral and social justice point of view, the effect of mass incarceration has been to inflict harm on individuals and communities in the name of justice, and the political machinery has so affected the legal system that these harms have the sanction of law and are accepted as justifiable responses to crime. The result has been the creation of an underclass without prospect of meaningful opportunity in employment or education and, for many convicted felons, little realistic likelihood of escaping poverty. The responsibility for this result rests with policy makers who have pursued a tough-on-crime drug war, even as persons of color and especially black males have been subjected to the damaging repression that can also be interpreted as social, political, psychological, and spiritual violence against persons.

Cultural violence is apparent in the symbols and justifications that support a criminal justice system that sanctions harms against persons in the name of justice. The ideals of liberal democratic societies—equality of opportunity and equality before the law—are still the ideas that most challenge cultural violence. These ideas are the basis for a social ethic that seeks to challenge the harms and address the damage created by a retributive system that has thus far placed the possibility of societal harmony, racial understanding, and peace beyond reach.

51 Rebecca U. Thorpe, "Republicans and Democrats Support Sentencing Reform. This is What Stands in Their Way," *The Washington Post,* October 5, 2015, accessed January 25, 2015, https://www.washingtonpost.com/blogs/monkey-cage/wp/2015/10/05/republicans-and-democrats-support-sentencing-reform-this-is-what-stands-in-their-way/.

Bibliography

Alexander, Michelle. "The New Jim Crow: How Mass Incarceration Turns People of Color into Permanent Second-class Citizens." *The American Prospect* 22, 1 (Jan/Feb, 2011): A19–A21.

Alexander, Michelle. *The New Jim Crow: Mass Incarceration in the Age of Colorblindness.* New York: New Press, 2012.

Bonczar, Thomas P. "Prevalence of Imprisonment in the U.S. Population, 1974–2001," Washington, dc: Bureau of Justice Statistics, 2003. Accessed July 30, 2016. http://sentencingproject.org/wp-content/uploads/2016/01/Trends-in-US-Corrections.pdf.

"Byrne JAG Program." The National Criminal Justice Association Center for Justice Planning. Accessed January 24, 2016. http://www.ncjp.org/byrne_jag.

Cantu, Aaron. "How the Government Bribes Police to Arrest People for Smoking Pot." *Alternet* (June 5, 2014). Accessed September 30, 2015. http://www.alternet.org/civil-liberties/how-government-bribes-police-arrest-people-smoking-pot.

CNN Wire Staff. "Obama Signs Bill Reducing Cocaine Sentencing Gap" August 3, 2010. Accessed January 3, 2016. http://www.cnn.com/2010/POLITICS/08/03/fair.sentencing/.

Cullen, Francis T., and Paul Gendreau. "Assessing Correctional Rehabilitation: Policy, Practice, and Prospects." *Criminal Justice 2000: Policies, Processes, and Decisions of the Criminal Justice System* 3 (2000). Accessed January 16, 2016. http://www.d.umn.edu/~jmaahs/Correctional%20Assessment/cullen%20and%20gendreau_CJ2000.pdf.

DeKeseredy, Walter, Shahid Alvi, Martin D. Schwartz, and Andreas E. Tomaszewski. *Under Siege: Poverty and Crime in a Public Housing Community.* Lanham, MD: Lexington Books, 2003.

"Drug Policy," The Sentencing Project. Accessed October 3, 2015. http://www.sentencingproject.org/template/page.cfm?id=128.

"Drug Possession Penalties and Sentencing." *FindLaw.* Accessed July 29, 2016. http://criminal.findlaw.com/criminal-charges/drug-possession-penalties-and-sentencing.html.

Galtung, Johan. "Cultural Violence." *Journal of Peace Research* 27, 3 (August, 1990): 291–305.

Gao, George. "Chart of the Week: The Black-White Gap in Incarceration Rates." Pew Research Center, July 18, 2014. Accessed November 19, 2015. http://www.pewresearch.org/fact-tank/2014/07/18/chart-of-the-week-the-black-white-gap-in-incarceration-rates/.

Ghandnoosh, Nazgol. *Race and Punishment: Racial Perceptions of Crime and Support for Punitiver Policies.* The Sentencing Project, 2014. Accessed July 31, 2016. http://www.sentencingproject.org/wp-content/uploads/2015/11/Race-and-Punishment.pdf.

"The Impact of the War on Drugs on U.S. Incarceration." Human Rights Watch. Accessed January 18, 2016. https://www.hrw.org/reports/2000/usa/Rcedrg00-03.htm.

"Incarcerated Women." The Sentencing Project. Accessed October 2, 2015. http://www.sentencingproject.org/doc/publications/cc_incarcerated_women_factsheet_sep24sp.pdf.

James, Nathan. "Is Violent Crime in the United States Increasing?" Congressional Research Service. Accessed July 28, 2016. https://www.fas.org/sgp/crs/misc/R44259.pdf.

Kearney, Melissa S., Benjamin H. Harris, Elisa Jácome, and Lucie Parker. "Ten Economic Facts about Crime and Incarceration in the United States." The Hamilton Project, The Brookings Institute Policy Memo (May 2014): 2. 2015. Accessed December 10, 2015. http://www.hamiltonproject.org/assets/legacy/files/downloads_and_links/v8_THP_10CrimeFacts.pdf.

LoBianco, Tom."Report: Aide Says Nixon's War on Drugs Targeted Blacks, Hippies," CNN, March 25, 2016. Accessed, July 28, 2016. http://www.cnn.com/2016/03/23/politics/john-ehrlichman-richard-nixon-drug-war-blacks-hippie/.

"Mass Incarceration: The Whole Pie 2015." Prison Policy Initiative. Accessed January 10, 2016. http://www.prisonpolicy.org/reports/pie2015.html.

McClesky v. Kemp, 481 U.S. 279 (1987).

NAACP Criminal Justice Fact Sheet. Accessed November 23, 2015. http://www.naacp.org/pages/criminal-justice-fact-sheet.

Paltrow, Lynn. "Punishment and Prejudice: Judging Drug-Using and Pregnant Women." In *Taking Sides: Clashing Views on Bioethical Issues.* 12th ed., edited by Carole Levine. 164–172. Dubuque, IA: McGraw-Hill, 2008.

Pope Francis. *Laudato Si': On Care for Our Common Home,* paragraphs 113, 133. Accessed December 10, 2015. http://w2.vatican.va/content/francesco/en/encyclicals/documents/papa-rancesco_20150524_enciclica-laudato-si.html.

"Prisoners in 2014." *Bureau of Justice Statistics, Summary/NCJ248955,*" September 2015. Accessed July 30, 2016. http://www.bjs.gov/content/pub/pdf/p14_Summary.pdf.

"Recidivism." National Institute of Justice, June 17, 2014. Accessed July 28, 2016. http://www.nij.gov/topics/corrections/recidivism/pages/welcome.aspx.

Roberts, Dorothy. "The Social and Moral Cost of Mass Incarceration in African American Communities." *Stanford Law Review*, 56, 5, *2004 Stanford Law Review Symposium: Punishment and Its Purposes* (April 2004): 1271–1305.

Roberts, Dan, and Ben Jacobs, "Donald Trump Proclaims Himself 'Law and Order' Candidate at Republican Convention." *The Guardian*, July 22, 2016. Accessed July 31, 2016. https://www.theguardian.com/us-news/2016/jul/21/donald-trump-republican-national-convention-speech.

Rodriguez, Michelle Natividad, and Nayantara Mehta. "Ban the Box: U.S. Cities, Counties, and States Adopt Fair Housing Policies." National Employment Law Project

(December 1, 2015). Accessed, January 15, 2016. http://www.nelp.org/publication/ban-the-box-fair-chance-hiring-state-and-local-guide.

Rothwell, Jonathan. "Drug Offenders in American Prisons: The Critical Distinction between Stock and Flow." The Brookings Institute (November 25, 2015). Accessed July 28, 2016. https://www.brookings.edu/2015/11/25/drug-offenders-in-american-prisons-the-critical-distinction-between-stock-and-flow/.

Saad, Lydia. "Most Americans Believe Crime in U.S. Is Worsening," Gallup (October 31, 2011). Accessed July 30, 2016. http://www.gallup.com/poll/150464/americans-believe-crime-worsening.aspx.

Saxe, Leonard, Charles Kadushin, Andrew Beveridge, David Livert, Elizabeth Tighe, David Rindskopf, Julie Ford, and Archie Brodsky. "The Visibility of Illicit Drugs: Implications for Community-Based Drug Control Strategies." *American Journal of Public Health* 91, 12 (December 2001): 1987–1994. Accessed January 14, 2016. http://www.ncbi.nlm.nih.gov/pmc/articles/PMC1446920/pdf/0911987.pdf. (PMCID: PMC1446920).

Steffen, Lloyd. *Executing Justice: The Moral Meaning of the Death Penalty*. Eugene, OR: Wipf and Stock, 2006.

Steffen, Lloyd. *Ethics and Experience: Moral Theory from Just War to Abortion*, Lanham: Roman and Littlefield, 2012.

Thorpe, Rebecca U. "Republicans and Democrats Support Sentencing Reform. This Is What Stands in Their Way." *The Washington Post* (October 5, 2015). Accessed January 25, 2015. https://www.washingtonpost.com/blogs/monkey-cage/wp/2015/10/05/republicans-and-democrats-support-sentencing-reform-this-is-what-stands-in-their-way/.

Tonry, Michael. "Racial Politics, Racial Disparities, and the War on Crime." *Crime and Delinquency* 40, 4 (October 1994): 475–494.

Tonry, Michael. *Malign Neglect: Race, Crime, and Punishment in America.* New York: Oxford University Press, 1996.

U.S. Bureau of Justice Statistics. *Correctional Populations in the United States*, 2011, 1, 3 tbl2, November 2012. Accessed July 29, 2016. http://sentencingproject.org/wp-content/uploads/2015/12/Race-and-Justice-Shadow-Report-ICCPR.pdf.

U.S. Bureau of Justice Statistics. "Prisoners in 2014," *Bureau of Justice Statistics, Summary/NCJ24 8955*, September 2015. Accessed July 30, 2016. http://www.bjs.gov/content/pub/pdf/p14_Summary.pdf.

Walmsley, Roy. "World Prison Population List, 10th Edition." *International Center for Prison Studies* (University of Essex). Accessed January 5, 2016. http://www.apcca.org/uploads/10th_Edition_2013.pdf.

West, Heather C., and Sebastian Sabol, "Prisoners in 2007," *Bureau of Justice Statistics Bulletin*. Revised February 2, 2009. Accessed July 29, 2016. http://www.bjs.gov/content/pub/pdf/p07.pdf.

"Written Submission of the American Civil Liberties Union on Racial Disparities in Sentencing: Hearing on Reports of Racism in the Justice System of the United States, Submitted to the Inter-American Commission on Human Rights, 153rd Session." (October 27, 2014: 5). American Civil Liberties Union. Accessed January 7, 2016. https://www.aclu.org/sites/default/files/assets/141027_iachr_racial_disparities_aclu_submission_0.pdf.

Ye Hee Lee, Michelle. "Does the United States Really Have 5 Per Cent of the World's Population and One Quarter of the World's Prisoners?" *The Washington Post* (April 30, 2015). Accessed November 23, 2015. https://www.washingtonpost.com/news/fact-checker/wp/2015/04/30/does-the-united-states-really-have-five-percent-of-worlds-population-and-one-quarter-of-the-worlds-prisoners/.

CHAPTER 7

Terrorism and the Necessity of Oppositional Clarification in the "War" Against It

Sanjay Lal

> Just as one must learn the art of killing in the training for violence, so one must learn the art of dying in the training for nonviolence. Violence does not mean emancipation from fear, but discovering the means of combating the cause of fear. Nonviolence, on the other hand, has no cause of fear. The votary of nonviolence has to cultivate the capacity for sacrifice of the highest type in order to be free from fear. He recks not if he should lose his land, his wealth, his life. He who has not overcome all fear cannot practice ahimsa (nonviolence) to perfection.[1]
>
> —M.K. GANDHI

Though the need for clarifying who the West is at war with has not gone unnoticed in the post 9/11 world, a glaring lack of clarity regarding what, exactly, is being fought against is noticeable even among leaders (e.g. President Obama) who have taken great pains to avoid creating the impression that Westerners are fighting Islam in their current war efforts. I maintain that such an absence of clarity allows cultural violence to continue unimpeded insofar as it prevents us from noticing important insights that challenge our tendency to readily accept violence and that are therefore essential for realizing a more peaceful world. I will show that a deeper consideration of key questions related to the violence committed on behalf of citizens in the West lead to conclusions that (at the very least) should make us all less willing to regard this violence as morally acceptable—even on the grounds that it is committed to protect innocent life. Specifically, I hold that the uncritical acceptance of the rationale that we must perpetuate violence on the grounds that it will prevent "our own" from being killed by our enemies blinds us to the indispensability of moral standing

1 M.K. Gandhi, writing in *Harijan,* September 1, 1940.

 | DOI 10.1163/9789004361911_009

in conflicts. I will partially rely on a Gandhian framework in making my arguments but intend to justify my conclusions in a way that does not hinge on sharing Gandhi's specific metaphysical commitments. I call for the consideration of questions that go well beyond the commonly asked, "Who are the good guys?" and "How are we not terrorists ourselves?" that instead relate to our own responses to acts committed by those we are said to fight against. I maintain that pursuing issues related to our present day causes of conflicts at a higher, "meta" level of inquiry will enable understanding essential for achieving a peaceful order.

I will specifically focus on the need for clarifying what it means to fight a battle of ideologies (as I implicitly take for granted widespread agreement that current wars are ultimately about ideology). I hope to show the importance defining the nature of our present problems and grievances with "radicals" has for imagining new ways forward. We will see that careful attention to this matter seemingly leads to the conclusion that much of what passes for accepted forms of violence in Western culture is no more ethically defensible than indiscriminate attacks on civilians or wanton torture practices performed solely to satisfy urges for retribution. Though my points have much broader implications for issues of peace and nonviolence, I will discuss them in the context of present day conflicts with "radical" Islam. Ultimately, consideration of actions in these particular conflicts provides openings by which much greater insights on peace can be attained. I also do not find it problematic, for my purposes, to discuss the so-called "radicals" in a way that makes no distinctions among the different strands of Islam that can be noticed among them given that my focus is entirely on how Western culture responds to perceived outside threats. Thus, demarcations and nuances among these groups have no bearing on my conclusions here. What is important for my points in this chapter is that the conflicts we are engaged in as a culture, in which we feel justified in inflicting violence in our handlings of, can ultimately be understood as battles of ideology. Furthermore, my points should be seen as truly going beyond commonly heard leftist criticisms (à la Chomsky) of Western foreign policy. My aim is not so much to give a historical indictment of Western policy toward the Muslim world, but to offer insights that can be noticed even by those who would say ultimately we are not at fault for "radicals" hating us.

Regarding the Present "War on Radicalism"

Before proceeding further, it is important to recognize key facts about, what is commonly referred to, as the "war against terrorism" (also often called the "war on radicalism"). In spite of insistences from two consecutive American presidents that we are not fighting a holy war against Islam, it is quite clear that Western actions in this on-going conflict (however we name it) have (at the very least) contributed to greater so-called "radicalism" becoming present in the Muslim world. As of this writing, ongoing coverage of the November 13th 2015 Paris attacks (occurring, not incidentally, right after Western officials hailed the killing of "Jihadi John"), terror warnings bringing about the lock-down of Brussels, "homegrown" radicals (including Western educated girls going abroad to join terror groups), as well as the overall rise of the so-called "Islamic state" have dominated Western airwaves. The Islamic state is indeed said to be more even more barbaric and radical than Al Qaeda—who, according to the mainstream Western narrative, are the original instigators of the seemingly never-ending fight against Muslim radicals. What's more is that the extent to which Westerners (particularly young women in the West) are willingly going overseas or are being recruited while at home and joining forces with the radicals of the "Islamic state" is seemingly unprecedented. It is widely accepted that the origins of the "Islamic state" is linked to the treatment of Muslims in Western countries (which is in turn linked to perceptions spawned by institutional responses to "radicalism") as well as the American led invasion of Iraq. In other words, despite professed objectives, Western reactions to the "radicals" seems to yield (or at least not stopped) even greater radicalization. As Robert Pape chronicled in 2005, this dynamic was indeed evident well before the advent of the "Islamic state."[2] Pape noted that in the two years immediately following 9/11 (or the time period which includes the start of the war in Afghanistan and the beginning of the Iraq invasion) Al Qaeda conducted more suicide attacks than all the years before 9/11 combined.

Western born and bred self-professed former Islamic radical Maajid Nawaz partly attributes "violence of white racists … experienced at home"[3] to his becoming ripe for radicalization. Indeed, it is readily apparent that members of Muslim communities have become drawn to the ideology our leaders denounce largely out of feeling threatened by common, taken for granted acts committed by Western societies. Janet Reitman, writing in *Rolling Stone* (a publication known for relaying dominant cultural attitudes), chronicles a central aspect of the effectiveness so called Jihadi recruitment efforts have is inextricably tying the cause of the fighters to the idea of persecution.

2 Robert Pape, "Dying to Win: The Strategic Logic of Suicide Terrorism" in *Approaches to Peace: A Reader in Peace Studies*, ed. David Barash, 3rd ed. (Oxford: Oxford University Press, 2014), 196.

3 Maajid Nawaz, "The Education of Jihadi John," op-ed *New York Times*, March 3, 2015.

Reitman states, "one of the conditions that makes hijra mandatory for Muslims is oppression by the country or system under which they live."[4] Notably in the same piece Reitman mentions the Obama administration's acknowledgement of the importance of "countering ISIS's effective social-media message" and quotes a now former perplexed Assistant Attorney General John Carlin as saying, "It's a war of ideas—we ought to be able to win. How do we explain that an ideology that's based on enslaving other people, killing women and children, is fundamentally nihilistic is one you shouldn't join?"[5] I hope to show that the tendency of assuming, while in battle, that one's ideology is morally sound without taking great pains to constantly make such superiority evident to a broader world underlies Carlin's perplexity.

Specifically, my points are meant to indicate that regrettable and unintended consequences like the rise of ISIS are an unsurprising result of Westerners lacking a clear cultural understanding of what they are actually fighting. I maintain that such a lack of clarity underscores and is largely responsible for their general willingness to uncritically accept morally questionable behavior which ultimately hampers achieving their professed objectives.

Issues in Present Need of Clarification

Before discussing my points further, it is helpful to first identify some such basic issues that are in need of clarification. Foremost among these is the question of how preservation of individual bodily existence is essential for winning an ideological battle. Western culture's uncritical acceptance of the latter as being necessarily connected to the former underlies and perpetuates the acts of violence we in the West are collectively responsible for. Indeed we can understand the loss of moral worth in terms of a scaffolding process that is ultimately spawned by the assumption that individual bodily existence should be preserved at all costs (even at the cost of clear moral standing). It is this assumption which underlies things like the permitting of torture, drone strikes that kill civilians, the denial of due process and so much else that ultimately makes attaining our professed objectives in fighting "radicals" more and more elusive. "We must kill them before they kill us" is a commonly accepted rationale made most prominent in recent years by the Bush doctrine of preemption which was an underlying basis of attempts made to galvanize the

4 Janet Reitman, "Teenage Jihad: Inside the World of American Kids Seduced by ISIS," *Rolling Stone,* April 9, 2015, 47.

5 Carlin quoted in Reitman, 42.

public to support the Iraq war as well as by America's use of rampant drone strikes—two readily accepted catalysts for the emergence of greater radicalism. I will show that the tendency to readily accept the notion that success in an ideological battle requires constant pursuit of individual physical survival (or doing all a people can to avoid the death of their individual members at the hands of "radicals") obfuscates the primary importance of moral worth in such a battle. What, in other words, we should clarify is the matter of why preserving physical existence (and thereby committing the violence that such efforts inevitably entail) is necessary for winning an ideological war.

For the purposes of my arguments, it is adequate to think of moral worth as being the absence of the performance of actions that can reasonably be thought of as seriously blameworthy insofar as they impact the well-being of others who are widely seen to possess moral standing. I do not mean to imply that moral worth can be understood solely in terms of what is absent from it but this minimal definition is most suitable for my purposes here of reaching conclusions that can be easily accepted by diverse members of Western society. From the above definition it would follow that torturing the family members of terrorism suspects simply to satisfy a public blood lust would be among the class of actions that undermines a country's moral worth.

It is notable that prima facie agreement in Western culture on the points that preserving individual bodily existence is not essential for winning an ideological battle yet the maintaining of moral worth is can be readily seen. Those willing to sacrifice themselves by dying for their country are, if nothing else, conventionally and institutionally revered as heroes. Furthermore, it is because Westerners have great confidence in their own culture's moral worth that relatively few of them question the overall legitimacy of Western countries having nuclear arms or launching drone strikes on unsuspecting targets—after all they are "the good guys" so such things are o.k. for them. This point is well noted in William Gay's discussion of the U.S. government's double standard regarding the atomic bomb.[6] It is clear that if those in the West did not place such a high premium on moral worth, we could not maintain the overall collective mental content and freedom from a burdening conscience about the violent acts committed in our name by our leaders. Uncritical acceptance however of the notion that preserving individual corporeal existence is essential in an ideological battle actually works against maintaining moral standing and thus realizing a peaceful order. This follows since such an acceptance enables

6 William Gay, "The New Reign of Terror: The Politics of Defining Weapons of Mass Destruction and Terrorism" in *Philosophical Perspectives on the War on Terror*, ed. Gail Presby (Amsterdam: Rodopi Press, 2007), 23–ff.

an attitude of complacency and also encouragement toward a culture's acts of violence which, in turn, tends to inevitably reduce moral standing. Consequently, this loss of moral standing intensifies an already existing violent dynamic which makes conflict resolution evasive.

Ultimately, to put my point in Gandhian terms, seeking individual physical preservation entails acting within the realm of physical force and not soul force.[7] It is only by remaining steadfast within the realm of soul force that we can keep from compromising (and thus muddying) our moral legitimacy. Maintaining moral legitimacy is essential for winning hearts and minds and thus succeeding (through clarifying and then resolving conflict) in a battle of ideology. Ultimately, all should agree, it is only the presence of moral legitimacy which can illuminate for all the good combatants from the bad ones (like those guilty of persecuting innocents) when different sides feel justified disrupting each other's peace. I maintain that once sufficient widespread consensus is reached on which combatants have the greater moral standing conflicts can be, if not resolved, at least pursued more fruitfully.

To summarize my main argument here: By uncritically accepting the notion that threats to our physical existence give us adequate reason for doing the things we do in our conflicts with "radicals" (a notion in tension with so much of our behavior and professed values) we inevitably sacrifice the moral standing needed for providing clarity and thus for resolving and prevailing in these conflicts. Such standing requires, if not outright eschewal of the above notion, much more serious consideration of its merits than we see in our culture.

On the Link between Seeking Physical Preservation and Compromising Moral Standard

Since a connection between the aim of preserving individual physical existences and losing moral standing is not immediately obvious, it is necessary here to offer an argument showing said connection. The seeking of continued individual physical existence involves primarily emphasizing, not adherence to moral principles, but the pursuit of consequences which are ultimately beyond our control (namely freedom from dying at the hands of our opponents). Given the myriad ways in which opponents can threaten our individual corporeal existences, seeking the continuation of on-going personal physical survival entails necessary departure from clear moral principles.

7 M.K. Gandhi, *Hind Swaraj*, quoted in Jack Homer, *The Gandhi Reader* (Bloomington: University of Indiana Press, 1956), 114.

Therefore, it is not surprising that our actions against "radicals" (motivated as we are by seeking to preserve physical existence) have involved violating norms like those calling on us to respect universal rights (e.g. not to be tortured or to be allowed due process). Nor is it surprising that the rationales offered for such violations typically involve scenarios like the ticking time bomb one which contain appeals to keep people from dying. Morality by its very nature, after all, calls on us to move away from thoughts of our own personal self-interests. An emphasis on personal physical survival (even when it is not on one's own) cannot but harbor a mentality that gives primary focus on satisfying personal self-interests given that no such interest is more basic than that of survival. Thus, such an emphasis tends to inevitably undermine moral standing.

That seeking, above all else, continuation of ongoing physical survival necessarily entails departure from clear moral principles is evident by the ease with which introductory students of ethics can think of situations in which it seems violating a given rigid moral principle is obviously justified. Alternatively, this point is evident by the standard problems that have confronted crude forms of utilitarianism. Invariably, such situations involve either keeping oneself or another from dying or violating cherished principles in pursuit of some supposed greater end. Thus, seeking continuation of on-going personal physical survival necessarily entails sacrificing moral standing (insofar as it implies that somethings are more important than moral standing). Moral standing, however, is something all sides accept the indispensable importance of. By now a paradox should be noticeable—by pursuing the goal that is moving us in our present day conflicts against "radicalism" we are undermining the prospect of having a legitimate basis for engaging in such conflicts in the first place. Therefore, Carlin's aforementioned perplexity seems inevitable given the nature of the actions of Western societies in their conflicts with "radicals."

The strength of the above argument can be illustrated by analogy. In arguing in favor of upholding absolute restrictions in war (and thus against torture and the killing of civilians to realize a greater good), Thomas Nagel enunciates the principle that "hostile treatment of any person must be justified in terms of something *about that* person which makes the treatment appropriate"[8] (emphasis in original). Accordingly, Nagel holds, "a perfectly natural" distinction between fighting clean and fighting dirty follows.[9] Nagel states:

8 Thomas Nagel, "War and Massacre," in *The Norton Introduction to Philosophy*, eds. Gideon Rosen, Alex Byrne, Joshua Cohen, and Seana Shiffrin (New York: Norton, 2015), 906.

9 Nagel "War and Massacre," 906.

> To fight dirty is to direct one's hostility or aggression not at its proper object, but at a peripheral target which may be vulnerable, and through which the proper object can be attacked indirectly.

From these points, Nagel concludes what is really wrong with, say, running an overly negative, "dirty" political campaign. The problem, Nagel says, with such campaigns is not related to issues of legality or the integrity of the electoral process, but that the methods of attack they involve are "irrelevant to the issue between you and your opponent, that in taking them up you would not be directing yourself to that which makes him an object of your opposition."[10] In other words, on this view we act morally wrong when in a conflict we are not directing our attack to the true target of our hostility (like, say, by harming civilian noncombatants) and focusing on what it is, exactly, that we find disagreeable about this target. If we are indeed fighting "a war of ideas" (as Carlin put it above), it cannot be the case that any group of flesh and blood, replaceable humans can be our true target. After all, no matter what the horrible things are that such a group does, unless the ideology motivating their actions is eradicated, we have not dealt with our true problem. As Nagel puts it further, in such situations we are not treating opponents as subjects but rather directing our hostile actions to them as individuals free from a wider moral context.[11] Indeed moral considerations are notably not evident (and certainly not treated as having the highest priority) when Western nations devise plans for engaging with individual "radicals." It cannot be overemphasized that it is ultimately (or should be) differences of morality that underlie the fight against "radicalism." Indeed the extent to which a culture moves away from seeing their conflicts as primarily moral ones is the extent to which their actions are not unequivocally seen to be those of the "good guys" and thus have a tendency to become recruiting tools for opponents. Ultimately, the lack of attempt to realize a real issue of contention enables Westerners to feel justified in engaging in the violent behavior that undermines their moral standing and thus perpetuates antipathy from others toward them.

Of course, it may be argued that some violence (e.g. killing) is morally acceptable provided that it is committed in situations that can legitimately be understood as exceptional (like when our lives are at risk) and are therefore such that otherwise binding moral codes that rule out violence do not apply. Indeed, this is the dominant understanding in Western culture of the violence

10 Nagel, "War and Massacre," 907.
11 Nagel, "War and Massacre," 907.

committed on our behalf toward "radicals" given the widespread belief that such individuals threaten our lives. The problem though for this argument is that, first, empirically it is clear that whenever violence has been collectively resorted to as a response to perceived threats from others, it has been virtually impossible to limit its presence to only the supposed clearly morally acceptable situations. Historic examples of cultures that have so limited their violent acts seem nonexistent. Furthermore, as I will argue below, it is not likely that our real issue with the "radicals" is that they pose threats to our continued physical existence. Therefore, focusing on these threats in our responses to the "radicals" becomes problematic in the way Nagel illustrates. Thus, even if it were granted that situations in which our physical existence is threatened are such that violence is morally permissible in them, by resorting to violence in the particular situations posed by our conflicts with "radicals" we are not addressing (and likely perpetuating) what the actual underlying issues are with them. Given these points, it is hardly surprising that we in the Western world see a seemingly never-ending cycle of violence and counter violence that our culture stays wrapped up in. As Gandhi puts it:

> To use brute-force ... means that we want our opponent to do by force that which we desire but he does not. And if such a use of force is justifiable, surely he is entitled to do likewise by us. And so we should never come to an agreement. We may simply fancy, like the blind horse moving in a circle around a mill, that we are making progress.[12]

Indeed one can find, in the great corpus of Gandhi's writings, many passages that indicate the disavowal of seeking physical existence above all else as the underlying basis of his thoughts on peace. He states, "The soul is omnipresent; why should she care to be confined within the cage-like body, or do evil and even kill for the sake of that cage?"[13] Elsewhere, in discussing the viability of responding nonviolently to Hitler, Gandhi states, "If Hitler is unaffected by my suffering, it does not matter. For I shall have lost nothing of worth. My honor is the only thing worth preserving. That is independent of Hitler's pity."[14] Given that there has been no shortage of attempts to compare present day "radical" leaders to Hitler, Gandhi's words seem no less relevant to our own present day conflicts than to a world riveted by World War II.

12 Gandhi quoted in Homer, 113–114.

13 Raghavan Iyer, ed. *The Moral and Political Writings of Mahatma Gandhi*, vol. 3, (Glocestershire: Claredon Press, 1986), 474.

14 Gandhi quoted in Homer, 334.

Takeaway for the Present-Day "War Against Radicalism"

The above points show, at the very least, the importance of clarifying what our issue really is with the "radicals" we are in conflict with. In other words, instead of pursuing the commonly asked question, "Who are we really fighting?" it would be more fruitful to determine what our issue really is with those we believe we should be fighting. Such a project can serve to allow us to notice previously unnoticed insights. Surely, the attractiveness of a new way of proceeding forward cannot be denied. Is there anything about such individuals as persons that makes the kind of hostile treatment Westerns administer to them justified?

Standard answers to this question, based on conventional understandings, lack clarity—a fact noticeable when these answers are considered more seriously. To reiterate, the common and visceral response to this question says "they are trying to kill us." However, this does not actually seem to be our true, underlying problem with the so-called "radicals" for if it were it would not seem that those willing to sacrifice their own physical existences (e.g. soldiers) could be thought of as upholding and defending what those in Western culture hold most dear. In other words, it is difficult to see how our hostile treatment of radicals can be justified on the grounds that such individuals are trying to kill us when we think of those of us who are willing to be killed by them to be doing something deserving of our greatest respect and honor. Therefore, dying at their hands cannot (or so it seems) be the kind of evil that justifies our hostile treatment.

As already noted, it seems likely that us assuming that our problem with the "radicals" consists entirely of them wanting to kill us has made the goal of realizing a world free of people trying to kill one another all the more elusive. Thus our commonly and uncritically accepted response to the question of what is it about the "radicals" that makes our hostile treatment of them justified actually seems to aggravate the underlying tensions we claim we seek to resolve. This is reason enough for this response to be reconsidered. Furthermore, no one worthy of listening to would seriously hold that it is simply their acceptance of certain beliefs that justifies such treatment on the part of the West.

It may seem that a more plausible response to the above question would say that the hostile treatment of "radicals" by the West is justified given the threat they clearly pose to innocent others (and not to any specific Western individuals). Thus, our actions can be said to be based on the non-selfish and morally acceptable effort to seek the personal well-being of others. We should consider however the degree to which those in Western society are able to accept civilian killings when they are perpetuated by their own leaders as well as the lack of consideration they show for the above mentioned issue of whether their attempts in dealing with "radicals" actually endanger more innocents than were ever initially threatened by the "radicals" themselves. These considerations make it difficult to think that it is really the protection of innocent life that can justify our hostile treatment of "radicals" as the value of such life can hardly be said to be our highest priority. In other words, our overall actions and beliefs regarding the deaths of innocent others make it difficult to believe that we really think harm to innocents is a wrong of such a magnitude that it justifies what we commonly do in fighting "radicals." It seems that as long as we believe the right ideology triumphs, we are willing to accept the loss of innocent life as necessary (and maybe even justified).

What's more is that an examination of the history of violently seeking the protection and defense of innocent life shows the actual pursuit of this objective by those in the West has been, if not counterproductive, then not ultimately effective. Thus it is not clear (even if we take a consequentialist view) how the hostile treatment we inflict on "radicals" is conducive to reaching the state of affairs we claim to seek and is therefore justified. The current example of the "war on radicalism" seems clearly to bear this out. By treating "radicals" in a hostile manner and thus violently seeking to protect the innocent lives of others, it seems plausible to think that at least as many (and probably more) innocent lives have been endangered than would be by non-hostile responses. There is no prima facie reason for thinking the innocent lives we endanger by our hostile responses should count any less than the ones we may be able to save by acting in a hostile fashion. Uncritically assuming that we are acting toward realizing moral goals without doing all that's possible to make our moral standing clear seems to make it inevitable that we will do things like launch drone strikes that kill civilians and indefinitely detain individuals without honoring their basic due process rights and thus engender greater hostility toward us. The current enemies of the West, after all, are said to be even more brutal toward innocents than the supposed original instigators of their hostile actions as these actions on the part of Westerns (allegedly in response to the threat posed by radicals) have seemingly served to elicit even more viciousness toward innocent others than those thought of as the original instigators. It is difficult to see any basis for thinking non-hostile responses toward the original instigators would have led to any worse kind of evolution (or even any such evolution at all). As Travis Meyer put it in commenting on the irony of how incidents like the My Lai and My Khe killings bolstered support for the Viet Cong and thus made the American mission in Southeast Asia all the more difficult, "Wars don't silence propagandists; they encourage them."[15]

15 Travis Meyer, "My Lai Remembered," letter to the editor, *New Yorker*, May 11, 2015, 3.

Thus even if we accept the assumption that Western responses to the "radicals" have been driven by the desire to protect the greatest amount of innocent life, it is unclear how the actual responses themselves have not undermined Western moral standing and have therefore actually threatened more innocents than would have otherwise been endangered. Moral standing indeed seems necessary for us to succeed in protecting the innocent in a way that is not marred by negative and worse (yet inevitable) consequences. Ultimately, it is difficult to see how our hostile treatment of "radicals" is justified on the basis of the threat they pose to the innocent lives of others (who are different from us) if the hostile treatment, itself, has made the goal of protecting innocent life, if not harder to reach, than no more of a reality. Therefore, it is questionable whether hostile treatment can be justified even by the threat "radicals" pose to the innocent lives of non-Westerners.

I want to be clear that my argument here is not intended to be a consequentialist defense of my position but rather based on how the clouding of moral standing has followed from the hostile treatment of "radicals" (even when that treatment is supposed to result from our quest to defend the innocent lives of others). Hostile treatment, at least the kind typically inflicted by the West, does not seem to be ultimately conducive to establishing overall moral worth (which we rightly hold to be of the greatest priority) and so it actually seems to hamper the realization of whatever moral goals (like saving as many live as possible) we may think justifies it. As noted above, this may be the case because once hostility is inflicted toward opponents, it is impossible to keep it in any kind of "proper" check.

A Better Understanding of Our Issue with the "Radicals"

It is, in fact, common for grievances in the West about "radicals" to be expressed in terms of their eschewal of modern values (e.g. giving science an honored place in society or respecting the tenets of a pluralistic society). Indeed, it is plausible that it such eschewal and the impacts it is perceived to have on others that is really underlying Western clashes with the "radicals" (that this, in other words, is the basis of our ideological conflict). This point relates to Mar Peter-Raoul's points concerning democracy as a remedy for terrorism.[16] Just as we can say it is a lack of democratic values that makes individuals ripe for engaging in terrorist activities, it makes sense to think that it is the perceived threat "radicals" pose to such values that underlies our grievances with them.

16 Mar Peter-Raoul in Presby, 67-ff.

Furthermore, Pape's extensive survey of terrorist acts over a 23 year period led him to conclude that democratic states are "uniquely" targeted by the kinds of radicals we claim to be at war with.[17] This point underscores the notion that our conflicts with "radicals" (in some real, underlying sense) stem from their rejection of liberal democratic values. Consider Emanuela Ceva's characterization of the liberal project:

> (The) basic idea I take to be un-controversially essential to the liberal project (is) of public justification. This idea concerns the standard liberal rationale for the public order as consisting of the establishment of a stable framework within which individuals, understood as the holders of rights and the bearers of the corresponding duties, can jointly pursue their possibly diverging life plans (and related interests and conceptions of the good). The public order is, therefore, justified to limit the arbitrary power of individuals and to secure cooperation among them, as free and equal persons, in the pursuit of their different and possibly conflicting life plans on terms they can accept on moral grounds. All participants in the public order hold a moral claim right against the institutions constitutive of that order (the state's institutions) that all social and political rules be justified to them.[18]

It is crucial to consider in what ways "radicals" really threaten modern values and how we can ensure the triumph of these values given the supposed threats posed. As Ceva's characterization and subsequent discussion makes clear, since the liberal project necessitates justification that is public this kind of justification need also be minimal (in the sense of not depending on complicated systems of metaphysics and values). Only this kind of justification can be in line with the liberal affirmation of freedom and equality of all. It is clear that this kind of understanding of the proper society is absent within the ideology of the "radicals" we are fighting against.

It stretches credulity however to claim such "radicals" can ever gain institutional power to such an extent that they will be able to impose their fundamentalist values (through, say, the mechanism of Sharia law) on the world at large. Therefore, responding to the perceived threat "radicals" pose to Western values in a way akin to how we would respond to a worldwide killer virus outbreak (e.g. attempting to physically eradicate it from existence) is neither

17 Pape in Barash, 195.

18 Emanuela Ceva, *Interactive Justice: A Proceduralist Approach to Value Conflict in Politics* (New York: Routledge, 2016), 16.

warranted nor (as we've seen) productive (given facts about recruitment tools). Moreover, in seeking to create a world of widespread adherence to correct values (of any kind) force seems powerless. Force, after all, is unable to influence the inner desire for having the correct ideological understanding. Together these points and the earlier point that preserving individual physical existence cannot be thought of as the main goal in battling radicals have profound implications for how the West should go about administering current conflicts.

Specifically, Westerners cannot base their strategies in such conflicts primarily on considerations of individual physical survival. Such a focus seemingly does nothing to help in advancing liberal values. Indeed it is not surprising that commonly adopted methods of fighting "radicals" (motivated as they are by the aim to preserve bodily existence) have been criticized for undermining liberal values. Doctrines of pre-emption (based as they are on the "kill them before they kill us" rationale) seem particularly difficult to justify if our actual problem with the "radicals" we are fighting is their eschewal of liberal values. What's more is that even considerations of the individual physical survival of others cannot be what Westerners primarily base their strategies of dealing with the "radicals" on. Any viable strategy must be able to satisfactorily account for what the real threat is that "radicals" represent. Thus formulating such a strategy would require strong departure from current conventional ways of thinking in the West.

Central to this different way of thinking would be a focus on determining how to handle threats posed by others without needlessly compromising moral standing. Thus such thinking would involve consideration of how to develop ideal character traits like fearlessness regarding our own mortality and freedom from bitterness (which underlies our desire to kill off opponents) toward those seeking to harm us. Given that it is ultimately moral worth that should characterize the triumphant side (above any other qualities), this changed way of thinking would surely be most conducive for ultimate victory.

More concretely, for Western societies to pursue a better way forward in dealing with "radicals" it is incumbent on our social institutions to play a more proactive role in developing, among citizens, stronger fealty to liberal values. When strong and fearless adherence to such values is in place, it seems clear that individuals would be less likely to compromise the moral principles that spring from those values and also be willing to sacrifice at the highest level to protect them. It is beyond the scope of this chapter to discuss specific things that can be done in developing the types of citizens I have in mind. However, given the commonly heard lament that Western societies are comprised of individuals who are content to allow a tiny few to engage in the necessary sacrifices for the greater whole, the viability of the new way forward I suggest would seem uncontroversial.

Conclusion

Constant media bombardment of images of beheadings and hostage sieges notwithstanding, uncritically accepting the idea that we in the West are the "good guys" (or have genuine moral standing) when we engage with "radicals" is damaging to our prospects for realizing a more peaceful order. Clarification of issues related to what we are actually fighting can make our moral standing more evident and thus us less prone to perpetuate the very things we claim to be fighting against. Specifically, it is crucial to understand that regarding the preservation of physical existence as the proper motivation of our efforts in fighting "radicals" is both counterproductive and not in line with the actual nature of present day realities. Additionally, regarding moral standing (in contrast to continued physical existence) as something worthy of preserving at all costs seems to hold great and largely unnoticed promise. Thinking beyond the immediate survival of individuals and adopting this kind of broader, contextual perspective is necessary for moving beyond the seemingly endless cycles of violence and retaliations we have been living in. As long as we remain stuck in cycles of this sort the prospects for more fully realizing a peaceful order will inevitably stay dim.

Bibliography

Barash, David, ed. *Approaches to Peace: A Reader in Peace Studies*. 3rd ed. Oxford: Oxford University Press, 2014.

Ceva, Emanuela. *Interactive Justice: A Proceduralist Approach to Value Conflict in Politics*. New York: Routledge, 2016.

Homer, Jack, ed. *The Gandhi Reader*. Bloomington: University of Indiana Press 1956.

Iyer, Raghavan, ed. *The Moral and Political Writings of Mahatma Gandhi* Vol. 3. Glocestershire: Claredon Press, 1986.

Presby, Gail, ed. *Philosophical Perspectives on the War on Terror*. Amsterdam: Rodopi Press, 2007.

Rosen, Gideon, Alex Byrne, Joshua Cohen, and Seana Shiffrin, eds. *The Norton Introduction to Philosophy*. New York: Norton, 2015.

CHAPTER 8

Just War Perspectives on Police Violence

David Speetzen

Introduction

The increasingly common spectacle of police violence in the American media has, at long last, sparked a national conversation about the use and abuse of force by law enforcement officers. Much of this conversation has rightly focused on structural problems in the American criminal justice system; militarization, overcriminalization, and racial discrimination all have a role to play in explaining at least some of the highly publicized cases of violence that have put law enforcement in the spotlight. But these cases and the discourse surrounding them have also made evident deep disagreements in our society about the purposes and limits of police force. Two people viewing the same use of force can come away with dramatically divergent evaluations of the suspect's and the officer's actions—where some see an entirely appropriate response to resistance, others see police brutality and excessive force. The phenomenon is persistent, and striking. It suggests that many citizens, and even some police, harbor serious misconceptions about when the use of force is justified, and how much force is justified when it is.

This is hardly surprising. Even in the academic sphere, the ethics of police force is undertheorized.[1] In this paper, I aim to set out a normative account of police force that relies on some general limitations on the acceptable use of force borrowed from the Just War Tradition.[2] The Just War Tradition is a body of thought comprising centuries of scholarship on the ethical evaluation of violence at all levels of conflict. One of its central achievements is to have identified, analyzed, and consolidated most, and perhaps all, of the many factors relevant to determining whether uses of force are just (morally permissible)

1 The philosophical literature lacks much in the way of sustained and direct attention to the issue—although see Joseph Betz, "Police Violence," in *Moral Issues in Police Work*, eds. Frederick A. Elliston and Michael Feldberg (New Jersey: Rowman and Allanheld, 1985), 177–196, and John Kleinig, "Legitimate and Illegitimate Uses of Police Force," *Criminal Justice Ethics* 33, no. 2 (2014): 83–103.

2 See Gregory M. Reichberg, Henrik Syse, and Endre Begby, eds., *The Ethics of War: Classic and Contemporary Readings*. (Malden, MA: Blackwell Publishing, 2006).

 | DOI 10.1163/9789004361911_010

or unjust (morally wrong). Although large-scale uses of force, like war, are the central preoccupation of most Just War Theory, scholars working in the field have always recognized that violence between states and violence between individuals are subject to some of the same conditions. While acknowledging that other moral categories may be relevant, I generate my normative account of police force from the concepts of necessity, proportionality, and just cause.

After this account is in place, we will be in a better position to diagnose some of the misconceptions that inform public discourse about police violence in American society today. Exposing these misconceptions is crucial because, when widely shared, they support and sustain police violence. First, they directly contribute to police violence by influencing officers' behavior on the job. Like everyone else raised in and living in our society, police officers absorb the messages that society sends them about the appropriate use of force in ways that training cannot alter completely. Of course, the vast majority of police officers have good intentions, and indeed, become officers out of a desire to help others and a respect for justice. But when they misunderstand their role and the moral limitations on their uses of force, they are prone to make mistakes—sometimes tragic mistakes—when interacting with citizens. I hasten to add here that it is precisely because these misconceptions are so widespread that we should hesitate before placing blame on police officers specifically. To say that an officer engaged in an unjust act of force is to say that the officer has done something wrong—but it is not yet to say that he is morally culpable for it. We can hardly place full blame on police officers for certain instances of brutality or excessive force when current popular, and even legal, understandings of these concepts permit them.

Second, and to my mind even more problematic, is the way misconceptions about police violence affect public opinion and, in turn, public policy and legislation. If many people have mistaken and unacceptably permissive attitudes toward the use of force by police, they will be unable to recognize police brutality and excessive force when it occurs and so will feel no need to hold political leaders, police agencies, or individual officers to account. Worse, they may lead privileged members of society to dismiss or even ridicule the legitimate complaints of disempowered minorities who suffer a disproportionate amount of police violence.

In the end, I will suggest that these misconceptions, combined with structural issues mentioned above, point us toward a "contingently pacifist" approach to police violence.[3] While traditional pacifism is widely rejected because of its

3 Contingent pacifism is still an emerging line of inquiry; terminology differs between authors. See Andrew Fiala, "Contingent Pacifism and Contingently Pacifist Conclusions," *Journal of*

complete eschewal of all violence, contingent pacifists concede that violence is sometimes morally justified.[4] What sets contingent pacifism apart is its avowedly skeptical stance toward particular wars (on the grounds that they will only rarely satisfy standard criteria for a just war), and its avowedly abolitionist stance toward the institutional forces pushing society into unjust wars. I am unsure whether we have license to draw contingently pacifist *conclusions* about police force—we should not, I think, be convinced that the use of force by police is *only* justifiable in theory, or that it is *almost never* justified in practice, as contingent pacifists say about wars. But I do think the misconceptions and structural issues surrounding police violence in American society certainly warrant enough skepticism to claim that the amount of force put to use by police in the United States today is much, much higher than it should be.

Police Force: A Normative Account

For a war to be just, it must be necessary, it must be proportionate, and it must have a just cause. A *just cause* is a reason or purpose that could license a war, at least in principle. The term is ambiguous between two related ideas: on one reading, a just cause is the injury or wrongdoing to which war might be a permissible response, the rationale or grounds for which the war is to be fought. On another reading, a just cause is a legitimate purpose or aim for which a war may be fought.[5] The two are related, because the only aims that may be pursued by means of war are those that involve averting or rectifying some injury or wrongdoing. The general consensus, for instance, is that a state may permissibly use war in order to defend itself from aggression. In the first interpretation, the just cause for war is the act of aggression itself—a wrongful attack on one's country could potentially license the resort to war. In the second interpretation, the just cause for war is defense—protection of one's country against attack is a legitimate purpose for fighting a war. Likewise, if

Social Philosophy 45, no. 4 (Winter 2014): 463–477; Larry May, *After War Ends: A Philosophical Perspective* (Cambridge: Cambridge University Press, 2012); James Sterba, "Reconciling Pacifists and Just War Theorists," *Social Theory and Practice* 18, no. 1 (Spring 1992): 21–38.

4 For the classic rejection of absolute pacifism, see Jan Narveson, "Pacifism: A Philosophical Analysis," *Ethics* 75, no. 4 (1965): 259–271.

5 Cf. Jeff McMahan, *Killing in War* (Oxford: Clarendon Press, 2009), 5. "The notion of a just cause is variously understood in the literature. As I understand it, a just cause is an aim that satisfies two conditions: (1) that it may permissibly be pursued by means of war, and (2) that the reason why this is so is at least in part that those against whom the war is fought have made themselves morally *liable* to military attack."

a humanitarian intervention is just, its just cause would be either the target state's aggression against its own people, or the aim of ending that aggression.

The use of force by police is also subject to a just cause condition, which is only to say that specific instances of police force require a legitimate ground or purpose. Two just causes are immediately evident, and parallel just causes for war: self-defense and defense of others. Police officers have a right to defend themselves and others against aggression. Similar rights are afforded to private citizens. It might be argued that on-duty police officers' rights to self-defense should extend further than those of ordinary citizens. For instance, while some jurisdictions impose a duty of retreat on citizens who can escape an attack without resorting to the use of force, a case could be made for allowing officers the privilege of "standing their ground" even when it is possible for them to retreat. A case might also be made for officers having more extensive rights to defend others. But I want to set these issues aside here, because even if there are some differences between officers' and private citizens' defensive rights to use force, there is a more important difference to consider.

Many people appear to believe that self-defense and defense of others are the *only* just causes for the use of police force. This is a mistake. Unlike ordinary citizens, police officers are charged with enforcing laws, and doing so may require the use of force against suspects even when they are not directly threatening the officer or anyone else with harm. To see why, consider the case of a trespasser who refuses to vacate another's property. The trespasser might take no aggressive action, but simply refuse to move. If property rights are to be enforced in such cases, police must be authorized to physically remove even a passively resisting suspect at some point. Or, consider a suspect who has been detained and tries to escape. The escape might involve no threat to the officers or to bystanders—but without permission to physically restrain him, it would be impossible to keep him in custody.

My suggestion, therefore, is that resistance to legal commands be taken as a kind of provisional just cause for the use of force by police; in fact, it would appear to be *the* distinctive just cause for police force, because of the significant overlap between officers' and private citizens' defensive rights. "Legal commands" here refers to commands that police officers are legally authorized to give a citizen, under the circumstances in which the command was given. Thus, resistance to an officer's command to a homeowner to "open the door and let me in" would be a just cause for the use of force if the officer had a warrant, and if not, then not. I say that resistance to legal commands should be taken as only a "provisional" just cause, because it is certainly possible for a legal system to grant police officers the authority to issue commands that, from a moral perspective, they should not have. Imagine, for instance, that police officers were given the authority to arbitrarily detain and search citizens or enter their homes without any probable cause. Under such a legal system, resistance to legal commands would not necessarily constitute a just cause for the use of force, since those commands, however legal, remain unjust. But an inquiry into the morally appropriate limits on police authority would take me beyond the scope of this paper, so in this instance I will use the current—although surely imperfect—legal standards as an approximate baseline for the discussion here.

Police commonly divide "resistance" to commands into four broad (and admittedly vague) categories: passive resistance (e.g., not moving when and how police command), verbal resistance (vocally refusing to obey, making threats), passive physical resistance (running away, going limp), and active physical resistance (struggling against, striking, or using firearms or other projectile weapons).[6] Resistance to police officers' legal commands, in any of the above senses, provides them with just cause to use force.

But, as with war, the possession of a just cause is only one condition on the use of force: resistance to legal commands does no more than make a suspect *potentially* liable to its use. Two limiting conditions on police violence remain: necessity and proportionality.[7] The necessity condition requires that police officers use force against resisting suspects only as a last resort. Now, this does not necessarily imply that officers must actually attempt other means to overcome a suspect's resistance, if it is clear that no other means would be sufficient to ensure compliance. Nevertheless, whenever actions besides the use of force could ensure compliance, the use of force is unnecessary, and so morally impermissible. Additionally, the necessity condition applies not only to the initiation of violence, but also to its escalation. The assumption here isn't simply that the use of force should be a last resort, but that the minimum amount of force necessary to ensure compliance should be used, and no more.

The proportionality condition requires that the use of force be "worth it," in the sense that the morally relevant benefits of that use of force outweigh its morally relevant harms. This is crucial, because it is possible for the use of police force to be necessary to secure compliance with a legal command, and yet be too harmful to be just. Suppose that an officer encounters a robbery suspect

6 Characterization of the categories of resistance differ from one agency to another. See William Terrill, *Police Coercion: Application of the Force Continuum* (New York: LFB Scholarly Publishing, 2001), esp. 62–63.

7 On the application of necessity and proportionality to self-defensive uses of force, see David Rodin, *War and Self-Defense* (Oxford: Clarendon Press, 2002), 40–43.

who flees with stolen goods when he is ordered to stop. Suppose further that the only way for the officer to make the suspect stop and recover the goods is to shoot him.[8] In such a case, the proportionality condition requires us to weigh the morally relevant benefits of allowing the suspect to flee against the morally relevant harms of shooting him. Presumably, however much harm would be prevented by recovering the goods does not outweigh the value of the suspect's life. There are some potential exceptions: particularly dangerous criminals might threaten so much harm to others that killing them would do far less harm than good—but these are not the usual cases. When killing a fleeing suspect is justified, it is so because it satisfies not only the just cause and necessity conditions but the proportionality condition as well.

Before using this account to highlight some of the problems with the way American society conceptualizes and institutionalizes the use of force by police, I want to introduce stipulative definitions for the terms "police brutality" and "excessive force." These terms are used in different ways in different contexts. But one advantage of offering a philosophical account of police violence framed at a high level of generality is that it can clarify the main ideas behind terms such as these. I will understand the term "police brutality" to refer to the use of force by police in the absence of a just cause. In such cases, police are using force for reasons other than defense of self, defense of others, or even in response to legal commands. It is a straightforward case of abuse of power, and so warrants the harsher term "brutality." "Excessive force," on the other hand, presupposes that some level of force might have been justified, if only in principle, but that the amount of force actually used exceeded the permissible amount. So I shall use the term "excessive force" to refer to police violence that is unnecessary to secure safety and compliance, or disproportionate relative to the threat of harm.

Misconceptions about Just Cause

Several misconceptions about just cause for police force inhabiting public discourse lead to more permissive attitudes toward police force than are warranted. Perhaps the most common misconception concerns what qualifies as "resistance" by a suspect. Many people, including some police officers, appear to take disrespect as a just cause for police force.[9] Of course, there is an

8 Cf. Betz, "Police Violence," 179.

9 For a useful empirical treatment, see William C. Pizio, *Police Officers' Encounters with Disrespectful Citizens* (El Paso: LFB Scholarly Publishing, 2012).

impersonal understanding of "respect" that simply identifies it with "compliance," from which we can reach the tautological conclusion that all disrespect is noncompliance, and so is a just cause for the use of force by definition. But other forms of disrespect—offensive gestures, profanity, personal insults, derogatory remarks, eye rolling, and so on—are sometimes taken to justify the use of force when they should not be. Call these forms of disrespect "personal" disrespect. Personal disrespect often accompanies resistance, but it is not the same thing.

The claim is not that suspects do nothing wrong when they insult police. Most police officers in most situations are entitled to basic courtesy. Nor is the claim that suspects can't make themselves liable to force through words alone: a verbal refusal to comply with an officer's legal command is a just cause for force (although force is not often fully justified; immediately responding to verbal resistance is often unnecessary and/or disproportionate). Instead, I am claiming that personal disrespect does not provide a just cause for the use of force. This is important, because the phrase "he had it coming" is a common one in discussions of particular cases of police violence, and it often seems to indicate that the speaker believes that the suspect's disrespectful attitude, demeanor, or actions somehow justified physical retaliation by an officer or, at any rate, that the suspect should have anticipated the officer's violent response and so has brought it on himself.

Another common misconception about applying the just cause condition to police force concerns the use of force to deter future resistance. It is sometimes argued that a "show of force" against one suspect will convince other suspects not to resist, thereby lessening the total amount of force officers will need to use overall. The argument can be applied to both individual uses of deterrent force, and to the general use of force by whole agencies. At the individual level, officers in a particular scenario might use force against one suspect in order to prevent onlookers or other suspects from intervening or resisting, now or in the future. At the broader municipal and federal level, officers can be assured of more compliance from the public at large by making their willingness to use force generally known. So it might be thought that the purpose of "keeping people in line" could, at some level, provide a just cause for the use of force.

But we should not accept deterrence as a just cause for two reasons. First, because the concept of a just cause presupposes that the one made liable to the use of force was made liable through injury or wrongdoing that he committed—the person who incurs the just use of force incurs it because of his own actions. To argue that deterrence is a just cause is to render people liable to the use of force, or to the use of more force, by reference to the wrongdoing of other people. It is not that this suspect's resistance doesn't justify force—it's that other people's resistance doesn't justify using force against him, and it doesn't justify using more force against him than is necessary to overcome his own resistance.

Second, it is important to notice that the resistance by others that is taken to justify force against this suspect is only possible, and not actual, resistance.[10] Allowing the just cause condition to include the prevention of resistance that has not even occurred yet establishes a very permissive and overly flexible rationale for resorting to force. On the one hand, it is impossible to know how much, or even whether, an act of force will deter future resistance, and so it is impossible to demonstrate, even in retrospect, whether that force was necessary or proportionate. On the other hand, it is worth pointing out that deterrent uses of force can backfire, and provoke the very resistance they are trying to prevent. Onlookers and surrounding suspects, even entire communities, can be moved to resist by seeing police use force against suspects they do not perceive as liable to violence, or liable to as much violence as was used against them.

Likewise, criminality, or having committed a crime, does not by itself make someone liable to the use of police force.[11] This is another common misconception: that those who have committed a crime *deserve* harsh treatment at the hands of the police—what is sometimes referred to as "street justice." In some cases of police violence, police departments have been known to release evidence of the suspect's criminality to the public when their officers are accused of brutality in an effort to sway public opinion. Such appeals would be ineffective if many people did not assume that the commission of a crime renders one liable to the use of punitive police force. To be sure, criminal actions may make one liable to harsh treatment at the hands of the state; but suspects have strong rights preventing such treatment until after they have been convicted through the due process of law. Even if retribution is a viable justification for legal punishment, police are not judges or juries, and they are likely at times to be acting out of aggression, bias, self-interest, or other motives inappropriate to the administration of retributive justice. The list of just causes for the use of force by police does not include punishment.

10 I do not mean to exclude the permissibility of preemptive uses of force against imminent threats. For a standard just war treatment of anticipatory attack and the impermissibility of uses of force against merely *possible,* rather than imminent or actual threats, see Michael Walzer, *Just and Unjust Wars: A Moral Argument with Historical Illustrations,* 5th ed. (New York: Basic Books, 2015), 74–85.

11 Betz, "Police Violence," 177–179.

Misconceptions about Necessity

Discourse about police violence is also prone to a number of important misconceptions about how to understand the necessity and proportionality conditions. Before addressing them directly, it will be useful to explain how necessity and proportionality are operationalized in police practice through the widely used framework of the "force continuum."[12] In its most basic form, the force continuum ranks specific kinds of police force, or "methods of control," along a continuum from least to most forceful. At the low end of the continuum—or perhaps at its logical limit—are verbally "forceful" means of gaining compliance: requests, outright commands, and threats. Although not technically "force" in the sense I am using here, these are the starting point for escalation. Beyond verbal means are various kinds and degrees of physical force: (1) restraint, including pat downs, grabs, holds, and the use of handcuffs or zip ties; (2) pain-compliance techniques such as joint locks, pushing, and takedowns; (3) bodily impact methods, like punching, kicking, and so on; and (4) object impact methods, in which officers use pepper spray, batons, tasers, or firearms. As with the categories of suspect resistance, these levels of violence are broad and can be made more precise by examining different techniques within each level, as well as contextual elements of an encounter that might make certain techniques more harmful than they would otherwise be.

In principle, the force continuum provides a useful framework for ensuring that officers are more likely to respond to resistance with necessary and proportionate force. By proceeding from least to most forceful means of overcoming resistance, officers can assess whether escalation from one category of force to the next is necessary and proportionate. However, in some instantiations and training programs, it can mislead officers about the amount of force that is actually justified during encounters with resisting suspects. Many portrayals of the force continuum correlate different levels of force with the different kinds of resistance outlined above. For instance, some portrayals of the force continuum associate passive resistance with restraint and pain-compliance techniques, and active or aggressive resistance with bodily impact methods and lethal force.

This is problematic for two reasons. First, it can lead some to believe that active resistance *automatically* justifies, or should even trigger, the use of high

12 See Terrill, *Police Coercion,* and William Terrill, Eugene A. Paoline III, and Jason Ingram, *Assessing Police Force Policy and Outcomes* (final technical report draft, National Institute of Justice, 2012), accessed September 25, 2016, https://www.ncjrs.gov/App/Publications/abstract.aspx?ID=259826.

levels of force, when lower levels of force might have successfully overcome even very violent levels of resistance. This interpretation amounts to disregarding the necessity condition altogether. Second, it can lead some to think of proportionality solely in terms of the amount of force being used on either side of the confrontation, rather than the overall balance of morally relevant benefits and harms the officer's use of force is likely to produce. I explain these problems in more detail below, but it is worth noting that the primary instrument for instructing officers in the use of force can be easily misunderstood in ways that support the following misconceptions.

Consider an armed suspect who has been cornered by police, who have him surrounded. The suspect is pointing a gun in the general direction of the officers, who have taken cover behind their vehicles and nearby buildings. Perhaps the suspect has already fired a few shots at them, but is not presently shooting. Many people appear to believe that the police would be morally justified in returning fire and killing the suspect. After all, he is resisting and is using deadly force to do so. On some interpretations of the force continuum, moreover, the mere fact that he is engaged in lethal resistance automatically licenses the use of deadly force against him. But the necessity condition is not a blunt instrument. It does not license the use of equal or superior force against any resisting suspect in all cases—instead, it requires that no less forceful means be sufficient to overcome the resistance. In the scenario described, it might still be possible to persuade the suspect to drop the weapon and surrender, and if it is, then the police violate the necessity condition by firing on him.

Naturally, we can add details to the case to make the resort to force appear more or less necessary. If the officers have no cover, or if there are innocent citizens around who are in immediate danger, and if attempts to persuade the suspect to surrender are likely to result in the death of officers or those citizens, then wounding or killing the suspect with firearms might be the only viable way to ensure compliance with their commands (without violating the proportionality condition, discussed more below). On the other hand, if no citizens are at risk and the officers are well protected, then there is ample time to engage the suspect through less forceful means, notwithstanding his use of a lethal weapon to resist. Obviously, the details matter.[13] But the point I am

13 A common refrain in this connection holds that when the use of firearms is called for, police should attempt to wound suspects rather than kill them. But the kind of accuracy and precision needed to reliably shoot a suspect in the arm or the leg, rather than the torso, is impossible except in the most favorable conditions—a calm, stationary officer firing at an immobile target at close range—and difficult even then. In general, conditions that license the use of firearms would have to be urgent and extreme enough that

making here is that the fact that the suspect is using a lethal weapon does not *automatically* license deadly force against him, as many appear to believe.

This point is essential to understanding contemporary discourse about police force, because in the opposing view, being able to categorize a suspect's resistance as potentially lethal (however broadly that term is understood) allows discussants to ignore the morally relevant particularities of the case at hand. "The suspect raised his gun and so I shot him," even if true, does not necessarily justify the killing if other means of gaining compliance were at the officer's disposal—a fact often neglected in discussions of particular cases of police violence. As I said, the force continuum contributes to this misunderstanding when it correlates general categories of resistance with forceful responses that, in the final analysis, might not have been necessary in a given case.

But our discourse about police violence commonly ignores the necessity condition for two other reasons as well. On one hand, commentators (and some officers) frequently downplay, dismiss, or simply fail to recognize possible alternatives to the use of force—including de-escalation, negotiation, and retreat—because they view force as the only, or at any rate the primary, instrument for dealing with resistance at police disposal. Second, and perhaps more importantly to police practice, officers are under no legal obligation to seek non-forceful or less forceful means of overcoming resistance.[14] In short, the problem I am identifying with the force continuum—that it makes no demands on officers to use force, or higher levels of force only as a last resort—is manifested in the law itself. Officers who are not held legally liable for failing to pursue de-escalation or non-forceful means of dealing with active resistance from suspects are much less likely to seek out and use those means, and so much more likely to use unnecessary levels of force.

Misconceptions about Proportionality

Finally, the discourse surrounding police violence harbors some misconceptions about the proportionality condition. Some of these misconceptions are

---

the likelihood and the risks of missing the suspect entirely are already unusually high, and so most police are trained to fire at a suspect's center mass. While I concede that aiming elsewhere might be called for in some scenarios, I believe it is much more important to focus on officers' decisions to use firearms in the first place.

14 Urey W. Patrick and John C. Hall, *In Defense of Self and Others: Issues, Facts & Fallacies—The Realities of Law Enforcement's Use of Deadly Force,* 2nd ed. (Durham: Carolina Academic Press, 2010), 47–50.

more superficial than others. As I mentioned above, an oversimple reading of the force continuum encourages many to believe that proportionality is a matter of matching force with force—an officer's use of a firearm against a suspect is proportionate *because* the suspect is also using a firearm; or, alternately, the officer's use of deadly force is proportionate *because* the suspect is also using deadly force. The intuitive appeal of this morally problematic stance is inscribed in the adage, "Don't bring a knife to a gun fight." But it is important to see that it is not the quanta of force on either side of the confrontation, at least not in any direct sense. What the proportionality condition requires is that the morally relevant benefits of using a firearm against the suspect outweigh the relevant harms. This means that even if an officer has a just cause to use force (a suspect is resisting), and even if a given level of force would be necessary to secure compliance (no lesser force would achieve that end), the use of that kind of force may simply do more harm than good.

Even when the proportionality condition is correctly understood by reference to force's benefits and harms, rather than its degree of forcefulness, considerable misconceptions remain. These misconceptions result from a failure to appreciate the full range and weight of the relevant considerations. First, many people appear to sharply discount or dismiss entirely the benefit of preserving a suspect's life and well-being. As I mentioned above, one impulse is to assume that criminality alone makes one liable to force or liable to more force, because if one has committed a serious crime one deserves punishment, including harsh treatment by police. Or, more disturbingly, some people believe that by committing crimes one thereby diminishes the moral worth of one's own life. An implication of this view is that it is less wrong to murder a criminal than it is to murder someone who obeys the law. I will not argue against this view here, although I think it is clearly wrong. Instead, I will point out only that in conjunction with another common impulse, it becomes very dangerous. It is surely a mistake to equate those *suspected* of crimes with those *convicted* of crimes. And for all the use the expression "innocent until proven guilty" receives in discussions about how our criminal justice system operates in other respects, many people believe that police officers are usually in a position to know whether suspects are guilty. When disregard for the lives and well-being of criminals is joined to a general assumption that all suspects are justly treated like criminals, anyone detained by police becomes worthy of harsh treatment for that reason alone. This, I hope it is evident, is an approach to police violence practically begging for brutality and excessive force.

A second misconception results from a failure to look beyond the suspect when weighing the harms of the use of force against its benefit. Of course, no one neglects to consider bystanders. Opening fire in a crowd of people in order to prevent a dangerous suspect from escaping is precisely the kind of situation most people recognize as a genuine moral dilemma, one whose resolution depends on: How thick is the crowd? How dangerous is the suspect? Is hitting the suspect without hitting innocents even possible, and if so, how likely? And so on.

What I have in mind are the broader harms that result from the use of police force—harms primarily to the suspect's family that may result from the suspect's injury or death, but also to the community and to the effectiveness of future law enforcement. Even if the suspect were to have made himself a criminal and therefore (on the erroneous view above) devalued the moral worth of his own life by committing a crime, his actions would not thereby lessen the moral weight of his family and friends' grief. Nor would his actions negate the moral importance for officers and agencies to preserve positive and constructive relationships with the communities they police. Although these harms may be relatively slight in comparison to direct physical harm to suspects, officers, and bystanders, they are not negligible. At the margins, the way police officers use force has an impact beyond those immediately involved in the confrontation. Harms that might have seemed proportionate within that narrow context could, in the long run, decrease trust and confidence in the police to such an extent that it provokes higher levels of resistance—and in some situations, active aggression—against law enforcement and its institutions. From the perspective of police agencies and their longstanding presence in a community, particular instances of police force cannot and should not be assessed in isolation from their broader effects.

Third, public discourse surrounding police violence displays misconceptions about the benefits of using force in response to resistance. On the one hand, it is easy to slip into the too-easy assumption that once a suspect is resisting, it does not matter what the content of the officer's command was, so long as it was a command the officer was legally authorized to give. What is important, at that stage of the process, is ensuring compliance—it is the resistance to a command itself that has become the problem, rather than the purpose for which the command was given. But, in fact, compliance with legal commands is of greater moral benefit in some cases than in others; in some cases, very little or no harm at all will result from a suspect's failure to comply with a legal command, while in others, compliance might be a matter of life of death. It would be a mistake to think that differences in the moral importance of the command make no difference to the justifiability of the use of force. Police force can be excessive even when it is a necessary means to overcome resistance to a legal command, if the amount of force far exceeds the relative importance of compliance with the command.

The Contingent Pacifist Approach

Within the Just War Tradition, so-called "traditional" pacifism is widely regarded as an implausible approach to the moral questions surrounding war because its prohibition against the use of force is both absolute and categorical: force is *never* acceptable at *any* level of conflict. But few pacifists actually adopt such a strong stance. Contingent pacifism is the view that (1) war is not wrong *in principle*; but (2) most or all wars do in fact happen to be wrong. So described, contingent pacifism is neither absolute (because it concedes the possibility of actual just wars), nor categorical (because it makes no claims about the use of force at lower levels of conflict). I do not want to suggest that we ought to draw contingent pacifist *conclusions* from my arguments above; but I do want to suggest that those arguments justify a contingent pacifist *approach* to questions surrounding police violence. To see the difference, it will be helpful to articulate two different strands of contingent pacifism that have come to the fore in contemporary just war literature: just war pacifism and anti-war pacifism.

Just war pacifists focus on analyzing the general moral conditions under which war could be justified, and then offer arguments for the conclusion that no actual wars—or, more usually, no *modern* wars—are likely to satisfy those conditions. A just war pacifist approach to international armed conflict, then, will be particularly keen to show that the weapons, tactics, and strategies of modern war are likely to be unnecessary and disproportionate, and to show that individual citizens have very strong reasons to doubt the rationales their governments give them for participating in such wars. This strand of contingent pacifism adopts an avowedly skeptical stance toward particular wars, solely on the basis of recognizing that just war criteria are much more difficult to meet than is commonly supposed. While some wars might be just, just war pacifists start from the (defeasible) presumption that they generally are not, and refuse to give those who wage wars the benefit of the doubt.

Anti-war pacifists, on the other hand, focus on the social and political forces responsible for pushing and pulling states into wars, regardless of whether those wars are just. They argue that the reason so few wars are likely to be justified according to standard just war conditions is that widespread militarism and the institutions that support it—the "war system"—inevitably lead states into waging wars irrespective of their justice.[15] An anti-war pacifist

---

15 Cf. Fiala, "Contingent Pacifism." Fiala's taxonomy, in contrast to my own, holds that contingent pacifism, properly speaking, must involve "a broad critique of war and the war system" (472), rather than just argument for the claim that modern wars are generally unable to satisfy just war criteria. Fiala would deny that "just war pacifism" is a form of

approach to international armed conflict therefore seeks to demonstrate the ways in which a state's military forces, arms industries, and politicians pursue hawkish foreign policies in pursuit of their own interests, as well as the ways in which the glorification of war and military service, and a widespread acceptance of violence among the state's citizens support those policies. This strand of contingent pacifism adopts an avowedly abolitionist stance toward these institutional forces and begins from the (defeasible) presumption that most, if not all, wars are a product of those forces, rather than being motivated by or intended to pursue matters of justice.

Contingent pacifists about war draw the general conclusion, then, that the actual wars we fight are generically unjust, and that we fight them almost entirely because of the unjust institutions inscribed in domestic and global society. But even if one rejects these conclusions, the approach such pacifists adopt and the strategies of argument they pursue are useful in revealing unwarranted assumptions about just war criteria, about the likelihood of actual wars meeting that criteria, and about the relevance of those criteria to explaining the number and kinds of wars we fight.

The parallels to police violence are clear. I opened this paper making reference to structural problems in the American criminal justice system: militarization, overcriminalization, and racial discrimination. Although I cannot examine these issues here, it is worth pointing out that increased use of military tactics and equipment, the additions and reprioritizations involved in the War on Drugs, and the continuing issues of racial profiling at both individual and institutional levels of law enforcement have almost certainly intensified, expanded, and concentrated the use of force by police over the last several decades. The "anti-war" equivalent of the contingent pacifist approach to police violence starts from the recognition that modern law enforcement is geared, in an important way, *toward* using significantly more force than can be justified from a moral perspective.

More in line with the major theme of this paper is an analog to the just war pacifist approach to war. In diagnosing the wide range of misconceptions prevalent in our cultural discourse about the justification of police force, we have uncovered a range of reasons to support a stance of skepticism when it comes to particular instances of that force. Was there a just cause to use force, in that a suspect was actually resisting, or have we mistaken disrespect, mere criminality, or the goal of preventing future resistance by others as a reason for violence? Was the use of force really necessary, and has the officer exhausted all other feasible means of overcoming a suspect's resistance (given the contingencies

contingent pacifism at all, although he would concede that its characteristic arguments arrive at contingently pacifist conclusions.

of the situation), or was the suspect's refusal to comply, or his escalating resistance, used as a kind of "trigger" for the use of force? And finally, was the use of force proportionate, not to the level of resistance encountered, but to the benefits likely to result from coercing compliance with the particular command that was given, and have all the relevant harms, including those to the victim, to other individuals, and to the broader community, been taken into account? To be sure, many uses of police force are necessary and proportionate means to ensuring compliance with legal commands by officers. But given the range and weight of the misconceptions under which our national conversation about police violence has proceeded so far, it would seem that we are warranted in taking a very skeptical stance toward particular instances of police force. When we adopt this stance, I suspect we will recognize many more of these as cases of police brutality and excessive force than we would have before.

Bibliography

Betz, Joseph. "Police Violence." In *Moral Issues in Police Work,* edited by Frederick A. Elliston and Michael Feldberg. 177–196. New Jersey: Rowman and Allanheld, 1985.

Fiala, Andrew. "Contingent Pacifism and Contingently Pacifist Conclusions." *Journal of Social Philosophy* 45, no. 4 (Winter 2014): 463–477.

May, Larry. *After War Ends: A Philosophical Perspective.* Cambridge: Cambridge University Press, 2012.

McMahan, Jeff. *Killing in War.* Oxford: Clarendon Press, 2009.

Narveson, Jan. "Pacifism: A Philosophical Analysis." *Ethics* 75, no. 4 (1965): 259–271.

Patrick, Urey W., and John C. Hall. *In Defense of Self and Others: Issues, Facts and Fallacies—The Realities of Law Enforcement's Use of Deadly Force.* 2nd ed. Durham: Carolina Academic Press, 2010.

Pizio, William C. *Police Officers' Encounters with Disrespectful Citizens.* El Paso: LFB Scholarly Publishing, 2012.

Reichberg, Gregory M., Henrik Syse, and Endre Begby, eds. *The Ethics of War: Classic and Contemporary Readings.* Malden, MA: Blackwell, 2006.

Rodin, David. *War and Self-Defense.* Oxford: Clarendon Press, 2002.

Sterba, James. "Reconciling Pacifists and Just War Theorists." *Social Theory and Practice* 18, no. 1 (Spring 1992): 21–38.

Terrill, William. *Police Coercion: Application of the Force Continuum.* New York: LFB Scholarly Publishing, 2001.

Terrill, William, Eugene A. Paoline III, and Jason Ingram. *Assessing Police Force Policy and Outcomes.* Final technical report draft, National Institute of Justice, 2012.

Walzer, Michael. *Just and Unjust Wars: A Moral Argument with Historical Illustrations.* 5th ed. New York: Basic Books, 2015.

CHAPTER 9

Cultural Violence and Gender Injustice in Africa: The Necessity for Enlightened Self-Interest

Laleye Solomon Akinyemi

Introduction

African society is a plural society, and as a plural society it is devoid of a perfectly equivalent belief system. The variations are of degree and not of kind. Although there is some specificity associated with each of the different groups in the fifty-three countries that make up the continent, the heterogeneity does not preclude some common denominators in the cultural beliefs and practices, which is more so when the continent is populated mainly by people with similar "culture, custom, common history of colonial experience and tutelage."[1] The shared values, belief systems, and experience carve a niche that defines the common identity of the people.

Culture is a complex phenomenon; its meaning goes beyond art, song, and dance to include all that is connected with a people's way of life. It manifests in their work, recreation, worship, and courtship; in the manner of interrogating nature and the utilization of nature's possibilities; and in their ways of knowing themselves and interpreting their places in nature. It is also seen in the manner in which people house and clothe themselves; their methods of conducting war and peace; their systems of statecraft, of education, of rewards and punishment; the way they regulate personal relations generally; and the ideas underlying these institutions and practices.[2]

One of the features of culture is that it binds a group of people together like the umbilical cord binds the foetus with the mother and carves a unique identity for the group based on common language, shared history, values, experiences, and sometimes geographical location. In other words, culture is a parameter by which a group of people can be differentiated from another. The culture of a people patterns the people's way of life. It dictates how members

1 Godwin Azenabor, *Understanding the Problems of African Philosophy* (Lagos, Nigeria: First Academy, 2002), 9.

2 Kwasi Wiredu, *Philosophy and an African Culture* (London: Cambridge University Press, 1980), 10.

 | DOI 10.1163/9789004361911_011

of a group are to behave and the duties, responsibilities, rights and privileges[3] they owe themselves as well as other members of the group. Culture, according to Makinde Moses, is the people's traditions, manners, customs, religious beliefs, values, and social, political, or economic organization.[4] In this sense, culture does not refer to an individual but to a people or group that consists of individuals.

The global space consists of a multiplicity of cultures—for instance, most Americans eat beef whereas most Indians do not. Female circumcision is prevalent in some countries of Africa but is viewed as a deplorable custom in most other countries. The death penalty was abolished in Germany but is retained in China. Recreational use of marijuana is legal in the Netherlands but illegal in South Korea. In Tibet, a dead body is neither buried nor cremated but is thrown to the vultures to eat. Doctor-assisted suicide is regarded as moral in Switzerland but immoral in Korea. Polygamy is an acceptable form of marriage in Saudi Arabia but not in China.[5] The heterogeneity of culture in the world does not imply the impossibility of overlap in cultural practices among the different groups of the world; two or more cultural groups could exhibit a particular cultural trait. For instance, polygamy is an acceptable form of marriage in Saudi Arabia as well as in African society, and hospitable actions are valued greatly in most human society, although the *modus operandi* can differ from one cultural group to another. In the same vein, some societies exhibit cultural practices that are regarded as misnomer by others. In spite of the plurality of cultures in the world, no culture is superior or inferior to another. The worldview of a group of people has an incontestable positive truth-value to the bearers of that worldview, but to others it may be value-neutral or possess the same positive truth-value. This forms the crux of tolerance as an indispensable factor in the sustenance of peaceful social coexistence in society.

The belief systems of Africans are of two different but related categories; the first is the autochthonous practices and norms that predate the people's contact with other cultures. Some of these cultural practices have endured and survived the ravaging influence of colonialism, capitalism, globalization, and modernization. They include mode of dressing, communal ownership of

---

3 Gbenga Fasiku, "Nature of Culture and the Question of National Identity" in *The Humanities, Nationalism, and Democracy* eds. Sola Akinrinade, Dipo Fashina, David O. Ogungbile, (Ile-Ife, Nigeria: Obafemi Awolowo University Press, 2006), 29.

4 Moses Akin Makinde, *African Philosophy: The Demise of a Controversy* (Ile-Ife, Nigeria: OAU Press, 2007), 13.

5 Seungbae Park, "Defence of Cultural Relativism," *Cultura: International Journal of Philosophy of Culture and Axiology* 8 no1. (2011):159.

property, belief in the interrelatedness of natural and supernatural events, inherent goodness of man, ethical relation with nature, and the shared beliefs in the pivotal role of music,

> Music in African culture features in all emotional states.
> When we go to work, we share the burdens and pleasures
> of the work we are doing through music. This particular facet,
> strangely enough, has filtered through to the present day.[6]

The second category of African culture is a product of acculturation between indigenous African culture, hitherto mentioned, and Anglo-Boer cultures. This category has its historical antecedent in the colonial through the post-colonial periods of African experiences. African culture or modern African culture in this sense is a synthesis of the indigenous and the modern.

The cultural beliefs, norms, and practices of the African people, as in every other society, are expected to be directed at fostering individual and social peace by regulating the conduct of the stakeholders, thereby minimizing the occurrence of conflicts. Unfortunately, both the autochthonous and the modern cultural perspectives highlighted encouraged unequal social relation between the genders, foisted unjust situations that debased the dignity of the female, and consequently engendered conflicts. By gender, reference is to the classification or distinction often drawn between the two sexes based on their biological compositions.[7] Efforts have been directed at liberating women through the establishment of institutions of empowerment such as the Convention on the Elimination of All Forms of Discrimination Against Women (CEDAW) and the Committee for the Defence of Human Rights (CDHR). The strengthening of existing instruments for the protection of rights and dignity such as United Nations and African Union Charters, are all incapacitated by the cultural beliefs and have, therefore, yielded marginal benefits.

To discern the myriad ways in which the female is discriminated against—exposed to unequal social relation, denied rights, and consequently inflicted with varieties of violence—the chapter is divided into three sections. The first section makes reference to a historical development that predates colonial Africa. The section examines some cultural beliefs and practices in pre-colonial Africa that subsist to the contemporary period, even though they inflict violence on girls or women.

6 P.H. Coetzee and A.P.J. Roux, eds. *Philosophy from Africa: A Text with Readings* (Oxford: Oxford University Press, 1991), 27.

7 H.M. Lips, *Sex and Gender: An Introduction,* 2nd ed. (New York: Mayfield, 1993), 3.

In the second section, the work examines the impact of contacts with alien cultures on the female through colonialism, capitalism, and globalization and how these resulted in the exacerbation of violence on women in Africa.

In the third section, the necessity for the ethical principle of enlightened self-interest as a panacea for gender egalitarianism and peaceful coexistence in Africa is stressed. The final section is a summary of the work.

The Cultural Construction of the Female Gender and the Culture of Violence in Pre-colonial Africa

Jean Jacque Rousseau observed that a unique feature of humans is that they are born equal. Equality, therefore, is a biological feature shared by all humans irrespective of the gender affiliation. Humans are not only biological beings, they are also social beings. The social nature of human beings foisted another distinctive feature on man through cultural norms and practices that culminated in the male/female dichotomy. The social constructions of the African woman are molded into the traditions, customs, and religious worldview, which are conceived as sacrosanct by the people. To therefore challenge any of the cultural dictates that inflict violence on the African woman is considered sacrilegious. By "violence against women," this paper refers to "any act of gender-based violence that results in, or is likely to result in, physical, sexual, or psychological harm or suffering to women … whether occurring in public or private life (Declaration on Convention on the Elimination of All Forms of Discrimination Against Women (CEDAW), adopted 20 December 1993). This includes but is not limited to wife-battering, sexual abuse of female children, rape, female genital mutilation, and other traditional practices harmful to women.[8]

Critique

The first cultural practice directed at the female at birth is the removal of the external female genitalia. The practice is anchored in the belief that the act prepares the girl-child adequately for adulthood and marriage as well as ensures marital fidelity. This cultural practice known as female genital mutilation (FGM) subsists in most African societies to date. The practice, although not unique to Africa, encroaches on the fundamental rights of the female to health, security, and physical integrity, as well as the right to be free from

8 Faedi Benedetta, "Domestic Violence and Human Rights Violation: The Challenges of Regional Human Rights Approach in Africa" in *Domestic Violence and the Law in Colonial and Postcolonial Africa,* ed. Emily S Burrill, Richard L. Roberts and Elizabeth Thornberry (Athens: Ohio University Press, 2010), 261.

torture. A woman who is against this cultural practice could be accused of witchcraft.

The belief in the reality of witchcraft is pervasive in Africa, and it forms the basis of explanation for social evils or unusual occurrences in the society. Every social evil in African society is explained in terms of witchcraft. Such evils include but are not limited to diseases, poverty, misfortune, inability to have children, and inability to find a husband or a wife.[9] More importantly, the belief of Africans with respect to witchcraft is discriminatory against the female; the practice is credited to this gender. For instance, the Akambas of Kenya, the Yoruba of Southwestern Nigeria, and the Zulus of South Africa to mention a few, believe that witches are women.[10] It is a widely held belief that witches hold their nocturnal meetings at night, where their clandestine activities are carried out. They are presumed to have metaphysical power with which they can turn their victims into edible animals or prey for consumption. Given the Africans' fervent belief in the phenomenon, it follows that physical and/or psychological violence is presumed to be inflicted on the victims of witchcraft. Although it may not be possible to scientifically, or logically, substantiate the infliction of violence on victims of witchcraft, the physical violence often unleashed on women in cases of "established" witchcraft levied against them could be stoning to death. This is a "deliberate violation of the right to life on the grounds of false metaphysics."[11] These cultural beliefs and practices in traditional Africa have outlived colonialism and subsist till present time.

In modern times, it would take the frantic efforts of law enforcement agents to rescue a witch. If they do, there is the conviction among Africans that the Western-imposed law that emphasizes empirical justification is not in tandem with the traditional beliefs that are predicated on metaphysical or spiritual justifications, as witches are often left off the hook for want of evidence. The advent of alien religions (Christianity and Islam) as well as Western education have not appreciably stemmed the tide, both in the beliefs and the practices of witchcraft. Not a few Africans (even with the relatively better literacy level compared with the pre-colonial past) want protection from "spiritual

9 J. Mbula Bahemuka, *Our Religious Heritage* (Edinburgh: Thomas Nelson, 1982), 105.

10 Lawson Thomas, *Religions of Africa* (New York: Harper and Row, 1984), 23. Also in J. Mbula Bahemuka, *Our Religious Heritage*, 107; E. Geoffrey Parrinder, *African Traditional Religions* (London: Shedlon Press, 1974), 124; and Omosade Awolalu and P.A. Dopamu, *Yoruba Beliefs and Sacrificial Rites* (London: Longman, 1974), 124.

11 Benson Igboin, "Human Rights in the Perspective of Traditional Africa: A Cosmotheandric Approach," *Sophia-International Journal for Philosophy of Religion, Meataphysical Theology and Ethics* 50 (1), (2011): 160.

attack"—the euphemism for the onslaught of witches. Most religious priests (prophets and imams) exploit the situation for their financial advantage. The question that often comes to mind in the discourse on the phenomenon of witchcraft is why it is the female who is accused of witchcraft. Male counterparts are rarely accused, and when they are sparingly accused of wizardry, they are not subjected to the ill-treatment meted out to the witches. Why is this so? Why is it that in any African society, the numeric strength of witches outweighs that of wizards? The questions could go on. This discrimination against the female concerning witchcraft is often used to blackmail any woman who has the courage to challenge the rationality of any cultural practice that is against the gender, as she could easily be labeled a witch. The onus would then lie on the woman to prove the contrary.

To convincingly demonstrate that an accused woman is not a witch requires other violent cultural practices. For instance in some African cultures, women are made to drink the water used in washing the corpses of their deceased husbands to prove their innocence in the death of the husbands.[12] In other cultures, a woman could be cleanly shaved, barred from having a bath for some specified number of days, and made to sleep alone with the corpse of the deceased for some specified days. It is noteworthy that similar measures are not in place when the wife dies—it is mostly practiced when the man is the deceased.

The denial of rights is also extended to ownership of property. The denial of rights to property as it relates to the female gender is not restricted to land. The Ikwerre culture of Rivers State in Nigeria requires that a woman who inherits her father's property has to remain unmarried. An Ikwerre woman forfeits her right to any inheritance whenever she marries. On the contrary, a man may marry as many wives as he wishes and retains the right to inheritance.[13] Rather than permitting a woman to inherit property, the cultural practices of some African communities portray the female as an object herself to be inherited.

A study by the U.S.-based Human Rights Watch on domestic violence in Uganda reveals that families justified forcing widows to be inherited by other males in the family on the grounds that the whole family contributed the bride price paid on the woman, and the woman therefore remained the "family property." Once inherited, a widow lost the right to her husband's property, which went to the new husband. And if a woman sought separation or divorce,

12 Reginald O Arisi and Patrick Oromaregbake, "Cultural Violence and the Nigerian Woman," *African Research Review: An International Multidisciplinary Journal* vol 5 (4) serial no 21: (2011):371.

13 Arisi and Oromaregbake, "Nigerian Woman," 370–371.

the dowry had to be reimbursed. Upon the unwillingness or inability of the family to repay, the brothers may beat her to force her back to her husband or in-laws because "they don't want to give back cows."[14]

These and other forms of discrimination, denial of rights, and infliction of violence (physical, psychological, and emotional) on the female occasioned by the cultural beliefs and practices in African society are what the author perceives as a culture of violence that requires a second thought by Africans. That is the essence of the dynamism of culture; it is a phenomenon that should evolve with time.

Cultural Contacts and the Entrenchment of Patriarchy

Culture is not a constant phenomenon; it evolves with time and events. Any aspects of a people's cultural belief can be consciously interrogated by critical minds with the aim of making necessary adjustment, in compliance with reality.[15] As rightly observed by C.B. Okolo, "culture is ... dynamic and fleeting, it can be lost with time, with incursion of alien cultures and values as exemplified by the interplay of industrialization and urbanization."[16] In other words, the changes that took place in the cultural patterns of traditional Africans are traceable to the contacts with other cultures. In addition, "no society can successfully dominate another without the diffusion of its cultural patterns and social institutions, nor can any society successfully diffuse all or most of its cultural patterns and institutions without some degree of domination."[17] So cultural contacts often result in one culture influencing or dominating the other. In the case of Africa, the contacts the indigenous culture had with alien cultures influenced the social relation among the male and the female, so much so that "the feelings of mental inferiority and habits of subservience and obedience developed ... and rendered the African woman irrelevant in public

14 Mary Kimani, "Taking on Violence Against Women: International Norms and Local Activism Start to Alter Laws, Attitude," *Africa Renewal,* special edition (2012), accessed September 9, 2016, www.un.org/. special.

15 Moses Akin Makinde, *African Philosophy: The Demise of a Controversy* (Ile-Ife, Nigeria: OAU Press, 2007), 15.

16 C.B. Okolo, *What Is to Be African? Essays on African Identity* (Enugu, Nigeria: Cecta, 1993), 32.

17 Rosamund Billington, Strawbridge Sheelagh, Lenore Greensides, and Annette Fitzimons, *Culture and Society: A Sociology of Culture* (London: Macmillan, 1991), 64.

spheres and also reduced them to second class citizens who live to serve man, her superior, her master, decision maker."[18]

Colonialism in conjunction with religion, capitalism and globalization introduced changes in the traditional life of Africans and consequently redefined the cultural perspective of feminine and masculine relations. They reconstructed the matriarchal/patriarchal relation in such a manner that the women were further subordinated to their male counterparts. Religion, that is, Christianity and Islam, seem to concur with the view that women could be a threat, particularly to their male counterparts as well as the society in general if accorded unrestricted freedom. For instance, the Holy Quar'an is emphatic that, "men are the managers of the affairs of women for that Allah has preferred in bounty one of them over the other."[19] In the same vein, the Holy Bible is unequivocal in the creation story of man and woman; not only was the woman was created after the man but the construction was accomplished using the man's ribs. Furthermore, the biblical narration of the Garden of Eden and the role played by Eve, Adam's wife, in seducing him to eat the forbidden fruit, which resulted in their expulsion from the garden, is often interpreted to portray the evil creature and the destructive elements that women are, hence the need for the man to constantly regulate her "excesses." Given the inferiority portrait of woman by both Islam and Christianity, the female is further subordinated to the authority of the male counterpart, who is seen as her master, her crown, and her decision maker. The Islamic culture further subjugated women under the control of men in most African countries such as Algeria, Morocco, Sudan, Chad, Niger, and northern Nigeria through the imposition of specific dress codes for women; the dress codes are presumed to reflect the modesty, piety, and domesticity of the female. Those who do not comply are sanctioned. Also, in many African societies, Muslim women are disenfranchised from the electoral process because Islamic culture disapproves of their presence in the public sphere where elections are carried out and the political sphere where opinions are expressed. According to T. Ebijuwa, when women are denied the right to decisional representation in the political sphere, it contradicts the right of everyone to vote and be voted for.[20] Suffice it to say that all measures are directed at protecting the interests of Muslim men who do not want

18 F. Jameson, "Third World Literature in the Era of Multinational Capitalism," *Social Context* 15. (1986): 76. Also in Sanusi Ramonu and Olaynka Wunmi Ibadan, *Journal of Humanistic Studies* no 21 and 22 (2012): 274.

19 Sura 4:34.

20 Temisanren Ebijuwa, "The Future of the Present: A Philosophical Investigation of Women and Political Participation in Africa," *Journal of Philosophy and Development* vol, 2 and 3 (2001):20.

undue exposure of their wives. In the northern part of Nigeria, it is not uncommon for Muslim parents to withdraw the girl-child from school and marry her off at a tender age to guard against this "undue exposure."

Marriage under both religions invades the autonomy of women; the religions prohibit divorce, even when there are threats to the life of the woman in a marital relation. The biblical arithmetical idea that "the two become one flesh"[21] is practiced when the marital relationship is in favour of the man.

The doctrines of Christianity and Islam are so ingrained in the psyche of Africans that they strive to be more Catholic than the Pope or more Shari'ah than the Qur'an; a blasphemous comment against Islam in the United States or Britain, for instance, that might not result in violence in Saudi Arabia, the spiritual headquarters of Islam, would easily reach a high magnitude of violence on lives and properties in most African societies. In cases of violence, it is the female who bears the most physical and psychological trauma. They are vulnerable to becoming widows, orphans, or victims of rape in violent situations, as exemplified in the numerous religious conflicts and insurgencies that have characterized African countries like Nigeria, Chad, Mali, Kenya, Niger, and Somalia, and the sociopolitical conflicts that define contemporary Africa. Susie Jacobs observes that women's positions deteriorated under colonialism while men's positions were enhanced. This was largely the result of both capitalist development and the creation of customary laws that legally subordinated women to men.[22]

Capitalism imposes the quest for wealth and material accumulation, which has led to the noticeable gulf between the "haves" and the "haves not" in modern Africa. It introduced private ownership of property and class stratification[23] so much so that the traditional communitarian spirit of Africans has been eroded. Africans are no longer their brothers' keepers as demanded by their traditional communalism. The attempt to make ends meet by individuals in contemporary Africa has resulted in the abuse of the dignity of girls through child marriage, hawking, neglect, and child labour. The vicious circle of poverty imposed by capitalism exposes the female to dangers that undermine her dignity. In an attempt to reduce the poverty level of a family, the child becomes either the breadwinner or subsidy provider to salvage the family's precarious financial situation. This is done through hawking, hiring out as a domestic servant, or exporting to foreign land for prostitution—a modern form of slavery.

21 Gen. 3.

22 Susie Jacobs, "Gender and Land Reform: Zimbabwe and Some Comparisons," *International Sociology* 7, (1992): 20.

23 K.A. Hoppe, "Gender in Africa History" in *Africa—Colonial Africa 1885–1935*, ed. Toyin Falola, vol. 3 (Durham: Carolina Academic Press, 2002), 230.

Twenty-first-century human society, especially African society, has witnessed the acceleration of conflicts and violence through the manufacturing, procurement, and deployment of weapons of mass destruction. This scenario has great effects on females, who are at the receiving end of every conflict situation, like rape. Women who admit to having being raped besmirch the honour of their men. Many communities reject these women and throw them out; in this case, women have lost their lives and many feel they might as well be dead. Indeed, men often kill women who return with children born of rape, and suicide rates for women are on the increase.[24]

Justice, Inequality, and Peaceful Social Coexistence

The quest for justice will remain on the front burner of interpersonal relations for a very long time, partly because people are concerned with how the self or others are treated within the sociopolitical arrangement in society. Although the analysis of justice or rights in modern African society is better appreciated within the context of the culture of the people, there ought to be a standard of justice that transcends the inherent shortcomings of the multiplicity of cultures. It is against this background that this section of the work is predicated.

Justice, as enunciated by some philosophers, particularly John Rawls, is burdened by the problem of distribution—Who gets what? Or who has a right to some primary social goods in the society, and what measure is his or her due? Contextualizing this within African society, especially as it relates to gender, a level playing ground devoid of discrimination of either sex should be available for everyone to meet his or her needs and aspirations. Gender inequality and the quest to narrow its gap, therefore, is one of the challenges confronting twenty-first-century Africa society.

Philosophers such as Jean Jacque Rousseau, Plato, and John Rawls, among others have consistently argued for equality of both sexes. For instance, Rawls's theory of justice as fairness envisions a society of free citizens holding equal basic rights cooperating within egalitarian economic systems. In furtherance of this position, various conferences and summits have been held and institutions and committees established, to reduce to the barest minimum discrimination and gender inequality where they exist in the world, particularly in Africa. Notable is the Beijing Conference of 1995 and the New York Conference of 2005

24 Sheila Meintjes, Anu Pillay, and Meredeth Turshen, *The Aftermath: Women in Post-Conflict Transformation* (London: Zed Books, 2002), 12.

of the Convention on the Elimination of All Forms of Discrimination Against Women (CEDAW).

The thrust of the conferences and convention is to ensure that "the cultural norms that regard woman as inferior to man perpetuate a structure of subordination and generate patterns of gender-based violence, which ultimately impairs or nullifies woman's enjoyment of human rights and fundamental freedoms,"[25] are eliminated in human society.

Most African nations were in attendance and are signatories to the convention and conferences. As signatories, African countries, therefore, have the moral duty to protect women from the physical and psychological violence engendered by discrimination and inequality. Unfortunately, religious considerations have continued to hamper the implementation of the articles of the convention and conferences; some Islamic countries, such as Morocco, Egypt, Lesotho, have expressed reservations about some of the articles of the convention, claiming that "they are incompatible with Islamic shar'iah, which guarantees to each of the spouses rights and responsibilities within a framework of equilibrium and complementarity in order to preserve the sacred bond of matrimony."[26] Lesotho argued against Article 11 of the convention on the grounds that it conflicts with her constitutional provisions on succession to chieftainship and the throne of the kingdom of Lesotho.[27]

In spite of the moral commitments of other African countries, marginal achievements have so far been recorded in women's participation in the sociopolitical sphere. Women are still underrepresented in the governance of most African countries, although they recorded marginal improvement in political participation in South Africa, Liberia, and Nigeria during the tenure of President Goodluck Ebele Jonathan.

Helen Clark lamented the marginal benefits of these measures with respect to agriculture and productivity level of Africa during the just-concluded International Conference on African Development in Kenya, when she remarked that Africans are not harnessing the full potential of women, because of gender inequality at the family level, community level, and national level, and this has cost the continent an estimated 95 billion dollars a year.[28] She observed

25 Faedi Benedetta, "Domestic Violence and Human Rights Violation: The Challenges of Regional Human Rights Approach in Africa," in *Domestic Violence and the Law in Colonial and Postcolonial Africa,* ed. Emily S Burrill, Richard L. Roberts, and Elizabeth Thornberry (Athens: Ohio University Press, 2010), 258–260.

26 Benedetta, "Domestic Violence and Human Rights Violation," 261.

27 Benedetta, "Domestic Violence and Human Rights Violation," 261.

28 Helen Clark is the Director of United Nations Fund and former Prime Minister of New Zealand. The extract is an address delivered at the Tokyo International Conference on African Development (TICAD V1) in Nairobi, Kenya, August 27–28, 2016.

that in some African nations women are banned from owning land or inheriting land, so they are less productive.

The various empowerment programmes geared towards enhancing the status of the African woman and narrowing the inequality gap, such as Better Life for Rural Women in Nigeria, Affirmative Action in South Africa, the Gender Commission in Zimbabwe, have also yielded only marginal benefits. Domestic violence caused by inequality is increasing. Depriving girls of the right to education is pervasive, female genital mutilation remains largely uncurbed, and a high incidence of rape in conflict situation is common, to mention these few. There is, therefore, the need for a review of the strategies put in place to promote gender equality.

Inequality and discrimination with respect to the female gender in Africa are caused by some of the indigenous cultural beliefs and practices as well as the foreign cultures the autochthonous culture had contacts with. Given this, an ethical principle that can further enhance the culture that promotes masculinity without necessarily undermining femininity is required. Simply put, the ethical principle of enlightened self-interest is instructive to forestalling the culture of violence being aided by the violence in the cultures of religions, colonialism, and capitalism.

Enlightened self-interest is the understanding and the trust that what is done to enhance the quality of life of another person or group also enhances one's own quality of life.[29] A patriarchal society focuses on the interests of the male without a concomitant consideration for the interest of the female. It is both sexes that constitute the human race; peaceful social coexistence, therefore, must accord due recognition to the interests of both parties. When the action of an individual or group of individuals discriminates against the other in social relations, it debases the humanity in the other because it surreptitiously classifies the other as inferior. It is more so when such action inflicts physical, structural, or psychological violence on others. It widens the gap of inequality among equals and threatens harmonious living between the male and the female. Harmonious relation between the genders thrives when both sexes realise the indispensability of the other rather than one despising or treating the other with scorn. To make soap, oil is required, and to clean oil, soap is required. The human person, irrespective of gender, has the same worth in terms of dignity. The dignity of a human person is better protected when he

29 Linda Bloom and Charlie Bloom,"Enlightened Self-Interest: The Ultimate Self-Interest Lies in Being Good to Others," *Psychology Today*, https//www.psychologytoday.com/ 25/9/2016.

or she is not deliberately denied his or her rights, or, in the words of Immanuel Kant, when the person is not treated as a mere means in the achievement of another's end. Women's rights are no less than human rights. Gender equality, therefore, is not a contest for supremacy but the recognition of the equality of rights available to both male and female.

To act in accordance with the principle of enlightened self-interest is to act on the basis of the virtues of doing what is right and desiring what is right. It is morally repulsive to treat someone as less simply because she happens to be a woman or he happens to be a man. The interest of the female gender must be reconciled with that of the male and vice versa in social relations for peaceful coexistence.

A patriarchal or matriarchal society is an egocentric and biased society that tends towards the male or the female, thereby emphasizing masculine or feminine individualism and interest. Such society will constantly be at conflict. The practical adoption of the principle of enlightened self-interest, which can facilitate the coexistence of the genders, is effective education that emphasizes the interests of the stakeholders.

Conclusion

The work examines sociopolitical relations in Africa with emphasis on gender relations. It observes that some of the cultural practices and belief systems in pre-colonial Africa orchestrated the marginalization of the female. The contacts with foreign cultures also encouraged patriarchy. Both cultures inflict physical and psychological violence on the female gender and consequently promote conflicts and violence at the family level, community level, and national level of contemporary African existence. The paper argues for the promotion of the ethics of enlightened self-interest as a means of facilitating individual and social peace in African society. The practical adoption of this principle is through a process of peace education that focuses on the reconciliation of male interests with those of the female without necessarily undermining any of the diverse interests.

Bibliography

Arisi, Reginald O., and Patrick Oromaregbake. "Cultural Violence and the Nigerian Woman" *African Research Review: An International Multidisciplinary Journal* 5 (4) serial no 21 (2011): 369–381.

Awolalu, Omolade, and P.A. Dopamu. *Yoruba Beliefs and Sacrificial Rites.* London: Longman, 1974.

Azenabor, Godwin. *Understanding the Problems of African Philosophy.* Lagos: First Academy, 2002.

Bahemuka, J. Mbula. *Our Religious Heritage.* Edinburgh: Thomas Nelson, 1982.

Benedetta, Faedi. "Domestic Violence and Human Rights Violation: The Challenges of Regional Human Rights Approach in Africa." In *Domestic Violence and the Law in Colonial and Postcolonial Africa,* edited by Emily S. Burrill, Richard L. Roberts, and Elizabeth Thornberry. 256–276. Athens: Ohio University Press, 2010.

Billington, Rosamund, Strawbridge Sheelagh, Lenore Greensides, and Annette Fitzsimons. *Culture and Society: A Sociology of Culture.* London: Macmillan, 1991.

Bloom, Linda, and Charlie Bloom. "Enlightened Self-Interest: The Ultimate Self-Interest Lies in Being Good to Others." *Psychology Today,* (December 17, 2012). https//www.psychologytoday.com/ 25/9/2016.

Clark, Helen. Address delivered at Tokyo International Conference on African Development (TICAD VI), Nairobi, Kenya. August 27–28, 2016.

Coetzee, P.H., and A.P.J. Roux, eds. *Philosophy from Africa: A Text with Readings.* Oxford: Oxford University Press, 1991.

Ebijuwa, Temisanren. "The Future of the Present: A Philosophical Investigation of Women and Political Participation in Africa." *Journal of Philosophy and Development* 2 and 3 (2001):18–32.

Fasiku, Gbenga. "Nature of Culture and the Question of National Identity." In *The Humanities, Nationalism, and Democracy,* edited by Sola Akinrinade, Dipo Fashina, and David O. Ogungbile. 87–102. Ile-Ife, Nigeria: Obafemi Awolowo University Press, 2006.

Hoppe, K.A. "Gender in Africa History." In *Africa,* vol. 3, *Colonial Africa 1885–1935,* edited by Toyin Falola. 219–234. Durham: Carolina Academy Press, 2002.

Igboin, Benson. "Human Rights in the Perspective of Traditional Africa: A Cosmotheandric Approach." *Sophia-International Journal for Philosophy of Religion, Metaphysical Theology and Ethics* 50 (1) (2011):159–173.

Jacobs, S. "Gender and Land Reform: Zimbabwe and Some Comparisons." *International Sociology* 7, (1992): 5–34.

Jameson, F. "Third World Literature in the Era of Multinational Capitalism." *Social Context* 15(1986):65–88.

Kimani, Mary. "Taking on Violence Against Women: International Norms and Local Activism Start to Alter Laws, Attitude." Special issue, *Africa Renewal* (2012). www.un.org/. special 20/9/2016.

Lips, H.M. *Sex and Gender: An Introduction.* 2nd ed. New York: Mayfield, 1993.

Makinde, Moses Akin. *African Philosophy: The Demise of a Controversy.* Ile-Ife, Nigeria: OAU Press, 2007.

Meintjes, Sheila, Anu Pillay, and Meredeth Turshen. *The Aftermath: Women in Post-Conflict Transformation*. London: Zed Books, 2002.

Okolo, C.B. *What Is To Be African? Essays on African Identity*. Enugu: Cecta, 1993.

Park, Seungbae. "Defence of Cultural Relativism." *Cultura: International Journal of Philosophy of Culture and Axiology* 8 no 1 (2011): 159–170.

Parrinder, E. Geoffrey. *African Traditional Religions*. London: Shedlon Press, 1974.

Rawls, John. *A Theory of Justice*. Cambridge: Harvard University Press, 1971.

Sanusi, Ramonu, and Wunmi Olayinka. "Religio-cultural and Poetic Constructions of the Subaltern African Woman." *Ibadan Journal of Humanistic Studies* no 21 and 22 (2012): 273–294.

Thomas, Lawson. *Religions of Africa*. New York: Harper and Row, 1984.

Wiredu, Kwasi. *Philosophy and an African Culture*. London: Cambridge University Press, 1980.

CHAPTER 10

War is America's Altar: Violence in the American Imagination

Alessandro Rovati

Killing for the Telephone Company[1]

> The modern nation-state, in whatever guise, is a dangerous and unmanageable institution, presenting itself on the one hand as a bureaucratic supplier of goods and services, which is always about to, but never actually does, give its clients value for money, and on the other as a repository of sacred values, which from time to time invites one to lay down one's life on its behalf .... It is like being asked to die for the telephone company.[2]

Alasdair MacIntyre has helped us see that contemporary institutions are constituted by two distinctive characteristics. They claim to be limited in their scope, power, and reach because of the supportive role they play in facilitating the pursuit of individual interests and in protecting popular sovereignty and

1 A work-in-progress version of this chapter was presented at the 28th Concerned Philosophers for Peace Conference held at Loyola University on October 22–24, 2015. I thank Dr. Fuat Gursozlu for the kind invitation to present at the conference and all those who worked to make the gathering possible. I also want to thank Dr. Andrew Fitz-Gibbon and Dr. Jane Fitz-Gibbon for their insightful comments on my paper and Dr. Andrew Fiala for the engaging conversation we had during the conference, discussing the set of issues that are at the heart of my argument. I learned a lot from their suggestions, and their criticisms forced me to think harder about what I need to say in order to make a case for what I want to say. Fuat Gursozlu, the editor of the volume, and a blind reviewer offered indications that made my work better. Mary Burazer and Susan Mayes of Belmont Abbey College, as always, provided much needed help gathering the materials that I needed for my research, and Leo and Lourdes White were kind enough to welcome me in their home in Baltimore: I am very grateful for their hospitality and friendship. My wife, Rachelle Ramirez, offered her usual support and help along the entire process; my work would not be possible without her.

2 Alasdair C. MacIntyre, "A Partial Response to My Critics," in *After Macintyre: Critical Perspective on the Work of Alasdair Macintyre*, ed. John Horton and Susan Mendus (Notre Dame, IN: University of Notre Dame Press, 1994), 303.

 | DOI 10.1163/9789004361911_012

personal rights. At the same time, though, their involvement in guaranteeing their citizens's rights vests democratic institutions with a somewhat sacral aura and creates the basis to justify the extreme sacrifices that some need to make to ensure their survival. There is a fundamental incoherence at the heart of political liberalism and its justificatory theory, for the insistence on the limited and neutral nature of democratic institutions inadvertently downplays and hides the sacrificial elements that actually sustain and make possible the kind of society that political liberalism creates. The nation-state presents itself and the set of commitments that it embodies as an ultimate value for which the citizens may be asked to arrive at the supreme sacrifice of their lives, and an adequate theory of our political beliefs must offer an explanation of such sacrifice.[3] Following this line of reasoning, theologian Stanley Hauerwas has made the reflection over the role war plays within the nation-state one of the signature contributions of his own scholarship. War is a constitutive element of our current social arrangement, and confronting its reality is one of the most urgent tasks for concerned scholars. In fact, by ignoring the way in which the nation-state as a source of ultimate meaning claims our total allegiance, political liberalism has made us blind to the power that war has over our imaginations, thus making us incapable of questioning some of our society's deeply held commitments and blind to the structure of violence they legitimize.[4]

The philosophers of the Enlightenment assumed that war could be eliminated, if only people would start to cooperate on the basis of rational principles sanctioned by the law. They shared the presupposition that the conflicts that afflicted Europe during modernity were caused by the intellectual disagreements over theological doctrines originating in the Reformation, and they argued that, to create a society where conflicts short of war are allowed and where peace is secured, a political arrangement in which religion is privatized and the state is given monopoly over the use of violence had to be created. History, though, shows all too well that, even after the institution of nation-states, war not only did not stop but actually escalated and became more destructive. As theologian William Cavanaugh has argued at length, "there is no reason to

3 Paul W. Kahn, *Putting Liberalism in Its Place* (Princeton, NJ: Princeton University Press, 2005), 13.

4 While to my knowledge Hauerwas has never engaged extensively with the scholarship of Johan Galtung, their projects clearly follow parallel paths. For Galtung's classic description of cultural violence as an "aspect of a culture that can be used to legitimize violence in its direct or structural forms," see his "Cultural Violence," *Journal of Peace Research* 27, no. 3 (August 1990).

suppose that people are more likely to kill for a god than for a flag."[5] Religious ideologies and institutions are thought to be more prone to violence because of their absolutist, divisive, and irrational character, but, says Cavanaugh, "no one provides a coherent argument for supposing that so-called secular ideologies such as nationalism, patriotism, capitalism, Marxism, and liberalism are any less prone to be absolutist, divisive, and irrational than belief in, for example, the biblical God."[6] As a matter of fact, he continues, American Christians "are far more willing to kill for their country than for Jesus."[7] Nevertheless, the "myth of religious violence,"[8] as Cavanaugh calls it, still serves a fundamental purpose, namely, that of legitimizing the nation-state's right to wage war. The myth, according to Hauerwas, creates a "story of salvation in which the nation-state claims a monopoly on legitimate violence to save us from the violence of religion" to reinforce the idea that "secular orders are inherently peaceful."[9] This story holds a great power over our imagination, and it fundamentally shapes our way of looking at the world and of justifying our current political arrangements, for political liberalism has succeeded in convincing us that we ought to do whatever it takes to let democratic institutions succeed, lest we all slide back in the latent conflict caused by opposing comprehensive doctrines.[10] Accordingly, Hauerwas notes that a nation like the United States

5 William T. Cavanaugh, "Religious Violence as Modern Myth," *Political Theology* 15, no. 6 (November 2014): 486–487.

6 Cavanaugh, "Religious Violence as Modern Myth," 488.

7 Cavanaugh, "Religious Violence as Modern Myth," 488.

8 Cavanaugh has developed his arguments at length in the book *The Myth of Religious Violence: Secular Ideology and the Roots of Modern Conflict* (New York, NY: Oxford University Press, 2009). As the author makes abundantly clear, the point of challenging the myth of religious violence is not to deny the actual violence that has been committed in the name of religion, but to challenge the assumption that religion is especially prone to violence. "People kill for all sorts of things," explains Cavanaugh, and the "distinction between secular and religious violence is unhelpful, misleading, and mystifying." 8–9.

9 Stanley Hauerwas, *Approaching the End: Eschatological Reflections on Church, Politics, and Life* (Grand Rapids, MI: W.B. Eerdmans, 2013), 132.

10 This is a concept famously introduced by John Rawls, who defined comprehensive doctrines as "conceptions of what is of value in human life, and ideals of personal character, as well as ideals of friendship and of familial and associational relationships, and much else that is to inform our conduct, and in the limit to our life as a whole." John Rawls, *Political Liberalism* (New York: Columbia University Press, 1996), 13. Given the great variety of incommensurable and competing comprehensive doctrines that human beings adhere to, one of the main tasks of Rawls's political philosophy is to find a method that allows individuals with different accounts of the good to deliberate about matters of justice. Rational standards ought to be discovered and imposed over public debates in order

that "spends more on its military than all the other nations of the world combined prides itself with being a peace-loving country."[11] What we face is a deep divide between the theory and the reality of political liberalism because, as Kahn explains, "to see sacrifice as the core of the political strikes the liberal theorist as characteristic of fascist political theory. But even liberal political orders rest upon an understanding that the state can call upon the individual to kill and to be killed."[12]

Hauerwas identifies three ways in which war characterizes and determines the life of contemporary democracies.[13] First, war is essentially connected with the modern establishment of the rule of law. Let me turn once again to Kahn.

> Law and war have not been antithetical forces, but common expressions of the modern political culture of the sovereign nation-state. That state writes itself into existence by drafting a constitution. It expresses the historical permanence of that law by defending it at all costs. It demonstrates its own ultimate significance in the life of the individual citizen through the act of sacrifice that war entails .... All citizens become appropriate subjects of sacrifice and all history becomes coterminous with the continuation of the state.[14]

Second, war is a necessary by-product of the formation of nation-states and of the cooperation based on self-interest that sustains the life within and

---

to avoid the emergence of unsolvable conflicts over ultimate values. Romand Coles has emphasized the role that this fear of the tragic plays in the justification of the various versions of political liberalism in his book *Beyond Gated Politics: Reflections for the Possibility of Democracy* (Minneapolis, MN: University of Minnesota Press, 2005), 1–41. Fuat Gursozlu has traced the evolution of Rawls's thought on these matters in his "Political Liberalism and the Formative Political Elements," *Review Journal of Political Philosophy* 11 (2014).

11 Hauerwas, *Approaching the End*, 132.

12 Kahn, *Putting Liberalism in Its Place*, 241.

13 Drawing on Hauerwas's arguments, but pushing them a step forward, Stan Goff has given us a compelling account of the way war has also become the formative practice that shapes our idea of masculinity. The fundamental link between maleness and the practice of war explains our society's celebration of domination and violence, which, in turn, is at the root of the contempt for and devaluation of women that characterizes our culture. As he puts it, "war is implicated in masculinity. Masculinity is implicated in war. Masculinity is implicated in the contempt for and domination of women. Together, these are implicated in the greatest sins of the church." Stan Goff, *Borderline: Reflections on War, Sex, and Church* (Eugene, OR: Cascade Books, 2015), 392.

14 Kahn, *Putting Liberalism in Its Place*, p. 279.

among them. The absence of an authority that might prevent and settle the conflicts among states, in fact, makes war inevitable. The reason for this is that, as Hauerwas explains, "the nation-state gains its legitimacy from the claim that it is doing something unique in history, that is, maintaining, nurturing, and improving the conditions of its citizens. That is why the nation-state ... depends on the success of maintaining modern life."[15] When the time comes, the nation-state has to put its own survival above every other concern and does not hesitate to use all the resources necessary to achieve it. Third, war is a moral institution within the life of modern liberal democracies, for it inserts people who otherwise would not share much in common into a community that has a sense of purpose and unity.[16] According to Hauerwas, the tireless pursuit of freedom as an end in itself that characterizes liberal societies has brought us to the paradoxical result that "most of us do not have the slightest idea of what we should do with our freedom,"[17] so that despite being well off, we seem to coexist with a sense of "deep despair and loss of purpose."[18] The result is that people find themselves living in a state of boredom and dire loneliness that makes them desperately long for forms of community that give them a sense of identity, purpose, and closeness. War's power is that it promises to build such a community. Chris Hedges has put it beautifully.

> The enduring attraction of war is this: even with its destruction and carnage it can give us what we long for in life. It can give us purpose, meaning, a reason for living. Only when we are in the midst of conflict does

15 Hauerwas, *Approaching the End*, 123. Hauerwas is here drawing on the arguments of Bobbitt's *The Shield of Achilles*.

16 Consumerism, argues Hauerwas, is the other fundamental binding experience within liberal societies, which are polities based on self-interest and consent, rather than on shared stories. Accordingly, people assume that "our political task is to pursue our self-interests aggressively and fairly," so much so that "competition is one of our most important moral endeavors. For all societies need to provide a sense of participation in an adventure. Insofar as many feel they lack such an adventure, all that is left is beating the next person." *A Community of Character: Toward a Constructive Christian Social Ethic* (Notre Dame, IN: University of Notre Dame Press, 1981a), 248.

17 Hauerwas, *Community of Character*, 80.

18 Hauerwas, *Community of Character*, 79. In his encyclical *Laudato Si*, Pope Francis has pointed out a similar issue. Our throwaway culture, explains Francis, is based on the lie that people "are free as long as they have the supposed freedom to consume," (no. 203) as if the continuous accumulation of goods were able to fulfill the human heart. Reality shows us that what happens is quite the opposite, as the "constant flood of new products coexists with a tedious monotony." (no. 113).

> the shallowness and vapidness of much of our lives become apparent .... And war is an enticing elixir. It gives us resolve, a cause. It allows us to be noble.[19]

Nowhere is the power that war has of capturing our imagination and bringing us together in a liberal society more evident than in the United States.

War and the American Difference

While war's power over people's imaginations is not limited to the United States, Hauerwas argues that "war has a role in the American story that is quite unique .... America is a society and a state that cannot live without war. Though a particular war may be divisive, war is the glue that gives Americans a common story."[20] Let me put this claim in its context. According to Hauerwas, America is the perfect embodiment of the modern attempt to produce a people who should have no story except the story that they chose when they had no story,[21] which implies that American freedom consists primarily in the illusion that we get to make up our own story, culture, and selves. Not only is this belief deceptive—given that we have not chosen the story that tells us that we get to make up our own story—but it also makes it difficult for people to have a sense of a common belonging. War has such a unique role in this kind of society because, in the absence of other communities, it remains the most determinative common experience of Americans.[22]

The history of the wars America has fought has given Americans a common story that unites people with very different backgrounds. The Civil War, first, and the two World Wars, later, contributed substantially to the constitution of a national identity and a sense of common purpose. In his remarkable moral history of the Civil War, historian Harry Stout shows that before the

19 Chris Hedges, *War Is a Force That Gives Us Meaning* (New York, NY: Public Affairs, 2002), 3.

20 Stanley Hauerwas, *War and the American Difference: Theological Reflections on Violence and National Identity* (Grand Rapids, MI: Baker Academic, 2011), xvi.

21 This is a recurring thought in Hauerwas's scholarship. One example of the argument can be found in his *Dispatches from the Front: Theological Engagements with the Secular* (Durham, NC: Duke University Press, 1994), 166.

22 In their erudite analysis of the American identity and its totemic characters, Carolyn Marvin and David W. Ingle have argued that a nation "is the shared memory of blood sacrifice, periodically renewed." Carolyn Marvin and David W. Ingle, *Blood Sacrifice and the Nation: Totem Rituals and the American Flag* (Cambridge, UK: Cambridge University Press 1999), 4.

war began there were few symbols of national unity, for state and local associations governed American life. The American flag, for example, was barely visible, and it was confined to merchant and naval ships. Everything changed with the advent of war. "Churches, storefronts, homes, and government buildings all waved flags as a sign of loyalty and support .... On both sides, flags assumed a transcendent significance as symbols of their respective nation's sacred importance."[23] Something similar happened during the First World War. As Hauerwas explains, drawing on the scholarship of Jean Bethke Elshstain, "nation-states can exist on paper before they exist in fact. Accordingly, ... the United States was a historical construction that visibly came into being as a cause and consequence of the 'Great War.' ... The First World War reintegrated not only the South into the Union, but also the immigrants who had flooded into America in the nineteenth century."[24] William Cavanaugh substantiates these claims by noting that war has been the first factor that brought about not only the creation of a sense of nationhood, but also the actual growth of the federal government. Interestingly enough, in fact, all but five government departments have come into being during wartime—the last case being the massive investments in the creation of the Department of Homeland Security after 9/11.[25]

The insistent emphasis on individual autonomy and freedom from tradition that is typical of political liberalism leaves us with a society that, Hauerwas argues, "shares no good in common other than the belief that there are no goods in common other than avoiding death."[26] It is exactly the presumption that death needs to be avoided at all costs that accounts for the constant demand for safety and security that characterizes American society. Such a

23 Henry S. Stout, *Upon the Altar of the Nation: A Moral History of the Civil War* (New York: Penguin Books, 2006), 28.

24 Hauerwas, *War and the American Difference,* 59. Once again, this is not something that is unique to America. After the Savoias accomplished the unification of Italy under their kingdom, Massimo d'Azeglio, one of those who contributed to the process, famously said that, "we have made Italy, now we have to make Italians." Even in Italy's case, the First World War and the national mobilization that it entailed were a determining factor for the creation of a unity among people who, at the time, did not even speak the same language.

25 William T. Cavanaugh, *Migrations of the Holy: God, State, and the Political Meaning of the Church* (Grand Rapids, MI: W.B. Eerdmans, 2011), 27–28. For another fascinating history of how the welfare state and the federal tax system were mostly the fruits of military efforts as well, see James Wright, *Those Who Have Borne the Battle. A History of America's Wars and Those Who Fought Them* (New York: Public Affairs, 2012).

26 Hauerwas, *War and the American Difference,* 18.

constant demand has a great impact on policy and budgetary decisions[27] that are made in the United States, and often times people seem willing to give up their basic civil liberties and some of their deeply held moral commitments in order to allow the government to protect them from all threats to their comfort and wealth. The system of intrusive surveillance put in place by the NSA after 9/11, the use of torture in the fight against international terrorism, and the creation of an expensive security infrastructure for air travel are but a few signs of the impact that the fear of death and the desire to be kept safe have in determining our life in the United States. Americans, argues Hauerwas, "are determined to live in a world of safety even if we have to go to war to make the world safe."[28]

There is another reason why war is a moral institution in the American imaginary: war helps Americans preserve virtues that would otherwise be lost. The military is the last social group based on honor that exists in US society. Furthermore, the capacity for self-sacrifice that is learned in war, together with the sense of cooperation that the devotion to a higher cause makes possible, are the elements that make war so compelling and somewhat exhilarating. While most would probably recognize the horror of war, it is undeniable that the prospect of war is also perceived by many as exciting. "The myth of war entices us with the allure of heroism," says Hedges, and "the admiration of the crowd, the high-blown rhetoric, the chance to achieve the glory of the previous generation, the ideal of nobility beckon us forward. War," in fact, "usually starts with collective euphoria."[29] There is something oddly beautiful about the sacrifices, struggles, and heroic actions that are involved in war. While there are many novels, poems, and movies centered around war, no one wants to hear a story about peace. Accordingly, says Hauerwas, "we cannot get rid of war because war has captured the habits of our imaginations. We quite simply cannot comprehend a world without war."[30] War is a force that gives us meaning because of the sense of purpose it provides for the nation. War makes the world coherent and understandable: there is a just cause sustained by good people on one side and enemies of freedom and justice on the other. The attempt to question this description by introducing elements that make it more complex

27 Kelly Denton-Borhaug details the "permanent war economy" that characterizes the United States in her book *US War-Culture, Sacrifice and Salvation* (Sheffield, UK: Equinox, 2011), 14–55.

28 Hauerwas, *War and the American Difference*, 11.

29 Hedges, *War Is a Force*, 84.

30 Hauerwas, *War and the American Difference*, 54.

is usually condemned as unpatriotic, for "the cause, sanctified by the dead, cannot be questioned without dishonoring those who gave up their lives."[31]

For most Americans war is, at least in principle, unproblematic. The reason for this, Hauerwas argues, is that "war is a moral necessity for America because it provides the experience of the 'unum' that makes the 'pluribus' possible. War is America's central liturgical act necessary to renew our sense that we are a nation unlike other nations."[32] This is very significant, for despite all the talk about the great separation between religion and politics, America still maintains a religious understanding of its own nature. "Americans are said to be the beacon of hope for all people. They must be ready, therefore, to make sacrifices, for example, to go to war for the good of the world .... Even though the church has been relegated to the 'private' realm, the nation is still conceived and legitimated in salvific terms."[33] America is even understood as the destiny of the world, that is, as what all people would want to be if only they had the education that America makes possible. Quite cleverly, Kahn observes that the political culture of the United States pursues a practice of proselytizing with its own contemporary missionaries who "preach democracy, free markets, and the rule of law—all institutions founded on our belief in the equality and liberty of every person."[34] When America fights a war, it does so for the universal ideals that America stands for—no matter if the war happens to be caused by national self-interests. Americans want their wars to be commensurate with the commitments that their democracy embodies, which is the reason why wars are usually justified in the name of individual freedom and tolerance, with the goal of protecting and spreading democracy, for the sake of upholding the rights of minorities and human rights, and so on. That America justifies its wars in this way is first and foremost due to the need to honor the sacrifices of those whom it asks to fight and die; for while it might not seem worth fighting for oil or for the stability of the power balance in the Middle East, sacrificing for freedom and democracy is perceived as a noble thing. The problem is that the United States struggles to keep its wars limited, for once concepts such as democracy, freedom, and human rights are invoked, wars stop being wars and become crusades. At the same time, Americans also find it hard to avoid waging new wars to show that the United States of today is still worthy of the sacrifices that were made in the past by those who fought for American values. As the former Dartmouth President John Wright argues,

---

31 Hedges, *War Is a Force*, 145.

32 Hauerwas, *War and the American Difference*, 4.

33 Hauerwas, *War and the American Difference*, 10.

34 Kahn, *Putting Liberalism in Its Place*, 6.

"sacrifice not only leads to more sacrifice; it requires more if we are to fully honor our heroes."[35] Think of the powerful words Lincoln spoke after the cruel battle of Gettysburg: "We here highly resolve that these dead shall not have died in vain—that this nation, under God, shall have a new birth of freedom and that government of the people, by the people, for the people, shall not perish from the earth." Hauerwas claims that a nation shaped by "such elegant and powerful words, simply does not have the capacity to keep war limited .... After the Civil War, Americans think they must go to war to ensure that those who died in our past wars did not die in vain. Thus American wars are justified as a 'war to end all wars' or 'to make the world safe for democracy' or for 'unconditional surrender' or 'freedom.' ... Wars, American wars, must be wars in which the sacrifices of those doing the dying and the killing have redemptive purpose and justification."[36] This is why Hauerwas claims that "war is America's altar."[37]

War and the American Imagination

Let me briefly mention what I take to be the most important consequences of the role war plays in the American imagination. First, the material sources that cause conflicts—money, territories, resources, and so on—do not fit into the moral narrative that claims that wars are fought in the name of universal ideals such as democracy and freedom. Accordingly, all the various actors involved in war—academics, the military, politicians, and the media (with very few exceptions)—continuously distract us and redirect our attention from the political and material bases of power to compelling war stories that are designed to reinforce our presuppositions about the righteousness of our aims and the heroism of our soldiers. The result is a climate of constant manipulation and deception where, as Churchill observed, truth is "always attended by a bodyguard of lies."[38]

Second, the greatest sacrifice asked of soldiers is not so much that of risking their lives, but actually the sacrifice of killing other human beings—sacrificing their unwillingness to kill.[39] The added cruelty is that after having

---

35 Wright, *Those Who Have Borne the Battle*, 82.
36 Hauerwas, *War and the American Difference*, 32–33.
37 Hauerwas, *War and the American Difference*, 32–33.
38 Quoted in Goff, *Borderline*, 201. Goff reflects extensively on Churchill's insight in Chapter 19 of the book.
39 Hauerwas, *War and the American Difference*, 67.

been trained and deployed to kill, soldiers "are told to return to their first rules," explains Wright, "to forget that which they have just learned, and to wipe from their memory contrary experiences. In each instance, this is impossible."[40] The problem is that our wars are supposed to be good wars, which means that as far as we, the public to whom they return, are concerned those who have fought them have done no wrong, for their actions were justified. Veterans, explain Robert Meagher, "are expected to deny their own pain, ignore what war has taught them, and take up their civil status as heroes."[41] This is why civilians completely fail to understand the kinds of moral injuries that war has carved in those we have sent to fight it.

Finally, Carolyn Marvin and David Ingle have helped us see that "what is really true in any community is what its members can agree is worth killing for, or what they can be compelled to sacrifice their lives for. The sacred is thus easily recognized. It is that set of beliefs and persons for which we ought to shed our own blood, if necessary, when there is a serious threat."[42] On this account, it is clear that American nationalism represents a powerful religion that grips the imagination of people in the United States and all around the world. The problem is that once such a sacralization of the nation and its ideals is accomplished, there is no limit to the allegiance we owe it. We are left at the mercy of those who rule over us and we lose the capacity to say "no."

The Church as an Alternative Community

Drawing on Iris Murdoch's scholarship, Hauerwas has argued that the moral life "is more than thinking clearly and making rational choices. It is a way of seeing the world."[43] Thus, formation is at the core of our lives because the quality of our habitual objects of attention determines the quality of our acts. In fact, we are shaped by what we pay attention to. Nowhere is this character of

40 Wright, *Those Who Have Borne the Battle*, 16.

41 Robert Emmet Meagher, *Killing from the Inside Out: Moral Injury and Just War* (Eugene, OR: Cascade Books, 2014), xv.

42 Carolyn Marvin and David W. Ingle, "Blood Sacrifice and the Nation: Revisiting Civil Religion," *Journal of the American Academy of Religion* 64, no. 4 (1996): 767.

43 Stanley Hauerwas, *Vision and Virtue: Essays in Christian Ethical Reflection* (Notre Dame, IN: University of Notre Dame Press, 1974; 1981b), 35. Hauerwas substantiates such a claim by developing a complex account of the interconnection between agency, language, and morality that I do not have time to address in the present context. For a good discussion of this set of issues, see Charles Robert Pinches, *Theology and Action: After Theory in Christian Ethics* (Grand Rapids, MI: W.B. Eerdmans, 2002).

the moral life more evident than in the life of soldiers, for, as explained by former special operations officer Stan Goff, "if you practice playing cards every day, you will think about cards a good deal of the time .... Likewise, if you practice killing every day, you'll think a lot about killing. You'll dream about killing. You'll construct hypothetical situations in your mind for killing, and for not being killed. You *become* killing."[44] We become what we do, and war inevitably makes soldiers do things that cause a great deal of moral degradation in them: hatred, hostility, and cruelty are not incidental to the practice of war, but are intrinsic aspects of it. That is why, argues Goff, just as a soldier is inevitably transformed into a brute,[45] a society that has accepted the logic of war is inevitably transformed "into a brutalized and brutalizing society," and "the more totalizing the military is in any society, the more likely that society will generally manifest the kinds of degradation associated with war."[46] The use of the word "brutalization" is harsh. I use it not to indict those who have conscientiously devoted their lives to military service, but to properly frame the cry of someone like Goff who has been involved in the practice of war. In this way, we who are outsiders are given a chance to appreciate the cost of the militaristic culture to which we ourselves contribute.[47] Of course, that war grips our imaginations in such a powerful way is not a sign that we are a people easily coopted or influenced by societal pressure, but rather that we lack any alternative capable of so capturing our attention that it frees us from the violence of our society. This means that the only chance we have to resist the power war exercises over our imagination is to be part of an alternative community that shapes our way of looking at the world by introducing us to habits of peace.

While being open to the fact that such peaceable modes of life might exist beyond it, according to Hauerwas the *church* is what stands as an alternative

44 Goff, *Borderline*, 78–79.

45 The main role of boot camp, a true initiation rite that forever marks the lives of those who enter the military, is to be "fundamentally re-embodied." Marvin and Ingle, *Blood Sacrifice*, 109. A new way of looking, seeing, talking, and behaving is forced upon the recruits, and, in the process, civilians are transformed into soldiers through a shock treatment that changes them. "Something happens to men's thinking when they study war. They become antagonistic beings." Goff, *Borderline*, 148.

46 Goff, *Borderline*, 102–103.

47 Hauerwas has always been aware that one of the challenges for Christian pacifists is to speak about nonviolence in a way that avoids the temptation of self-righteousness, on the one hand, and recognizes the sacrifices of those we have sent to war, on the other. On the topic, see the chapter "Sacrificing the Sacrifices of War" in his *War and the American Difference*, 53–70.

to the world.[48] It is so by being a community of peace in a context dominated by self-interest, distrust, fear, and—ultimately—war. The church is a "contrast model,"[49] a community formed by trust that refuses to "resort to violence to secure its own existence or to insure internal obedience."[50] By being such a community, the church manages to provide the space and time necessary to develop the skills we need to interpret and discern what the possibilities and limits of our society are, thus freeing us from the necessities[51] that the world imposes on our lives and releasing our imagination from the grips of war. "Christians are people whose imagination has been challenged by a God who has invited us into an otherwise unimaginable kingdom."[52] Only God, in fact, could have created a world where forgiveness rather than force is a possibility and a duty. Only God could have challenged us to see the other as a gift rather than a threat, or to trust in His care rather than in our strength and power.

48 As he says, "as Christians we may not only find that people who are not Christians manifest God's peace better than we ourselves, but we must demand that they exist. It is to be hoped that such people may provide the conditions for our ability to cooperate with others for securing justice in the world." Stanley Hauerwas, *The Peaceable Kingdom: A Primer in Christian Ethics* (Notre Dame, IN: University of Notre Dame Press, 1983), 101. It is worth noting that Hauerwas describes the existence of such people as "a testimony to the fact that God's kingdom is wide indeed." The church cannot predetermine the boundaries of the kingdom, for it is its task to "acknowledge God's power to make his kingdom present in the most surprising places and ways," which is why Hauerwas's insistence on the role of the church does not coincide with an utter closure and enmity toward everything that comes beyond it. Hauerwas, *Peaceable Kingdom*, 101. The examples abound; with their work as foster parents, for instance, Jane Hall Fitz-Gibbon and Andrew Fitz-Gibbon testify to the fact that habits of peace that create communities of love in fact exist beyond the church. They have described their experience in the book *Welcoming Strangers: Nonviolent Re-Parenting of Children in Foster Care* (Piscataway, NJ: Transaction Publishers, 2016).

49 *A Community of Character*, 84.

50 *A Community of Character*, 85.

51 The main problem when violence is justified in principle as it is in our society is that such justification "stills the imaginative search for nonviolent ways of resistance to injustice." *The Peaceable Kingdom*, 114. Andrew Fiala has thoughtfully challenged our imaginations in his *Against Religion, Wars, and States: The Case for Enlightenment Atheism, Just War Pacifism, and Liberal-Democratic Anarchism* (Lanham, MD: Rowans & Littlefield, 2013). While disagreeing with him upon the all-encompassing rejection of religion as fundamentally irrational, I find his relentless criticism of the main assumptions of contemporary political theory and practice very engaging, as it shows us that many of the necessities that shape our lives are rooted in acquiescence, deception, and coercion, not in reason.

52 Stanley Hauerwas, *Against the Nations: War and Survival in a Liberal Society* (Minneapolis, MN: Winston Press, 1985), 57.

> Because we have been called to discipleship in a community of the new age proclaimed by Jesus of Nazareth, we have become capable of the unimaginable: forgiveness of enemies even unto death, loving service knowing no boundaries or limits, trust in the surpassing power of God's peace. In short, God has invited us to learn the skills, disciplines, and necessities of his kingdom through which we may display to the world the unceasing innovations made possible by being his people.[53]

Hauerwas has become famous for his commitment to nonviolence and reconciliation,[54] but it is important to notice the deep theological roots of such commitment. Christians are not called to nonviolence because of some humanistic commitment to individual dignity, nor for some utopian vision about a warless society. This kind of pacifism was especially popular in Christian circles in the aftermath of World War I. It received a scathing critique from Reinhold Niebuhr—arguably the most influential theologian in the United States in the past century—for having "rejected the Christian doctrine of original sin as an outmoded bit of pessimism, hav[ing] reinterpreted the cross so that it is made to stand for the absurd idea that perfect love is guaranteed a simple victory over the world, and hav[ing] rejected all the other profound elements of the Christian gospel as 'Pauline' accretions which must be stripped from the 'simple gospel of Jesus.'"[55] Hauerwas himself has been critical of this form of pacifism that treats peace as a "realizable ideal harmony among nature, people, and nations that our [Christian] theological commitments underwrite

---

53 Hauerwas, *Against the Nations*, 58. The often-made criticism against Hauerwas is that the church he describes does not actually exist. Hauerwas's answer to such charge is twofold. On the one hand, he has provided multiple examples of communities that actually embody the theological ideals he talks about. For example, see his *Where Resident Aliens Live: Exercises for Christian Practice* (Nashville, TN: Abingdon Press, 1996) and the book he coauthored with Jean Vanier, the founder of L'Arche, *Living Gently in a Violent World: The Prophetic Witness of Weakness* (Downers Grove, IL: InterVarsity Press, 2008). On the other hand, Hauerwas has also reflected at length on the eschatological character of the Christian call to discipleship. It is no surprise that the church does not live the way of the kingdom at its fullest and that Christian witness is stained by incoherence and sin. The kingdom, in fact, is already present but not yet fulfilled, which is why Christians live like pilgrims on the road to sanctification. Among others, see his *Approaching the End*.

54 Hauerwas was nominated "America's Best Theologian" by *Time* magazine just a few days after the attacks of 9/11. In the aftermath of that tragic event, many news sources turned to Hauerwas for comments, thus making his pacifist stance popular even beyond the academy.

55 Robert McAfee Brown, ed. *The Essential Reinhold Niebuhr: Selected Essays and Addresses* (New Haven, NJ: Yale University Press, 1986), 104.

but play no decisive role in determining."[56] Instead, following John Howard Yoder,[57] Hauerwas has insisted that Christians are a nonviolent community because they are disciples of Christ,[58] whose ministry was a ministry of peace that renounced the use of violence.[59] That is why Christian pacifism must be Christological and eschatological in nature;[60] as Hauerwas explains, in fact, "Christian nonviolence is necessary not because it promises us a world free of war; but because in a world of war as faithful followers of Christ we cannot be

56 Stanley Hauerwas, "A Pacifist Response to the Bishops," in *Speak Up for Just War or Pacifism: A Critique of the United Methodist Bishops' Pastoral Letter "in Defense of Creation,"* ed. Paul Ramsey (University Park, PA: Pennsylvania State University Press, 1988b), 155.

57 Perhaps no book has had a greater influence on Hauerwas's theology than John Howard Yoder's *The Politics of Jesus* (Grand Rapids, MI: W.B. Eerdmans, 1994). Yoder has engaged in extensive conversations with critics of his Christian pacifism in the book *Christian Attitudes to War, Peace, and Revolution* (Grand Rapids, MI: Brazon Press, 2009).

58 The longstanding just war tradition stands in contrast with this claim. For a beautiful overview of the tradition that focuses on the relationship between just war and the Christian life, see Daniel M. Bell, *Just War as Christian Discipleship: Recentering the Tradition in the Church Rather Than the State* (Grand Rapids, MI: Brazos Press, 2009). Hauerwas has engaged just war thinking on multiple occasions; for example, see his "Why War Is a Moral Necessity for America? or, How Realistic Is Realism" in *War and the American Difference: Theological Reflections on Violence and National Identity*, 21–34.

59 Hauerwas has described his Christological commitments in various works. In particular, I would point the reader to Stanley Hauerwas, *Cross-Shattered Christ: Meditations on the Seven Last Words* (Grand Rapids: Brazos Press, 2004a) and *The Peaceable Kingdom.*

60 The theological bases of Hauerwas's pacifism have been questioned. This is not surprising because the debate on whether a faithful reading of the Gospel requires a pacifist stance on the part of disciples has kept the church busy for its entire history, and it is still far from settled. Joseph Capizzi provides a helpful account of just war ethic in his *Politics, Justice, and War: Christian Governance and the Ethics of Warfare* (New York: Oxford University Press, 2015). A collection of texts that shows the Christian commitment to peace is Michael G. Long, ed. *Christian Peace and Nonviolence: A Documentary History* (New York: Orbis Books, 2011). Given the long history of controversies about these issues, Hauerwas's arguments too have been at the center of many theological disputes. For example, Nigel Biggar has argued that Hauerwas's pacifism lacks a strong biblical foundation; see Nigel Biggar, *In Defence of War* (New York: Oxford University Press, 2013), 16–60. Paul Ramsey, instead, has questioned Hauerwas's Christology and his account of the cross and redemption; see Paul Ramsey, *Speak Up for Just War or Pacifism: A Critique of the United Methodist Bishops' Pastoral Letter "in Defense of Creation"* (University Park, PA: Pennsylvania State University Press, 1988), 111–115. A book that addresses this set of criticisms by engaging in careful exegesis of the New Testament is Richard B. Hays, *The Moral Vision of the New Testament: Community, Cross, New Creation* (New York: Harper San Francisco, 1996).

anything other than nonviolent."[61] Christian nonviolence cannot be described as a position about the use of force abstracted from discipleship to Jesus Christ the Lord, because "nonviolence is not a position you can or should take prior to or subsequent to the answer given to Jesus' question, 'But who do you say that I am?' (Lk 9:20)."[62] The church is not committed to nonviolence because it believes it is a good strategy to avoid conflicts, but rather the church is aware that it might well happen that its refusal to use violence might make the world more violent. As a matter of fact, the painful awareness that innocents might suffer because of the Christian commitment to nonviolence is the most demanding feature of this call to discipleship. To put it in Hauerwas's words: "to be nonviolent does not make the difficulty of reality disappear. Indeed, it may intensify the difficulty, given that the nonviolent may have to watch the innocent suffer for their convictions."[63] But then again, what could the disciples of a crucified God expect? In Jesus God has inaugurated a kingdom founded on servanthood rather than power, forgiveness rather than revenge, and gentleness rather than and even in the face of anger and fear.

Hauerwas actually does not like to be identified with the label "pacifist," for the language of pacifism and nonviolence seems to imply a passive stance, while, instead, peacemaking names the activities that are intrinsic to the life of the church.[64] For a Christian, "peace is not the name of the absence of conflict, but rather peacemaking is that quality of life and practices engendered by a community that knows it lives as a forgiven people."[65] Peace is a demanding

61 Stanley Hauerwas, *Performing the Faith: Bonhoeffer and the Practice of Nonviolence* (Grand Rapids, MI: Brazos Press, 2004c), 181.

62 Hauerwas, *Performing the Faith,* 173.

63 Hauerwas, *Approaching the End,* 150. It is worth noting that this is not a challenge only for Christian pacifism. Every moral perspective, in fact, imposes demands on others because, to say it with Hauerwas, "there is *no* morality that does not require others to suffer for our commitments." The problem, continues Hauerwas, is not "asking others to share and sacrifice for what we believe to be worthy. A more appropriate concern is whether what we commit ourselves to is worthy or not." *The Peaceable Kingdom,* 9. For example, even just warriors need to be willing to let innocents die in order to avoid fighting a war unjustly. See "Just How Realistic Is Just War Theory? The Case for Christian Realism," accessed September 18 2016, http://www.abc.net.au/religion/articles/2013/09/02/3839028.htm.

64 Another frequent charge against Christian nonviolence is of being sectarian and apolitical. Examples of such criticism can be found in D.B. Robertson, ed. *Love and Justice: Selections from the Shorter Writings of Reinhold Niebuhr* (Gloucester, MA: Peter Smith, 1976), 260–267, and Paul Ramsey, *The Just War: Force and Political Responsibility* (New York, NY: Rowan and Littlefield, 2002), 259–278.

65 Stanley Hauerwas, *Christian Existence Today: Essays on Church, World, and Living in Between* (Durham, NC: Labyrinth Press, 2001), 91.

activity, for it requires that we be a people who is not afraid to speak the truth and who is willing to confront one another about our sins. This is why the peace of the church is so different from the peace of the world for, while the former is built on truth, the latter is built on power, which means that often the world needs to resort to war to keep its peace. What the church needs to do is "help the world find habits of peace whose absence so often makes violence seem like the only alternative. Peacemaking as a virtue is an act of imagination built on long habits of the resolution of differences .... Without an example of a peacemaking community, the world has no alternative but to use violence as the means to settle disputes."[66] Christian pacifism does not entail a withdrawal from the world, for Christians are in fact called to make their contribution to society.[67] They do so by embodying the unity to which the church is called so that the world may "have the means to recognize the irrationality of the divisions resulting in violence and war."[68] Christian nonviolence is not a theory but is the way a community called to mutual forgiveness and reconciliation lives, which is why Christians, who are "a people who must learn to live without control,"[69] cannot offer the world a definitive solution to bring all conflicts to an end, but only "a witness that we think is the truth of our existence. That witness requires the existence of a body of people who provide an alternative so that we may be able to see the violence that so grips our lives. Given the violence of the world in which we live, it may be thought that that is not much. For those of us who believe that God has made us part of the kingdom of peace through cross and resurrection, however, it is everything."[70]

Bibliography

Bell, Daniel M. *Just War as Christian Discipleship: Recentering the Tradition in the Church Rather Than the State*. Grand Rapids, MI: Brazos Press, 2009.

Biggar, Nigel. *In Defence of War*. New York: Oxford University Press, 2013.

66 Hauerwas, *Christian Existence Today,* 95.

67 Hauerwas has explored the connection between Christian nonviolence and democratic practices of common deliberation in the book he co-authored with Romand Coles, *Christianity, Democracy, and the Radical Ordinary: Conversations between a Radical Democrat and a Christian* (Eugene, OR: Cascade Books, 2008). I build on such connection in my forthcoming volume *Putting Hauerwas in His Place* (Eugene, OR: Pickwick, forthcoming).

68 *Peaceable Kingdom,* 100.

69 *Peaceable Kingdom,* 105.

70 *Dispatches from the Front,* 135.

Capizzi, Joseph E. *Politics, Justice, and War: Christian Governance and the Ethics of Warfare*. New York: Oxford University Press, 2015.
Cavanaugh, William T. *The Myth of Religious Violence: Secular Ideology and the Roots of Modern Conflict*. New York: Oxford University Press, 2009.
Cavanaugh, William T. *Migrations of the Holy: God, State, and the Political Meaning of the Church*. Grand Rapids, MI: W.B. Eerdmans, 2011.
Cavanaugh, William T. "Religious Violence as Modern Myth." *Political Theology* 15, no. 6 (November 2014): 486–502.
Coles, Romand. *Beyond Gated Politics: Reflections for the Possibility of Democracy*. Minneapolis, MN: University of Minnesota Press, 2005.
Denton-Borhaug, Kelly. *U.S. War-Culture, Sacrifice and Salvation*. Sheffield, UK: Equinox, 2011.
Fiala, Andrew. *Against Religion, Wars, and States: The Case for Enlightenment Atheism, Just War Pacifism, and Liberal-Democratic Anarchism*. Lanham, MD: Rowans and Littlefield, 2013.
Fitz-Gibbon, Jane Hall, and Andrew Fitz-Gibbon. *Welcoming Strangers: Nonviolent Re-Parenting of Children in Foster Care*. Piscataway, NJ: Transaction Publishers, 2016.
Galtung, Johan. "Cultural Violence." *Journal of Peace Research* 27, no. 3 (August 1990).
Goff, Stan. *Borderline: Reflections on War, Sex, and Church*. Eugene, OR: Cascade Books, 2015.
Gursozlu, Fuat. "Political Liberalism and the Formative Political Elements." *Review Journal of Political Philosophy* 11 (2014): 58–81.
Hauerwas, Stanley. *A Community of Character: Toward a Constructive Christian Social Ethic*. Notre Dame, IN: University of Notre Dame Press, 1981a.
Hauerwas, Stanley. *Vision and Virtue: Essays in Christian Ethical Reflection*. Notre Dame, IN: University of Notre Dame Press, 1981b.
Hauerwas, Stanley. *The Peaceable Kingdom: A Primer in Christian Ethics*. Notre Dame, IN: University of Notre Dame Press, 1983.
Hauerwas, Stanley. *Against the Nations: War and Survival in a Liberal Society*. Minneapolis, MN: Winston Press, 1985.
Hauerwas, Stanley. *Christian Existence Today: Essays on Church, World, and Living in Between*. Durham, NC: Labyrinth Press, 1988; 2001.
Hauerwas, Stanley. *Dispatches from the Front: Theological Engagements with the Secular*. Durham, NC: Duke University Press, 1994.
Hauerwas, Stanley. *Cross-Shattered Christ: Meditations on the Seven Last Words*. Grand Rapids, MI: Brazos Press, 2004a.
Hauerwas, Stanley. "A Pacifist Response to the Bishops." In *Speak Up for Just War or Pacifism: A Critique of the United Methodist Bishops' Pastoral Letter "in Defense of Creation,"* edited by Paul Ramsey. University Park, PA: Pennsylvania State University Press, 2004b.

Hauerwas, Stanley. *Performing the Faith: Bonhoeffer and the Practice of Nonviolence.* Grand Rapids, MI: Brazos Press, 2004c.

Hauerwas, Stanley. *War and the American Difference: Theological Reflections on Violence and National Identity.* Grand Rapids, MI: Baker Academic, 2011.

Hauerwas, Stanley. *Approaching the End: Eschatological Reflections on Church, Politics, and Life.* Grand Rapids, MI: W.B. Eerdmans, 2013.

Hauerwas, Stanley. "Just How Realistic Is Just War Theory? The Case for Christian Realism." ABC Religion Accessed September 18, 2016. http://www.abc.net.au/religion/articles/2013/09/02/3839028.htm.

Hauerwas, Stanley, and Jean Vanier. *Living Gently in a Violent World: The Prophetic Witness of Weakness.* Downers Grove, IL: InterVarsity Press, 2008.

Hauerwas, Stanley, and Romand Coles. *Christianity, Democracy, and the Radical Ordinary: Conversations between a Radical Democrat and a Christian.* Eugene, OR: Cascade Books, 2008.

Hauerwas, Stanley, and William H. Willimon. *Where Resident Aliens Live: Exercises for Christian Practice.* Nashville, TN: Abingdon Press, 1996.

Hays, Richard B. *The Moral Vision of the New Testament: Community, Cross, New Creation.* New York: Harper San Francisco, 1996.

Hedges, Chris. *War Is a Force That Gives Us Meaning.* New York: Public Affairs, 2002.

Kahn, Paul W. *Putting Liberalism in Its Place.* Princeton, NJ: Princeton University Press, 2005.

Long, Michael G., ed. *Christian Peace and Nonviolence: A Documentary History.* New York: Orbis Books, 2011.

MacIntyre, Alasdair C. "A Partial Response to My Critics." In *After Macintyre: Critical Perspective on the Work of Alasdair Macintyre*, edited by John Horton and Susan Mendus. Notre Dame, IN: University of Notre Dame Press, 1994.

Marvin, Carolyn, and David W. Ingle. "Blood Sacrifice and the Nation: Revisiting Civil Religion." *Journal of the American Academy of Religion* 64, no. 4 (1996): 767–780.

Marvin, Carolyn, and David W. Ingle. *Blood Sacrifice and the Nation: Totem Rituals and the American Flag.* Cambridge, UK: Cambridge University Press, 1999.

McAfee Brown, Robert, ed. *The Essential Reinhold Niebuhr: Selected Essays and Addresses.* New Haven, NJ: Yale University Press, 1986.

Meagher, Robert Emmet. *Killing from the Inside Out: Moral Injury and Just War.* Eugene, OR: Cascade Books, 2014.

Pinches, Charles Robert. *Theology and Action: After Theory in Christian Ethics.* Grand Rapids, MI: W.B. Eerdmans, 2002.

Ramsey, Paul, *Speak Up for Just War or Pacifism: A Critique of the United Methodist Bishops' Pastoral Letter "in Defense of Creation."* University Park, PA: Pennsylvania State University Press, 1988.

Ramsey, Paul. *The Just War: Force and Political Responsibility*. New York: Rowan and Littlefield, 2002.

Rawls, John. *Political Liberalism*. New York: Columbia University Press, 1996.

Robertson, D.B., ed. *Love and Justice: Selections from the Shorter Writings of Reinhold Niebuhr*. Gloucester, MA: Peter Smith, 1976.

Rovati, Alessandro. *Putting Hauerwas in His Place*. Eugene, OR: Pickwick, forthcoming.

Stout, Henry S. *Upon the Altar of the Nation: A Moral History of the Civil War*. New York: Penguin Books, 2006.

Wright, James. *Those Who Have Borne the Battle: A History of America's Wars and Those Who Fought Them*. New York: Public Affairs, 2012.

Yoder, John Howard. *The Politics of Jesus*. Grand Rapids, MI: W.B. Eerdmans, 1994.

Yoder, John Howard. *Christian Attitudes to War, Peace, and Revolution*. Grand Rapids, MI: Brazon Press, 2009.

CHAPTER 11

Michel Foucault's Theory of Practices of the Self and the Quest for a New Philosophical Anthropology

Edward Demenchonok

"Crisis" is the term perhaps most frequently used in characterizing the state of the contemporary world, which is suffering global problems, such as weapons of mass destruction, Third World underdevelopment, deteriorating ecology, and global warming. Homogenizing globalization has resulted in the marginalization or disappearance of many unique cultures. There is also evidence of the traumatic and degenerative impact of dehumanizing conditions on human beings. The socio-economic, cultural, environmental, and anthropological crises are symptoms of a contemporary civilization disease syndrome.[1] The possibility of its "treatment" depends on whether or not humankind will be able to regain its humanity and culture, thus establishing more harmonious

1 Philosophers detect the root cause of the conflicted character of the contemporary world in the calculative "instrumental reason." Its economic-political consequences included colonialism and new forms of exploitation and alienation, epistemological and political violence, and the exclusion of the other. The techno-economic progress was at the cost of depersonalization and dehumanization. The humanistic tradition presents an in-depth critique of this calculative reason and its objectivising instrumentalisation of the world. Martin Heidegger criticized the instrumentalisation of humanity's proper thinking and the "enframing" of modern technology that reveals the world only insofar as it is a thing to be used, a *"standing-reserve." See* Martin Heidegger, "The Question Concerning Technology," in *Basic Writings: from Being and Time (1927) to The Task of Thinking (1964)*, ed. David Ferrell (New York: Harper and Row, 1977), 287. The philosophers of the Frankfurt School developed a critique of the instrumentalisation of reason under the guise of civilisational modernity. According to Theodor Adorno and Max Horkheimer, because the Western Enlightenment has become "totalitarian," the world has become intelligible to humankind only insofar as to make its multiple forms calculable: "Now that self-preservation [of humanity] has been finally automated, reason is dismissed." See Max Horkheimer and Theodor W. Adorno, *Dialectic of Enlightenment: Philosophical Fragments*, ed. Gunzelin Schmid Noerr, trans. Edmund Jephcott (Stanford, CA: Stanford University Press, 2002), 24–25. Not only is reason dismissed, but reason itself becomes subsumed under calculative or instrumental reason. This type of reason and technology become a means of control, domination, and exploitation, and their abuse threatens the survival of humanity.

 | DOI 10.1163/9789004361911_013

relations of the human being with himself or herself, with others, and with nature.

Culture provides the context in which human beings develop into distinct individuals. An individual depends on interpersonal relations and on cultural traditions in the formation and development of personal identity. However, in culture, negative tendencies are shown in the loss of spirituality and the weakening of the role of human values, which is supposed to counterbalance politics as a struggle for power and self-serving interests.

Culture in relation to power can be used for either emancipation or subjection. Culture is liberating in that it frees human beings from the material dependencies of nature and liberates us from the restrictive fate of being only "political," "economic," or "technical" human beings. However, it also creates new, symbolic dependencies—on customs, traditions, conventions, and values—that constrain persons as members of particular groups. Culture can also be used for the ideological justification of politics. The distorted and ideologically abused culture imposes limitations with its own idiosyncrasies, manias, phobias, ideological indoctrination, and information filters, which have the potential to create an oppressive cultural environment for its members. Such a distorted culture, instead of being an antidote to politically organized or structural violence, becomes complicit with it. Cultural violence refers to aspects of a culture that can be used to legitimize structural violence. This can be seen in religion, ideology, and language, as well as in the prevailing attitudes and beliefs that justify structural violence, making it seem natural.

Philosophers draw attention to the growing tendency of man toward extreme experiences, such as virtual practices, extreme psycho-practices, and transgressions, as well as unprecedented violence, including mass shootings (even in schools) and suicidal terrorism. All of this shows changes occurring to man. Michel Foucault, Georges Bataille, Maurice Blanchot, and Gilles Deleuze, among others, all study these extreme experiences.

Philosophers see this as an anthropological phenomenon and try to understand the problems facing humankind and possible solutions. Thus, a better understanding of the human being as such and a new philosophical anthropology are needed. Today's philosophers—similar to the Stoics during the decline of the Roman Empire or to the existentialists at the time of the two World Wars—try to find in the inner intellectual and spiritual resources of individuals the fortitude to resist the depersonalizing and violent tendencies of the social system. With the inner self-transformation of individuals, including the "practices of the self" and "spiritual practices," philosophers connect their hopes for the path toward inner harmony, the humanization of culture, and peace.

The works of Michel Foucault have made a significant contribution to the ongoing discussions regarding the subjectivity and power, as well as ambivalent role of culture, which can be used as either an instrument of domination or a resource in human striving for freedom. His late works outline the ideas for a new philosophical anthropology. Foucault introduced an anthropological and philosophical concept of the practices of the self (*pratiques de soi*). In his study of the historical development of the practices of the self, Foucault distinguishes three major models of practices of the self: the Platonic, the Hellenistic, and the Christian.

In this chapter, I start with some observations on Foucault's analysis of the history of practices of the self in Christianity, mainly of the practices of confession and of pastoral power, paying special attention to his critique of the Western "morality of asceticism" and "self-renunciation" as a form of control of individuals and domination. Foucault sees an alternative in the Hellenistic model of practices of the self, which inspires him to the idea of an ethics of taking care of oneself. Next, I will focus on the contribution of Foucault's theory of the practices of the self to the emergence of a new philosophical anthropology. Finally, I will examine how some of the insights of a new philosophical anthropology have found their original development in "synergic anthropology."

The Subject and Power

Foucault describes the main objective of his lifelong philosophical project as "to sketch out a history of the different ways in our culture that humans developed knowledge about themselves," analyzing any science of man as "games of truth" (and as "imaginary sciences" in the sense that their foundations do not lie in the things themselves but are derivative of man's relations with himself) related to "specific techniques that human beings use to understand themselves."[2] He distinguishes four major types of interrelated technologies, which people use to understand who they are, each representing a matrix of practical reason: technologies of production, of signs systems, of power, and of the self. He is interested mainly in the last two, technologies of power and of the self. In his late works, he focuses on:

2 Michel Foucault, "Technologies of the Self," in *Technologies of the Self: Seminar with Michel Foucault*, eds. Luther H. Martin, Huck Gutman, and Patrick H. Huttman (Amherst: University of Massachusetts Press, 1988), 17–18.

> technologies of the self which permit individuals to effect by their own means or with help of others a certain number of operations on their own bodies and souls, thoughts, conduct, and way of being, so as to transform themselves in order to attain a certain state of happiness, purity, wisdom, perfection, of immortality.[3]

Foucault's concern with subject vis-à-vis power is a leitmotif of his works. As he notes, "it is not power, but the subject, that is the general theme of my research."[4] He explores the different ways in which contemporary society has expressed the use of power to "objectivize subjects." The subject is studied mainly in relation to power, as dominated but also as striving for freedom. He considers his objective to be the study of the history of the different modes by which, in our culture, human beings are made subjects, dealing especially with "three modes of objectification that transform human beings into subjects."[5] The study of these modes marks the major phases in the development of Foucault's project: a theme of the subject is examined in relation to discourse, power, and self-formation.

In the first phase, Foucault analyzes the modes of inquiry that try to give themselves the status of sciences. In the second, he studies the objectivizing of the subject in what he calls "dividing practices." In the third, he concentrates on "the way a human being turns him- or herself into a subject."[6] The novelty of his latest works is the change of the focus from the practices of power to the "practices of the self." He makes a theoretical shift to those forms of understanding that the subject creates about himself or herself, to "the forms and modalities of the relation to self by which the individual constitutes and recognizes himself *qua* subject."[7]

After his earlier study of practices of power and knowledge, in his latest works, Foucault focuses on the immanent constitution of the subject and "practices of the self" as practices of the self-transformation of the subject. In terms of his inquiry of what he calls "the games of truth," his initial study of their interplay with one another in sciences and their interaction with power relations later on shift to the study of "the games of truth in the relationship

3 Foucault, "Technologies of the Self," 18.

4 Michel Foucault, "The Subject and Power," in *Power*, ed. James D. Faubion (New York: The New Press, 2000b), 327.

5 Foucault, "Subject and Power," 326.

6 Foucault, "Subject and Power," 327.

7 Michel Foucault, *The History of Sexuality*, vol. 2, *The Use of Pleasure* (New York: Vintage, 1990), 6.

of self with self and the forming of oneself as a subject." For his field of investigation, he takes "the history of desiring man."[8] This is considered as Foucault's anthropological turn, outlying a new, nonclassical philosophical anthropology.[9]

While in his previous works, Foucault examines the discursive and nondiscursive practices of the disciplinary power that governs individuals through techniques of controlling their conduct, in his later works, he studies individuals' reaction to coercive power, of the way in which they appropriate these manipulative techniques and internalize the prescribed truth and identity, and thus, how the outer manipulation becomes transformed into a self-imposed tutelage and an inner self-control. In particular, he unmasks the essential connection between power-knowledge relations and moralization.

Foucault explores the constitution of subjectivity through power relations. He distinguishes two meanings of the word "subject": one is "subject to someone else by control and dependence," the other is the subject "tied to his own identity by a conscience or self-knowledge."[10] Both meanings indicate a power that shapes the subject through external and internal influence.

He examines the first meaning in his studies of the power techniques oriented toward individuals. In *Discipline and Punish*,[11] he sheds light on individuals' ways of existing and knowing themselves. He describes a "micro-physics" of power, the techniques that target individuals, scrutinize the details of their behavior, and mold their conduct. The individual impact of power relations combines repression with manipulation and tutelage (ideological brainwash). The dignity of individuals' self-concern and self-knowledge as human beings is threatened by their modern condition as individuals whose conduct and normality is subject to supervision and manipulation.

The second meaning is articulated in Foucault's later studies of the "individualizing power," which imposes forms of self-awareness and identities, determining the way individuals perceive themselves. Foucault shows the danger of:

> this form of power that applies itself to immediate everyday life, categorizes the individual, marks him by his own individuality, attaches him to

8 Foucault, *Use of Pleasure*, 6.

9 Cf. Sergey S. Horujy, *Practices of the Self and Spiritual Practices: Michel Foucault and the Eastern Christian Discourse*, ed. Kristina Stoeckl, trans. Boris Jakim (Grand Rapids, MI: William R. Eerdmans, 2015), xxiii–xxv.

10 Foucault, "Subject and Power," 331.

11 Michel Foucault, *Discipline and Punish* (New York: Vintage Books, 1995).

> his own identity, imposes a law of truth on him that he must recognize and others have to recognize in him. It is a form of power that makes individuals subjects.[12]

In Foucault's later works, the themes of subject and power become more related to the problematic of governance. The exercises of power are analyzed in terms of government in a broad sense. This includes not only the political-ideological and institutional mechanisms of power, but also the government of individuals, the specialized practices and knowledge of the individual (such as punishment or psychiatry), the ways in which power makes contact with individuals, and the techniques for controlling their conduct and manipulating their self-consciousness. In his later works, Foucault "was particularly concerned with the forms and modalities in which individuals themselves appropriate such techniques, how external coercions become 'self-control,' how government becomes 'self-government.'"[13] His studies of the technologies of the self focus attention on the relationship of oneself to oneself through which the individual identifies himself or herself in particular ways and appropriates certain ideologies and rules of conduct in the process of self-formation.

Foucault pays particular attention to so-called pastoral power, with which he associates the individualizing power of the modern state. He traces the origins of this modality of power and its technique of subjection to Christian institutions and the concept of the deity or the leader as a shepherd followed by his flock of people. Later on, this became broadly spread in modernized forms. The "technology of the self," which was traditionally developed as means for self-formation and spiritual growth, then was adopted by the pastoral power for ecclesiastic control over the individual's soul and conduct. In contrast to political power, which recognizes sovereignty and other legal principles, pastoral power is salvation-oriented, obligatory, and individualizing. It involves an obligation of truth of the individual exercised through confession, exploring the soul, and seeking to know and to control one's conscience. Christian pastorship implies a peculiar type of knowledge between the pastor, who must know what goes on in everyone's soul, and his flock, who must know themselves and unveil the depths of their souls, confessing their sins. Foucault attributes to the origin of Christianity "the emergence of a very strange phenomenon in

12 Foucault, "Subject and Power," 331.

13 Michael Clifford, *Political Genealogy after Foucault: Savage Identities* (New York: Routledge, 2001), 65.

Greco-Roman civilization, that is, the organization of a link between total obedience, knowledge of oneself, and confession to someone else."[14]

With societal secularization since the eighteenth century, the pastoral power of the ecclesiastical institution has substantially diminished, but its function was spread and assimilated by the state as a "modern matrix of individualization," which became a new kind of state-related pastoral power. The modern Western state has integrated the traditional pastoral power technique into its political structure. The technology of the self, originally developed for spiritual purpose, was, in the modern state, transformed into "the political technology of individuals" and used by a secular government to control and manipulate its citizens' way of thinking and living. The so-called new pastoral power is a power practiced by the modern state and, in addition to the institutional means of control, includes an ideological manipulation and control of the individual's mind and conduct, modeled on the traditional ecclesiastic pastoral power inherited from Christianity.

In his studies of sexuality, Foucault shows how modern control of sexuality as a form of power is associated with allegedly scientific disciplines of sexuality and their norms. Individuals internalize those norms and try to conform to them, thus becoming controlled not only as *objects* of disciplines but also as self-scrutinizing *subjects*.

Along with his critique of pastoral power, Foucault analyzes other forms of rationalization of power: the doctrine of the rationality of state power as expressed in the concepts of "the reason of state" and "the theory of police." Foucault draws caustic conclusions about political rationality and the centralized state regulating the individual's life, qualifying such ideas of intervention in man's activities as "totalitarian." He argues that from the very beginning of its emergence, the modern state has been indifferent to both the interests of individuals and the requirements of community; however, it keeps both under control, and thus "the state is both individualizing and totalitarian." He concludes that "liberation can come only from attacking not just one of these two effects but political rationality's very roots."[15]

Individuals can be integrated into a sophisticated state structure "under one condition: that this individuality would be shaped in a new form, and submitted to a set of very specific patterns."[16] The new form of pastoral power becomes a matrix of such integration. The power of a pastoral type is no longer limited

14 Michel Foucault, "'*Omnes et Singulatim*': *Toward a Critique of Political Reason*," in *Power*, ed. James D. Faubion (London: Allen Lane, 2000a), 310.

15 Foucault, "'*Omnes et Singulatim*,'" 325.

16 Foucault, "Subject and Power," 334.

to religious organizations, but is spread out to a multitude of institutions and the individualizing "tactics" that permeate family, education, psychiatry, mass media, etc. Individuals are caught in a political "double bind" of "the simultaneous individualization and totalization of modern power structures."[17]

These observations help us better understand the hidden mechanisms of power. Foucault mentions fascism and Stalinism as pathological examples of extreme control of the system over individuals. At the same time, he warns that they are not quite original; they use mechanisms already present in most other societies: "in spite of their own internal madness, they used, to a large extent, the ideas and the devices of our political rationality."[18] Those totalitarian states were the most brutal, paradigmatic examples of power that went too far in manipulating individual citizens' minds and in totalizing them into a homogeneous mass blindly following their leaders. However, a similar pattern of power domination can also be practiced in more subtle and pseudo-democratic neo-totalitarian forms: Big Brother can wear different masks.

In today's high-tech society, sophisticated electronic technologies of surveillance and information collection are the powerful means abused by the state and other institutions for unprecedented control and manipulation of citizens. Excessive control over the individual self undermines individuals' human freedom and creativity at the cost of human degradation, thus aggravating the anthropological crisis. Thus, Foucault's observation—that never in the history of human societies has there ever been "such a tricky combination in the same political structure of individualization techniques and of totalization procedures"[19]—is quite relevant.

Domination generates resistance and desire for liberation. In addition to the traditional types of social struggles against forms of domination and exploitation, there is a struggle against ideological structures that determine the form of subjectivity. Foucault notices newly developing oppositions: "opposition to the power of men over women, of parents over children, of psychiatry over the mentally ill, of medicine over population, of administration over the ways people live."[20] All these multifaceted struggles revolve around the question of identity: Who are we? They express a refusal of both ideological state violence—ignoring our individuality—and of "scientific and administrative inquisition that determines who one is."[21] There is an increasing struggle against the forms

17 Foucault, "Subject and Power," 336.
18 Foucault, "Subject and Power," 328.
19 Foucault, "Subject and Power," 332.
20 Foucault, "Subject and Power," 329.
21 Foucault, "Subject and Power," 331.

of domination—"against that which ties the individual to himself and subjects him to others in this way,"[22]—namely against the submission of subjectivity. These forms are the more fundamental mechanisms of domination.

Foucault's critical analysis is his philosophical contribution to this struggle for human freedom and dignity. He considers how to get rid of this kind of political "double bind" of individualizing and totalitarian power, concluding with his call for liberation. An immediate critical task is to refuse an image of "what we are" that has been traditionally imposed on us, in order to liberate us "both from the state and from the type of individualization linked to the state." We need to discover what we are, "to promote new forms of subjectivity."[23]

Further in this chapter, I will examine how, in his late works, Foucault explores the possible new forms of subjectivity and envisions a new ethics of care for oneself as an exercise of freedom.

The State Ideology of Asceticism and Moral Demagogy

In his latest works, Foucault shifts his attention from the relations of power to knowledge to the relationship of power to morality. He makes a breakthrough in unmasking the essential connection between a certain kind of morality and power. Morality is used as a form of subjection. Foucault analyzes this kind of morality in Western societies, which he calls a morality of asceticism and self-renunciation. Among the historically rooted components of this morality, which shaped its main characteristics, he indicates the tradition of Christian morality, which makes self-renunciation a condition for salvation. This morality also inherited the legalism of "a secular tradition which respects external law as the basis for morality." Another inheritance is a conformist "social morality which seeks the rules for acceptable behavior in relations with others." Each of these components represents an external norm, whether religious, legal, or social, imposing restrictions on an individual's self-knowledge and care for oneself. The combination of these components results in a morality of asceticism, which "insists that the self is that which one can reject."[24] This morality is based not on respect for the self, but rather on the external norms which are incompatible with and hinder the concern for oneself. This morality imposes a straitjacket of austere principles on individuals, thus limiting the possibility of individuals exercising care for themselves.

22 Foucault, "Subject and Power," 331.

23 Foucault, "Subject and Power," 336.

24 Michel Foucault, "Technologies of the Self," 22.

The morality of asceticism, adopted and enhanced by official ideology, becomes for politicians a field of moral demagogy. First, it indicates the main parameters of power relations, in which an individual is insignificant by comparison to supra-individual entities, like the State, to which the moral authority is attributed. The individual's true individuality is said to reside in the political universal, the State. The individual is considered to be like Hegel's character in the world's historical drama: the process of merging the Absolute Spirit with itself, using the individual as a means of attaining its own goals, which justify its victims and sacrifices. Second, "ascetic" in this morality means a moral obligation of obedience to those considered to be "authorities." In this sense, asceticism means conformism rather than any restrictions on materialistic consumerism or exercise of power and domination over the others. The conformist, obedient attitude (including in a consumerist society) can result from fear of the oppressive State power or from internal pressures such as guilt over moral transgressions.

The morality of asceticism, transmitted through culture, instilled in the mass consciousness by the official ideology of the establishment, and orchestrated from the top, can have differing political implementations. It can be translated into a set of prohibitions (regarding way of life, sexuality, information, etc.) or prescriptions (hard work, patriotism, support of governmental policy, the sacrifice of one's economic interests, or even one's life in time of war), which are used for the political control and manipulation of the people. Authorities, exercising their power, claim to have also *ex officio* moral authority and possession of the "truth."

In moral demagogy, everything can be labeled as "good" or "evil"—the differences in social status, race, gender, ethnicity, religion, intellect, values, ideology, etc.—and be used as issues in the policy of "*divide at impera.*" This kind of "moral categorizing," which appeals to prejudices and emotions of fear and intolerance, is used to avoid any rational discussion of issues or justification of policy. Politicians, under the banner of morality, justify their power by campaigning and mobilizing the masses to fight against the "unbelievers," "class enemies," "non-patriots," "dissidents," "foreigners," "immigrants" and many other "others." They stir up racism, supremacism, and hegemonic exceptionalism. Proclaiming "America First" implies that the other nations are secondary and that the interests of humanity as a whole are of little interest at all.

Political demagogy equates policy with moral obligation; thus, loyalty to authority (and conformity to its rules) is imposed as a moral imperative. To disobey the morally dressed commands of authority is equivalent to challenging morality itself. Since the government claims to speak on behalf of morality, opposition is, therefore, portrayed as lacking moral qualities. In this context,

Foucault goes to the heart of the matter by stating, in his delicate manner, that "taking care of ourselves" is considered "an immorality, as a means of escape from all possible rules."[25]

Let us be clear: at issue is not morality itself, but its abuse by those in power. If the appeal to morality is invoked not for its own sake, and not from the moral motive, then it has no moral worth. If the intention of such an appeal is to coerce and dominate people, it is fundamentally immoral.

The appeal to morality can be (and actually is) used in power games as moral demagogy. This is a form of political demagogy, which plays on popular prejudices, moral feelings, and emotions, for the purpose of seizing political power. Moral demagogy is an abuse of the moral evaluation, in which an individual portrays himself or herself as the restorer of national morality and attributes moral degradation to others. Politicians, who select people (or even whole nations) by moral criteria, dividing them into "good" and "evil," presume God's role. Moral demagogy is used as a justification of violence. Politicians who practice moral demagogy usurp the right to represent the "good," while marking their opponents as "evil," thus demonizing them and portraying them as enemies, and then sanctioning hatred and violence against them. Religious and ideological fundamentalism, nationalism, supremacism, xenophobia, and hegemonic ambitions are facets of moral demagogy, when any nation or group presents their particular interest as an allegedly universal one and claims to have a monopoly on universal "freedom," "democracy," or "faith," thus dividing peoples and nations into good and evil.

An Ethics of Taking Care of Oneself as a Practice of Freedom

Foucault's attempt to critically overcome the Western morality of asceticism and to find an alternative to it led him to study the genealogy of ethics. In his historical research, he explores the roots of the modern ethical concepts. In the three-volume *The History of Sexuality*,[26] Foucault turns to Greco-Roman antiquity (Hellenistic and early Christian period). Placing Christianity in a historical perspective, he compares it with Hellenistic culture. In particular, he compares views of morality and the use of the technologies of the self in

25 Foucault, "Technologies of the Self," 22.

26 Michel Foucault, *The History of Sexuality*, 3 vols. (New York: Pantheon, 1978–1988). The first volume, *The Will to Knowledge*, was originally published in 1976; that appeared first in English translation in 1978. Volume 2 is titled *The Use of Pleasure*, and Volume 3 is titled *The Care of the Self*.

the context of the two cultures. This reveals the historical relativity of many modern concepts that had been considered absolute. In addition, a historical approach to Christianity shows significant differences between the first Christians and the later evolution of this religion, which became increasingly institutionalized and connected to power.

In his studies of the moral content of the "aesthetics of existence" in classical antiquity, Foucault finds a historical example of an alternative to the model of morality as obedience to a code of prohibitions and commandments (like morality of asceticism), and this alternative, as a form of ethics, shows the possibility of a new ethics as "the conscious practice of freedom."[27]

Foucault challenges the traditional view of morality in Western society, opposing to it his concept of ethics. He introduces some innovative methodological approaches. First of all, he views morality historically, in its historical-cultural transformations and different forms. He challenges the simplistic view of morality as obedience to a dogma or set of rules that are considered absolute. In contrast to such one-dimensionality, he examines differences. Second, instead of traditional studies of the moral theories, he turns the focus on *moral practices*, the behavior of individuals. He undertakes to study the forms and transformations of morality. He indicates the ambiguity of the term "morality" and distinguishes two meanings for it. One refers to "moral code," a prescriptive set of values and rules of action, enforced through family, educational institutions, churches, and other prescriptive agencies. Another meaning refers to "acts," to the real behavior of individuals and the manner in which they react to the moral code imposed on them. A rule of conduct does not automatically determine an individual's conduct. An individual may respect or disregard a given set of values, obey or resist a prescription, comply with a standard of conduct or transgress it. This is a matter of the individual's personal choice. This is the battlefield between external law (which can be used by the dominating power) and the inner world of an individual's thoughts and desires, the realm of an individual's freedom of choice and action.

Foucault emphasizes an important other side of the moral prescriptions: the relationship with the self. He distinguishes four major aspects of this relationship with the self that are common to all techniques of the self: the ethical substance, the types of subjection, the forms of elaboration of the self, and the *telos* (ultimate aim) or moral teleology.[28] He focuses on the study of the

27 Michel Foucault, "The Ethics of the Concern of the Self as a Practice of Freedom," in *Essential Works: 1954–1984*, vol. 1 *Ethics: Subjectivity and Truth*, ed. Paul Rabinow (New York: The New Press, 1997a), 281.

28 Foucault, *Use of Pleasure*, 32.

differences in each of these aspects of individuals' relation to themselves and to a prescriptive system operative in their culture. He shows such differences in comparison of Greek and Christian cultures. According to him, for example, in Christianity, the rules of sexual behavior were justified through religion, having become a kind of judicial form, and imposed through religious institutions. But in ancient Greece, there were no such obligations; mode of conduct was mainly a matter of personal choice. For the Greeks, the ethical substance was the *aphrodisia* (acts, desire, and pleasure); the mode of subjection was an aesthetic mode of building one's beautiful existence as a personal choice; the form of "practice of the self" was *tekhnē* about the body; and *telos* was to achieve mastery of oneself.[29]

Telos plays the central role in determining the techniques of self-forming activity (the practice of the self), and the other aspects of the relationship with the self. In other words, end determines means. He shows that in Christianity the *telos* and the technologies of the self became different than in ancient Greece.

In search for an alternative to the Western morality of asceticism, Foucault sketches some of the ideas of a new ethics. This ethics is supposed to help the individual liberate oneself from goals that have been hijacked by the power structure and imposed through the morality of asceticism, and to regain the individual's *telos* of taking care of oneself and exercising freedom. The new ethics implies a new relationship between an individual and the self and a new view of human beings, which potentially can help individuals transform themselves into free and responsible, ethical subjects of their own actions.

In his analysis of Plato's *Alcibiades*, Foucault points out the central role of the principle of care for oneself, to which everything else is related: political activity, education, knowing oneself, philosophical love, and relation to master. These relationships became the major themes of thought during the Hellenistic and later periods (in Seneca, Plutarch, Epictetus, among others), with quite different interpretations by the various schools. The view of taking care of the self became broader, eventually becoming for everybody a universal principle, a way of living throughout one's life.

Foucault pays attention to the development of a certain culture of taking care of oneself. It becomes a common philosophical theme, elaborated by Epicureans, Stoics, Cynics, and Pythagoreans. Their ideas are related to the practice of the self and are guides in the way of life, promoting activities to

29 Michel Foucault, "On the Genealogy of Ethics: An Overview of Work in Progress," in *Essential Works: 1954–1984*, vol. 1 *Ethics: Subjectivity and Truth*, ed. Paul Rabinow (New York: The New Press, 1997b), 267.

serve the soul through self-reflection, meditation, introspection, and reading and writing activities. In the culture of taking care of oneself, more attention is paid to sensitivity to the nuances of life, cultivating a subtlety of mind, delicacy of feeling, and more detailed introspection in various forms, including through self-expression in notes, letters, and treaties. By attending to the self, one is preparing oneself to confront the vicissitudes of life or death.

Foucault compares the meaning of *askēsis* (variant of "ascesis," from the Greek *ασκήσεις* "exercises") in Stoicism and in the Christianity. For both, the goal of *askēsis* is self-examination and purification. But the practice is quite different in each culture. For the Christian, it means the strictly devout ascetic life of struggle against the desires of the flesh, through prayer, fasting, and self-denial. Through practicing excessive rigor and self-denial the Christian fights the temptation to sin and thereby grows in spiritual strength. For the Stoics, *askēsis* means the mastery over oneself in order to transform oneself, the practices by which one can acquire truth and apply it as a principle for action. Thus, *aletheia* becomes *ethos*. Through a system of ascetic exercises, one can test one's strength and verify an ability to confront events. In Stoic ethics, each correct choice and action is a step toward our eventual *telos* of living in accordance with nature and in harmony with divine plan. An initial concern with yourself can be later extended to those close to you and eventually to all of mankind, paving the road toward justice.

According to Foucault, the interrelation of the care of the self and the knowledge of the self is decisive for the state of the individual, culture, and society. The famous Delphic maxim "know thyself" (*gnōthi seauton*) directs the individual to focus knowledge first of all on oneself and thus is related to the care of the self (*epimeleia heautou*). Their dynamic interaction has changed through the different historical epochs. In Greco-Roman culture, the care of the self was closely related with knowledge of the self. Knowledge was subordinated to the practical end of self-mastery, which in turn was a condition for access to the truth. Greek philosophy held that "a subject could not have access to the truth if he did not first operate upon himself a certain work that would make him susceptible to knowing the truth—a work of purification, conversion of a soul by contemplation of the soul itself."[30] Ascesis was a price for access to truth.

The dynamic interaction of the care of the self and the knowledge of the self has changed through the different historical epochs. In the history of Western culture, there was also a kind of link between asceticism and access to truth up

30 Foucault, "Genealogy of Ethics," 278–279.

to the sixteenth century, but it was broken with the emergence of Descartes's rationalism, according to which direct evidence is enough, and evidence "is substituted for ascesis at the point where the relationship to the self intersects the relationship to others and the world."[31] Self-transformation was no longer considered necessary to access the truth, resulting in "a nonascetic subject of knowledge." Thus, one can be immoral and know the truth. The principle of knowledge of the self became disconnected from the principle of the care of the self. The connection between spirituality and rationally grounded reflection was broken. This change made possible the institutionalization of modern science. In the thought of Western Modernity, the dominant principle of knowledge, separated from spirituality, became the only requirement to access the truth. This led to the predominance of instrumental rationality and its dehumanizing effects.

In his study of morals, Foucault distinguishes between moral code and acts, the real behavior of people in relation to the moral prescriptions imposed on them. He emphasizes that all moral action is not merely conformity to a law or a value, but it also involves a relationship with the self: the self-formation as an "ethical subject." A moral action usually refers to moral conduct, which calls for forming oneself as an ethical subject, and this self-formation involves modes of subjectivation—the way a subject freely relates to himself or herself—which is supported by ascetics or practices of the self. This self-formation is characterized as a process, structured in accordance with the modes of subjectivation—the ethical substance, the mode of subjection, and the ethical work, all oriented toward the *telos* of the ethical subject. This is a process of self-transformation, which involves several steps, in which the individual focuses in the object of his or her moral practice, defines his or her position regarding a rule of conduct, and then decides on a certain mode of being that will serve as his or her moral goal: "And this requires him to act upon himself, to monitor, test, improve, and transform himself."[32] He stresses an important aspect of the moral prescription "the kind of relationship you ought to have with yourself, *rapport à soi*," which Foucault calls ethics. This relationship to oneself "determines how the individual is supposed to constitute himself as a moral subject of his own actions."[33]

A moral obligation in relation to self is not a mere derivative or "function" of an external code internalized by an individual, but rather a moral obligation

31 Foucault, "Genealogy of Ethics," 279.

32 Foucault, *Use of Pleasure*, 28.

33 Foucault, "Genealogy of Ethics," 263.

that he or she establishes for himself or herself and that gives form to the self. To constitute oneself as a subject means to establish a moral obligation regarding a domain of one's own experience. This is the inner realm of the freedom and creativity of self-formation. In contrast to the morality of asceticism and self-renunciation—in which apparent altruism leads to limiting the individual's ability to take care of himself or herself and therefore of others, and at the same time makes the individual vulnerable to the new pastoral power and domination, which masks its self-interest by the hypocritical altruism—Foucault emphasizes the priority of taking care of oneself as a pivotal point of the ethics of a free person. As he writes, "the care of the self is ethically prior in that the relationship with oneself is ontologically prior."[34]

"Take care of yourself" and "know thyself" are the maxims of classical Greek culture, which concentrate the whole philosophy of life. Foucault reveals the depth of their ontological, ethical, and political meanings through studies of the representative texts of Plato and of the late Stoics, in which moral reflection is interwoven with the theme of taking care of the self. Such texts are a reflection on practices, and a type of ethical manual for individuals to appropriate certain values and techniques of self-formation and to define a mode of being. Foucault creatively assimilates some of these tenets in sketching his outline for a new ethics.

Taking care of the self is the mode in which individual freedom is reflected as an ethics. It is the ethical axis for the proper practice of freedom, of right conduct, of knowing oneself and of forming oneself, mastering one's appetites in order not to be their slave. As Foucault writes, "in antiquity, ethics as the conscious practice of freedom has revolved around this fundamental imperative: 'Take care of yourself.'"[35]

Foucault in his analysis of the relationship between freedom and ethics indicates that the Greeks problematized their freedom as an ethical problem. He uses the original Greek term *êthos* (*ēthos*), which has had a much more personal and deeper meaning than the contemporary term *ethics*. For ancient Greeks *ēthos* meant not only a certain way of acting but also a mode of being for the subject. A person who practiced freedom in a certain way, possessed a splendid *ēthos*, which was evident in his appearance and behavior, and it was praised and honored as an example. This was the concrete form of freedom and the way Greeks problematized freedom as *ēthos*. This *telos* could be achieved only as the result of practice and of efforts at self-formation.

34 Foucault, "Concern of the Self," 287.

35 Foucault, "Concern of the Self," 285.

As Foucault emphasizes, “extensive work by the self on the self is required for this practice of freedom to take shape in an *ēthos* that is good, beautiful, honorable, estimable, memorable, and exemplary.”[36]

Taking care of the self is frequently misinterpreted as being tantamount to selfishness and immorality. In response, Foucault asserts that taking care of the self is ethical in itself; but at the same time, it implies ethical relationships with others. The Greeks' *ēthos* of freedom is also a way of caring for others, insofar as the care of the self enables one to form interpersonal relationships and to occupy one's position in the community. One needs a counselor, a friend. Thus, the problem of relationships with others is present throughout the development of the care of the self. Taking care of the self always aims for the well-being of others, which implies that power relations should be managed in a nonauthoritarian manner. The postulate of this morality is that free persons properly caring for themselves are able to relate properly to others. Foucault views in this historical experience of ethical development elements that can serve today's search for a new ethics, opening possibilities for individuals to regain their freedom and humanity.

Philosophy is characterized by openness to all questions and possibilities, taking nothing for granted. As critical thinking, philosophy calls into question all authority that takes itself for granted, ideological positions that are presented as having no need for further examination, and domination. In this regard, Foucault emphasizes the critical role of philosophy, relating it to the Socratic maxim “take care of yourself.” This means, “make freedom your foundation, through the mastery of yourself.”[37] Foucault himself follows this path, warning of the dangers of power, calling into question domination in every form in which it exists, and thus helping individuals free themselves and become creators of their own aesthetics of existence.

Toward a New Philosophical Anthropology

In Foucault, the concept of the care of the self is interrelated with his anthropological and philosophical concept of the practices of the self. Both concepts provide the basic orientation regarding the self and the others, which requires focusing on oneself and performing upon oneself certain actions in order to change and transform oneself. The practices of the self are the anthropological core of the care of the self, while at the same time “the care of the self

36 Foucault, “Concern of the Self,” 286.

37 Foucault, “Concern of the Self,” 301.

extends the practices of the self into an integral cultural and social strategy."[38] Foucault's theory of the practices of the self became the groundbreaking work for a new philosophical anthropology.

Foucault's project was unfinished at the time of his untimely death, and as such, it has certain limitations. Pierre Hadot, whose studies on spiritual exercises in antiquity Foucault considered beneficial for his own project, praises Foucault's meticulous description of the practices of the self articulated by Stoic philosophers, but at the same time delineates "differences of interpretation."[39] Hadot believes that a "conversion toward the self" leads to "the higher psychic level" and "a new being-in-the-world," in which "one identifies oneself with an 'Other': nature, or universal reason, as it is present within each individual."[40] This implies a radical transformation of perspective, which has a universalist, cosmic dimension: "interiorization is a going beyond oneself; it is universalization." In Hadot's opinion, Foucault "did not sufficiently insist" on this.[41]

Another limitation of Foucault's project is that his "Christian model" relates mainly to Western Christianity, ignoring the theological and ascetical experiences of Eastern Christianity. His model of practices of the self is limited by the analysis of early Christian ascesis as it is described by John Cassian and Augustine. His analysis of the sacrament of confession is based mainly on examples from the Catholicism of the sixteenth and seventeenth centuries. This project can be broadened toward the reconstruction of the history of subjectness as a process of the change of formations of practices of the self up to the present. The inclusion into this reconstruction of the ascetical experiences of Eastern Christianity sheds an additional light on the rich history of Christian spiritual traditions.

Nevertheless, the groundbreaking innovations of Foucault's philosophy remain relevant. His theory of practices of the self is rightly considered an important step toward nonclassical anthropology. The main theme of Foucault's philosophy is the immanent constitution of the subject and the practices of the self-transformation of the subject. These practices are constitutive for human beings and they are at the anthropological level of reality.

Some philosophers have begun to rethink Foucault's theory of the practices of the self in their search for a new anthropology. For example, similarly to Foucault, Sergey Horujy develops an alternative to classical philosophical

38 Horujy, *Self and Spiritual Practices*, 18.

39 Pierre Hadot, *Philosophy as a Way of Life: Spiritual Exercises from Socrates to Foucault*, ed. Arnold Davidson, trans. Michael Chase (Oxford UK: Blackwell, 1995), 206.

40 Hadot, *Way of Life*, 211.

41 Hadot, *Way of Life*, 211.

anthropology, which is based on principles of subject, essence, and substance, using a methodology of abstract postulates and speculative essentialist constructions. As he writes, "Foucault's theory of practice of the self is the most significant contemporary essay in anthropological thought; perhaps it is also the first substantial outline of a new anthropology."[42]

Horujy's philosophical project aims to elaborate upon an anthropology that would overcome the limitations imposed by Western metaphysics. He offers his own philosophical and anthropological proposal: "synergic anthropology." It shares several common basic features with Foucault's theory: both are based on nonclassical and nonessentialist principles; they reject a Cartesian conception of the subject and epistemology; and they characterize anthropological reality not by abstract categories, but by anthropological practices. Synergic anthropology represents a particular approach to the hermeneutics of the subject, focused on the constitutive practice of the self-transformation of man. Horujy writes about Foucault's project: "As far as the idea of the practices of the self is concerned, it merits nothing but the most respectful praise; in our opinion, this idea, which is revolutionary with respect to classical anthropology, is extremely relevant, extraordinary rich, and exceptionally full of promise. Moreover, it has a whole web of connections with synergic anthropology, and these connections are useful and valuable for the latter."[43] The distinctive characteristic of synergic anthropology is that it relates these aforementioned common features to the Eastern Christian discourse.

Horujy compares Foucault's theory of practices of the self and the Eastern Orthodox Christian ascetical tradition of hesychasm (from Greek *ἡσυχία, hesychia*: stillness, rest, quiet, silence—an ancient mystical tradition of prayer and spiritual practices), revealing an affinity between their insights into new approaches to philosophical anthropology.[44] This broadens the experiential basis of studies. For example, Foucault characterizes the practices of the self of the Roman Stoics as anthropological experiences in which a human being practices self-transformations involving all the levels of human organization aimed at achieving a goal.[45] Horujy's approach to a new anthropology is close to that view in its logic and methodology, but it is based on the experiences of world spiritual traditions, and foremost on the spiritual practices of Eastern

42 Horujy, *Self and Spiritual Practices*, xxv.

43 Horujy, *Self and Spiritual Practices*, 164.

44 Horujy, *Self and Spiritual Practices*, 99–102, 123–131.

45 Michel Foucault, *The Hisotry of Sexuality, vol. 3, The Care of the Self* (New York, Pantheon, 1986).

Orthodox Christian hesychasm. In the spiritual tradition of hesychasm, he finds a viable model of "practices of the self" and the ground for developing an alternative to the traditional anthropology, which would think beyond the classical subject and toward the human being.

The hesychast tradition is rooted in the earliest Christian asceticism and, despite having undergone many crises and interruptions, it continues now. This ascetic tradition can open a new horizon of a culture of personality, of a specific mode of existence, of transformative practices of the self. The hesychast tradition also represents an original view of human beings, of their consciousness and actions. The reconstruction and philosophical reflection on hesychast practices and spiritual tradition, in the light of the quest for a new anthropology, can provide heuristically valuable insights. They serve as the basis for the development of synergic anthropology.

Horujy develops synergic anthropology with a reconstruction of hesychasm, focusing on its anthropological meaning and insights for a new approach to philosophical anthropology. Synergic anthropology asserts that a relationship of synergy (Greek *synergia*, "cooperation") exists between God and human beings, resulting in harmony and cooperation between Divine and human energies. Synergic anthropology is oriented toward the exploration of the rich philosophical and psychological potential of hesychast and other traditions of spiritual practice and applying it to the development of a new comprehensive anthropological model. In synergic anthropology, several new programmatic ideas are formulated as follows:

> (1) Instead of any essentialist concepts, the new anthropology is based on the concept of *energy* and presents an approach to the phenomenon of man as an "energic formation." (2) The new approach to the comprehension of anthropological reality is not speculative but rather an experiential discourse based on human practices. It is focused on "anthropological experience," which includes religious experience of faith, such as the hesychast mystical experience. (3) Instead of the postulated "nature" or essence of man, synergic anthropology uses the notion of the "constitution of man," which is pluralistic and experiential, and includes all man's manifestations and structures of personality. (4) Human constitution is formed up in "extreme experience," in which human beings reach the limits and the horizon of human consciousness.

Horujy further elaborates on these ideas in light of his concept of "anthropological unlocking." The unlocking or the openness is any kind of human being's encounter with the Other, including another person or surrounding reality.

The unlocking, understood energically, occurs during the encounter of the configuration of the energies of a human being with energies of the Other.[46]

The unlocking is constitutive for the human being as such. Horujy distinguishes different kinds of extreme experience, producing different types of man's constitution or anthropological formations. In all extreme anthropological manifestations, which he terms the "Anthropological Border," he describes three areas corresponding to the three basic kinds of the constitutive anthropological unlocking: ontological, ontic, and virtual.

This reminds us of Marin Heidegger's distinction between the categories of ontological and ontic.[47] His distinction is used in synergic anthropology to describe a variety of human manifestations: a contrast between an authentic horizon of being which constitutes the "ontological border of man," and the horizon of the empirical human existence with the "ontic border of man" defined by the unconscious. Below it there is virtual reality.

The first and highest kind of unlocking, related to spirituality, is the *ontological* unlocking, in which man attains his openness to the Other-being, actualizing his relation to being as distinct of present empirical being (the ontological difference). The main sphere of such unlocking is religious life. Individuals' task is to open themselves to Divine energies and achieve synergy with them: unlocking themselves toward the other mode of being (or, more correctly, toward genuine being). In hesychast practice, in ontological unlocking, "human energies achieve openness to the Other-being, to 'personal being-communion' playing the part of the meta-anthropological *telos* of the practice."[48] The hesychast practice serves as a prototype of ontological unlocking. A similar kind of anthropological unlocking can be found in spiritual practices of other world religions.

The second kind of unlocking is the so-called *ontic* unlocking. Its extreme experience does not actualize the ontological difference but is restricted to present being. Its examples are related to the area of unconscious, such as neuroses, manias, etc. The third kind is the *virtual* unlocking, which is realized in virtual practices, for example in cyberspaces.

These ideas and concepts outline the starting ground of a nonclassical, nonessentialist, and subjectless anthropological model, based on the synergic paradigm of unlocking. It can serve as the basis for exploring the issue of the constitution of personality and identity. Synergic anthropology identifies three principal types of the constitution of man as such, corresponding to the

46 Horujy, *Self and Spiritual Practices*, 124.

47 Martin Heidegger, *Being and Time* (New York: Harper, 1962).

48 Horujy, *Self and Spiritual Practices*, 124.

three basic mechanisms of anthropological unlocking: ontological, ontic, and virtual.

Ontological man is constituted by the synergy of man's energies and of energies of the Other-being. Constitutive experience is that of the actualization of man's relation to being, distinct from empirical being. This is the experience of man's openness to being. His identity is formed "in the process of ascent on the ladder of energic forms, a ladder oriented toward the Other-being as the meta-anthropological *telos* of the whole process."[49] The identity constituted in this way is called "participative identity," because it is achieved through participation in the energies of the Other-being as the supreme source of the identity. This identity is formed through the ascending spiritual-anthropological process, which takes place in a "personal communion": in the encounter with the energies of the Other-being and in the transindividual, intersubjective technologies of the spiritual practice. In this communion, a building up of personality takes place—with the increase of self-consciousness, strengthening of character and growth.

"Personal communion" is not connected with relations of power. It is different from the practices of confession, described by Foucault as related to pastoral power and someone's domination. "'Personal communion'—in the sense in which we are using it, i.e., oriented toward 'personal being-communion,' toward interchange of being—and the discourse of power, the power relation, are mutually exclusive."[50]

There is also another difference. Foucault describes how "renunciation of the self" became distorted as a kind of morality adopted by official ideology. In contrast to that, the meaning and the content of ascetic spiritual practices (including repentance, fasting, and so on) are directly opposite to that distortion: they are not destructive but constructive. Conversion to the self is a choice of strategy alternative to the ordinary mode of existence and entails a total self-transformation. Spiritual practices are the creative processes in which a new type of subjectiveness is actualized. It starts with renunciation of one's "old self" as a necessary premise of self-unlocking and person-creation in acquiring one's "true self" at the end, as the path aiming to ascent to *theosis*, deification.[51]

"Personal communion," becoming ever deeper, gradually approaches interchange of being—the paradigm of the trinitarian Divine Being, called in

49 Horujy, *Self and Spiritual Practices*, 126.
50 Horujy, *Self and Spiritual Practices*, 122.
51 Horujy, *Self and Spiritual Practices*, 110.

Greek "*perichōrēsis*" (from the Greek *perichōrein* "to go around"), and in Latin "*circumincession*" (from the Latin *circum-*, "around," and *incedere*, "to go along"). The term means the "interpenetration" of the three persons of the Trinity. It describes a "timeless process of permanent mutual exchange of being" that is called "ontological or absolute communication."[52]

Ontic man is radically different from the ontological man, and is characterized as the result of the replacement of ontology by topology.[53] It is constituted in patterns of the unconscious (social pathologies, such as "neuroses of civilizations" and phobias, studied by Sigmund Freud), which generate disorders and dysfunctions, showing defects of identity. *Virtual man* is characterized by "underactualized identity," which is incomplete and deficient. The present-day situation is characterized as "the beginning of the period of Virtual Man's dominance."[54]

Horujy characterizes the current situation as a successive decline: "man's downward slide on the Anthropological Border" from the ontological, to the ontic, to the virtual.[55] This process is reflected in the predominance of commercialized "mass-culture" and politicized simulacra of religions. Persons in spiritual practice (regardless of their tradition) feel a part of all of humanity in their orientation toward meta-anthropological *telos*. In contrast, persons with ontic, reduced identities identify themselves only with some "group" or "minority," thus diminishing their humanity. This tendency can lead to the transformation of humanity into a conglomerate of conflicting minorities waging religious-cultural wars among themselves.

This downward slide is evident in transgression, going beyond social limits, violence (including the phenomenon of suicide terrorism), extreme psycho-practices, genetic- and gender-related issues, and virtual experiences. The increasing "virtualization" of human existence leads to the degeneration of actual reality: "virtualization, when it becomes more deeply implanted, will inevitably turn into the scenario of euthanasia, the virtual death of humankind."[56] In warning about the dangers of these tendencies, Horujy does not diminish or trivialize the gravity of the crisis at the anthropological level, which erodes the very core of humanity.

---

52 Sergey S. Horujy, "Contribution of the Eastern-Orthodox Tradition to the Formation of the Dialogical Civilization," (Moscow, 2012), accessed July 22, 2017, http://synergia-isa.ru/wp-content/uploads/2013/03/hor_dialog_cicvlization.pdf.

53 Horujy, *Self and Spiritual Practices*, 128.

54 Horujy, *Self and Spiritual Practices*, 146.

55 Horujy, *Self and Spiritual Practices*, 142.

56 Horujy, *Self and Spiritual Practices*, 146.

In search for possible solutions, he critically disavows deterministic conceptions of man and society. The new anthropology opposes the deterministic view of a human being, as, for example, developed by the twentieth-century tradition known as "philosophical anthropology" in its biological (Arnold Gehlen) and cultural (Erich Rothacker) versions, with its negative view of "human nature." In contrast to the traditional conceptualization of man as an essence and a center, Horujy describes man as an energic constellation and pluralistic being interacting with the energies of the "Other." Instead of a single "human being," he writes, "there exists an 'anthropological space' in which is actualized a collection of beings having fundamentally different constitutions of personality and identity and unceasingly undergoing transformations into each other of all kinds."[57] He holds that the development of the current situation of decline is by no means *pre*-determined: "the factors shaping the situation include man's will and freedom" and the possibilities to influence the situation, and thus "the fate of the fundamental structures of the Ontological topic is also by no means predetermined."[58]

The diagnosis of the problem already contains insights for the search for its possible solutions. Horujy suggests directing the analysis of the anthropological situation "to those still-preserved elements that are connected in one way or another with the Ontological topic" and to investigate the possibilities of the strengthening of these positive elements and of the creation of new elements enhancing the human ascendance toward becoming *Ontological man*. Instead of the degeneration to "cyborgs and mutants," a man, through the practices of the self and spiritual practices, can undergo self-transformation, aiming for "the (trans-) goal of actual transcending into the Personality, i.e. 'deification.'"[59]

Philosophers have been pondering possible solutions to this problem of extreme actions and transgression. They warn against the traditional pattern of "socialization," neototalitarian surveillance, control, and external prohibition. The discipline and punishment used by a State are unable to solve this human problem and are counterproductive because some of these destructive impulses are motivated by the natural human protest and rebellion against the depersonalizing and excessively controlling socioeconomic system, which deprives the individual of the necessary space for freedom and self-realization. Human beings always strive for full self-realization, but in contemporary society, this

57 Horujy, *Self and Spiritual Practices*, 131.
58 Horujy, *Self and Spiritual Practices*, 152.
59 Horujy, *Self and Spiritual Practices*, 150.

natural desire clashes against the stone wall of an extremely sophisticated individualized and totalized system of power. Thus now, individuals seek the complete actualization of their identity and full self-realization in the extreme character of personal experiences, striving to the limits of possibilities, to the border of the horizon of their existence.

As a solution, philosophers try to find constructive alternatives, suggesting the creation of different anthropological possibilities and strategies, capable of satisfying the individual's needs for full self-realization in a nondestructive, positive way. This should also include the construction of new institutions and fostering new possibilities for individuals. An alternative anthropological strategy should give an individual the necessary space for self-realization and actualization of one's complete identity in its integral form. Such a strategy, for example, is represented by the personal paradigm of the inner practice of the self. Spirituality is the realm of individual's inalienable freedom. Synergic anthropology shows the radically new, "maximally plastic, changing, and polyphonic image of Man—of Man who is capable of choosing stunningly different scenarios of self-realization."[60] An individual's choice of personal identity and future rests in one's own hands, and in this way an individual can find an inner peace.

Spiritual practice contains transindividual aspects, which include participation of another individual or of a community. Inner practice is an individual occurrence, but it is inseparably connected with some comprehensive superindividual, historical and social wholesomeness of spiritual tradition. The main reason for this lies in ontological and meta-anthropological nature of the inner practice. Spiritual tradition includes organization, interpretation, and examination of the experience that provide direction and individual help in the movement toward a meta-empiric goal. Spiritual tradition is inner-personal, transindividual, and a result of efforts of many generations in forming this experience, in developing many psychical and hermeneutical procedures and methods. Spiritual tradition lies between the anthropological reality and the global one, bridging both. The concepts of inner practice and spiritual tradition are considered the way to transfer the anthropological phenomena onto broader levels of the global reality.[61]

60 Horujy, *Self and Spiritual Practices*, 131.

61 Hesychasm at its mature stage tended to translate itself into the surrounding Christian world, playing an ameliorating role in the society. This characteristic is reflected in Russian hesychasm, which developed a new transindividual practice and the active interaction between ascetic tradition and society, as shown in the phenomenon of eldership. The monastic elders were hesychasts with inexhaustible love and the ability to see deeply into

The inner practice and a spiritual tradition, being a meta-anthropological strategy, constitute a sphere of anthropological manifestations, which are positive and creative. In relation to that there are so-called associate practices of a spiritual-cultural tradition (as expressed in literature and arts). This broad scope of practices and strategies can be spread in the contemporary world as a means to counter its current crisis.

Many spiritual traditions have several similarities. In comparing spiritual traditions such as classical yoga, Tibetan Tantric Buddhism, Taoism, Zen, Islamic Sufism, Roman Catholic spiritual exercises, or Eastern-Orthodox hesychasm, Horujy shows that despite their differences, spiritual practices share some universal ontological, methodological, and anthropological elements. He indicates some characteristics of a general "paradigm of spiritual practice," describing the anthropological foundations of the mystico-ascetic practices created in the world religions.[62] First, spiritual practice is a holistic practice of the Self oriented to a meta-anthropological telos ("higher spiritual state"), the goal of which is actual ontological transformation, transcending man's mode of being. It deals with the configuration of spiritual, psychical, and physical energies of a human being and their controlled and directed transformation. Second, spiritual practice has a progressive "ladder" structure as a series of steps from the initial step corresponding to Spiritual Gate, to the final one corresponding to the *telos* (the *telos* may be different for each spiritual tradition). Third, the central block of spiritual practice (the "anthropological mover") is a certain school of prayer or meditation with concentration of attention that functions as an ontological auto-training. Fourth, in the highest big block of spiritual practice there appear manifestations of the approaching change of the fundamental predicates of Man's horizon of being. Finally, the necessary condition of the achievement of the *telos* of spiritual practice is the participation of the "energies of the Other-being, Divine energies."[63] For example, Christian hesychasm and Buddhism both represent the meta-anthropological strategies and well-developed methodologies of spiritual practice. They have also substantial similarities in how their practitioners view reality.

---

a person's inner soul. They served as spiritual counselors of individuals through personal contact, not only helping to solve personal problems but also introducing them to the hesychastic way of life. Elders, such as those in the Optina Pustin Monastery, combined individual work of spiritual self-transformation with social life, mainly through the power of Christian love, bestowed by the grace of God. Optina Pustyn's Monastery became known worldwide through Fiodor Dostoevsky's novel *The Brothers Karamazov*.

62 Horujy, *Self and Spiritual Practices*, xxiv.

63 Horujy, *Self and Spiritual Practices*, 114.

Although each spiritual tradition is unique, spiritual traditions are not isolated; they are dialogically related.[64] The universal elements of spiritual practice can facilitate communication among people from different religious backgrounds and dialogue between their respective traditions. Personal communication is helpful for enhancing dialogue between diverse spiritual traditions. It involves face-to-face communication of living persons who possess unique personal and spiritual experience. Horujy calls this the "encounter in the depths."[65] Although divergences of participants can provoke mutual estrangement, participants' differences do not hinder communication; rather, they spark mutual interest and make dialogue more meaningful and profound; it opens the opportunity of complete self-realization to its participants. Spiritual tradition is the core of any religion. An advancement of a dialogue of spiritual traditions is essential for paving the way toward the interreligious and intercultural dialogue.

Horujy offers a philosophical anthropology that is open to religious experience and reflects the postsecular nature of our contemporary period. As he writes, "in postsecular dialogue many old ideological labels and barriers are removed, including, in the first place, the barriers between secular and religious consciousness, thought, spheres of social and cultural life." Such dialogue helps us to reduce growing threats and "it increases the chances for mutual understanding and survival of all of us in the global village."[66]

The practices of the self and spiritual practices, philosophically conceptualized in a new anthropology, promote the ideas of human freedom, justice, and peace. They represent an alternative to the ideologies of domination and "culture wars," which justify the vicious circle of violence.[67]

64 David Lochhead, *The Dialogical Imperative: A Christian Reflection on Interfaith Encounter* (Eugene, OR: Wipf and Stock Publishers, 2012).

65 Horujy, "Eastern-Orthodox Tradition," 6.

66 Horujy, *Self and Spiritual Practices*, xxi–xxii.

67 Philosophers point out the obstacles to dialogue created by monological thinking and domination, which is obvious in fundamentalism, supremacist exceptionalism, and authoritarian power. Less evident, while also damaging, is the abuse of universalistic notions, such as dialogue, once they are trivialized and downgraded to mere clichés in political demagogy or pseudo-philosophical sophistry. This can ruin even a learned organization if it fails to live up to democratic principles and instead falls prey to an internal power struggle. An example of this is shown in Jovino Pizzi's analysis of the crisis of the notorious "International Society for Universal Dialogue" (ISUD), demonstrating its demagogy and "the gap between the pretensions of 'universal dialogue' and the undemocratic monologic attitude of the parochial group controlling ISUD," which is neither international nor dialogical, and which "disgraces the whole idea of dialogue." Disappointed members demanded that the hijacked through the coup and fake organization be dissolved.

Johan Galtung, who introduced the term "cultural violence," denies that human nature condemns us to violence.[68] He opposes theories that cultural differences are the source of violence, such as Huntington's concept of "the clash of civilizations." In his recent works, Galtung stresses that the different cultures and civilizations have common ground for mutually beneficial cooperation, complementing each other. He lists the unique and positive characteristics of major world religions and ideas, which can constructively contribute to the progress of Humanity: "Let us focus on their positive aspects, for cooperation, not for clashes:

- Judaism: dialogues as truth not final declarations; intellectuality;
- Orthodoxy: long-term optimism Sunday Christianity—'Christ arisen';
- Catholicism: forgiving the sinner who confesses and rejects his sin;
- Protestantism: individualism/I-culture, individual responsibility;
- Americanism: freedom to innovate in science, culture, economy;
- Islam: collectivism/We-culture submission sharing rich to poor;
- Africanism: women in power distribution more than growth ubuntu;
- Hinduism: celebrating birth-protection-death linguistic communities;
- Buddhism: society as nets of relations-networks not individual knots;
- Daoism: reality as holisms forces/counterforces *yin/yang* dialectics;
- Confucianism: both rights and duties both at the top and the bottom;
- Chinaism: synergy buddhism-daoism-confucianism lifting the bottom up;
- Humanism: humans as the measure of all things (Protagoras);
- Naturism: nature—diversity-symbiosis—as the measure of all things.

Stimulate cooperation based on positives, and not paranoid security based on negatives: 'security studies' being academic paranoia."[69]

"The hijacking of a learned association and its detrimental consequences created a dangerous precedent, which is deeply troubling and unacceptable in the eyes of the international scholarly community." As he concludes, dialogue is a noble ideal, but "it can be (and is) a magnet attracting opportunists with hegemonic instincts who may cynically exploit it for their self-serving interests of power and money ... Thus, the adherents of genuine democratic dialogue need to be aware of this, to be able to separate the wheat of genuine dialogue from the chaff of pseudo-dialogic simulacra." See Jovino Pizzi, "Parochial monologuism under the guise of 'universal dialogue' (ISUD)," *Topologik* 21 (First semester 2017): 43, 57–58.

68 Johan Galtung, "Cultural Violence," *Journal of Peace Research* 27(3) (1990): 291–305. doi: http://www.jstor.org.gate.lib.buffalo.edu/stable/423472.

69 Johan Galtung, "The World Beyond Global Disorder," keynote address at the 13th World Public Forum "Dialogue of Civilizations," October 9, 2015, Rhodes, Greece, accessed July 22, 2017, http://www.wpfdc.org/images/2015_blog/Johan_Galtung_13RF.pdf.

Philosophers, who argue for harmony in diversity, see in the enhancement of sustained dialogue and of cross-cultural and interreligious interaction the possibility of a cosmopolitan perceptive for the humanity. Fred Dallmayr, reflecting on an emerging global city or community, views it as a historical journey of humanity toward cosmopolis: "Going beyond the narrow confines of anthropocentrism, the journey has to make ample room for dialogue and listening, for the humanizing demands of education, ethics, and spiritual insight. Differently put: *homo faber* has to yield pride of place to *homo loquens, homo quaerens,* and *homo symbolicus*."[70]

Bibliography

Clifford, Michael. *Political Genealogy after Foucault: Savage Identities.* NewYork: Routledge, 2001.

Dallmayr, Fred. "After Babel: Journeying toward Cosmopolis." In *Intercultural Dialogue: In Search for Harmony in Diversity*, 2nd ed., edited by Edward Demenchonok, 365–378. Newcastle upon Tyne, UK: Cambridge Scholars Publishing, 2016.

Dallmayr, Fred. "Introduction. The Courage to Hope." In *A World Beyond Global Disorder: The Courage to Hope,* edited by Fred Dallmayr and Edward Demenchonok, 1–15. Newcastle upon Tyne, UK: Cambridge Scholars Publishing, 2017.

Demenchonok, Edward, ed. *Intercultural Dialogue: In Search for Harmony in Diversity*, 2nd ed. Newcastle upon Tyne, uk: Cambridge Scholars Publishing, 2016.

Foucault, Michel. *The History of Sexuality*. 3 vols. New York: Pantheon, 1978–1988.

Foucault, Michel. "Technologies of the Self." In *Technologies of the Self: Seminar with Michel Foucault,* edited by Luther H. Martin, Huck Gutman, and Patrick H. Huttman, 16–49. Amherst: University of Massachusetts Press, 1988.

Foucault, Michel. *The History of Sexuality.* Vol 2, *The Use of Pleasure*. New York: Vintage, 1990.

Foucault, Michel. *Discipline and Punish*. New York: Vintage Books, 1995.

Foucault, Michel. "The Ethics of the Concern of the Self as a Practice of Freedom." In *Essential Works: 1954–1984*. Vol. 1, *Ethics: Subjectivity and Truth,* edited by Paul Rabinow, 281–302. New York: The New Press, 1997a.

70 Fred Dallmayr, "After Babel: Journeying toward Cosmopolis," in *Intercultural Dialogue: In Search for Harmony in Diversity,* ed. Edward Demenchonok (Newcastle upon Tyne: Cambridge Scholars, 2016), 366. See also Fred Dallmayr, "Introduction. The Courage to Hope," in *A World Beyond Global Disorder: The Courage to Hope,* eds. Fred Dallmayr and Edward Demenchonok (Newcastle upon Tyne: Cambridge Scholars, 2017), 1–15.

Foucault, Michel. "On the Genealogy of Ethics: An Overview of Work in Progress." In *Essential Works: 1954–1984*. Vol. 1, *Ethics: Subjectivity and Truth*, edited by Paul Rabinow, 253–280. New York: The New Press, 1997b.

Foucault, Michel. "*'Omnes et Singulatim'*: Toward a Critique of Political Reason." In *Power*, edited by James D. Faubion, 298–325. London: Allen Lane, 2000a.

Foucault, Michel. "The Subject and Power." In *Power*, edited by James D. Faubion, 326–348. New York: The New Press, 2000b.

Galtung, Johan. "Cultural Violence," *Journal of Peace Research* 27(3) (1990): 291–305. http://www.jstor.org.gate.lib.buffalo.edu/stable/423472.

Galtung, Johan. "The World Beyond Global Disorder." Keynote address at the 13th World Public Forum "Dialogue of Civilizations," October 9, 2015. Rhodes, Greece. Accessed July 22, 2017. http://www.wpfdc.org/images/2015_blog/Johan_Galtung_13RF.pdf.

Hadot, Pierre. *Philosophy as a Way of Life: Spiritual Exercises from Socrates to Foucault*. Edited by Arnold Davidson. Translated by Michael Chase. Oxford UK: Blackwell, 1995.

Heidegger, Martin. *Being and Time*. New York: Harper, 1962.

Heidegger, Martin. "*The Question Concerning Technology*." In *Basic Writings: From Being and Time (1927) to The Task of Thinking (1964), edited by David Ferrell.* New York: *Harper & Row,* 1977.

Horkheimer, Max, and Theodor W. Adorno. *Dialectic of Enlightenment: Philosophical Fragments*. Edited by Gunzelin Schmid Noerr. Translated by Edmund Jephcott. Stanford, CA: Stanford University Press, 2002.

Horujy, Sergey S. *Practices of the Self and Spiritual Practices: Michel Foucault and the Eastern Christian Discourse*. Edited by Kristina Stoeckl. Translated by Boris Jakim. Grand Rapids, MI: William R. Eerdmans, 2015.

Horujy, Sergey S. "Contribution of the Eastern-Orthodox Tradition to the Formation of the Dialogical Civilization." Moscow, 2012. Accessed July 22, 2017. http://synergia-isa.ru/wp-content/uploads/2013/03/hor_dialog_cicvlization.pdf.

Lochhead, David. *The Dialogical Imperative: A Christian Reflection on Interfaith Encounter*. Eugene, OR: Wipf and Stock Publishers, 2012.

Pizzi, Jovino. "Parochial monologuism under the guise of 'universal dialogue' (ISUD)," *Topologik: International Journal of Philosophy: Educational and Social Sciences* 21 (First semester 2017): 43–58.

CHAPTER 12

Toward a New Conception of Socially-Just Peace

Joshua M. Hall

Introduction

In this chapter, I approach the subject of peace by way of Andrew Fiala's pioneering, synthetic work on "practical pacifism." One of Fiala's articles on the subject of peace is entitled "Radical Forgiveness and Human Justice"—and if one were to replace "Radical Forgiveness" with "Peace," this would be a fair title for my chapter. In fact, Fiala himself explicitly makes a connection in the article between radical forgiveness and peace.[1] Also in support of my project, Fiala's article names four of the six historical figures who are central to my chapter, namely Marcus Aurelius, King, Arendt, and Nietzsche. Moreover, Fiala also insists there that "forgiveness must be held in creative tension with justice," and it is this very tension that forms the basis of my new conception of socially-just peace. To wit, I propose that socially-just peace is lovingly generous reimagining (peace) through intuitively self-overcoming tension (social justice).

To elaborate, peace is the result of imagining things to be different from our usual ways of seeing them, which requires a kind of generosity, which in turn requires a loving comportment. And social justice is the result of tapping into an intuitive knowledge, in order to catalyze a process of self-overcoming on the part of the oppressed, which self-overcoming allows them to channel the tensions produced by oppression into the fight against that oppression. Put briefly, socially just peace is sustainable tranquility (peace) through organismic empowerment (social justice). As will be clearer in my discussion of Marcus Aurelius below, by "tranquility" here I mean the Stoic sense of a calm, peaceful contentment. And by "sustainable," I intend the sense in contemporary ecological ethics, one crucial feature of which is the ability to prolong a given way of life indefinitely into the future.

The structure of this chapter is as follows. First, I will briefly summarize my conception of socially-just peace. Second, to elaborate and support this new

1 Andrew Fiala, "Radical Forgiveness and Human Justice," *Heythrop Journal: A Bimonthly Review of Philosophy and Theology* 53:3 (2012): 494–506, accessed August 31, 2016, doi: 10.1111/j.1468-2265.2010.00637.x.

 | DOI 10.1163/9789004361911_014

conception, I will offer etymological analyses of "peace" and "social justice." Third, I will sketch three historical conceptions germane to both terms (from Dr. Martin Luther King Jr., Marcus Aurelius, and Hannah Arendt, and from Benedict Spinoza, Friedrich Nietzsche, and Frantz Fanon). And finally, I will conclude with an application of this new conception to contemporary debates regarding feminism.

In recognition of the aforementioned tension that Fiala notes between peace and forgiveness (and that I am claiming applies also to peace and social justice), each of these four phases of my analysis will reframe this tension as a dialectical challenge—namely, by attempting to resolve the dialectical challenge of the preceding stage.[2] Regarding the first phase of my analysis, which involves a conceptual analysis, I describe peace as "sustainable tranquility" and social justice as "organismic empowerment." The dialectical challenge here becomes how to empower all organisms (social justice) without permanently disturbing the tranquility of the environment (peace). Put simply, how can we increase individuals' ability to overcome social injustice without making them more dangerous both to themselves and (nonthreatening) others?

Regarding the second phase of my analysis, its etymological analysis resolves this first dialectical tension (from the conceptual analysis), only to introduce a new dialectical tension, by revealing peace to be an imaginative fabrication of those armed for violence. Put as a question, how can we motivate individuals with an *actual* capacity for violence to engage in the collective production of a *potential* imaginative artwork of peace? Or, more simply, if violence is immediate and real, while peace is futural and imaginary, how can people be persuaded to abandon present certainty for future possibility?

Regarding the third phase, its historical analysis resolves this second (etymological) dialectical tension by revealing that (a) love can be polemical, (b) generosity flows from viewing oneself as divine, and (c) reimagining violent others requires imagining them as themselves insufficiently imaginative/thoughtless. And yet this too introduces a new dialectical tension. To wit, how can we tap into these hidden dimensions of love, generosity, and reimagining and render these complex conceptions of them accessible to an audience large enough to actually bring about peace?

2 By "dialectical" here, I mean the philosophical method introduced by Plato and most fully developed in Hegel and his successors. For the reader unfamiliar with it, in a dialectical method, one interlocutor posits a position, which a second interlocutor attempts to challenge and undermine, in response to which challenge the first interlocutor (or a third) modifies the initial position (typically in the direction of greater subtlety and sophistication).

And regarding the final phase, I will suggest that the resolution of this last dialectical tension is a concrete example of how a controversial public debate might be reframed by my new conception of peace. More specifically, on the subject of contemporary feminism, I will follow Alison Jaggar in calling for a lovingly generous reimagining of the battlefield over gendered justice, specifically by construing that field as containing—not only feminists and anti-feminists—but also what Jaggar terms "non-feminists."[3] It is the individuals constituting the latter group, who (per her definition) have not explicitly rejected feminism but who have not yet endorsed it either, whom we could most beneficially reimagine—as insufficiently imaginative or thoughtful to have understood the discrimination women continue to face in our global society. Insofar as this reimagining is valid, we would perhaps do well to direct a larger percentage of our pedagogical and socializing energies on this non-feminist group. As a result, we might be able to persuade them to join the feminist cause, thereby tipping the scales of social justice further to the good.

Conceptual Analyses of Peace and Social Justice

My new conceptions of peace and social justice draw on the discourses of biology and ecology. Beginning with peace, as "sustainable tranquility," it involves an understanding of peace as restfulness—in the etymological sense of being "filled with rest." Here, one could link peace to John Dewey's concept of "undergoing."[4] Central to this concept is the idea that animals are constantly active, even when we appear motionless, and that even something as apparently passive as sense-perception involves organismic activity. Translated into the human realm in general, we must actively choose to engage in activities that appear passive, including listening, waiting, sleeping, etc. Applied to the arena of peace in particular, this means that we must allow ourselves to undergo peace, which includes allowing other things and people to provoke us, and to stimulate the expansion of our imaginations.

By contrast, social justice as "organismic empowerment" could be linked to Dewey's complementary (to "undergoing") concept of "doing." In this way, social justice becomes something that we have to go out and actively pursue, instead of merely hoping that it will arrive one day on its own, or assuming

3 See, for example, Allison Jaggar, "Feminist Ethics: Projects, Problems, Prospects," in *Feminist Ethics*, ed. Claudi Card (Lawrence, KS: University Press of Kansas, 1991), 78–106.

4 See, for example, John Dewey, *Art as Experience* (New York: Penguin, 2005), 23.

thoughtlessly that we already have enough of it (or as much of it as one can hope for in a "fallen" world, etc.). As "organismic empowerment," social justice involves a sense of flourishing, in the etymological sense of an outward-spreading display, such as the feathers of a peacock, the panels of a Spanish fan, or the limbs of a trained dancer. (This inclusion of nonhuman examples is meant to recall that a flourishing world includes diversity, plurality, and heterogeneity, including of species). Put differently, social justice is a bottom-up, grassroots activity in which each organism is enabled to be its best self. This conception is not, therefore, a top-down, centralized imposition of just relations from above. Nor is social justice, on this account, a reductive affair in which one merely subtracts (as it were) "units" of injustice, as identified perhaps by some governing body or institution.

Seen in this comparative light, and continuing to draw on Dewey's thought, peace becomes a matter of the environment (or community), whereas social justice is more concerned with the organism (or individual) in that environment. In other words, peace is like a web, which requires multiple lines of connection in order to exist at all (since just one or two strands are insufficient to make a web). Social justice, however, amounts to nothing if it is merely connections and abstractions, and must instead be grounded in acts of social justice performed for each individual in a population.

This position is counterintuitive, in the Western tradition at least, where peace is often understood (in part due to the influence of Jewish and Christian theology) as first and foremost a state of mind or soul in the individual, whereas justice (at least since Plato's *Republic*) is often considered the paradigmatic sociopolitical virtue. It is precisely these more traditional conceptions of peace and justice, however, that have produced the thus-far irresolvable tensions between peace and social justice. That is, we Westerners tend to try to create peace individually and internally, and then become frustrated at our inability to expand internal peace into peaceful relationships with others. Complementarily, we devise schemes of abstract justice which have certain beauties qua images but which remain insubstantial when we attempt to tether them to the individuals who are actually suffering injustice.

The dialectical challenge of my new conceptions, though, involves how to facilitate and support organisms' constant creative exertion toward social justice, without those organisms' environments completely succumbing to exhaustion and/or frenzy. Put dramatically, if everyone starts seeking justice individually, and tries to coordinate peace among all the other justice-seekers, then it looks a bit like a typical superhero story line, in which a large number of exceptionally powerful individuals rip the world apart while trying to save it from one another.

Etymological Analyses of Peace and Social Justice

To resolve the aforementioned tension, it is necessary to explore the etymologies of the two central phrases being deployed in this discourse. For both etymologies, I draw on the discourses of myth and religion, locating the first in Jesus of Nazareth's conception of peace.[5] "Peacemaking" is based on a compound Ancient Greek word—*eirene-* + *poiesis*—which betrays a connection to the analyses of poetry as theatrical creation in Plato (through which connection the disciplined activity of peace could be understood as a kind of theatrical artwork).[6] In other words, peace is not only social (as the conceptual analysis already revealed) but artificial and fabricated as well. In contrast to this, social justice takes the form of Dike, the sword-bearing Greek goddess of human justice (or Dike's Roman counterpart, Iustus, with her famous blindfold, scales, and sword). In other words, social justice is not only individual (as the conceptual analysis already revealed) but also natural and real.

What follows from these new etymological understandings is that (a) peace will no more exist on its own than a novel or symphony that has never been imaginatively composed; and (b) social justice is so natural and actual that its denial will ultimately lead to violence, which entails that it requires something like self-restraint in regard to one's capacity for force (rather than as direct assertion of that capacity). These etymologies thus resolve the dialectical tension I identified in my conceptual analyses, namely by identifying the sources of that tension as (a) the artificiality/fabricated-ness of peace, and (b) the necessity of the discipline of self-restraint within effective fighters for social justice. Put differently, we must stop waiting for a peace that will never arrive by nature, and we must attempt to keep sheathed the swords with which social justice empowers us. This, however, begs the question as to how this fabrication and self-discipline can be attained, which constitutes the next dialectical challenge, and which requires a reinvestigation of alternative conceptions from the history of philosophy germane to peace and social justice.

Historical Analyses Germane to Peace and Social Justice

To resolve the aforementioned tension—as to how we can imaginatively compose peace (as sustainable tranquility) among the just (as empowered

5 See Matthew 5:9.

6 See for example, *Ion*, in *Plato: Statesman, Philebus, Ion* (Cambridge, MA: Harvard University Press, 1925).

organisms), who necessarily have the capacity for divisive harm—it is necessary to explore our history, to which the majority of the present chapter will be devoted. More specifically, I will consider three marginalized historical conceptions germane to peace, and three such conceptions germane to social justice. To foreshadow my analyses below, everything turns on the role of illusion, imagination, and even deception; and the common thread in the six thinkers is an emphasis on metaphors drawn from dance and poetry (as script and performance) in the context of the theatrical arts.

To clarify, what follows below are not all, or at least not necessarily, conceptions *of* peace and social justice, but rather conceptions that are useful for and/or illuminating of peace and social justice. Thus, I am not claiming that the first three theorists are "peace theorists" (or peace advocates) per se, nor that the latter three theorists are "social justice theorists." But that does not mean that the six thinkers do not offer insights potentially invaluable for those who do endorse these two causes. By implication, moreover, both clusters of theorists do not necessarily have much in common, because it is not necessary for two theorists who illuminate the same concept (like King and Aurelius regarding peace) to share a similar worldview. The synthesis of the six occurs, instead, in my own hybrid concepts of peace and social justice.

For peace, I will draw on the anthology of King's writings entitled *A Testament of Hope*, on Marcus Aurelius's *Meditations*, and on Hannah Arendt's *Eichmann in Jerusalem*.[7] Their respective conceptions of peace are as follows: (a) *agape* love torsioned away from god and toward the community (from King), in order to fund (b) divinely tolerant generosity toward others (from Aurelius), in the form of (c) imagining evil as merely banal and thus the others as forgivable (from Arendt). Put in terms of peace as "lovingly generous reimagining," King offers *love*, Aurelius *generosity*, and Arendt *reimagining*.

As for social justice, I will draw on Spinoza's *Ethics*, Nietzsche's *Thus Spoke Zarathustra*, and Fanon's *Wretched of the Earth*.[8] Their respective conceptions of social justice are as follows: (d) an intuitive maximization of one's being as a mode (or stylization) of the cosmos (Spinoza), (e) which maximization erupts

7 Martin Luther King Jr., *A Testament of Hope: The Essential Writings and Speeches of Martin Luther King Jr.*, ed. James M. Washington (New York: HarperOne, 2003); Marcus Aurelius, *Meditations*, trans. Martin Hammond (New York: Penguin, 2006); and Hannah Arendt, *Eichmann in Jerusalem: A Report on the Banality of Evil* (New York: Penguin, 2006a).

8 Baruch Spinoza, *Spinoza's Ethics*, ed. and trans. G.H.R. Parkinson (Oxford: Oxford University Press, 2000); Friedrich Nietzsche, *Thus Spoke Zarathustra*, ed. Adrian Del Caro and Robert Pippen (Cambridge: Cambridge University Press, 2006); and Frantz Fanon, *The Wretched of the Earth*, trans. Richard Philcox (New York: Grove, 2005).

in a self-transformation (Nietzsche), that (f) converts the literal muscular tension of oppressed communities into liberating art (Fanon). In one word each, Spinoza offers *intuition* Nietzsche offers *self-overcoming*, and Fanon *tension*, to form my hybrid conception of social justice as "intuitively self-overcoming tension." I will now offer more detailed analyses of all six texts.

King on "Lovingly"

I begin with King, whose conception of *agape* constitutes the "lovingly" adverb in "lovingly generous reimagining." Here I will utilize King's article, entitled "An Experiment in Love" (excerpted from King's *Stride toward Freedom: The Montgomery Circle*, originally appearing in the September 1958 edition of the magazine *Jubilee*). Despite significant overlap with many other texts by King, this article is distinguished by a more extended reflection on love, and contains three primary insights relevant to my chapter. The first insight is that King describes the concept of love, which he traces to Jesus of Nazareth, in the following surprising terms: "the creative weapon of love."[9] Two things here are worthy of note. To begin with, love is traditionally understood as the opposite of violence (like the opposing principles of *eros* versus *polemos* [strife] in Empedocles's metaphysics), and thus contrary to weapons per se. Also, weapons are traditionally understood as destructive, rather than creative. Perhaps this is a subtle allusion (among many others) in King to Nietzsche, in this case to the *Gay Science*'s famous claim that "only as creators can we destroy."[10] Thus, love for King means reimagining (like Arendt) certain things to be their apparent opposites. This connection to reimagining, moreover, helps clarify the precise nature of love's creation for King. To wit, it is theatrical creation, which is also true of Aurelius's concept of generosity, and of Arendt's concept of reimagining. Finally on this point, the stated purpose of King's theatrical creation (as he repeats in other writings, including the article "Nonviolence: The Only Road to Freedom") is to dramatize real-world injustices, specifically for audiences who were (a) committing violence against the nonviolent protestors, or (b) reading and viewing media coverage of said injustices and violence.[11]

The second insight relevant to my investigation in "An Experiment in Love" concerns a quote that King takes from Gandhi, regarding the fighter for civil rights entering jail "as a bridegroom enters the bride's chamber." Here again (as with his weapon metaphor) King invokes the metaphor of love (specifically

9 King, *Hope*, 16.
10 King, *Hope*, 58.
11 King, *Hope*, 58.

the *eros* of marital consummation) to describe another phenomenon generally regarded as antithetical to love (in the present case, prison). More precisely, this antithetical relationship between prison and love (like that between weapons and love) also involves violence.

In both of these metaphors (weaponry and imprisonment) then, King provokes us to reconceive love itself as a kind of active, forceful, even aggressive power vis-à-vis some object. I use the word "object" here deliberately—as opposed to the more obvious choice of "opponent" or "enemy"—because King repeatedly insists (here and elsewhere in his writings) that "the attack" in his nonviolent method of civil disobedience "is directed against forces of evil rather than against persons who happen to be doing the evil."[12] This means, finally from King, that his concept of love is also generous (including in the etymological sense in which generosity "generates" the next generation, consequent upon the bridegroom's entry into the bride's chamber). In short, love is not a passive feeling, but rather an active giving. On this note, I turn to Aurelius's peace-facilitating emphasis on generosity.

Aurelius on "Generous"

Aurelius, to repeat, contributes the "generous" adjective to "lovingly generous reimagining." As I explore in detail elsewhere, Aurelius's treatment of the theatrical art of dance in his *Meditations* reveals a political ethics constituted by (a) an ethics of patient tolerance, and (b) the generosity flowing from the micro-political power created by cultivating one's inner divinity.[13] In brief, beginning with the ethical partner in this "dance" of political ethics, the word "tolerance" (according to the *OED*) comes from the Latin *tolerare*, meaning "to bear, endure," and the word "patience" derives from the Latin *patior*, meaning "to suffer." As for the dance's political partner, "generosity" derives from the Latin *generosus*, meaning "of noble birth, noble-spirited, of good stock or breeding (of animals or plants), superior." It is on the latter that I will focus here, with a brief consideration of Aurelius's references to "generosity" in the *Meditations*.

To begin, in the first section of the text, which amounts to a catalogue of thanksgiving to his teachers and other loved ones, Aurelius praises the following three different people for their generosity: (a) his mother, for her "generosity" per se; (b) a fellow philosopher-politician, for his "unstinting generosity"; and

12 King, *Hope*, 18.

13 See Joshua M. Hall, "A Divinely Tolerant Political Ethics: Dancing with Aurelius," *Epoché: A Journal of the History of Philosophy* 20 (2): 2016, 327–348.

(c) the Stoic senator Claudius Maximus, for his "generosity in good works."[14] To connect these remarks to my previous subsection, the reference to Aurelius's mother reinforces the connection between generosity and love as noted by King (given the traditional association between maternity and love).

In Aurelius's second reference in the text to generosity, he writes that there is something "agreeable" in "generosity" itself. One could perhaps interpolate here the synonym for agreeable, "lovable."[15] Third, Aurelius argues that his possession of reason entails that he should treat "dumb animals and generally all things and objects with generosity."[16] This expanded notion of generosity clearly involves both a loving attitude (as in King), and also a significant reimagining (as in Arendt) of every single thing in the cosmos as an appropriate object of said generosity. Fourth, Aurelius describes his own "character" as "generous."[17] Finally, Aurelius advises himself to be "generous with" himself, parsed as the following imperative: "leave all the past behind, entrust the future to providence, and direct the present solely to reverence and justice."[18] I will now attempt to condense these points, and Aurelius's political ethics of patient tolerance and divine generosity, into a scenario involving Aurelius's privileged metaphor of humans as puppets.

Imagine, if you will, finding yourself on a theatrical stage, as a life-size puppet, from which long strings rise up into the rafters above you. Then imagine that, on this same stage, there are a number of other life-size puppets, whose sole important difference from you is that their strings are all being controlled by one indifferent puppeteer. Your strings, by contrast, are wrapped around a beam above the stage and dropped back down and attached to the top of your head, such that, by moving your head in complex ways, you control the movements of the rest of your body. Finally, imagine that the puppeteer of the other puppets always keeps some music playing, and continuously makes the other puppets dance to it.

There you are, suspended from the artificial heavens, bound by strings to a stage that is your only possible home, and all the other puppets are dancing. What, then, should you do? Before you answer, keep in mind that you are armed with the following two vital truths: (1) you are in the minority of puppets with the godlike power to move yourself, and (2) the non-self-moving puppets

14 Aurelius, *Meditations*, Book I: paragraphs 3, 14, and 15.

15 Aurelius, *Meditations*, Book V: paragraph 10.

16 Aurelius, *Meditations*, Book VI: paragraph 5.

17 Aurelius, *Meditations*, Book 10: paragraph 36.

18 Aurelius, *Meditations*, Book 12: paragraph 1.

are essentially the same as you, except that they are powerless to resist the movements of the puppeteer. According to Aurelius, the only rational and politically virtuous course of action is to channel your divinely based thoughtful power into the generosity necessary to dance with the other puppets—who, after all, share your spark of rational divinity—as beautifully as you can. For some helpful stage directions regarding this challenging task, I now turn to my third and final historical thinker in connection to peace.

Arendt on "Reimagining"

Hannah Arendt, to repeat, contributes the "reimagining" noun to my conception of peace as "lovingly generous reimagining." I will approach this concept of reimagining primarily indirectly, through Arendt's reflections on thoughtlessness, as thoughtlessness is arguably the phenomenon that results from a lack of reimagining. The primary example of such thoughtlessness in her oeuvre is Adolf Eichmann, whom she treats—with a surprising degree of humor—as a comical figure. Arendt describes the "horrible" phenomenon of Eichmann's thoughtlessness as "outright funny."[19] For example, she writes that "officialese," as she terms it, "became his language because he was genuinely incapable of uttering a single sentence that was not a cliché."[20] As such, Eichmann's role as an actor in the theater of his trial, according to Arendt, is "not a 'monster,'" but rather "a clown."[21]

As to the reason for this clownishness, Arendt concludes that Eichmann was—shockingly—too completely "normal," specifically in a horrific Nazi context in which "only 'exceptions' could be expected to act 'normally.'"[22] Zeroing in further on the problem, Arendt observes that Eichmann showed an "inability to ever look at things from the other fellow's point of view."[23] In short, Eichmann dramatizes for Arendt the horrendous potential of the clownish thoughtlessness of the average modern person. As the aforementioned reference to "comedy" already hints (and as I noted above in my discussions of King's theatrical art of civil disobedience, and of Aurelius's dance of tolerant generosity), the theatrical is equally central for Arendt. In fact, she even goes so far (in her essay, "What Is Freedom?") to compare political speech to a dance

19 Arendt, *Eichmann*, 48.
20 Arendt, *Eichmann*, 48.
21 Arendt, *Eichmann*, 54.
22 Arendt, *Eichmann*, 27.
23 Arendt, *Eichmann*, 48.

performance, while *Eichmann in Jerusalem* describes his trial as a theatrical performance in its opening pages.[24]

The opposite of such thoughtlessness, as Arendt writes in her *Lectures on Kant's Political Philosophy*, is a maximally "enlarged mentality."[25] Such a mentality, Arendt explains, "by the force of the imagination makes the others present."[26] By this, Arendt means that reimagining incorporates, when forming a political judgment, indefinitely many other peoples' perspectives. Her analogy for this incorporation is the ideal theatrical spectator, who incorporates various figurative angles on a given performance in order to judge its merits.[27] To return to *Eichmann in Jerusalem*, Arendt there offers, as a contrast case to Eichmann the thoughtless clown, the equally theatrical heroism of the people of Denmark.

Facilitated by their thoughtful imagination of their Jewish "others" as fully human, and (Arendt notes) "unique among the countries of Europe," the Danish people openly defied the Nazis' attempts to forcibly evacuate the Jewish people from Denmark.[28] The story of how they did so, Arendt claims, should be "required reading in political science for all students who wish to learn something about the power inherent in nonviolent action and in resistance to an opponent possessing vastly superior means of violence."[29] The outline of this story is as follows. First, Arendt notes that "only the Danes dared speak out on the subject [of "the Jewish question"] to their German masters," whereas all the other European nations held their tongues, and resisted (if at all) in secret.[30] Second, when the Nazis proposed the infamous yellow badge be used to identify Jewish people, the Nazis "were simply told that the King would be the first to wear it."[31] Third, the Danes argued that, "because the stateless refugees [non-Danish Jewish people] were no longer German citizens, the Nazis could not claim them without Danish consent."[32] Fourth, as a consequence—and one that Arendt describes as "truly amazing"—"everything went topsy-turvy."[33]

24 Hannah Arendt, "What Is Freedom?" *Between Past and Future* (New York: Penguin, 2006b), 152; and Arendt, *Eichmann*, 4.

25 Hannah Arendt, *Lectures on Kant's Political Philosophy*, ed. Ronald Beiner (Chicago: University of Chicago Press, 1989), 44.

26 Arendt, *Kant*, 55.

27 Arendt, *Kant*, 55.

28 Arendt, *Eichmann*, 171.

29 Arendt, *Eichmann*, 171.

30 Arendt, *Eichmann*, 171.

31 Arendt, *Eichmann*, 171.

32 Arendt, *Eichmann*, 172.

33 Arendt, *Eichmann*, 172.

For example, "riots broke out in Danish shipyards, where the dock workers refused to repair German ships and then went on strike."[34] Fifth, when the Nazis came to kidnap the Jewish people and begin their deportation from Denmark (ultimately intended for the concentration camps), the Danish police allowed the Nazis to take only those Jewish people who were "at home and willing to let them in"—which figure ended up being merely 477 of the 7,800 Jewish people there.[35] Sixth, the Jewish authorities in Denmark publicized the impending kidnappings openly in the synagogues, giving the people "just enough time to leave their apartments and go into hiding" among a Danish community in which every citizen welcomed them.[36] Finally, in regard to the last phase of Denmark's response, the secret evacuation of the hidden Jewish people to safety in Sweden, Arendt notes that the extensive cost of this evacuation "was paid largely by wealthy Danish citizens."[37]

Even more surprising to Arendt than the actions of the Danish, is the fact that their imaginative thoughtfulness proved contagious, in that "the German officials who had been living in [Denmark] for years were no longer the same" as they had been back in Germany.[38] In fact, Arendt elaborates, even "the special s.s. units employed in Denmark frequently objected to 'the measures they were ordered to carry out by the central agencies.'"[39] In conclusion, Denmark was "the only case we know of in which the Nazis met with open native resistance," and "the result seems to have been that those exposed to it changed their minds."[40] In other words, the Danish citizens imagined themselves in the Jewish people's place, and then acted politically on the basis of this reimagining, which managed to inspire even some of the Nazis, also, to reimagine the Jewish people as fully human.

Having thus considered all three thinkers on the dancingly theatrical artwork of peace, I now turn to my final three thinkers, in order to explore the poetic discipline of social justice.

Spinoza on "Intuitively"

My first thinker germane to social justice, Spinoza, contributes the "intuitively" adverb to my conception of social justice as "intuitively self-overcoming

34 Arendt, *Eichmann*, 172.
35 Arendt, *Eichmann*, 173.
36 Arendt, *Eichmann*, 173, 174.
37 Arendt, *Eichmann*, 174.
38 Arendt, *Eichmann*, 172.
39 Arendt, *Eichmann*, 173.
40 Arendt, *Eichmann*, 175.

tension." It is imperative, at the outset, to note that Spinoza introduces a unique, technical definition of "intuition." To clarify that definition, I will preface my discussion of it with a brief overview of Spinoza's thought regarding knowledge in general. As I explore in detail elsewhere, for Spinoza, the first kind of knowledge, which he calls "imagination," is a kind of sense-experience of particulars.[41] The second kind of knowledge, which he calls "understanding," involves the rational grasp of universals. And the third kind of knowledge, in Spinoza's words, "proceeds from an adequate idea of the formal essence of some of the attributes of god to an adequate knowledge of the essence of things."[42] I will now unpack this difficult quote word by word, and then argue that the medium of poetry constitutes a privileged locus for Spinoza's intuition. More specifically, I will focus on the subgenre of poetry that is theatrical dramatic poetry, drawing on Hasana Sharp's feminist analysis of Spinoza on embodiment.[43]

To begin, an "idea" for Spinoza denotes, not a mental representation or the content of such a representation, but rather "an action of the mind … involving judgment."[44] By an "adequate idea," in turn, Spinoza means "an idea which, insofar as it is considered in itself without relation to its object, has all the properties, or the extrinsic denominations, of a true idea."[45] Adequacy, then, could be paraphrased as truth minus correspondence, or truth that remains at the level of generality, without any relation to a concrete object. Regarding the second concept in Spinoza's definition of intuition, namely essence, he describes a being's essence as that which is distinctive of that type of being, which essence thereby defines said type of being. Spinoza defines the "actual essence"

41 Joshua M. Hall, "Poetic Intuition: Spinoza and Gerard Manley Hopkins," *Philosophy Today* 57:4 (2013): 401–407.

42 Spinoza, *Ethics*, 149. I will follow the system of citation used by Parkinson in his edition:
"A = Axiom
C = Corollary
D = Definition
DE = Definition of the Emotions (Part 3)
L = Lemma
P = Proposition
S = Scholium
(So, for example, 'e2p40s2' refers to *Ethics*, Part 2, Proposition 40, Scholium 2)".

43 Hasana Sharp, *Spinoza and the Politics of Renaturalization* (Chicago: University of Chicago Press), 2011.

44 Gilles Deleuze, *Spinoza: Practical Philosophy*, trans. Robert Hurley (San Francisco: City Lights, 1988), 52.

45 Spinoza, *Ethics*, e2d4.

of a thing (i.e., a thing's essence as we conceive it) as "the endeavor to persevere in its own being," condensed in the word *conatus*.[46] And the "formal" of "formal essence" in Spinoza's above definition equates, in contemporary terms, to "reality." Finally from the first half of the above quote, the third concept in Spinoza's definition of intuition, "attribute," he defines elsewhere in the *Ethics* as "that which intellect perceives of substance as constituting its essence."[47] Since (a) "substance" and "God" are synonymous terms for Spinoza, and (b) human beings can perceive only two of substance/god's infinite attributes (namely, thought and extension), the referent in the above quote of "some of the attributes of God" can only be "thought" and "extension." To paraphrase the first half of Spinoza's definition of intuition, substituting my elaborations for the original terms: intuition is a faculty of knowing that makes an inference or judgment on the basis of an internally consistent, general, and real truth about thought per se or extension per se.

Onward, then, to the second half of Spinoza's definition of intuition. To recall, it proceeds *from* "an adequate idea of the formal essence of some of the attributes of God ..." and *to* "an adequate knowledge of the essence of things." I have observed that adequate knowledge means the same thing as true knowledge, but without reference to the existing entity that is known. And I have noted that the essence of a thing for Spinoza is its *conatus*, its endeavor to persist in its being. As for the last phrase, "things" for Spinoza are what he terms "finite modes."[48] "Modes" in general for Spinoza are what he terms "affections of substance, or, that which is in something else, through which it is also conceived."[49] These modes are modifications of substance by way of being modifications of the attributes of substance (which for human knowledge are limited to thought and extension). And "finite modes"—that is, particular things—he describes as "nothing other than the affections, i.e., the modes, of the attributes of God, by which the attributes of God are expressed in a certain and determinate way."[50] For example, the attribute of extension is one way in which the intellect perceives the essence of substance, and a particular human body is simply one (finite) mode of extension. To paraphrase the second half of Spinoza's definition of intuition, substituting my elaborations for the original

46 Spinoza, *Ethics*, e3p7.

47 Spinoza, *Ethics*, e1d4.

48 G.H.R. Parkinson, "Editor's Introduction," in *Spinoza's Ethics*, ed. and trans. G.H.R. Parkinson (Oxford: Oxford University Press, 2000), 21.

49 Spinoza, *Ethics*, e1d5.

50 Spinoza, *Ethics*, e1p25c.

terms: intuition is a faculty of knowing that infers an internally consistent and general truth about the *conatus* of things.

Condensing the above analyses of both halves of Spinoza's definition, by intuition one arrives at a rationally correct conception of the *conatus* of a thing (i.e., a finite mode) by means of a rationally correct conception of thought or extension. Put differently, if one really understands thought and/or extension in principle, one can thereby infer the essence of a particular thing. Thus, if one understands that thought and extension are the intellect's perception of the essence of god/substance, then one can understand that particular things are conceived by human beings *in terms of* or *by means of* thought and extension. One must know what extension is in order to understand a particular extended thing, and one must know what thought is to understand a particular mental thing.

I will now attempt to flesh out the broader context in which Spinoza deploys this concept of intuition. Spinoza claims that intuition, like understanding, "is necessarily true" and "teaches us to distinguish between the true and the false."[51] He compares intuition to the intuitive grasp of a mathematical formula, which is achieved by considering the relationship among specific numbers plugged into the formula (as opposed to an understanding achieved by calculating the problem using variables). Spinoza also provides a few other scattered clues for understanding his concept of intuition. He describes it as being especially powerful in overcoming the negative effects of the emotions, and as inspiring the intellectual love of God as eternal and infinite.[52] Further, he claims that to "understand things by the third kind of knowledge" is the "highest endeavor of the mind, and its highest virtue," because "the more we understand things in this way [in their essence, i.e., reality] the more ... we understand God."[53] Spinoza describes this understanding as the mind's "power" and "virtue" and "nature" (all of which, for him, are synonymous). Additionally, the more things the mind grasps in this way, the more it wants to grasp things in this way. In such pursuits, Spinoza claims, the mind finds its greatest peace.[54] Finally in terms of these clues, it is also worth noting that Spinoza regards the mind itself (rather than, say, external things, or god), as the cause of the third kind of knowledge.[55]

51 Spinoza, *Ethics*, e2p41.

52 Spinoza, *Ethics*, e5p20s.

53 Spinoza, *Ethics*, e5p25, e5p25d.

54 Spinoza, *Ethics*, e5p26–27.

55 Spinoza, *Ethics*, e5p31d.

In light of these observations, one possible understanding of intuition is that it consists in a combination of the specificity and concreteness of the first kind of knowledge ("imagination") with the accuracy and generality of the second kind of knowledge ("understanding"). In other words, through intuition, the universal and the particular are understood through each other. Either thought or extension is grasped through the action of a specific idea. Conversely, a specific idea is enacted by grasping the nature of thought or extension in itself. Above all, it seems central for intuition that the relationship between generality and specificity is affirmed. And nothing, arguably, is more effective at affirming the generality-specificity relationship than language.

On the one hand, via its connection to thinking, language is a property or dimension of thought. On the other hand, via its connection to speech, language is also a property or dimension of extension. Language is thus distinctly capable of affirming, at an intuitive level, Spinoza's central claim that thought and extension are merely two different ways of representing the same substance. Furthermore, whenever language is used to denote particulars, it brings its nature as a universal medium to bear on those particulars, and thus affirms the resonance between generality (that is, rationality) and specificity (that is, phenomena in the world).

Moreover, this inherent power of language in general as a vehicle for intuition is even greater in poetry in particular. The reason for this is that poetry both utilizes language to describe particular situations, thoughts, feelings, observations, etc., and also manifests language as language. Especially in the subgenre of dramatic poetry, and even more especially when that poetry is performed, poetry foregrounds language's capacities for affirming the general-specific relationship at the same time as it refers to the phenomena in the world named by the language of the poem.

More precisely, in thinking about poetry, whether reading silently or hearing the actors speaking their poetic lines during a play, one is made aware not only of what the poem is describing about the world but also of the activity of the attribute of thought, or of thought taking place. Similarly, in scanning poetry with one's eyes, one is aware not only of how the words match up with things in the world but also of how language itself is an extended thing made of ink, a physical spread of words on a page. Finally on this note, when one hears poetry performed, one is made aware not only of the things in the world that the sounds evoke but also of language as itself a physically extended phenomenon, namely sound waves spun from vibrating vocal cords and inhabiting the surrounding air.

To bring this discussion of poetry and intuition back to social justice, intuition is the power that enables us to know each being, including ourselves, in those beings' relationship to every other being, and to the cosmic whole. Intuition thus shows us that we are all equal insofar as we are all modalities of the cosmos, as thinking and extended things. And dramatically performed poetry in particular has an enormous power to increase and reinforce this knowledge, by making vivid our metaphysical solidarity will all fellow beings (as for example with the Founding Fathers' favorite play, *Cato*).[56] In this way, poetry can inspire those engaged in the struggle for social justice, by uniting protestors, in voice and mind, in the common cause.

Nietzsche on "Self-Overcoming"

My second thinker illuminative of social justice, Nietzsche, offers the "self-overcoming" adjective to my conception of social justice as "intuitively self-overcoming tension." To repeat, I am not claiming that Nietzsche was an advocate of social justice. Although one could conceivably make the case that he is an advocate for a kind of hierarchized social justice—an unequal treatment appropriate to unequal beings—I will save this analysis for a separate inquiry. My discussion of this concept of self-overcoming will be briefer than those for the other five thinkers, on the assumption that most readers will already be familiar with the concept (given its central importance in Nietzsche's oeuvre).

The fullest exposition of self-overcoming is found in the section bearing that title in *Thus Spoke Zarathustra*. In addition to the obvious connection between this text and poetry—namely, the fact that *Thus Spoke Zarathustra* belongs in the genre of prose poetry—there is also a significant connection between its section "On Self-Overcoming" and dance, insofar as the latter section appears just pages after another section entitled "The Dance Song." In this dancing section, Nietzsche depicts Zarathustra as briefly joyful and reconciled to life as a result of watching the dance of a group of beautiful young women. Then, in the subsequent section, entitled "The Grave Song" (which immediately precedes the "On Self-Overcoming" section), Zarathustra expresses the melancholy that ensues when the dance ends. "Only in dance," Nietzsche writes, "do I know how to speak the parables of the highest things—and now my highest parable remained unspoken in my limbs!"[57] What survives this melancholy, however, is Zarathustra's "will," which "wants to walk its course on my feet," because

56 Joseph Addison, *Cato: A Tragedy, and Selected Essays*, ed. Christine Dunn Henderson and Mark E. Yellin (Indianapolis: Liberty Fund, 2004).

57 Nietzsche, *Spoke Zarathustra*, 87.

"Invulnerable am I only in the heel."[58] On this note, Nietzsche transitions to the section titled "On Self-Overcoming."

"On Self-Overcoming" begins by claiming that the will to truth is actually the will to power in disguise, and then Nietzsche suddenly swerves (or executes a dancing spin) to a discussion of Zarathustra's own truth-search into the nature of life itself. From this search, Zarathustra claims to have learned the following three things: (1) "All living is an obeying"; (2) "the one who cannot obey himself is commanded"; and (3) "commanding is harder than obeying." Zarathustra's inference from these three things, finally, is that all commanding involves "an experiment and a risk."[59] For example, Nietzsche writes, "the living" being "must become the judge and avenger and victim of its own law," and in so doing, this living being "risks—life itself."[60]

As an apparent reward for having thus boldly experimented with the truth of life, a personification of life grants to Zarathustra the privilege of hearing life's secret: "I am," Life says to Zarathustra, "that *which must always overcome itself*."[61] In order to perform this self-overcoming—and here Nietzsche returns to the metaphor of dance/walking—life must walk on "*crooked* paths."[62] Put more concretely, the life within one's self must oppose even that self's own creations, along with the love the self feels for its creations. The reason for this necessary opposition, according to Nietzsche, is that life values other things more highly than life. In particular, life values power. In the service of power, Nietzsche concludes the "On Self-Overcoming" section as follows: "And may everything break that can possibly be broken by our truths! Many a house has yet to be built!"[63]

To translate these insights into the discourse of social justice, those of us who desire it must also desire the increased empowerment of social justice even more than we desire the well-being of our own bodies and lives. From this perspective, these bodies will soon die, and our lives derive a majority of their value from the living force within them (rather than the span of time that we are alive as individuals). Our best, in other words, lies in becoming more than we are. As a result, we can in good conscience encourage ourselves to risk everything that belongs to us as individuals, in a grand experiment for the further empowerment of social justice.

---

58 Nietzsche, *Spoke Zarathustra*, 87.
59 Nietzsche, *Spoke Zarathustra*, 89.
60 Nietzsche, *Spoke Zarathustra*, 89.
61 Nietzsche, *Spoke Zarathustra*, 89.
62 Nietzsche, *Spoke Zarathustra*, 89.
63 Nietzsche, *Spoke Zarathustra*, 90.

Fanon on "Tension"

The final historical thinker in this chapter, Frantz Fanon, supplies the "tension" noun to my conception of social justice as "intuitively self-overcoming tension." In *Wretched of the Earth*, Fanon describes the embodied oppression of black peoples living under antiblack racism, specifically that of the era of European colonialism. Although his analyses therefore originate with a specific set of historical circumstances, those circumstances were sustained by ideological structures of racism that have survived, albeit in mutated forms, to the present day. From my detailed exploration, elsewhere, of Fanon's analysis, the most relevant portion thereof for the present chapter is his conception of "perpetual muscular tension."[64]

The first indication of this concept appears early in *Wretched of the Earth*, in Fanon's claim that "the dreams of the colonized subject are muscular dreams."[65] Repressing their rage toward their oppressors, he explains, the oppressed experience a buildup of stress in their very bodies, as a result of which the "muscles of the colonized are always tensed."[66] Much later, Fanon returns to the issue of muscular tension in his description of the colonized intellectual who "feels he must escape this white culture" by withdrawing from Westernization. The connection to muscular tension is that this movement, according to Fanon, "above all calls to mind a muscular reflex, a muscular contraction." For this reason, the colonized intellectual's style is an "energetic style, alive with rhythms, bursting with life," in preparation for a "swift, painful combat where inevitably the muscle had to replace the concept."[67]

To connect Fanon's insights back to the theatrical art of dance, to be a dancer is to be in constant muscular ready awareness, storing energy in tension to be released in a display of powerful grace or desperate aggression. Such a muscular, physiological awareness is important in the struggle of black persons and communities for genuine equality, as a significant marker or litmus test for the success of that struggle. In this way, dance could be used to foreground the importance of the physical/bodily dimension of being a raced being, as well as the importance of ensuring that theoretical insights can also be applied at the level of concrete human embodiment.[68]

---

64 Joshua M. Hall, "Revalorized Black Embodiment: Dancing with Fanon," *Journal of Black Studies* 43(3): 2012, 274–288.

65 Fanon, *Wretched*, 15.

66 Fanon, *Wretched*, 16.

67 Fanon, *Wretched*, 80, 84.

68 Given the easy applicability of Fanon's analyses of black embodiment in antiblack racist cultures to the experience of dancers, it is interesting that in the contemporary white

Admittedly, Fanon rarely discusses dance explicitly, including two brief references in *Black Skin, White Masks* and two in *Wretched of the Earth*. And in three of these four references the connotations are intensely pejorative. However, the fourth and final such reference (like the second and final reference in *Wretched of the Earth*) is unequivocally positive, appearing after Fanon's extensive discussion of what he calls "combat literature." To wit, he suggests that dance can be transformed into a kind of combat dance, much like ordinary literature can become combat literature, which prepares the colonized people for political liberation, and contributes to "the new national rhythm" that "drives the nation."[69] This transformation of cultural and religious dance into combat dance consists, essentially, of integrating contemporary political consciousness into dance artworks, creating dances whose rhythms inspire proud revolt.

In addition to Fanon's brief moment of explicit affirmation of dance, one can also find dance-resonance in Fanon's earlier analyses of "perpetual muscular tension." That is, the phenomenological similarities between dancing embodiment and Fanon's accounts of black embodiment in racist and colonized societies buttress his hopes for combat dance. More specifically, one might be able to channel the constructive and affirmative energy often directed toward dance qua art form into strategies for affirming and improving the lives of disempowered persons of color seeking social justice. Put more concretely, the beauty of tension as embodied by dancers (qua artistic performers) could be imaginatively extended to people of color (qua survivors of racism), for example by encouraging a recognition of tension's potential benefits for the ongoing struggle for social justice.

Recapitulation

Having thus considered these six texts, figures, and aspects—the historical dimension of my conceptions of peace and social justice—one is left with yet

United States, there is a stereotype that black persons are essentially better dancers than white persons. It is also interesting that dancing is generally understood to be the privileged province of other oppressed or disadvantaged groups as well, including women and gay men. Women more than men, alternatively oriented more than exclusively heterosexual, non-Westerners more than Westerners, rural folk more than urbanites, the conventional more than the unconventional, are perceived as being both interested and proficient in dance.

69 Fanon, *Wretched*, 157.

another challenge, namely how to love the agents and vehicles of oppression qua the not-yet-just. To resolve this final tension requires nothing less than real-time political action. Thus, I will close this chapter with a specific suggestion, and an invitation to further public discourse, regarding the fight for gendered social justice today. But first, I will briefly rehearse the insights of this chapter.

Overall, I have attempted in this chapter to sketch a new conception of socially-just peace. At a first, conceptual level, I defined social justice as sustainable tranquility through organismic empowerment. The counterintuitive implication of these conceptual analyses is that peace is predominantly external and social, whereas social justice is predominantly internal and individual. At a second, etymological level, I claimed that peace's sustainable tranquility is based on its being an artificial, artful construction (as in the peace "made" by Jesus of Nazareth's "peacemakers"), while social justice's organismic empowerment is based on its being the disciplined self-restraint of those armed for force (as in the Roman goddess Iustus, who stills her sword until her scales have rendered their verdict). The counterintuitive implication of these etymological analyses is that peace is unnatural and must be continuously created, while social justice requires that the oppressed restrain their own impulses to use violent force (unless this capacity for force has already been denied by their society, as is often the case).

And at a third, historical level, I claimed that (a) peace's sustainable tranquility through artful construction consists of polemical love, to facilitate divine-like generosity, deployed in a thoughtful reimagining of the other; while (b) social justice's organismic empowerment through disciplined self-restraint consists of an intuitively based knowledge of the universal via the particular, utilized to overcome the self in favor of empowerment per se, achieved by turning oppression's tensions against its own forces and institutions. The counterintuitive implication of these historical analyses is that (1) love can be an agonistic struggle, (2) humans can express transcendent generosity by imagining themselves gods, (3) even the worst evils can be reimagined as mere thoughtlessness, (4) universality shines fully through each particular being, (5) life and living beings naturally seek empowerment rather than a mere continuance of living, and (6) the most trivial and complicit movements of artistic expression involve tensions that can nevertheless be repurposed for liberation.

Conclusion: A Contemporary Feminist Application

One frequently hears various forms of feminism criticized on the grounds that they allegedly constitute a kind of "disturber of the peace"—the sword, if you will, in the hands of women in our communities. Put differently, many folks on the conservative side of the culture wars claim that men and women are naturally unequal (qua different), and thus that feminists' efforts at gendered justice are fundamentally misguided, and ultimately create unnecessary conflicts and tensions within heterosexual relationships, traditional families, etc. What one does not tend to hear, however, are the thoughts of those who occupy a space between the two warring camps, temporarily undecided, and avoiding the question or issue altogether while nevertheless pursuing goals that align with many feminists' goals. The latter include, notably, some race theorists, Marxian theorists, continental philosophers, and others who are independently invested in their work in the exploration of power differentials, but who do not necessarily identify as feminist.

Following Alison Jaggar, I will group the latter individuals under her umbrella term, "non-feminists," to differentiate those individuals from the outright opponents of various forms of feminism (whom Jaggar calls "anti-feminists"). Furthermore, I would argue that my conception of socially-just peace (to repeat, lovingly generous reimagining through intuitively self-overcoming tension) could be helpful in advancing Jaggar's strategy. To wit, my conception seems to suggest that, in public discourses regarding feminism and women's rights, it might be strategically beneficial to lovingly generously reimagine the linguistic productions of non-feminists, through intuitively self-overcoming tension, in order to resist cultural violence and promote sustainable tranquility.

Beginning with the above conceptual insights, peace as sustainable tranquility requires a move beyond a kind of civil war between roughly equal numbers of feminists and anti-feminists, which might be accomplished by offering non-feminists a more comfortable pathway to the feminist camp. And the organismic empowerment here involves empowering non-feminists to both express their current, controversial views openly, and also benefit from the information and education that we, as feminists, can provide them in the course of such conversations.

From the above etymological insights, if peace is an artificial construction, then we cannot simply wait for nature to take its course and establish peace between feminists and anti-feminists. Instead, we must use our creativity and imagination to see non-feminists differently, so they can learn to see themselves in a different way that is more consonant with our struggles for gendered justice. And if social justice is the self-restraint of our capacities for force, then we must resist the urge to merely condemn or "shout down" anyone who is not already an avowed feminist, and instead give those who occupy more complex—and potentially coalition-friendly—positions to participate in a substantive conversation, with less fear on the non-feminists' part of being silenced and demonized.

Finally, from the above historical insights, peace appears to require a striving, combative love for non-feminists, in order to fuel a seemingly divine degree of generosity (in the form of patience and the benefit of the doubt), and all in the service of reimagining non-feminists as potential allies rather than enemies. Social justice, complementarily, appears to require seeing feminists' spirit of gendered justice hidden within non-feminists. This could help us bracket our defensive self-labeling, and facilitate intensified life within our potential allies (and between us and them). And this, in turn, could channel the tensions of our potential allies' distrust, confusion, and skepticism into a more dynamic readiness to help fight for gendered justice.

In closing, I ask that the reader please join me in lovingly (with King), and generously (Aurelius), reimagining (Arendt), by channeling our intuitively (Spinoza) self-overcoming (Nietzsche) tension (Fanon), our non-feminist others. In so doing, we can cocreate the artwork that is socially just peace.

Bibliography

Addison, Joseph. *Cato: A Tragedy, and Selected Essays*, edited by Christine Dunn Henderson and Mark E. Yellin. Indianapolis: Liberty Fund, 2004.

Arendt, Hannah. *Lectures on Kant's Political Philosophy*, edited by Ronald Beiner. Chicago: University of Chicago Press, 1989.

Arendt, Hannah. *Eichmann in Jerusalem: A Report on the Banality of Evil*. New York: Penguin, 2006a.

Arendt, Hannah. "What Is Freedom?" In *Between Past and Future*. New York: Penguin, 2006b.

Aurelius, Marcus. *Meditations*. Translated by Martin Hammond. New York: Penguin, 2006.

Deleuze, Gilles. *Spinoza: Practical Philosophy*, Translated by Robert Hurley. San Francisco: City Lights, 1988.

Dewey, John. *Art as Experience*. New York: Penguin, 2005.

Fanon, Frantz. *The Wretched of the Earth*. Translated by Richard Philcox. New York: Grove, 2005.

Fiala, Andrew. "Radical Forgiveness and Human Justice." *Heythrop Journal: A Bimonthly Review of Philosophy and Theology* 53:3 (2012): 494–506. Accessed August 31, 2016, doi: 10.1111/j.1468-2265.2010.00637.x.

Hall, Joshua M. "Revalorized Black Embodiment: Dancing with Fanon." *Journal of Black Studies* 43, 3 (2012): 274–288.

Hall, Joshua M. "Poetic Intuition: Spinoza and Gerard Manley Hopkins." *Philosophy Today* 57, 4 (2013): 401–407.

Hall, Joshua M. "A Divinely Tolerant Political Ethics: Dancing with Aurelius." *Epoché: A Journal of the History of Philosophy* 20, 2 (2016): 327–348.

Jaggar, Allison. "Feminist Ethics: Projects, Problems, Prospects." In *Feminist Ethics*, edited by Claudia Card, 78–106. Lawrence, KS: University Press of Kansas Press, 1991.

King, Martin Luther Jr. *A Testament of Hope: The Essential Writings and Speeches of Martin Luther King, Jr.* Edited by James M. Washington. New York: HarperOne, 2003.

Nietzsche, Friedrich. *Thus Spoke Zarathustra*. Edited by Adrian Del Caro and Robert Pippen. Cambridge: Cambridge University Press, 2006.

Plato, *Plato: Statesman. Philebus. Ion.* Cambridge, MA: Harvard University Press, 1925.

Sharp, Hasana. *Spinoza and the Politics of Renaturalization*. Chicago: University of Chicago Press, 2011.

Spinoza, Benedictus. *Ethics*. Edited and translated by G.H.R. Parkinson. Oxford: Oxford University Press, 2000.

Index

Printed in the United States
By Bookmasters